"For the most complete overall picture of what genuine wilderness camping entails, the Sierra Club's *Walking Softly in the Wilderness* is the ultimate manual." HOUSTON CHRONICLE

"Walking Softly in the Wilderness is crowded with information on gearing up, on food and fuel, finding your way, making and breaking camp, and advice on trouble. A common-sense and literate approach." LOS ANGELES TIMES

"Author Hart is a thorough and fluid writer [and] *Walking Softly in the Wilderness* ranks with the best basic guides to backpacking." CAMPING JOURNAL

The Sierra Club Outdoor Activities Guides

BACKCOUNTRY SKIING *The Sierra Club Guide to Skiing off the Beaten Track*, by Lito Tejada-Flores

BIKE TOURING *The Sierra Club Guide to Outings on Wheels*, by Raymond Bridge

CAVING *The Sierra Club Guide to Spelunking*, by Lane Larson and Peggy Larson

THE COMPLETE BICYCLE COMMUTER *The Sierra Club Guide to Wheeling to Work*, by Hal Zina Bennett

EXPLORING UNDERWATER *The Sierra Club Guide to Scuba and Snorkeling*, by John L. Culliney and Edward S. Crockett

LAND NAVIGATION HANDBOOK *The Sierra Club Guide to Map and Compass*, by W. S. Kals

SIMPLE FOODS FOR THE PACK, by Vikki Kinmont and Claudia Axcell

STARTING SMALL IN THE WILDERNESS *The Sierra Club Outdoors Guide for Families*, by Marlyn Doan

WALKING SOFTLY IN THE WILDERNESS *The Sierra Club Guide to Backpacking*, revised and updated, by John Hart

WEATHERING THE WILDERNESS *The Sierra Club Guide to Practical Navigation*, by William E. Reifsnyder

WILDWATER *The Sierra Club Guide to Kayaking and Whitewater Boating*, by Lito Tejada-Flores

Completely Revised & Updated

Walking Softly in the Wilderness

The Sierra Club Guide to Backpacking

John Hart

**Sierra Club Books
San Francisco**

The Sierra Club, founded in 1892 by John Muir, has devoted itself to the study and protection of the earth's scenic and ecological resources—mountains, wetlands, woodlands, wild shores and rivers, deserts and plains. The publishing program of the Sierra Club offers books to the public as a nonprofit educational service in the hope that they may enlarge the public's understanding of the Club's basic concerns. The point of view expressed in each book, however, does not necessarily represent that of the Club. The Sierra Club has some fifty chapters coast to coast, in Canada, Hawaii, and Alaska. For information about how you may participate in its programs to preserve wilderness and the quality of life, please address inquiries to Sierra Club, 530 Bush Street, San Francisco, CA 94108.

for Julie

COPYRIGHT © 1977, 1984 BY JOHN HART

LIBRARY OF CONGRESS CATALOGING IN PUBLICATION DATA

Hart, John, 1948—
    Walking softly in the wilderness.
    Includes index.
    1. Backpacking. I. Sierra Club. II. Title.
GV199.6.H37 796.5 76-21620
ISBN 0-87156-813-6 (pbk)

Book design by Jon Goodchild/Triad
Front cover photograph by Art Twomey
Illustrations by Bonnie Laurie Russell

Printed in the United States of America
First revised edition: 1984

10 9 8 7 6 5 4 3 2

Acknowledgment is made for permission to reprint material from the following sources:

ANABASIS by St. John Perse, translated by T.S. Eliot. N.Y.: Harcourt, Brace Jovanovich, Inc. Copyright © 1938, 1949 by Harcourt, Brace & Co.

A WIZARD OF EARTHSEA by Ursula LeGuin. N.Y.: Ace Books. Copyright © 1968 by Ursula K. LeGuin. By permission of the author.

GERARD MANLEY HOPKINS, POEMS AND PROSE edited by W.H. Gardner. N.Y.: Oxford University Press. Copyright © 1953, 1963 by W.H. Gardner.

MOUNT ANALOGUE by Rene Daumal, translated by Roger Shattuck. Baltimore, Md.: Penguin Books. Copyright © 1952 by Librairie Gallimard. Reprinted by permission of Random House, Inc.

OREGON WINTER by Jeanne McGahey. Andes, N.Y.: Woolmer/Brotherson Ltd. Copyright © 1973 by Woolmer/Brotherson Ltd.

Patterns of Wilderness Use as Related to Congestion and Solitude by George H. Stankey *et al.* Published by the U.S. Forest Service, Intermountain Forest and Range Experiment Station.

ROUND RIVER by Aldo Leopold. N.Y.: Oxford University Press. Copyright © 1953 by Oxford University Press.

THIS IS DINOSAUR by Wallace Stegner. N.Y.: Alfred A. Knopf, Inc. Copyright © 1955 by Wallace Stegner. By permission of the author.

Trends in Recreational Use of National Forest Wilderness by Margaret E. Petersen. Published by the U.S. Forest Service, Intermountain Forest and Range Experiment Station.

The War Between the Rough Riders and the Bird Watchers by Wallace Stegner. Reprinted from the SIERRA CLUB BULLETIN (May, 1959) by permission of the author.

Wilderness Forever by Howard Zahniser, from WILDERNESS: AMERICA'S LIVING HERITAGE. Copyright © 1961 by the Sierra Club.

Acknowledgments

I OWE THANKS TO MANY PEOPLE for assistance on this book.

At the top of the list are the readers, who worked through the entire manuscript or reviewed selected chapters: Michael McCloskey, Jim Watters, Allen Smith, and Wendy Goldwyn, all of the Sierra Club; John Stanley, of the Club's Wilderness Impact Study team; Jim Owens; George D. Davis of the Wilderness Society; Phil Ward of the National Park Service; Bill Devall and his sociology students at Humboldt State University, Arcata, California; Gilbert Roberts, M.D.; Norman A. Wilson, snow consultant; Mike Hughes, George Malanson, Bill Riebsame, and Nick Van Pelt; and my parents.

Many others gave information and advice. Among them are Jim Absher, Gordon Benner, M.D., Garrett De Bell, Ann Dwyer, Michael J. Franzblau, M.D., Willie Fuller, Gaynor Franklin, Larry Gaudreau, Iris Noble, Tom Pillsbury, Harry Reeves, Alan Schmierer, Jerry South, Steve Ziman. Also Stephanie Atwood, Jordan Fisher-Smith, Christie Hakim, W. M. Harlow, Lelia Loban Lee, O. Granger; Bob Schneider, Sari Sommarstrom, and Shirley Taylor; Don M. Deck of Wilderness Digest Publications; Mike Harding of Mountain Traders; Reuben Rajala of the Appalachian Mountain Club; Floyd Wilson of the Wilderness Education Foundation; and MacPherson Brothers of San Francisco, tannery agents.

SECOND EDITION: I am indebted first of all to Oscar V. Lopp, First Aid Officer of the San Francisco Bay Chapter, Sierra Club (to list one credential) for his careful review of the chapters on wilderness first aid. Special thanks also to the staff of the Alpine House in Kentfield, Calif.; Samuel J. Brinton of W. L. Gore and Associates; Robert Camp; Jim Cohee; John C. Endahl, Jr., of Optimus; Pete Fitzinger of New Balance; Lew Gardner of the Boy Scouts of America, Bay Area Council; Pam Heath of Early Winters; John Hooper; Jon and Gail Hall and Denny and Marg May of the Boy Scouts of Canada, Northern Region; Mike Johnson; Julie Manson; Roderick Nash; Michael Scherer of Marmot Mountain Works; Mary Anne Stewart; and the many readers who have provided information and valuable criticism.

Numerous offices of the National Park Service, U. S. Forest Service, U. S. Fish and Wildlife Service, and Bureau of Land Management are of continuing help in this research.

—*J.H.*

Contents

Note to the Reader *xi*

A The Land Beyond the Roadhead
1: The Land Beyond the Roadhead *2*
2: Breaking In *11*

B Gearing Up
3: Gearing Up *16*
4: Boots *29*
5: Clothing *48*
6: The Pack *67*
7: The Bedroll *86*
8: Shelter *105*
9: Stove and Kitchen *127*
10: The Rest of the Load *153*

C Preparing the Trip
11: Designing the Trip *166*
12: Planning Food and Fuel *177*
13: Common Sense in Packing *188*

D Travel on the Trail
14: To the Trailhead *196*
15: Walking with Pack *202*
16: Finding the Way *214*

E Making and Managing the Camp
17: Making Camp *240*
18: Shelter and Bed *249*
19: Fire and Food *257*
20: Sanitation and Clean Water *274*
21: Breaking Camp *281*

F Variations
22: Cross-Country Travel and Other Variants *286*
23: The Winter Wilderness *313*
24: Hiking and Camping with Kids *349*

G Trouble and How to Deal With It
25: Trouble! *362*
26: Some Common Medical Problems *371*
27: Problem Animals and Plants *381*
28: Diseases of Heat, Cold, and Altitude *399*

H The Wilderness Regions
29: Wilderness in the East *414*
30: Western Wilderness *429*

I The Politics of Wilderness
31: Battle of the Wilderness: An Orientation *444*
32: The Backpackers: Who Are They? *462*
33: Problems in Wilderness Management *467*

Appendix: Resources *481*

Index *491*

Note to the Reader

WELCOME TO THE SECOND EDITION of *Walking Softly in the Wilderness*. Much has changed, especially in the area of gear, since this book first appeared in 1977. Hardly a page has escaped revision, and several chapters have been rewritten from scratch.

The changes in the backpacker's world, and the revisions they entail, are hardly likely to stop now. I would like to invite your help in keeping this book accurate. Does something in these pages seem wrong to you, or inefficient, or (once again) outdated? I would very much appreciate your letting me know about it, care of the Sierra Club. In revising the original edition, I have found reader feedback invaluable.

Of course, no book of manageable length and decent clarity can explore *all* the possible choices in wilderness gear and methods. Instead, a book must simplify. It must select. Often it must present only one way of doing things when there may be others just as good. Every backpacker works out a personal style; your style in the wilderness will be your own.

However, I hope that you will be slow to discount what this book has to say about *low-impact* methods in the wilderness: about the skills of using but not injuring the vulnerable land. For these are not merely points of "backcountry manners" or "wilderness etiquette." Not afterthoughts. Not optional finishing touches. Low-impact methods are the new necessities. And while there are legitimate disagreements about some of the details, the outlines are clear enough. There is little doubt about the things each hiker needs to know and do.

I hope you will help.

The Land Beyond the Roadhead

A

Where do the six trails go?
What are the mountains
named
That are colored like Iroquois?

—Jeanne McGahey

1:
The Land Beyond the Roadhead

THERE IS IN COLORADO a cold sky-colored lake, unchanging in its wilderness of stone. And from the nearest road it's two days' walk to be here.

In Washington a volcanic mountain glistens. You climb to its lasting ice and alpine flowers on miles of shady trail, up one of the greenest valleys in the world.

In South Carolina there is a waterlogged forest, an American jungle of vines and trailing moss and cypress trunks almost as big as California redwoods.

In Utah there is a branching canyon in red rock, an intricate path so narrow that with either hand you sometimes brush the wall.

And off the Michigan shore, on a primitive island that is fifty miles long, the timber wolves still hunt and moose are still the hunted.

These are the places we call *wilderness*, these and a thousand more. They are the unaltered landscapes of America, the places we have not reshaped with our machines, not stamped with our straight lines. They are the last survivals of the wildness beyond the old frontiers: the wildness that once was a continent wide.

When we learned to value these places—to recognize the benefits, practical and subtle, that we get from them—it was almost too late. It was almost too late when we realized that we actually *needed* them, that, in some important way, we cannot do without them. Nor is it a lesson we have fully learned. While some of our wild places have official labels and official protection—in federal wilderness units, in parks, in wildlife refuges—many others are unlabeled, unprotected. They have remained what they are only by fortunate accident. These wild places are disappearing fast and steadily: there was more wild country in America last year than there is today. Next year there will be, inevitably, somewhat less. Just how long the shrinking goes on and just how much wilderness is finally preserved depend on what Americans want and what they loudly ask for.

Wilderness belongs to everyone: it is a national possession. Its value is not only for those who make direct and obvious use of it. But wild country does inevitably have a particular meaning, a further meaning, to those who make the effort to go into it. It belongs, in a certain sense, to that very large yet very distinctive group: the backpackers.

Today there are millions of them, heading out from the roadheads. They are the people who don't mind walking, who are willing to carry moderate loads on their backs, who find a luxury in self-sufficiency. The backpackers earn their pleasure and would not find it so pleasant if it were not earned.

And yet the entry to the world of the trails is not hard. There are few Americans who are physically prevented from making the effort that the wilderness requires. There are many—indeed, the large majority—who have so far not tried. Some just aren't attracted and find the idea foreign. Others genuinely can't afford the gear. Others are content to have their wilderness secondhand, in books and photographs. But still others—who knows how many?—stay home because they simply don't know how to start or have an exaggerated idea of the difficulties, the discomforts, the expense.

Wilderness travel is not free—but it is, for most people, reasonably inexpensive.

Wilderness travel is not effortless—but it is, if you choose to make it so, quite easy.

Wilderness travel is not entirely without discomforts—but these are slight enough beside the rewards.

Wilderness travel is probably not for everyone. But it may be for a good number of people who have not yet found it out. There seems to be in many people a kind of hunger for wilderness, which, once aroused, is never to be satisfied by any substitute.

During the 1970s, backpacking became established as one of the major American outdoor pur-

Use of National Forest Wilderness 1965–1980

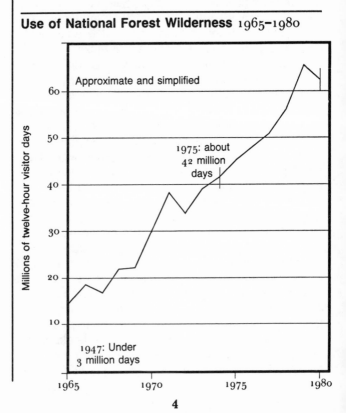

suits. The American Hiking Society estimates that 66 million hikers use the nation's trails, taking at least 5 million trips a year. The demand is still increasing, though not any more at the giddy pace of the early 1970s.

For those who have loved the wilderness all along, who have worked and fought to defend it from logging, mining, the endless thrusting-forward of the roads, this expanded audience for the wild places is a very hopeful sign. It suggests that the value of our wilderness will be more and more fully recognized. It suggests that there will be more voices every year asking that we preserve what still can be preserved.

The impact problem

But along with this hope has come a stirring of alarm. As more and more people seek out the wilderness, some of that wilderness is suddenly, unmistakably, *crowded.* Certain especially popular places are getting the worked-over look of run-down city parks.

In the Appalachians from the Smokies to the Catskills, the woods around popular campsites have been stripped of young growth by hikers hunting for fuel.

At popular lakes in any western range you may find shorelines trampled bare and spotted all around with blackened fire-rings.

On the famous High Peaks of the Adirondacks, the trampling of thousands of boots is destroying the moist alpine tundra that makes these peaks so much of another world. In Colorado's Rocky Mountain National Park, similar damage may take hundreds of years to reverse itself.

And so it is, on even the greatest mountains. The Forest Service has had to limit use of the trail up Mount Whitney in California, highest in the forty-eight lower states. And on 20,320-foot McKinley in Alaska, where any ascent is an expedition, rangers are cleaning up decades of accumulated junk.

The danger signs are everywhere, most obvious

in the East and in the Far West, where wild lands lie closest to great cities, but spreading fast to the remoter ranges of mid-continent. Today, in almost every well-known wilderness, there are places where the fabric of the land has visibly begun to fray.

About the permanent damage to the land—the long-term impairment of natural systems—ecologists tend to be somewhat reassuring. The genuinely spoiled places, they say, are (so far) small and few. But "wilderness" is a word that means not just the country itself but also our experience of that country. And this experience is, in its own way, a fragile, vulnerable thing.

When backpackers are asked what they desire most of all from wild places, the answer comes back: *solitude.* Not, to be sure, the total solitude of the single traveler: most backpackers travel in groups of two, three, or four, and like it that way. "Solitude," for them, means that they should meet few other groups; that they should meet no *large* parties at all; and that they should have no company at camp. Four or five meetings a day, for many, begins to spoil the experience. (This is not to say that larger groups have no place in the wilderness, but there is little question that the larger parties are resented by the smaller.)

Damage to the land, injury to the experience: these are the two dimensions of the "impact problem." If every hiker were scrupulously careful to make no mark on the land, to intrude on others as little as possible, the twofold problem would be far less difficult to solve. Unfortunately, too many backpackers are still relying on old methods, still maintaining outdated habits, still acting like lonely pioneers in an empty mountain world. Their weight on the land is heavy. It takes only a few of them to make a crowd.

The rise of the rules

It is not only the backpackers who are troubled by the changes they see in the backcountry. Government agencies manage our protected wilderness, and it is their charge to keep it authentically wild. But that means that the door to the wilderness cannot be endlessly, unconditionally open. In the 1970s, the authorities moved to regulate use as never before. Visitors to popular areas are now commonly required to pick up "wilderness permits" for their trips. At the moment only a few highly visited roadheads have actual daily quotas, but the time may come when it will be common to find, at the edge of wilderness, a "Come back tomorrow" sign.

It is hard to be comfortable with such restrictions. One of the chief pleasures of the land beyond the roadhead has always been the independence of the traveler and the freedom from formal rules. Quotas, certainly, should be a last resort. There is reason to complain, in some instances, that other, gentler methods have not been properly tried.

But for all that, there seems little chance that formal controls can be dispensed with now. And there is little logic in resenting them. Indeed, when the reasoning behind the limitations is made clear, most backpackers seem to accept them willingly. For more about the problems of wilderness management, see Chapter 33.

One thing is unmistakable. Restriction will come soonest, and in the most annoying form, in the places where the hikers themselves have failed. As an official at Yosemite National Park put it, "We have to plan everything with the *worst* backcountry user in mind." The job of protecting wilderness belongs largely to us who enjoy it. Each of us has the power to make the problem less.

First, each backpacker must make certain that his or her own way in the wilderness is a gentle and a thoughtful way. There is neither need nor excuse for adding new scars to the land. It is time to make a game, an ethic, a matter of pride, of walking softly in the wilderness world. We have to grasp the fact that no change we inflict on the changeless wilderness is trivial: each of us, now, is a thousand.

Second, we can seek out the less-known, less-used, and less-regulated areas. Even in such

7

crowded regions as the High Sierra and the Adirondacks you can find relatively empty lands. Crowding is still the exception, not the rule; it's easy enough to avoid the busy trails, the lakeshores and trailside camps, the busy days of the week, the busy times of the year.

And there is a third contribution that some may want to make. The demand for wilderness is great and growing—so much greater, then, the need to protect our only, irreplaceable supply. Each of us has the chance to speak out for wilderness. Each can lend some small individual weight to the cause of protecting what is unprotected now. If every second or third backpacker did so, the future of the wilderness would be immeasurably brighter. For more on this, see Chapter 31.

If wilderness has an essence, that essence is *room*. The more wilderness we have, the roomier it will be.

Going light: first points

This book is not just about backpacking. It is about that special kind and style of backpacking called "going light."

A few years ago, when you spoke of "going light," you were probably thinking of the poundage in your pack. "Going light" was the skill of paring down the load, of leaving at home every ounce that could be spared. And that is still an excellent thing to do.

But today "going light" has an additional meaning. Today you go light to spare the land. You choose your route, your gear, your destination with the welfare of the wilderness in mind. You camp and travel by the rules of "low impact."

Those principles are not complex. There are, indeed, different problems from region to region, as the landscape changes. There are questions that the different experts answer differently. Yet the main points are clear. Unfortunately, no more than a minority of today's backpackers seem to have heard even the most constantly repeated slogans of low impact. Before this book goes further, some of these points should be stated once more.

The go-light backpacker doesn't camp on meadows. This is a hard one; it seems to run against some instinct out of the Stone Age. The novice hurries to camp on the grass at the edge of the water or—a second choice—on the grass at the edge of the forest. But meadows, and especially high, moist meadows, are exceedingly fragile (they are also damp, cold, and full of mosquitoes). No matter how inviting that lakeside lawn appears, try for a camp in the woods or on barer, higher ground. Even in steep terrain three or four people can usually find a flat and pleasant spot.

The go-light camper avoids camps at timberline. Whether in Oregon or in Maine, the plants of timberline—the tiny stunted trees, the heathery, ground-pressed flowers—are already fighting to survive. It may take decades of short summers to bring measurable growth, and any damage you do will last a very long time. Try to plan your camps lower down, where living things have more margin, or higher up, where the rock and snow are barren.

Go-lighters take the landscape as they find it. The perfect camp is found, not made. If you want a laid-out campsite, choose an established one. If you pitch a tent, find a site with natural drainage. Don't cut limbs, dig ditches, pound nails, pile stones. The game is preservation, not pioneering.

Thoughtful backpackers carry out all their trash. Hikers are very conscientious these days about outright litter, but many still think it good practice to bury the junk they cannot burn. *Don't do it.* In most wild places the soils are shallow; animals and erosion often dig up what you bury. Whatever isn't burned should go out the same way it arrived—in your pack.

The go-lighter is sparing with fire. This is one of the more complicated matters: see Chapter 19. But note that in many wild areas fires are allowed only at certain sites or in certain zones. A light, portable stove gives you much more freedom to camp where you like.

The modern backpacker goes along with agency rules. In designated parks and wilderness areas, you may need a *wilderness permit:* see Chapter 14. With it you will get a list of regulations and suggested practices. Follow these, no matter what you may have read or what differing conclusions you may have formed. The agency workers aren't just hassling you: they are the people who watch the land; they see the changes, good and bad. Some of their rules are experimental, but the experiments have to be made. Play along—or go them one better in your efforts to spare the land.

Backpackers are anxious to do the right thing. In fact, as studies show, it would be hard to find another group of people so conscientious. It is misinformation, not any vandalistic instinct, that keeps bad habits going. To change those habits, the friends and users of America's wilderness need only to know what to do and why. And that is the most hopeful fact of all.

The freedom of the wilderness

We look back with something like sorrow to the days of the Great Wild: when Thoreau at Walden, a day's ride from Boston, could test the uses of utter isolation—when Muir could set out into the unknown Sierra, sleeping on beds of cut boughs, with no further provisions than a loaf of bread, a warm coat, and a billycan. That condition of the world could not last. But it is a pity that we have gone so far in the other direction—that we have pushed so far beyond what might have been the healthy balance point of civilized and wild.

Yet the wilderness we have—even that shrunken wilderness—is grand beyond description. And if it is no longer large enough to absorb and nullify whatever abuses we pour into it, it can be large enough for the delight of everyone who comes to visit it. It can be—if we can learn the self-restraint that makes it possible, in this our crowded world, to be free.

2:
Breaking In

WHOEVER YOU ARE, THE WAY IS OPEN.

Wilderness travel is not for the experts only, nor for the well-to-do, nor for the young. It is not only for the people who love to travel hard and count the miles behind them. It is not a competition. It is not a proving ground.

The way is open; yet it can be hard to know just where and how to begin. Some people choose to hurry themselves and make their first trip a considerable mountain journey. Others prefer to take it in slower stages.

The easy first step: *start hiking close to home.* You need not walk far, nor seek out rugged terrain: just start taking short walks, as easy as you like, on any available parkland trail. You will need no special gear at the beginning, and later only a light day-pack and a pair of boots or hiking shoes. If you would like to go with a group, get in touch with a local hiking club. These are found all over the country: the Appalachian Mountain Club and its chapters, the Mazamas, the Mountaineers, the Carolina Mountain Club, the Colorado Mountain Club, and endless others. The Federation of Western Outdoor Clubs and the Appalachian Trail Conference (see addresses in the *Resources* appendix) can give you information on their member organizations. The Sierra Club has chapters all over the United States and in much of Canada; most of these run local outings. Inquire also at the nearest backpacking store.

There are advantages to hiking with a group. For one thing, it hooks you into a grapevine, with the constant chatter about gear, experiences, places to go, problems encountered and solved. For another, you can watch how more experienced hikers handle themselves. And though most backpackers eventually choose to travel in family-sized parties, these group sessions are good social fun.

Now, as gradually as you like, begin building up your stock of gear and the skills that go with it. A good pair of boots or hiking shoes will be about the first on your list. As soon as you have them, set out to break them in. Wear them for short distances, then for long, until boot and foot have adapted each to the other. Try out the combinations of clothes you have in mind to wear on later overnight trips. When you buy your pack, try loading it and carrying it on a day-hike.

Spend time working with a compass and a topographic map on local, familiar ground; learn to translate from map to land and from land to map. This is important: even if you never plan to step off plain trails, you are bound to find places where you need to do a little navigation, and you might conceivably find yourself someday in a situation in which map and compass could save your life.

If day-hiking is Step One, Step Two (which many skip) is the organized, overnight backpacking trip. Most hiking clubs run these; in national parks you will find such trips run by concessioners as well. In such a group you have the support of experienced people, and if you've arrived without some small, crucial object, you can just about count on the party having a spare.

These sizable organized groups have a very special function. Many people never need them; some frankly detest them; but for many hikers they are the indispensable bridge into a wilderness that seems at first a bit strange and incalculable. Organized groups, some studies suggest, have more middle-aged people than you find elsewhere in the wilds, and more children; unlike smaller parties, they are made up about equally of men and women.

Step Three, for those who wish to make it, is the first independent trip with family or friends. The first time you head out, you may want to choose a well-known corner of the wilderness; inquire around the grapevine or check one of the trail guides sold in backpacking stores and in most general bookstores (see also Chapter 11). With that first trip behind you, you have known real self-sufficiency; you are no longer "breaking in." You are on your way.

Do you have to "get in shape"?

It depends.

Hiking with a pack is not, of itself, very hard. Anybody who is reasonably active at home can turn to the trails with no special preparation. But to people who have accustomed themselves to a life of physical leisure beyond the limits of what is healthy, backpacking can seem hard. To those who have spent years behind their desks—even though they golf or ski on weekends—it can seem hard. To the muscular man who regards himself as strong, yet seldom walks or bicycles or swims, it may come harder than he expects.

There are several ways in which one can be "fit." But there is one kind of "fitness" that matters most on the trail: the kind known variously as "stamina," "cardiovascular conditioning," or just plain "wind." This is not a matter of bulging muscles but a matter of efficient heart and lungs. When you are fit in this way, your heart will beat relatively slowly, even when you are working hard; you will be taking deep, satisfying breaths; you won't feel pressed for air. You get this stamina from lots of walking, lots of cycling, or from briefer periods of running or swimming. Anything that makes the heart and lungs work will strengthen them. Peak effort isn't important. The long haul is.

The only specific training for backpacking is backpacking; the second best preparation is hiking without a pack. Make sure that you can hike pretty vigorously without ill effects before adding the stress of an overnight load.

The first few times out (or the first time in a given season), many backpackers find their hips somewhat sore and abraded by the pressure of pack hip belts. This annoyance seems unavoidable, but the skin soon toughens. Sore knees are another frequent problem with beginners; knee braces, available in stores that sell athletic equipment, can help. If the problem persists, a doctor with experience in sports medicine can suggest exercises to strengthen the muscles that stabilize the knee.

It goes without saying that you need a doctor's advice if you suspect a heart problem or any other condition that might limit your backpacking; older people in particular should start very slowly and keep the doctor posted on what they're undertaking. But the chances are good that your physician will enthusiastically approve. The backpacker's kind of fitness is the kind that doctors most welcome in their patients, and nobody basically healthy needs to deny himself or herself the pleasure of the trails.

Gearing Up

Naturally, we also carried all the standard mountain climbing equipment: cleated shoes and nails of all kinds, ropes, screw rings, hammers, snap hooks, ice axes, crampons, snowshoes, skis and all accessories, as well as instruments for observation like compasses, clinometers, altimeters, barometers, thermometers, range-finders, alidades, and cameras. And arms: rifles, carbines, revolvers, short sabers, dynamite—in other words, enough to face any foreseeable obstacle.

—René Daumal

3:
Gearing Up

No MATTER HOW GRADUALLY you begin, you will soon have to start locating gear—*objects*, and quite a few of them. Even the lightest pack will contain seventy or eighty separate items. The novice, looking at a list like the one on the next few pages, sees a sizable job ahead.

Take a moment to scan this list. It allows something more than minimum comfort on a trip in hospitable western mountains in a hospitable season, late summer. Humidity is low, water plentiful, weather pleasant, trails plain.

Such conditions are by no means the rule in the American wilderness. This list is *not* a model to go by but only an illustration of the way one party packed for a particular journey. It is meant to show something of the *logic of gear*.

What do you need to travel safely and in comfort?

You need *boots or shoes* sturdy enough, and heavy enough, to support and protect your feet— and not one bit heavier than that.

Exhibit: A Typical Packlist for Dry-Summer Mountains

(For one person in a party of three. No price shown for items found at home.)

Item	Weight in pack	Cost
Clothing, worn		
stout cotton pants	—	—
belt	—	—
underpants	—	—
undershirt	—	—
cotton shirt	—	—
hat	—	$7
sunglasses	—	$10
inner socks	—	$3
outer socks	—	$4
hiking boots, ultralight	—	$90
Clothing, packed		
spare socks, one set	13 oz.	$7
hiking shorts	10 oz.	$15
rain chaps, urethane	6 oz.	$15
spare sunglasses in case	2 oz.	$15
knit cap	3 oz.	$8
polyester pile vest	12 oz.	$30
Gore-Tex wind/rain parka	24 oz.	$130
Sleeping gear		
mummy sleeping bag in stuffsack	59 oz.	$185
foam pad, short length	8 oz.	$10
groundsheet, 7' × 9'	9 oz.	$10
Kitchen and basic tools (individual)		
flashlight	3 oz.	$10
spare batteries, bulb	2 oz.	$2
matches	1 oz.	$1
cup	3 oz.	$2
spoon	1 oz.	—
pocketknife	2 oz.	$10
bandannas, two	2 oz.	$2
50' nylon cord	4 oz.	$2
candle	1 oz.	—
Office		
notebook, pencils	2 oz.	$1
maps	2 oz.	$5
compass	2 oz.	$10
cheap watch	—	—

Item	Weight in pack	Cost
Personal		
tooth care items	1 oz.	—
toilet paper	1 oz.	—
lip balm	1 oz.	$2
suncream	2 oz.	$5
Miscellaneous		
first aid kit	16 oz.	$20
sew and repair kit	2 oz.	$2
Haulage		
pack	72 oz.	$140
stuffbags	5 oz.	$15
plastic bags and closures	2 oz.	$2
quart water bottle	4 oz.	$4
Shelter (group)		
tarp, 12′ × 10′	44 oz.	$56
Kitchen (group)		
small white gas stove with screen	14 oz.	$39
two pots	16 oz.	$15
gripper	1 oz.	$1
liter fuel can	5 oz.	$6
funnel, eyedropper	1 oz.	$2
Consumables (group)		
food (three people, four days)	384 oz.	$70
reserve food	48 oz.	$10
fuel	18 oz.	$1
water (in canteens at any one time)	48 oz.	—

Weight of pack and contents

Personal gear	17 pounds 5 ounces
One-third of group gear	1 pound 11 ounces
One-third of consumables	10 pounds 6 ounces
Total	**29 pounds 6 ounces**

Cost of pack and contents

Personal gear	$774
One-third of group gear	$37
One-third of consumables	$27
Total	**$838**

You need *clothing:* garments to protect you from sun, from wind and cold, from rain and snow, from scratching brush and irritant plants, from mosquitoes and stinging flies.

You need *sleeping gear* for warmth at night and *shelter* to keep you dry.

You need *water and food,* and the tools of cooking and eating (unless you choose to rely on no-cook meals).

You need a *knife,* a *flashlight,* plenty of *matches,* and a good length of *cord.*

You need *emergency, medical,* and *repair* gear for problems, major and minor.

You need *navigation tools*—usually just maps and a compass.

You need *personal items*—toilet paper and a toothbrush at the minimum.

And you need *containers*—mostly bags, big and little, and a pack to put it all in.

One of the minor pleasures of wilderness travel is the comfortable feeling of dealing with good gear. You come to know that collection of objects almost like a language: the uses of each item, its faults, its limitations, the location in which it should be packed to be most easily at hand when you require it. This familiarity *can* lead to a kind of obsessive fussiness. It can also produce the "gear freak," the zealot who is restless when lacking the very latest innovation in every department. But for all that, the pleasure of gear is a genuine pleasure.

In buying gear, there's a Rule Number One: *Go slowly.* There is no reason to purchase everything at once, and unless you are unusually sure of yourself you should not try to. Borrow and rent equipment whenever you can. Make do with what you have on hand. Some expensive items—like stoves and tents—are shared, so you can rely at first on your companions; or you can begin with organized trips where these items are part of the package. It is almost never a mistake to put off buying equipment. The longer you delay, the better chance you have to find out what truly suits you.

Where to buy

If you can, get the help of a backpackers' specialty shop—or of several. There are now many of these nationwide. Department stores, surplus outlets, and general sporting goods stores also carry wilderness gear, but they seldom can answer the questions you need to ask.

Take a look in the Yellow Pages: first under "backpacking and mountaineering," then under "camping," "skiing," and "sporting goods." If you are lucky, you may have several competing specialty shops in your area. Use all of them. Consider. Shop around. No need to stay home while you're considering: many stores also rent packs, tents, and sleeping bags. And renting is not a waste of money—it's a valuable series of lessons in the merits of different brands and designs.

The salespeople in most of the specialty shops are knowledgeable, easy to talk to, and generous with their time. Don't feel you're imposing on them: the time they spend on you is reflected in the prices they charge. They always have opinions, and there is almost always disagreement from store to store; compare the versions, and you learn a good deal. A few backpacking stores are larger, somewhat cheaper, and less personal: take your pick. But there is something reprehensible about gathering all your advice from the smaller stores only to do all your buying at the larger ones.

If you don't have access to specialty shops, there's always mail order. It's worthwhile to collect the catalogs of the major outfits, in any case, for the information they contain. Some very good lines of gear are sold primarily by mail. But there is truly no substitute for seeing and handling the gear yourself.

In the last few years the choices in gear have doubled and redoubled. For every type of equipment there are not just competing brands but competing, fundamentally different, designs; and every one of them seems to have been tested on a trek across the

Sahara, or on some mountain wall in Asia. The days are gone when a mere backpacker can keep track of the changing technological scene. This makes the advice of the salespeople, biased though it often is, more important than ever.

For more help, you can turn to equipment-rating articles published in such magazines as *Backpacker* and *Outside.* These ratings are not beyond dispute. You must also keep in mind that a negative report on a product often causes the manufacturer to alter the design—thus all such studies tend to become rapidly dated. Nonetheless, they can help the buyer navigate the equipment labyrinth.

Faced with these complexities, some backpackers become obsessed with gear. They spend endless energy in the search for some pack or tent or sleeping bag that strikes them as "the ideal." While it's good to take your time, it's also good to remind yourself frequently that gear is only a set of tools: a means to an end. The backpacker does the work, not the backpack. And when you get out into the field, you're likely to find that different, competing models, if equally well made, do the job about equally well.

How much will it cost?

What about the first weekend trip? How *little* can you spend and still be safe and comfortable in the wild?

This depends, of course, on where you are going, how much useful junk you have around, and how many people you have with you to share common expenses. By renting some of the major pieces of gear and buying the cheapest adequate versions of other items, you can probably reduce the tab to under $200 the first time you go out. Lower than that it is difficult to go.

The cost of successive trips will depend on what new items of equipment you buy each time. The shopping never stops entirely; there are always minor objects to add or replace. Once you are past such major purchases as pack and boots, however, you will find yourself spending much less: seldom over $50 a trip, and often only a fraction of that.

What about the total cost of building your permanent stock of good equipment? It can no longer be said that backpacking gear is cheap. A pretty complete set of well-made summer gear is likely to set you back something like $750, 1983 prices, before you are through (but remember that this expense will be spread out over several years). More than half of the price tag will be for four major items—your *boots* (Chapter 4), your *pack* (Chapter 6), your *sleeping bag* (Chapter 7), and your *stove* (Chapter 9). If you need a *tent*—but you may not—that is the fifth major purchase (Chapter 8). There are also some very expensive items of wilderness clothing to be had—items that, however, you may well be able to do without (Chapter 5).

There are ways of beating down this entry price. A few stores handle secondhand gear; many have bulletin boards where sellers advertise. Then again,

---

Minimum cost of first weekend trip

Individual

rent pack	$10	
rent sleeping bag	$20	
buy cheapest boots	$50	
2 sets socks	10	
pad, groundcloth	20	
poncho, chaps, hat	40	
other items	20	
food	15	
Individual total	**185**	*(plus any restaurant meals)*

Group

rent tent (?)	18	
rent stove	5	
fuel	3	
pans or billy cans	(found at home)	
Group total	**26**	*(plus shared auto costs)*

you may be able to find *seconds*—items that come from the factory with harmless imperfections. These are sold at reduced prices, either at factory outlets or in special "seconds shops." Inquire at local stores.

If you're pretty sure of what you need, you can pick up excellent bargains at the seasonal sales that gear stores hold. Too, stores that rent gear eventually sell those items at cut prices. Large mail-order houses may be cheaper than your local mountain store. There are several mail firms that make a point of offering well-made wilderness gear at substandard prices (one such is Back To Basics in Emeryville, California).

Military surplus stores (many of which are not surplus at all but merely discount houses) have some good prices on good gear. They also stock flimsy products: go carefully here. The same goes for department stores, general sporting goods stores, and the like. It should be noted that both J. C. Penney and Sears Roebuck market fairly adequate lines of wilderness gear at attractive prices.

Whether you buy high or low, don't spend money needlessly on gear that's intended for heavier use than you plan to give it. Some shoppers look by reflex at the "top of the line." They buy the weightiest, costliest, most nearly "expeditionary" sleeping bags, packs, boots, tents, jackets. For almost all of them this is an error. The sleeping bag you could use in the winter in the Never Summer Range of Colorado is only hot and clammy in a normal wilderness summer. And a Himalayan-scale backpack is a poor container for a weekend's worth of gear.

The prices in this book

The prices of the things backpackers need are not immune from inflation; in fact, they seem to outpace it. Basic materials, notably leather and down, have taken several sharp price jumps in recent years. They will probably do it again. So please bear in mind that all prices given in these pages are both approximate and liable to change. They reflect the situation in 1983 and, like EPA mileage estimates, are best used for comparative purposes. It isn't just possible that you will find higher price tags when you go out to buy: it is nearly certain.

How much will it weigh?

Let's say you have a packload without too many extras: no paperback novels, no ropes, no cameras, no Monopoly games. Assume your load is for a lightweight summer trip. Forget for a moment about water, food, and fuel. And forget about shelter, stove, pots—the gear you will be sharing among companions.

Thus limited, the *basic dry weight* of your pack—including clothing, bedding, first aid kit, various oddments, and the pack itself—should be somewhere between sixteen and eighteen pounds. This does not count your boots or the clothes you start out wearing, but it does include clothes for rain and moderate cold, which will, with luck, be stowed away much of the time.

To get a notion of what the rest of the packload will weigh, you can apply these rules of thumb:

● For food, figure on two pounds per person per day. With expensive freeze-dried foods and an average appetite, you may find yourself happy with less. Most women eat less, most teenagers a good deal more.

● Add one pound for each pint of water you normally carry.

● Add twelve ounces for each pint of white gas or kerosene. A typical if economical allowance is one-quarter cup, or 1.5 ounces, per person per day; butane weighs more. See Chapter 12.

● If your group will use a tent or tents, figure about three pounds per person. But allow just one pound per person if shelter is a tarp or tarps.

● Finally, a group of two or three hikers will carry two to three pounds of cookware and stove.

So, if two of you were heading out for five summer days, in, say, the Adirondacks; if you carried, as you should for that trip, both stove and tent; and if each of you had a pint of water in a canteen, your theoretical share of the load would be something like this:

17.5 lbs. of personal kit
10 lbs. of food
1 lb. of water
1.5 lbs. of cooking gear
8 ozs. of fuel (1.5 oz. per person per day)
3 lbs. of shelter

for a theoretical total of thirty-three and a half pounds.

This, like the detailed list a few pages back, is merely an illustration. But it makes the point: on a trip of less than a week in a place and month not extraordinarily hostile, you won't need a load of more than thirty-five pounds.

But how much can you comfortably carry?

An old rule of thumb says you can carry a third of your body weight. And indeed, if you have to, you can; climbers often wind up toting that or more. But for most people on today's trails—people who come for the simple fun of it—that is far too much. With light, modern gear, it should be possible to limit your pack to a fifth of your own weight on trips of a few days.

So a 200-pound man might have a comfortable limit of 40 pounds; a 110-pound woman, by this formula, would be limited to 22. With loads of this order, experienced hikers may almost forget that they have packs on their backs. (But note: if you are overweight, your built-in extra poundage doesn't entitle you to a heavier pack.) If you hike in a group, as most people do, you can split up food, fuel, and community gear according to body weight. As to your personal gear, you're stuck with it. If you travel alone, your pack will include all "community" gear and ride a little heavier.

The one-fifth rule is only a starting point. It is possible to cut down this standard load, easier still to build it up. Every hiker makes a compromise between the advantages a light pack and the advantages (if any) of the extra gear.

Going light: old style and new

You will hear the most drastic advice about cutting the weight in your pack. People really do cut handles off toothbrushes. Whether or not this deadpan game makes a practical difference, it's true that the overloaded hiker gets ingenious at finding objects to leave home.

But "going light," that familiar slogan, has undergone a subtle change in meaning. Today it refers less to the load in your pack than to the weight—the impact—of your passage on the land. And in adopting this version of "going light," backpackers have learned to accept a few more ounces of weight on their shoulders.

The heaviest of the new necessities is the stove. Nobody should travel in today's wilderness without one. Don't put yourself in the position of *having* to kindle a fire when conditions are wrong. (Sometimes there is no down, dead wood to be had. Sometimes fires are not permitted, or permitted at certain sites only. In other cases your fire would leave ugly and unnecessary scars.) And a stove gives you a much wider choice of campsites—much more freedom to revise your plans.

Extra water containers, too, are carried more often now. In well-watered mountains like the Cascades or the Adirondacks, it may seem odd to keep more than a sip in your canteen. But if you have bottles you can fill toward evening, you no longer have to cling to stream and trail. You can, for instance, work your way up some lofty ridgeline and camp where dawn will strike you early and alone.

And of course you never plan to save weight at the expense of the land—by building, for instance, shelters of green branches. That was fine for the mountain men of the 1860s, but it has no place in the wilderness today. As for the famous natural foods to be found in the hills, they're there, all right, but you find them undisturbed only because not many people have yet thought of looking for them. Enjoy the trout, enjoy the huckleberries or wild onions, but count them as luxuries. "Living off the land" is an idea whose time has passed. This development is ironic and yet quite logical: the stronger our wish to preserve the wild places, the less we can meet them on their own terms; the more sophisticated, civilized, and complex become the gadgets we must bring into them.

The wilderness regions and the gear you take

From region to region and season to season, rules change. One list of gear won't serve for all landscapes, all weathers, all the different demands of the American wilderness.

Some places are pretty dry in summer; some are very wet. In the dry-summer mountains of the West, shelter and raingear can be simple and light; the occasional thunderstorm may be more an entertainment than a piece of serious weather. But in the Smokies or the North Cascades, summer rain is real, and much can be said for carrying a tent.

Humidity counts, too. If the air is dry between rains, cotton clothing and classic down sleeping bags are efficient. But in the Catskills or the Blue Ridge, even a cool, clear night may be damp enough to saturate your sleeping bag and chill you in cotton clothes. In such places, wool or fiberpile clothing and synthetic-filled or water-resistant sleeping bags have their advantages.

In the deserts, and on some ridge routes in less arid ranges, water is the factor that limits you. Springs and streams may be far apart, and unreliable at that. In Death Valley, for instance, two thirds of your load may be water.

In areas where winter brings snow, a whole new kind of wilderness, a white and challenging wilderness, appears with the first cold storm.

Problems with gear

Catalogs often contrive to give you the impression that wilderness gear is indestructible and perfect. Of course (as you'll find out soon enough) this isn't so. Some items and some brands hold up better than others; none are invariably trouble-free. Sleeping bags and tents get torn. Stoves balk and have to be tinkered with. Waterproofing wears off and has to be renewed. Zippers fail. On cheap packs—and even on some very costly ones—inadequate stitching may fray. As for flashlights, they fail about as often as they work.

Wilderness gear is indeed better made, on the average, than other consumer goods today. Yet much of it is made less well than it could be. When you shop for gear, pay special attention to the detail of construction: durability is perhaps the greatest virtue of all. (The gear industry began as a collection of tiny, independent makers. Now, like other fields of commerce, it is in the process of sorting out into a handful of big conglomerates. This may affect the quality of gear.)

Many minor repairs, of course, can be done on the trail. When the problem is too large for that, most reputable shops and manufacturers are very good about repairing items that were faulty to begin with. Some stores will do additional repairs very cheaply on items purchased from them. Shoemakers will sew on leather patches, replace hooks and grommets, and handle many other problems with leather and heavy fabric. And one equipment outlet, Eastern Mountain Sports, runs a nationwide mail-order repair service for most kinds of gear.

4:
Boots

SOONER OR LATER—and probably sooner, because this purchase is one of the hardest to put off—you will have to acquire some special footgear for backpacking. The choice is wide. In fact, for easy shopping, it is *too* wide. Dozens of different manufacturers make boots and specialized shoes, and every one of them claims special virtue for its product. You can get lost in the clamor of competing features and learned arguments for this or that cunning design.

And yet there are just two things you require from a hiking boot or shoe. The first is comfort: the footgear should be as light, well fitting, and easy on the flesh as it possibly can be. The second is protection: it must support and shield the foot and the ankle against incessant jarring, bruising stones, water and cold ground, and possible twisting falls. These two goals compete, and every boot or shoe is a compromise between them.

The trick is to choose footgear that is heavy

enough for the kind of hiking you will do—and not one ounce heavier. Only experience will tell you just where that balance point lies for you. For years, people wandered around the wilderness wearing vastly excessive amounts of leather, simply because it was the expected thing. Currently, ultralight-weight footgear is in vogue. What you need will depend on the type of hiking you do, the kind of loads you carry, and your personal agility and steadiness of ankle.

The lightest boots weigh as little as two pounds the pair in an average size; the heaviest can run five pounds or even more. We can divide the range into approximate thirds.

Smooth-trail boots and shoes are light and flexible. Many use materials other than leather: nylon cloth, and sometimes water-resistant Gore-Tex. They are fine for day-trips on well-surfaced trails when the climate is not too cold, and many backpackers find them adequate for hiking with pack as well. Typical weights, for a middle-range size, lie between two and three pounds the pair. Prices presently run from under $60 to well over $100.

General-purpose boots are heavier, more solid, and stiffer. Almost all have uppers made entirely of leather. They are suitable for cross-country travel, for heavy loads, and for cold weather. But there's a penalty in comfort and in weight: they range from just over three pounds to almost five pounds the pair. Prices run from $75 to more than double that.

Mountaineering boots begin at about five pounds and go on up—way up. Their leather is very strong, thick, and rigid. A few are made of tough plastic. The heavier models have extra-thick mid-soles, and some have totally rigid soles that make them great for certain kinds of climbing but terrible for ordinary walking. Most hikers need to know about these massive constructions only to guard against buying them by mistake.

The best boot is the lightest boot that will serve your hiking purpose. A pound on your feet, army research shows, is as hard to move as five pounds on your back. Stiff boots, though sometimes needed, are hard to break in and generally tough on the feet. Many people who wear massive boots have trouble with painful, inflamed Achilles tendons, caused by the incessant bruising of the flesh against the top of a rigid boot heel.

Now: how heavy should your first pair of boots be?

Your day-hiking experience should give you some feeling for your feet. If you've hiked in sneakers, running shoes, or other light footgear, what do your feet tell you at the end of the day? Are they bruised and sore from the hardness of the ground? Do you find that you keep your balance easily, or do your ankles tend to turn under you? If you feel vulnerable in light shoes, then a leather boot probably makes sense for you. If you feel competent in conventional shoes, you can reasonably look for boots at the lightweight end of the range.

Your ambitions obviously make a difference here, too. Do you expect to hike well-maintained trails in warm climates for the time being? Or do you plan to branch out soon into cross-country travel and cold-weather hiking?

I will now stick my neck out. To my mind, the ideal first boot for easy backpacking is one right at the boundary between the light and middleweight types, within a few ounces on either side of three pounds the pair. (Weights are usually given in "average" size, equivalent to a man's size 8 or 9.) Choose one of the stoutest of the lightweights, with a stiff heel counter, a stiff toe, and a high top. Or pick one of the lightest and most pliable of conventional leather boots. Such boots can hardly fail to be useful in quite a range of conditions, and you won't have to take out a loan to buy them. After a season or two, you will know much better what your real requirements are. Then you can replace your worn-out starter pair, or add other, more specialized footgear to your collection. Many backpackers wind up owning a whole row of diverse clodhoppers.

Some boot anatomy

All boots—leather and ultralight—have a basic structure in common.

A typical boot *sole* is a fairly complex structure of layers: the tread layer or *outsole* next to the ground; one or several *midsoles;* the *insole* next to the foot. All boots suitable for backpacking have midsoles. Without this layer, there is an inadequate cushion between foot and ground. In many boots a metal *shank,* a short, flexible band built into the midsole, adds support and springiness.

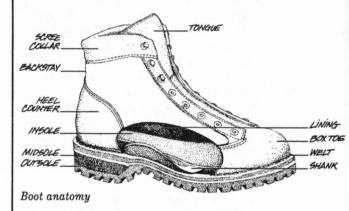

Boot anatomy

The margin where the sole joins the *upper* is called the *welt.* Uppers are fastened to soles in various ways. Leather boots, in general, are stitched; ultralight boots are likely to be cemented.

Whatever material makes up the body of the upper, there must be stiff reinforcement at both heel and toe. At these spots the boot must keep its shape for protection and proper fit. The *heel counter,* the reinforcing piece that wraps around the heel, is especially important.

Most boots have at least some foam padding around the foot, between the main leather wall and a thin inner liner. Padded boots are easier to break in. They are, however, harder to keep dry in wet climates, because the padding soaks up water.

There are several different ways of closing off the spaces between the tongue and the rest of the upper. You should make sure there is *something* there. Often it will be a bellows of thin flexible leather; or it can be two flaps under the tongue, which overlap.

Lacing varies, too. There may be grommeted *eyelets, D-rings* that rivet onto the leather, or *hooks*. Most often there is some combination. Eyelets break less often than the others but are a little harder to lace, especially with cold hands. Rings and hooks tend to break off, but any shoemaker can repair them for a small charge. Sometimes, midway in a row of hooks, one pair of normal hooks is replaced by a pair of "clinch hooks" or other devices that grip the laces and prevent them from sliding through. Using these, you can, in theory, tighten the laces firmly on one side of the clinch while leaving them loose on the other.

Many boots have leather or plastic *scree collars* sewn on around the top of the ankle opening. The idea is to keep the tiny rocks of "scree" from bouncing into your boots. These collars don't seem to accomplish their main purpose very well. The scree collar does have another function, however, at least on a rigid boot: it cushions the sensitive Achilles tendon. (Some boots lack collars but give you extra padding above the heel.)

More about ultralight boots

In the last few years, bootmakers have been thinking light. And the manufacturers of running shoes—struck by the fact that many experienced backpackers use their products happily—have branched out into the hiking shoe business. New Balance, Adidas and Nike are bootmakers now. The result is a pack of competing and rapidly changing ultralight designs.

Lightest of all are reinforced walking shoes that are almost indistinguishable from running shoes. As the weight per pair climbs past two pounds, recog-

Some ultralight boots

nizable boots appear, with high tops, extra padding, and more ability to shed water. The uppers are usually nylon packcloth or Cordura, to which pieces of leather are sewn for reinforcement. Soles may resemble those of traditional running shoes, those of traditional hiking boots, or something in between. Some have midsoles of shock-absorbing EVA (ethyl vinyl acetate) like those found in running shoes. Some have foam insoles that mold to the foot and can be removed for washing.

The advantages of these boots are clear. Lightness. Low cost. A short and easy breaking-in period. These soft materials adapt to the foot, not the other way around. Another good point is that many ultralights have soles of crepe or shallow-toothed Vibram that gouge the soil less than the deep-toothed Vibram familiar in traditional designs. (See *Lugs: a question of impact,* below.)

The new boots also have limitations. They are not very durable. An active cross-country hiker can demolish a pair in a season. They can't be recommended for cold or very wet places. They cannot offer the solid ankle support of conventional boots.

One material now being used in lightweight boots is Gore-Tex, a microporous membrane that, ideally, keeps liquid water out but allows the evaporation of sweat. (For much more about this fabric and its cousins, see Chapter 5.) In theory, Gore-Tex should allow boots to shed water as never before. In practice, there are problems. Gore-Tex is rather fragile stuff, however protected by cloth facings, and a boot gets rugged wear. If a boot has seams through the Gore-Tex, these must be carefully and repeatedly sealed in the hope of preventing leakage. Some boots are now made with one-piece Gore-Tex liners that surround the foot like a sock, and this design may prove more effective. In any case, there is probably little reason to seek out such refinements if your ultralight boots will be used chiefly in warm and moderately dry places.

More about leather boots

When you look at leather boots lined up in a store, one difference will jump out at you. Some boots have a rough, feltlike surface; others are smooth and shiny. These are called "rough-out" and "smooth-out" surfaces. There is little practical difference between them. (Don't consider looks. All leather boots look alike after the first few journeys.)

Much more important is the distinction between top-grain and split-grain leather. The tanned skin of the cow is thicker than it needs to be for boot leather. So, in the factory, it is split, and the layers pulled apart. The outer layer, the layer next to the hair, is rugged, pliable, naturally oily, and water repellent. The lower layers, split-grain leathers, are permeable and not so strong. Most hiking boots are made of top-grain material, but the lightest models use split-grain leathers. Such boots are excellent for trail hiking where water is not a problem. They do stretch and get a lumpy look, and they wear out more quickly than boots of top-grain leather.

There are other differences among leathers. Some pieces are tougher and cost more. Large chunks also cost more. Some boots are made from several pieces of leather and have many seams; some are made of a single piece, with just one seam.

Welt designs in leather boots

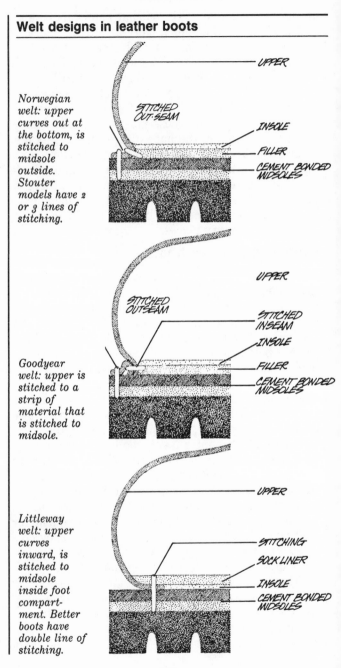

Norwegian welt: upper curves out at the bottom, is stitched to midsole outside. Stouter models have 2 or 3 lines of stitching.

UPPER

STITCHED
OUT-SEAM

INSOLE

FILLER

CEMENT BONDED
MIDSOLES

Goodyear welt: upper is stitched to a strip of material that is stitched to midsole.

UPPER

STITCHED
OUTSEAM

STITCHED
INSEAM

INSOLE

FILLER

CEMENT BONDED
MIDSOLES

Littleway welt: upper curves inward, is stitched to midsole inside foot compartment. Better boots have double line of stitching.

UPPER

STITCHING

SOCK LINER

INSOLE

CEMENT BONDED
MIDSOLES

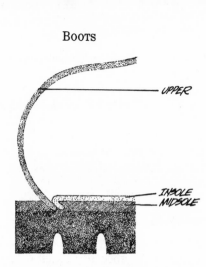

Injection molding: upper penetrates midsole and is bonded without stitches.

These one-piece are the most expensive, the most durable, the easiest to waterproof, and the hardest to break in. Though some perfectionists insist on them, backpackers can ignore the question.

With leather boots, the upper is almost always attached to the sole by stitching. There are several methods. When you can actually see stitches around the sole on the outside of the boot, you are looking either at a *Norwegian* welt or at a *Goodyear welt.* If you see more than one row of stitching, you can be sure it is Norwegian. The Goodyear, used on many American boots, is not so sturdy, but it's acceptable for light backpacking use. You can recognize this welt by the separate band of leather or plastic that runs around the groove.

If there are no visible stitches around the sole, it may mean that the stitching is inside (the *Littleway* method). There's quite a controversy between Norwegian and Littleway fans, but both methods, in truth, are good. On some boots the absence of visible stitching may indicate that another process, called *injection molding,* was used. This is acceptable provided that there is a midsole.

Metal shanks are standard in the soles of leather boots. To provide additional "spring," soles are designed with an upturned toe, so that the foot tends to roll forward as the hiker's weight shifts. This "rocker" pattern is very pronounced in some boots, less in others.

Recently boots of tough, stiff plastic have reached the market. The problem of rigidity is overcome by pronounced "rocker" soles, by ankle hinges, and by internal padding. Though these are effective, they seem at present to be better adapted to mountaineering and winter use than to general backpacking: like heavier leather boots, they weigh in at over four pounds the pair.

Shopping for boots

As with most gear, the case is good for buying your boots in the specialty outlets. There are a few bargains outside the backpacking stores, however, that you should consider. Almost any store selling shoes will offer two types of light boots that work well on easy trails. The ordinary "work boot," with a slick leather surface and a crepe sole, is an excellent bargain. The GI regular combat boot is also cheap, if you find it sufficiently comfortable (most people don't). Surplus stores also carry a lighter, ventilated "tropical combat" boot; these are much favored for travel in warm, wet places, such as low-lying regions of the South.

If you need a general-purpose boot, bargains are harder to find. A few backpacking stores sell used hiking boots, or take commissions for helping the owners to sell them.

Fitting

When you go shopping, make up your mind to insist on a good fit. When in doubt, don't buy. Some people find suitable boots quickly; others have to go through quite a few sessions of trying boots on.

Before you enter a store, have an idea of the type and weight of boot you want: that is, the loads you plan to carry in the near future and the kind of terrain you expect to traverse. Wear the combination of socks you plan to wear when you hike. (See *Socks* below.) Tell the salesperson your street shoe size and let him or her take it from there. (You need help on this—sizing is anything but standard—but the specialty store employees know their stock.)

Slide on your candidate pair. They should feel a good bit roomier than your normal shoes—at least half an inch longer than your stockinged foot, but less than an inch. Before you lace up, push your foot forward inside the boot as far as it will go. You should just barely be able to fit an index finger all the way down between your heel and the back of the boot. (Two fingers is too much room.)

Now kick back in the boot to settle the heel into the socket and lace the boots tightly. (If the laces draw the sides of the closure so close together that they almost touch, the boot is too loose.) Have the salesperson hold your heel to the floor and do your best to lift the back of your foot. The heel should rise no more than an eighth of an inch inside the boot. (That's not much. It should feel very firm.)

To check the fit of the toe, hook your heel over a rock, a wooden shoe-rack, or a street curb, so that your toe points sharply downhill. Kick forward inside the boot. If your toes feel stubbed against the tip, the boot is too short. (You can also kick against something hard, if the store will let you—some say it's bad for the boot.) You must be able to wriggle your toes freely when you wear the boot, or you risk cutting off the circulation of blood in your foot.

To make sure the boot is not too wide, have someone hold the boot to the floor and try to rotate your foot inside it. The ball of your foot shouldn't shift noticeably sideways. Don't worry if the sides of the boot feel tight—boots loosen up in this dimension. (But they don't get longer or shorter—heel and toe are crucial.)

You may hear it said that it is better to have a boot too large than too small, on the theory that you can always add socks. Don't count too much on this. A boot that is sloppy in the store will only get sloppier. And a loose heel is almost bound to give you blisters.

If the boots or shoes seem to pass these various

tests, make sure you have them laced up firmly and spend ten or fifteen minutes "hiking" around the store. Don't just stroll: speed up, slow down, go up and down stairs, swivel, do knee bends. Watch again for a feeling of tightness in the toes or of sloppiness in the heels. As foot and boot warm up, the fit may change.

Undecided between two sizes or models? Try wearing one of each. In a few minutes, one will start feeling markedly better than the other. Double-check by repeating the experiment with the two types on opposite feet. If you have a third model on your final list, compare it with the survivor of your first elimination round, using the same method. It's time-consuming, but the time spent is worthwhile. No competent salesperson will try to hurry your decision!

Most stores allow you to take a pair of boots home with you and walk around indoors until your mind is made up—then, if necessary, return them for a refund. Or you can climb up and down stairs in a city building. If you find nothing that fits you properly in a particular store, go elsewhere. Keep looking. Different brands of boots can be *very* different in configuration. (Boots are built on standardized patterns called "lasts." A last is nothing but a model foot—a hypothetical, average foot. Somewhere out there, somebody is probably building boots on a last that matches your foot shape reasonably well.)

Women's feet are, on the average, a little differently proportioned than men's. Many bootmakers now recognize this fact and manufacture women's sizes—which provide another last variation to be tested by hikers of either sex. In addition, there are some models designed and advertised as women's boots exclusively. The market for these does not seem to be large: a boot's a boot, and the only thing that matters is what fits *you*.

Buying by mail

If you have to, you can order boots by mail.

Many people do and are quite satisfied. The key thing, as every catalog will tell you, is to send an outline of your stockinged foot. (One foot is usually the larger; trace that one, or both.) It's a good idea to list several choices from the brands offered, so that the mail-order people can choose the "last" that best fits your foot outline. Here it makes sense to deal with the large houses, like Recreational Equipment, Inc. (REI) and Eastern Mountain Sports (EMS), because of their wide selection. When the boots arrive, do as you would with a pair found in a store: test the boots, wear them around indoors, and if you aren't satisfied, send them back for replacement or refund.

Other types of boots

Alongside the basic backpacking boots, there are perhaps a dozen different kinds of specialized shoes. *Rock-climbing boots* are light, tight, fragile, and generally unsuited for plain walking. *Shoepacs* are high boots with waterproof rubber around the foot and leather rising up the ankle; they are much used for winter travel in the East. *Cross-country ski boots* are built to attach to skis with light, simple three-pin bindings. *Ski-mountaineering boots* are heavier models for much more rugged skiing. For more about winter footwear, see Chapter 23.

Shoepac

Socks

Ask ten people, get ten answers. Most hikers start by wearing two pairs: a thinnish wool or cotton inner pair (say a medium-weight athletic sock) and a thick wool outer. Then, if they like, they experiment. If you blister easily, try wearing a very thin white sock—as thin as a normal dress sock but *not* made of nylon, which is hot—inside the others. Ultralight boots are often worn with a single, medium-weight sock.

Accessories

There are plenty of extras (always!) that you can take for your feet. The real necessity is *moleskin* or *molefoam,* sheets of protective padding, sticky on one side, that you can buy in any drugstore. Apply moleskin whenever you suspect an irritation that could lead to a blister. (Some people find ordinary adhesive tape works just as well.) A few hikers take *foot powder* to fight both blisters and athlete's foot; some like to carry tincture of benzoin, a sticky liquid that, applied to the skin, helps moleskin or tape to adhere; a very few take *rubbing alcohol. Soft shoes*—tennis shoes, moccasins, or whatever—are sometimes taken to use around camp, if the trail boots are heavy: for comfort, of course, but also because they disturb the ground less than toothy lug soles. (Light shoes are also sometimes useful for crossing streams.) *Booties* ($15 and up) are loose, high-topped slippers stuffed with insulation. A luxury in summer, they can make the difference between achingly cold feet and pleasantly warm ones on a cold winter night. Booties with heavy fabric soles cost more. *Gaiters* ($15–$40) are fabric coverings that fasten around the tops of your boots when you slog through snowbanks or wade through ankle-deep scree. They are also of value in rattlesnake country. On muddy trips you may want a *wire brush:* see below. *Spare laces?* Use your general-purpose cord.

Breaking in

Whatever sort of boots or shoes you buy, they will need at least a little breaking in before they are comfortable. (Ultralights adjust rather quickly to your feet; light split-leather boots, especially those with generous inside padding, settle in fairly quickly, too.) With heavier leather boots it will take ten miles for the first stiffness to disappear and fifty miles before the adjustment is complete. Allow several weeks for this. Start with easy walks and short distances. Don't be surprised if you get blisters—better now than later. You may find that you can help tender skin to toughen by massaging it with rubbing alcohol every day. Some people get good results with tincture of benzoin. Walking barefoot when you can helps also. Try leaving the upper hooks or eyelets in the lacing pattern unused for the first five miles; this may help to prevent heel blisters. Be sure to have *at least* ten miles of break-in hiking behind you before you head out on a more considerable journey.

If you don't have time for this method, there are some drastic shortcuts. This one's a classic: fill your boots with hot tap water; empty them immediately; then put them on over dry socks and hike until they are dry. I can only add that it didn't work for me.

If you're heading out on a big trip with blisters already started, or with boots that aren't really broken in, bring along some tennis or running shoes.

When you first start wearing your boots, make sure that the tongue lies straight under the lacing. If it gets twisted or lopsided at this stage, it will have a tendency to stay that way—forever.

Taking care of boots

A good leather boot should last five years or more. Light fabric boots wear out much faster, as do lightweight leather boots made of split leathers. But whatever kind of boot you have, you can get more wear out of it with a little care.

Ultralight boots. The weak points here are the

seams. When you have settled on your boots, pick up a tube of plastic shoe repair compound (available where boots or running shoes are sold). Follow directions, putting a thin protective layer along all seams. Whenever the seal scuffs off, recoat.

Sometimes soles will begin splitting apart layer from layer. These delaminations can be fixed with one of the super-strong instant-hardening glues. As soles begin to wear down, they can be patched or built up with a liquid cement designed for this purpose. A gear store or a running-shoe store can give you advice and sell you what you need.

Some ultralight boots are resolable; some aren't. This is a good question to ask when you shop. In some models, the uppers are unlikely to outlast the soles in any case. Generally speaking, only boots with a separate midsole can be resoled.

Leather boots. Leather is a marvelous material. It's like waterfowl down—nothing we can make works quite as well as the original. But leather is also fragile. Heat can damage it; so can excessive moisture; so can prolonged drying out. To get the longest life from your leather boots, you need to protect them by applying certain preparations.

Seams, and the welt where the uppers join the sole, are the most vulnerable areas in any boots. A number of good preparations on the market will seal these weak spots. Sno-Seal, for instance, makes a product called Welt-Seal. REI has Seam-Seal. Epoxy glue, often used in the past, is less than ideal, because it tends to chip off.

Hikers in most climates need not pay too much attention to the insides of their leather boots. But if you live in a moist climate or have a valued, expensive pair of boots, it's worth treating the interiors with one of several antimildew lubricating preparations available.

The treatment to be applied to the balance of the boot—the all important outer surface—is a matter of some controversy. Most bootmakers advise you to steer clear of pure greases, fats, and oils, which can soften leather unduly. Three frequently recom-

44

mended preparations are Sno-Seal, a paste containing, among other things, silicon; Bee-Seal, which uti-
lizes beeswax and lanolin; and Ultra-Seal by REI.
The debates concerning which is best are on the ab-
struse side. If care instructions accompany the boot,
by all means use the treatment they suggest.

On the trail

Keep your boots as dry as you can. Take them
off when you have an opportunity. Keep them under
cover at night. When they're seriously wet, the
quickest way of drying them is to wipe them inside
and then wear them with a pair of dry socks. In
winter, try to keep damp boots from freezing. Often
you must take them inside your sleeping bag with
you (in a plastic bag).

Never dry your boots at the edges of a campfire.
Don't even leave them in the hot sun any longer
than you can help. Leather is tender to heat and ultraviolet rays—as tender as human skin. The cemented or vulcanized soles of ultralight boots are
vulnerable to heat as well. Cooked boots fall apart
like cooked meat. Don't chance it.

The cleaner you can keep your boots, the better.
Wipe off surface dirt each evening. Don't leave mud
caked on a boot: it draws natural oils out of leather,
and can also damage glues. If you plan a muddy
trip, it's worth taking a small, stiff wire brush.

Between trips

When you get home, remove crusted dirt from
your boots with a stiff brush. Clean leather boots
with a sponge and a little cool water; saddlesoap,
used inside and out, is good. Light fabric boots can
simply be washed in warm water and nondetergent
soap. Rinse thoroughly. Let the boots dry gradually
but very completely. (You can stuff them with news-
papers to draw dampness out; a little Lysol sprin-
kled inside may keep mildew from forming in a
humid climate.) Finally, treat the leather portions
once more with whatever product you have been
using.

If you will be storing leather boots for a month

or more, it's a good idea to put them in a sealed
plastic bag. By inserting a pair of cheap department
store shoetrees—strips of springy metal with knobs
on the end—you can keep the soles from curling.
Some people go further and store their boots on
rigid ski boot racks.

Repairs and resoling

A shoemaker will make minor repairs on your
boots—restitch a fraying seam, replace a grommet
or a hook, reglue a separating sole—for a small
charge. It's good to catch such problems early.

Any boot with a midsole can be resoled. The
price is currently $20 to $40—probably a fraction of
the cost of your boot and very much worth it. All
but the lightest fabric boots are likely to make it
through two soles. Take this step before the soles
wear so thin that the midsole—the second layer
up—is exposed, which makes resoling much more
difficult. If you're hiking in a cold climate, you won't
want to let your soles get very thin.

Neoprene rubber lug soles come in many brands;
Galibier and Vibram are the two most familiar ones,
but all are good. They also come in different patterns. Vibram has thick, deep lugs in its *Montagna*
designs and shallower lugs, or none at all, in its
Voyageur, Roccia, and flat *Silvato* designs. By the
time you have worn out a sole, you should be in a
position to judge how badly you need the deep lugs.
If you aren't certain you need heavy lugs, consider
switching to one of the shallow-toothed or flat designs.

Lugs: a question of impact

It is clear that the lugs of typical boot sole, protecting like so many rows of teeth, do more than
their share of damage to the land. The lugs dig in
and grip—that's their great advantage. They also
tend to break up the soil surface, leaving fragments
that runoff can carry away the next time it rains.
This effect has been well documented. Heavy use
and lug soles together have made gullies out of

many miles of trail.

Some claim that lug soles, regardless of their impact, are essential for surefootedness. In certain situations they probably are. But on the trails that most of us walk, most of the time, a much less ferocious style of sole will do.

Fortunately, it is no longer hard to find boots with shallow lugs, widely spaced projections instead of lugs, or flat, crepe-style soles. There is no longer much excuse for buying conventional lugs if you don't need them. Even if your original boots do have lugs—and this is still the most common equipment—you can switch when it comes time to resole.

5:
Clothing

IN CHOOSING CLOTHING for the wilderness, there are two dangers to avoid. First is the danger of going underequipped. Second (if hardly parallel in seriousness) is the danger of spending more money than you need to. Many backpackers do.

The clothes on your back (and still more important, the reserves in your pack) are a large part of your comfort and safety. They are daytime protection from cold and from wind; from soaking, chilling rain and snow; from heat and burning ultraviolet rays; from mosquitoes and poison ivy and thick, scratching underbrush. An essential item not taken can mean discomfort, even danger, even death.

And yet, if wilderness clothing is all-important, it is also remarkably simple. You can go nearly anywhere, except in snowy winter, with rather ordinary clothes. For a summer trip you may already have everything you need.

There is no such thing as a standard list of clothing for the wilderness. People vary. Every hiker works out the combinations that are right for him or her. And the wilderness itself—from hot to cold, from wet to dry, from calm to battering wind— varies most of all.

To deal with these changes, wilderness hikers have two sets of clothing. First, there is a simple, almost universal, fair-weather outfit: boots and socks, cotton pants or hiking shorts, light cotton shirt, and a few other items. Second, there is a set of *reserve* clothing, more often in the pack than on the back, for dealing with cold, wind, rain, and snow. In spring, summer, and fall hiking, this reserve may be rather small, but it is always there. In winter travel, the basic outfit changes from cotton to wool or wool substitutes, and the reserves are more formidable.

The basic outfit: summer

The hiker dressed in just the basic outfit is traveling in the easiest conditions. You're striding along in sunlight; the air is warm, or hot; if there's a breeze, it comes as a relief. And in much of America's wilderness during the months when people visit it most, this is the way things usually are.

Any type of pants will do. Cotton/synthetic and plain cotton fabrics are cooler and more comfortable than others. Denims are popular and cheap, and they're fine if you don't find they chafe you in steady walking. (Wash them once, if they are new, to soften the fabric.) Pants should be loose fitting and not too close to the point of disintegration. Avoid bell-bottoms and dirt-catching cuffs.

Hiking shorts are a nice luxury; in hot, wet places everybody wears them. You have to watch out for sunburn, of course; burned legs can make walking painful. You should always have a pair of long pants along as well. You'll need them especially for any hiking off the trail, and wherever irritant plants are a problem. Mosquitoes, too, can make bare-legged walking unappealing.

There are some pants and shorts made specifically for hiking. Looser-fitting than the ordinary, they often have patch-type "cargo pockets." One useful feature is a pocket mounted low enough on the leg so that you can reach into it when the pack's hip belt is buckled. Some excellent garments are made of thin, soft canvas or other very durable fabrics. But such gear is really for the perfectionist.

The outer shirt, in this fair-weather outfit, is usually light cotton. It should have long sleeves and also pockets that button or zip. It shouldn't be too fragile, especially if you plan to do any bushwhacking. Some people use stout "chamois shirts" of a thick, feltlike cotton. In cooler climates, the basic shirt may be wool.

As for underclothes, whatever you wear at home is usually fine for backpacking—but garments should be cotton, not clammy, hot nylon.

Some hikers take no undershirt at all. Net undershirts—openwork constructions that look like "holes knotted together with string"—are traditional but hardly required. The advantage is that the shirt can be either very warm or very cool, as you choose. When your outer shirt is buttoned, the air trapped in the net is a warm, insulating layer. When you open the outer shirt, the gaps let the breeze reach your skin. If you buy a net shirt, make sure that your model has ordinary solid fabric over the shoulders; otherwise the pack straps will drive the netting painfully into the skin.

Spare underclothing? In good weather, it's your choice. Some people take several sets. Some wash them on the trip. Some just don't worry about it. In wet weather, however, it is important to have dry underwear and socks to change into.

Except maybe in forest walking, you will want a broad-brimmed hat to protect your head from heat, your face and neck from sunburn, and your eyes from glare. On snow and at high altitudes you must have sunglasses. In fact, you need not just one pair but two, in case you lose or break your primary pair. The glare from snowfields can actually blind you temporarily.

There are places where mosquitoes are so tormenting that some hikers add to the basic outfit a head net: a veil of mosquito netting. Most people make do with insect repellent and netted tents.

Bathing suit for swimming? Sure, if modesty requires.

Into the reserves

So much for the dry, balmy day. Now suppose the temperature begins to drop: from 70 to 50 to 40 degrees Fahrenheit or lower. Clouds move across the sun; a cold air is stirring. Or maybe it has been cool all along. You were warm when you were walking, but when you sit down to eat lunch, you feel a chill.

Or maybe the mists of a temperate morning are congealing into rain.

What do you pull out for what conditions?

It is useful to split the problem into parts. One environmental challenge is *cold,* and you respond to that by adding one or more layers of *insulation.* Another set of problems is posed by *wind and rain* (or snow), and you deal with that by adding *shells.* Some garments have both insulation and weather shells in one, but these are less versatile and generally less desirable.

Insulating garments

The first essential for warmth is a wool or polyester *stocking cap* ($8). More than a third of the heat the body loses into the air is radiated from the head. Conserve some of that, and you'll feel warmer all over. Some stocking caps are thick and fuzzy, others thinner and less formidable looking; either will do fine. For colder places and times, get a longer cap that rolls down to cover the neck, with a gap left for the face, helmet-fashion (called a *balaclava*). Hands also radiate a lot of heat; on chilly summer evenings, gloves or mittens ($8–$15) can be nice.

For the torso the simplest armament is one or two wool sweaters, or a wool shirt and a sweater, or two wool shirts, one large enough to be worn over the other. Shirts should have high collars, long tails, and closable pockets. Prices vary, with $30 to $40 typical. Cheaper ones, made of reprocessed wool, are not quite so warm.

In sweaters you have a choice between the pullover type and the type that opens at the front. The pullover is simpler and lighter, but a front closure lets you cool off without taking off the sweater. Zippers are better than buttons.

A good substitute for wool is polyester fabric, woven in nappy textures known as "pile" and "fleece." Polyester garments can be thought of as heavy sweaters or light jackets; $50 to $80 is typical. Like wool, polyester has the great virtue of retaining its insulating power when it gets wet; of the two, polyester absorbs less moisture and dries more readily.

Many people are now finding that pile garments are all the insulation they need, even on very chilly trips. Still available, however, are *insulated jackets* and *vests*. These come in a great variety of designs and weights. For most travel, one of the lighter, simpler versions will do.

Some jackets use a fill of waterfowl down. Others contain polyester fibers known as Polarguard, Quallofil, or Thinsulate. If you do most of your hiking in dry-cold areas, down is hard to beat. Nothing else insulates so well for the same weight. But if you expect to be in places both cool and wet, it's not wise to depend on down for warmth; once wet, it loses most of its insulating power. Polyester-filled jackets weigh somewhat more than down for the warmth they deliver but won't collapse when wet; they are also cheaper.

Thinsulate and Sontique are two fairly new materials that give the lie to an old axiom: the rule that insulating power depends simply on the thickness of the insulating substance. In both materials, the polyester fibers are spun very finely and arranged in a denser net than in any other kind of fill. Due to a phenomenon called still-air surface bonding, these fibers trap heat more effectively than do more loosely patterned ones. The result is insulation that is far more efficient than coarser competitors, *bulk for bulk*. But its very density makes the fine-spun network heavy. Thinsulate and Sontique do not outclass other synthetic insulators when weights are compared, and, on that basis, they cannot compare with down.

In the cheaper down-filled jackets, sewn-through seams separate the compartments that contain the fill. For most wilderness use—even in winter—this construction is warm enough. Most synthetic-filled jackets use a quilted construction without sewn-through seams. Shell fabrics vary, too. Generally speaking, the lightest alternative is best. Some jackets have built-in hoods; others come with separate hoods that attach with snaps. A hood can be spared in most summer use.

Along with the full-scale jackets, there are various cut-down versions, very light and versatile. Simplest of all is the insulated *vest* or armless jacket, with or without a collar. An extremely light jacket is known as an insulated *shirt.* Take away its front opening, and it becomes an insulated *pullover.*

Down-filled jackets with sewn-through seams sell in the $70–$90 range; synthetic-filled jackets run a few dollars cheaper, warmth for warmth. Down vests start at $30, with polyester-insulated vests again a little behind. Insulated "shirts" and "pullovers" cost more than vests, less than full jackets.

In choosing garments for warmth in the wilderness, never overlook one thing: someday, somewhere, that clothing is going to get wet. Plan accordingly.

Shells for rain

It is well to acknowledge at the outset that there is probably no such thing as fully *waterproof* raingear, at least not in lightweight garments. It's often hard to see where the weakness lies, but if it rains long enough and hard enough, some water is going to make its way in. To avoid disappointment, it's best to think in terms of *water-repellent* clothing.

Most raingear today is of two kinds. There are, first, garments coated with an impermeable layer, usually of polyurethane. Second are garments built of fabrics that incorporate a "one-way" microporous membrane such as Gore-Tex. First, let's look at the cheaper (and less controversial) urethane-coated garments.

Coated raingear

These garments have a traditional drawback. When moisture has a hard time getting in, it has trouble getting *out* as well. Sweat can't evaporate. Thus it is never fully comfortable to hike in such clothing. Even if the air is cold, you're likely to be hot and damp inside. A partial solution is to design garments with as much ventilation as possible.

The best-ventilated piece of raingear is certainly the *poncho*. This is simply a big rectangle of coated nylon with a hole for the neck and a hood. The short-tailed or regular poncho is really just a loose, untailored raincoat. More versatile is the *packboard poncho*, so long in back that it hangs over the pack and protects the load as well as the porter. Packboard ponchos can double as tarps for shelter if the rain is not too serious. Good ponchos cost $30 or more.

Because the pack is inside with you, so to speak, a packboard poncho isn't pinched in around your body by shoulder straps and hip belt. Thus ventilation is excellent; sweat gets some chance to evaporate. But if the rain is heavy, especially if there is wind, no poncho will be protection enough. Rain always works its way in at the sides. When the mist comes down in the hills and the sky closes over in a slow-arriving, slow-departing storm, you need a regular raincoat and a separate cover for your pack.

City-type rain *slickers* of rubberized cloth are very effective but too heavy. *Rain parkas* are raincoats of urethane-coated nylon, usually with a zipper at the front. An *anorak* is a short, hooded nylon coat with no front zipper—it pulls on over your head. Perhaps the most total protection possible is the full-length anorak, or *cagoule*, which covers you down to the knees.

All wilderness raincoats are full cut to leave room for layers of clothing underneath. Hoods are usually built in, sometimes detachable. (I prefer built in. And separate rainhats are little use because they don't protect the neck very well.) Some coats have drawstrings to tighten them at the waist or around the hem. The more vents, the better; an opening under each arm is especially important. Raincoat prices start at $35 in gear stores; cagoules run about twice that.

What about your legs? In warm country, many hikers wear shorts and let their legs get wet. In colder climates you'll need waterproofing all the way down. *Rain chaps* come in literal pairs, a separate tube for each leg, and tie on to the belt at the top. Full *rain pants* protect the crotch and waistline better. Whatever combination of coat and leg protection you work out, make sure there is a generous overlap at the waist. Chaps cost about $15 the pair, and rain pants run $5 or $10 more.

Gore-Tex and cousins

What the rain-soaked or sweat-soaked hiker longs for is raingear that would miraculously let sweat out without letting rain in. After decades of experimentation, the industry has come up with several fabrics that fill the bill to some degree.

First on the market was Gore-Tex, a thin fragile film with countless microscopic pores. Water vapor from evaporating sweat can pass out through these openings, but liquid water droplets, being larger, can't get in. To make a strong fabric with Gore-Tex, the film is bonded between layers of ordinary cloth. Such sandwiches are known as Gore-Tex laminates.

Gore-Tex has now been through three generations. The early models were disappointing, but the product has now established itself in the market and is used almost universally by gear makers. Meanwhile, several competitors—Stormshed, Klimate, and others—have appeared on the market and are going through a similar shaking-down process.

The microporous fabrics have many applications. They are being tried in tents, sleeping bags, even in boots. However, their most significant use, by far, is in clothing. Never before has it been so comfortable to wear water-resistant garments while actually hiking. Before Gore-Tex, a hiker wore raingear as little as possible, and many would carry separate wind shells for use when wind alone was the problem; now the extra clothing can be left at home. We can now speak of *all-weather shells.*

The new fabrics do, however, have their limitations—and their detractors. Complaints of failure have diminished in the last few years, but they have never ceased. People who spend a lot of time in the backcountry and who use their gear very hard—wilderness rangers and climbers, for instance—seem especially likely to report bad experiences. Even the boosters of Gore-Tex have backed off on initial claims. They now prefer to call the fabric "water-repellent" rather than "waterproof." They acknowledge that, in extremely wet climates, old-fashioned raingear will probably serve better. (In the forests of the Pacific Northwest, more than a few backcountry travelers fall back on a very traditional item indeed: the umbrella.)

Another frequent report is that the latest Gore-Tex is waterproof, all right, but that this version does not "breathe": sweat does not evaporate through it readily, and the chief advantage is lost.

I must add at this point that my personal experience with Gore-Tex has so far been quite good.

The commonest form of raingear using all-weather fabrics is the *parka.* This is a solidly made, unpadded coat, generally long enough so that you can sit down on the tail. It has a built-in hood with a drawstring; a rugged front zipper, with a flap of fabric behind it and a line of snaps to use if it fails; and usually several enormous pockets. Often, there's another drawstring to tighten the coat around the waist. Lighter coats are also made, and pants in various styles. All-weather clothing is usually bulkier and heavier than urethane-coated garments of similar design.

The new fabrics have one disadvantage that is beyond debate: they are expensive. Typical Gore-Tex raincoats cost $125 or more (though REI sells one lightweight model for $85); pants start at $50 and go over $100. Garments using rival all-weather fabrics cost somewhat less.

Seam-sealing

Seams are a weak point in any garment meant to shed rain. To be on the safe side, it is wise to coat all accessible seams, inside and out, with one of the many similar products that gear stores sell for the purpose. The most useful dispenser—much better than those the sealant-makers provide—is a Mono-ject–style plastic syringe. (REI sells them.) Otherwise, just follow package directions. Better repeat the treatment each season. It's a tedious, smelly business, but it pays.

(Some garments, including Gore-Tex items of recent manufacture, are seam-sealed in the factory by a fusing process. Unfortunately, the results are mixed—there are many reports of leakage. For the time being, at least, home sealing seems to be necessary insurance.)

After a few seasons, your urethane–coated raingear may begin to lose its waterproofness. Gear stores have preparations you can paint on to restore protection for a while.

Wind shells

If your budget isn't up to a wardrobe of all-weather garments, you may need to supplement your urethane-coated raingear with one or two pieces of gear designed to block out wind alone. (Your raingear will cut wind, of course, but you won't want to wear your sweaty coated nylon any more than you have to.)

The simplest wind shell, adequate for most three season hiking, is a nylon *wind shirt* weighing only a few ounces. Department stores sell these for $15 or so, though it can be hard to find them without cotton lining you don't need or want. For some reason, few gear stores carry these light, useful garments.

What you may see instead is the *wind parka,* a garment very like the all-weather parka described above but less versatile. Traditional wind parkas are made of polyester-cotton mixes known as "65/35" and "60/40" cloth. These fabrics are somewhat resistant to water as well as to wind; they may protect you in a sprinkle, or shed dry snowflakes. But, unlike Gore-Tex, these fabrics have no claim to be rainproof. (Cost: $80 and up.)

If it's cold and windy enough to require a parka, you may also want wind protection for your legs. *Wind pants* (as opposed to double-duty pants made of all-weather fabric) are now rather hard to find. Simple ones are loose and pajama-like with an elastic band around the waist. More elaborate ones have zippers up the legs so that you can get in and out of them without taking off (for instance) your skis. Cost: $15 to $25.

Winter and cool places

If it is wet but warm, raingear alone, added to your basic outfit, may be enough to keep you comfortable. (In the semitropical weather of the Southeast, hikers may actually shed clothing when the rain starts rather than adding it.)

But if it is cold, or even cool, and also wet, your whole costume must change. Cotton, like down, loses its power to insulate when it gets soaked. In fact, it sucks heat away from your skin. A cold wind, rain, and wet cotton clothing add up to serious danger.

This is the basic winter outfit: long johns; wool pants, or wool knickers and wool knee socks; one or more wool shirts and sweaters; wool cap; wool mittens; and goggles or sunglasses. Polyester pile garments can replace some of the wool.

Several types of long underwear make sense. A current favorite is polypropylene, available in different thicknesses. This material wicks water away from the skin without getting wet itself and keeps you feeling dry. Fishnet long johns are also used.

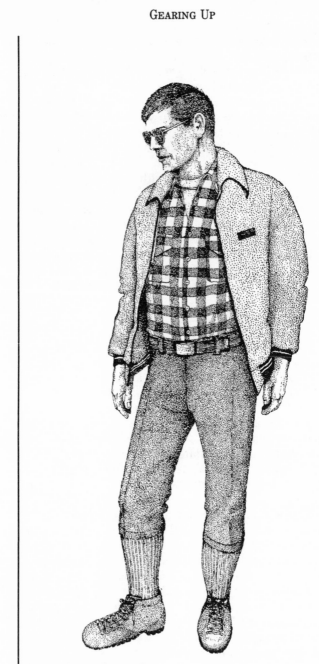

Basic cold weather outfit

Wool is okay but irritates some epidermises and gets soggy; types using cotton should be avoided strictly.

On your legs go wool or polyester pile pants. (Ski pants will serve but tend to bind at the knee.) Some gear stores sell full-length wool trousers, but you can find these at lower prices in surplus stores and thrift shops. The specialty shops carry knickers, loose-cut pants that stop at the knee; they are worn with high-topped wool socks. Skiers like this combination because it allows the leg to bend freely, and also because you roll down the sock when you're working hard and get some cool air on your calves. Knickers and pants should be made of heavy fabric (lighter versions tear). There should be a double seat and heavy reinforcement along the seam of the crotch. Good knickers cost $45 or more, and knee socks run $5–$10 a pair.

Cotton shirts are also ruled out in wet, cold places. Instead, the wool shirt is the standard. Two thin ones, or a thin one and a thin sweater, will give you more possible combinations to choose from.

Gloves and mittens are essential for winter. People wear different combinations. A typical one in very cold places is a light, fingered wool glove inside a heavier wool mitten with a water-repellent mitten shell on top of that: a combination costing $30–$40. Outer shells may be Gore-Tex.

Another winter essential is a pair of *gaiters.* These tough nylon sheaths fasten around the ankle, closing off the gap at the top of the boot where snow would otherwise get in. Some gaiters, for wading occasional snowbanks, are simple and collarlike. For real snow travel you need the fitted or "spat" type that covers the upper half of the boot and rises well up the leg. Most gaiters have zippers in front, and usually a line of snaps as well. A cord or buckle, running under the boot, keeps the gaiter from creeping up out of place. Gaiters may be waterproof or not, waterproof only in the lower part, or of waterproof/breatheable fabric; some wearers find that completely waterproof ones are clammy. Prices range from $15 to $40.

All of the summer garments for wet and cold and wind are useful also in winter. For extremes of cold, extra and specialized clothing may be added. For instance, some winter backpackers carry down jackets with extra fill and without sewn-through seams. These expensive, excellent garments, constructed like fine sleeping bags, weigh two to three pounds and cost $170 and up. Unless you have unusual trouble keeping warm, you should be slow to buy so massive a garment.

If the superthick insulated jacket is of doubtful usefulness short of an expedition, still more questionable is the insulated parka that stuffs filling inside a heavy shell. These are among the heaviest and clumsiest of wilderness garments. Better to do the job with a separate, lighter jacket and a separate, lighter shell. (Outdoor writers have been preaching this "layer system" doctrine for decades, yet heavy combination garments continue to dominate the catalogs. People like the look of them, I guess.)

Adjustability: why less is sometimes more

When you hike, whether in summer or winter, you burn a lot of fuel and produce a lot of heat. At the same time, you're losing that heat, mostly to the air. To stay comfortable, you have to maintain a rough balance between the heat you generate and the heat you give away. Retain too much, and you'll be hot; lose too much, and you'll be miserably cold. Not too far beyond misery, in either direction, is danger. (See Chapter 28 for more about these problems.)

Every moment you spend on the trail, something happens to shift the heat balance a little. Maybe at first you are walking along a flat, shaded valley, feeling comfortable. Then the trail climbs a ridgeline in the sun, and you are hot and sweating. Later, a chill takes you as you reach the windy height above. Wind, sunlight, temperature, terrain, your own metabolism—everything is constantly changing.

The body has certain built-in ways of managing heat, but the adjustments it can make are limited. Beyond that narrow range, what you adjust is your clothing. The change may be as simple as rolling your sleeves up or down or as complex as putting on a jacket and a stocking cap; the purpose is always the same.

And the easier it is to make these adjustments, the more comfortable you will be. In choosing clothes for the wilderness, look for garments that allow you to change your protection exactly as required when the heat balance shifts from too much to too little and back again.

For this reason, most hikers prefer several *thin* garments to one thicker layer. If you have two light shirts along, you can wear neither, or one, or both, for three degrees of warmth. If you have only a single, heavier shirt, it's either on you or in your pack; you've lost an intermediate choice.

In the same way, backpackers tend to favor pieces of clothing that do a single job to those that try to serve several purposes at once. If you have both a light insulated jacket and a shell, you can wear the jacket alone when it's cool and still; the shell alone when it is not so cold but blowing; both together when you need the greatest protection. But if you brought a monstrous down-stuffed parka that is shell and jacket in one, you have no choice. You either wear the thing or you don't.

A third principle: if each piece of clothing is *adjustable* in itself, you have an advantage. Thus most people prefer an open-front raincoat or sweater to a pullover style. If the pullover gets too hot for you, you can simply suffer. Or you can stop, take off your pack, take off the pullover, put it away, hoist your pack again, and go. By that time you may be chilled again anyway. But with a front closure, you can let a cool breeze in any time.

All of this matters, in typical summer weather, only to a degree. It is in really bad weather, and especially in winter, that ease of adjustment can make a striking difference. When you are traveling in a bitterly cold wind, you don't want to work up too much of a sweat; it will chill you the moment you stop. The world you are in, wonderful though it may be, is also hostile. You have to keep the balance to survive.

Putting it together

How, then, do you choose the clothes for a particular trip? Whether you're heading for the local woodland in June or for a 12,000-foot peak in December, the questions are the same. Start with the basic outfit appropriate to the season, and then ask yourself: what else, if anything, do I need to add for *cold?* What what insulation do I need to add for *cold?* What shell or shells should I add for *wind and wet?*

There are three or four typical climates that U.S. backpackers encounter and three or four typical lists of clothing that result.

First, there's the comfortable weather of the Southwest hiking season. In the wilderness lands of California and the mountain states to the east, temperatures may be hot or cool in summer, depending on month and elevation, but the air will seldom be wet for more than a day at a time. Humidity is almost always low; if rain comes, it is likely to be in brief, torrential thundershowers. Under these circumstances, the hiker is likely to wear and carry, besides boots and socks and underclothing:

> hiking shorts
> denims
> light cotton shirt
> sunglasses and spares (in some areas)
> hat
> bandanna
> one or two light sweaters or light insulated
>   jacket
> light rainshell
> light windshell (often omitted)
> stocking cap

At lower elevations, and in areas that are almost totally free of summer rain, this short list can be shortened still further.

Less hospitable, in some ways, is the moister, cooler summer landscape of Maine or western Washington or Minnesota. Really hot days are not common; storms can develop at any time and last for several days; the temperature can drop sharply and quickly. Under such conditions the hiker may well start out in cotton clothes but will carry wool or polyester pile.

    hiking shorts
    denims
    light cotton shirt
    sunglasses and spares (in some areas)
    hat
    bandanna
    sweaters or light jacket (not down)
    raincoat
    windshell (often omitted)
    wool pants (or knickers and knee socks)
    stocking cap

Different again are the regions where the normal hiking season is both humid and either warm or hot, with perhaps the relief of cool nights at higher altitudes. Here the usual hiking uniform is boots and shorts and as little else as possible. The clothing pack list grows shorter here.

    hiking shorts
    denims
    light cotton shirt
    hat
    bandanna
    sweater or wool shirt
    raincoat

In such places there's no need to carry wool (if wet cotton is cool, so much the better).

These lists could be varied—there are a thousand personal preferences, legitimate arguments for adding this, deleting that—but I hope they make the point: trail clothing, for most wilderness conditions, need not be complex. It is only in winter (or in places that are always wintry) that the whole range of wilderness clothing may have to be drawn on at once. One typical winter pack list looks like this:

polypropylene long johns
knickers
knee socks
weather pants (Gore-Tex)
insulated jacket with hood
parka (Gore-Tex)
wool cap
ordinary hat
goggles and spares
high gaiters
wool gloves
wool mittens
nylon overmitts

6:
The Pack

THE PACK MAKES THE BACKPACKER. Without it you remain a hiker, confined to a circle with a car at its center and a radius as long as you can walk in half a day. But with your pack on your back, you are a *traveler on foot;* you can go for a week or longer and cover, if you wish, several hundred wilderness miles. There is something formal, almost ceremonial, in the way an experienced packer hoists the load on the first morning of a trip.

And that moment should be a pleasant one. *A properly fitted pack is comfortable.* Nobody, on a wilderness trip of normal length and difficulty, should have to feel like a pack animal, struggling forward under a painful burden. While any pack is likely to seem heavy at the end of a long day, no pack should make you groan sincerely when you put it on (some people groan for show). If it does, something is wrong. Either you've filled the pack too full, or you have it wrongly adjusted, or—just possibly—

you have the wrong pack in the first place.

There are hundreds of different models of packs on the market. New designs are turning up each year. Many are just *daypacks*—hiker packs built for minor loads. If you take only the bare necessities and strap your sleeping bag on the outside, you *can* make a large daypack do for an easy weekend trip. But sooner or later you will want to put out the money for a full-sized pack, and here the complexities begin.

Buying a full-sized pack

Some people buy their first pack quickly, taking the first model that strikes their eye and seems to fit. Others like to dwell on the decision. Both methods work, but there is much to be said for going slowly. This is a major purchase, and the chances are you'll be traveling with the thing for many years.

Many gear stores have packs for rent. Take advantage of this if you can. Only experimenting on the trail permits you to know for sure what you like best, especially if you are deciding among fundamentally different designs. (A typical three-day rental fee is $10.) Check the specialty shops available to you for the lines they carry; read the catalogs; but trust nothing so much as your own comfort and convenience.

In buying a pack you have to watch out for some inferior products. Packs by "reputable manufacturers" (who's reputable? see *Resources* appendix for a partial listing) are usually well built. The specialty shops, not surprisingly, are your safest source. While general sporting goods shops often stock fine brands, they aren't always able to fit you properly, nor can they give you experienced advice. Department stores are risky places to purchase a pack. They often carry models that look quite rugged but don't hold up in the field: such packs have been known to fail the first time out. Unfortunately, no acceptable pack for an adult now sells for less than about $70, and $130 is a much more typical price.

Designs that are exceptionally well made, exceptionally elaborate, or both go for $150 or more.

One thing to be aware of, when buying a pack, is *weight.* The pack, after all, is part of the load you carry! Full-sized packs run from under three pounds to more than six. Heavy fabrics, large volume, and extra features are nice, but are they worth the penalty?

Now, more on the anatomy of backpacks and the choices to be made.

What kind of frame?

Modern full-sized backpacks are a genus with two species. First, there are the familiar *external-frame packs:* large, compartmented packbags attached to rigid frameworks. Second, and much newer on the scene, are the large *internal-frame backpacks:* these lack any outwardly visible skeletons.

Both types can be traced back to designs in use before World War II. But all the packs of that period had the same fault: they were supported entirely by the shoulders. The upper body carried the whole load. In fact, the upper body is not well adapted to carrying supporting weight. No pack that hangs off the shoulders, without any other point of support, is comfortable with a load of more than fifteen to twenty pounds; and the packs of that period—compressing the spine and dragging at the back—were uncomfortable indeed by current standards.

The full-size packs developed since World War II solve this problem. Their rigid frames transmit the weight of the pack down to a padded hipbelt; the pressure rests, not on the weak shoulders and back, but on the robust joints and powerful muscles of the hips, buttocks, and thighs. When you wear a properly adjusted backpack, your shoulders take only a small share of the burden. More than any other innovation, this change in pack design made wilderness hiking appealing to a wide public, and the wilderness a place where almost anyone could go.

Do you want a pack with an external frame, or one of the new internal-frame designs?

External frames are the trucks of backpacking. They can be built to hold more gear than any other type. And they are probably the most comfortable tools for carrying very massive loads on trails. They have a considerable advantage in warm weather: standing well out from the back, except at shoulder and hip, they give sweat plenty of chance to evaporate. Their disadvantage comes from their total rigidity. They tend to bounce and swing whenever the wearer makes a quick motion. When the hips swivel and dip, as they do when you hike downhill, the frame pack does the same—but in its own competing rhythm.

Internal-frame packs fit much closer to the body; their frames are much less massive and designed to flex. The capacity of their packbags is typically a little less (though still potentially large). Depending on the model, they may be warm on the back in hot weather.

What about the essential thing, comfort under a load? For any weight but the most extreme, there appears to be little difference.

You might summarize the pros and cons like this:

● If you plan to spend much time off the trail, going cross-country, especially over rugged ground; if you want to use the pack for scrambling or for climbing; or if you want a pack that you can carry when skiing, the choice is clear: the soft pack, with its flexibility and closer fit, is almost certainly for you. (For snowshoeing, too, a soft pack is preferable, though a frame is manageable.)

● If you plan to carry oversized loads, as for very long trips—and if you will do nearly all your travel on the trail, or in very easy cross-country—then a frame pack is a reliable choice.

● If you expect to carry moderate loads and to do most of your hiking on-trail—a description that fits most backpackers, most of the time—then either an external-frame or internal-frame pack will make sense. All you can do is rent differing kinds for a trial, and trust your experience.

More about external-frame packs

The typical exoskeletal pack has two distinct components. First is the frame itself, a structure of metal tubing commonly shaped like an "H" with several crossbars, along with the supporting straps: wide padded belts around the waist (to carry the weight) and over the shoulders (to steady it). Second, there's the packbag itself—tall, flat, and box-like, generally attached to the frame with metal pins. You almost always buy packbag and frame as a unit; you can't ordinarily mix and match different brands. But shoulder straps and hipbelts can be exchanged in many cases.

Not all frames are of the basic H pattern. Some close off the "H" at top or bottom. Some have an hourglass shape, consisting of a single squared-off curve of tubing pinched in at the sides. There are other variations. Nearly all frames have a slight double curve to match the shape of the spine.

Frame materials vary. Sometimes the tubing is aluminum, sometimes an alloy of magnesium. Coleman makes a controversial frame of molded plastic.

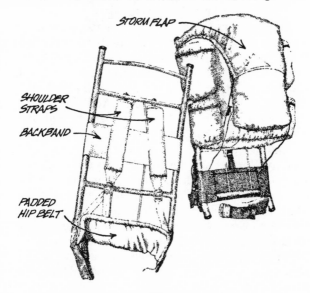

STORM FLAP

SHOULDER STRAPS

BACKBAND

PADDED HIP BELT

Joints are usually welded, sometimes mechanical. A few models are built to be adjustable for different wearers. Both plastic and adjustable frames are somewhat less rigid than other types, which may help to reduce the jostle-and-bounce typical of frames. If you'd like to hear the arguments for all these variations, ask a salesperson or consult the catalogs.

One dramatic variation is the so-called wraparound frame. Several companies market a variation of the standard H-shaped frame in which the sides of the frame curve sharply forward at the bottom. The result is that the two vertical tubes end right beside the hipbone (rather than on your back well behind the hip). Or else the frame sprouts metal extensions forward. Either way the point is the same: the shoulder straps and the hip belt attach to the frame much farther forward than with the standard H.

There are two advantages claimed for this arrangement. First, the variation may bring a still larger proportion of the total load onto the hips, leaving still less hanging from the shoulders. Second, and more important, these packs are a little less inclined to lurch on a rough trail.

Does it work? Some users are enthusiastic, others unimpressed. Evidently the pattern works best for people with broad hips. I have had good luck with it myself. (Wraparounds have some incidental features of interest. These frames will stand up by themselves, if set on flat ground. And if you sit down wearing one, the belt won't jerk up out of place, as always happens with a standard frame.)

Another variant is the flexible-linkage pack developed by North Face (they call theirs the Back Magic). In this design, the metal frame does not connect directly to the hip belt. Instead, the weight is transmitted through a flexible plastic column at the back. You can just about do the hula wearing this pack: hip motions don't jiggle the load much at all. I find, however, that the flexibility makes for an unstable carry: the upper part of the pack shifts disturbingly in response to torso movements. Again, consider carefully.

Belts and bands

When you wear a properly fitted frame, none of the tubing touches your body. The three parts of the pack that actually touch you are the shoulder straps, the hip belt, and the backbands.

Shoulder straps typically attach to the frame near the top, on one of the upper crossbars. They then diverge to pass over the shoulders and run down the sides of the body to attach at the two lower points of the H of the frame. A buckle in front of each shoulder adjusts them for length. Where they rest on the skin, they are padded with firm closed-cell foam.

The hipbelt—it should be a single band of tough cotton or nylon—attaches at those same two points, the bottom tips of the H, and runs around the waist, buckling securely at the front. (Most "buckles" today are plastic snap-in clamps, which seem to work very well.) Some belts are heavily padded, some aren't—experiment to find out which you like best.

When a frame pack is properly worn, the two shoulder straps do little more than hold the pack upright and steady on your back. (To convince yourself of this, try on a loaded frame pack with the hip belt cinched up tight; then unbuckle the belt so that all the load comes onto the shoulder straps. You'll instantly feel the backward-and-downward drag.)

Across the frame are stretched one or two backbands, the points at which the pack rests against your back. Most backbands are of mesh for easy ventilation. There is usually an adjustment—a metal turnbuckle or just criss-crossed cords—so that each backband can be tightened as it begins to stretch, or loosened for sliding to a more comfortable position. (On some packs the bands don't shift.)

The packbag

You wouldn't think there could be so many different ways to build a bag to haul a few pounds of gear in. Shape, size, fabric, zippers, compartments, closures, features: the list goes on and on. Fortunately, only a few of these distinctions matter much. It comes down to personal preference, convenience, even to style.

Most packbags are made of a smooth, tightly woven nylon duck. (Cotton is okay, too. It's cheaper but heavier and less resistant to water.) Others have a rougher nylon called *Cordura* or an ultra-strong fabric known as *ballistics cloth*. Almost all manufacturers now make their bags with water-repellent fabric. You can recognize it by the glossy inner surface. Water repellency, by itself, won't keep your gear dry in heavy rain or wet snow, but every little bit helps.

How *big* a packbag do you need? Full-size bags vary from under 2,000 cubic inches capacity to more than 6,000 cubic inches, though the really big bags fit only on long frames worn by long people. For comparison, a standard brown supermarket bag holds about 1,400 cubic inches.

For summer trips of a week or less, the smaller packbags should do fine. A small load rides more neatly in a small bag than in a big one. The sleeping bag is generally strapped on outside. Most wilderness trips are quite short—a few days, a few miles. You don't need a warehouse on your back.

For very long trips, for remote climbing trips, and for winter trips of more than a few days, even very large packs can become astonishingly full. But packs with a capacity of more than 4,000 cubic inches are really meant for expeditions, and most backpackers who buy them are spending too much money for too much pack.

Most packbags are *three-quarter length*—shorter than the frames on which they are mounted. The sleeping bag, stuffed in a storage sack and strapped to the lower crossbars of the frame, fills the remaining space. Some packbags are so designed that you can shift them up or down to change the center of gravity (a low center of gravity helps in cross-country scrambling).

How is the packbag *divided?* In the commonest design, there is a large upper compartment, held open at the top by a light metal framework. A long fabric *stormflap* pulls over the top opening and part way down over the front of the pack (that is, down the side away from your back). Underneath this top compartment there is commonly a smaller bottom chamber, with a zipper. Then there are zippered outside pockets, at least two, one on each side of the pack, and often many more (the more, the handier: it's a nuisance to have to dig too deep into the pack for things you need during the hiking day).

On this simple design there are endless variations. Some bags aren't divided but have a single deep compartment. This is less convenient for getting at things, easier for packing bulky or odd-shaped items. Some packs have zip-out dividers so that you can have it either way. Several have permanent dividers but leave corner gaps so that you can stick long objects down through.

Zippers are mostly made of hard nylon. Sometimes they run straight across the tops of the compartments they open; on other packs the zippers are vertical or arc-shaped. On some models the whole front of the pack zips out, so that you can pack it like a suitcase. Though I personally prefer straight-across zippers (less chance of losing things, and you still have a usable space if the zipper breaks), there's no advice to give but *suit yourself.*

Packbags can be attached to their frames in several ways. Most commonly you see stout metal pegs poking through holes in the metal and through grommets in the packbag. These "clevis pins" are held in place by metal lock-rings. Some packs clip on with fabric tabs.

Fitting an external-frame pack

A pack, like a pair of boots, must fit you. Fortunately, by comparison with the problems of fitting boots, the fitting of a pack is easy. The key thing is the length of the frame. Some models adjust, but most come in three or four sizes to match body length from shoulder to waist. A salesperson can help you locate the right size and make obvious adjustments to the hipbelt and shoulder straps. Next, load the pack with not less than thirty pounds. Most stores offer you sandbags or climbing ropes for weights.

Get the pack on your back and tighten the hipbelt firmly. It should lie just below the upper edge of the hipbone: not so high that the belt is really around your waist, but not so low that it slips off below the widest part of the bone. The lower part of the backband should fit snugly just beneath the small of your back. As you tighten the hipbelt, the whole pack should shift upward on your back so that the shoulder straps actually *rise* just slightly from your shoulders. You'll feel the weight leave your shoulders and come onto your hips. If this doesn't happen, the pack is probably too short for you.

Correct fitting of frame pack: shoulder straps rise over shoulders, hip belt rides on hip bone.

Next, tighten or loosen the shoulder straps to make them firm but not tight—you should be able to slide a couple of fingers between the strap and your shoulder with no trouble. Then take an indoor hike with your load. Climb stairs, bend, sit down, stride. Make sure that the hipbelt is comfortable and that it shows no sign of slipping up or down from its proper position (except when you sit). Satisfy yourself that the metal tubing of the frame doesn't touch your back at any point. Check that the buckles on the shoulder straps do not slip (on some cheap models they may). The waistbelt closure must also grip very securely. If it seems inclined to loosen in the store, it will be far worse on the trail.

What about fitting one of those wraparound packs? The tests are much the same. You must make very sure that the hipbelt stays in place. If it has any tendency to slip up into the hollow of the waist or down below the point of the hip, reject the pack. People with narrow hips often find they cannot wear packs of this design.

Internal-frame packs: general

Like exoskeletal packs, internal-frame packs come in significantly different types. The most important variation is in the type of internal frame: parallel, X-design, or load-pressure.

In the parallel design (pioneered by Lowe), two long thin bars of metal lie in pockets, one positioned on either side of the spine. Like an external frame, these shift the load down to a wide, padded hipbelt. This design permits a very close fit to the back and is very flexible.

In the X-design (pioneered by Gregory), the metal bars cross, making an X across the back. Necessarily, to avoid bruising the spine, the pack stands farther out from the back. The framework is somewhat more rigid, and is sometimes made even stiffer by the addition of crosspieces at the top or bottom of the X.

The third or "load-pressure" design is harder to describe because there is, in fact, no separate frame

True soft pack: contents serve as frame.

at all. Rather, the load itself—packed carefully and firmly in two side-by-side vertical compartments—becomes the rigid frame. The sleeping bag is stuffed balloon-tight into a wraparound bottom compartment that narrows to a belt and buckle at the front.

Again, what's to choose?

For most people, the load-pressure design is rather easily crossed off the list. It is finicky to pack and small in volume, thus not a very good general-purpose vehicle.

The parallel-frame design appears to be best in cases in which the virtues of a soft pack—flexibility, the ability to move easily with the body—are paramount. The same reasons that lead one to consider an internal-frame pack in the first place argue for the parallel-stay design.

The X-design, however, has some compensating advantages. For one thing, it tends to stay farther off the back, making it more suitable for hot-weather hiking. It is an excellent choice for someone who will be doing both on-trail and off-trail hiking in all seasons.

The type of frame is not the only thing to look at. One key point is the connection between the bottom ends of the frame and the hipbelt. The more rigid that connection is, the less flexible the pack is, and the more likely it is to jump about on your back like a conventional frame. Leading makers in the field have deliberately built their packs so that only fabric, rugged but still flexible, provides the link between frame and hipbelt.

Many soft packs have just one big compartment. Some open at the top, with a zipper, or drawstrings and straps. On others, the whole front of the pack unzips for easy loading. Layouts vary as much as those of packbags on external frames. There will frequently be an arrangement for carrying skis—straps, "ski sleeves" down the sides or a set of detachable pockets behind which skis are slid.

Straps and belts on these packs are typically elaborate. It is common to find *laminated hip belts*, with soft open-cell foam against the body and firmer closed-cell foam backing it up. *Hip stabilizer straps*

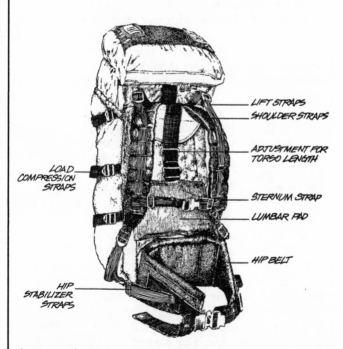

LIFT STRAPS
SHOULDER STRAPS

ADJUSTMENT FOR
TORSO LENGTH

LOAD
COMPRESSION
STRAPS

STERNUM STRAP

LUMBAR PAD

HIP BELT

HIP
STABILIZER
STRAPS

Anatomy of an internal frame pack

are added to hold the bottom of the pack firmly against the lower back, preventing sideways sway; *lift straps* (see *Fitting*, below) keep the load from settling on the shoulders. Many packs have *sternum straps* that buckle across the chest to add still more stability. Almost always there is a thick *lumbar pad* where the weight of the pack comes to bear on the base of the spine.

Fitting an internal-frame pack

Some soft packs come in just one size but offer multiple adjustments. Others come in several sizes with fewer movable buckles and straps. Whatever is most comfortable for you is, of course, the right thing.

To test the fit, do about as you would with a frame pack. Get a salesperson's help in locating the closest size or making the first rough adjustment of a harness. Load the pack heavily and get it on your back. The hip belt, as with any pack, should lie right across the hipbones—that is, around the widest part of the pelvic girdle. Tighten the belt firmly; then lengthen or shorten the shoulder straps to put most of the weight on the belt while still holding the pack firm.

Most soft packs have special lift straps. These connect the main shoulder straps to the top edge of the pack. As you tighten the lift straps, they raise the shoulder straps and help shift the weight to the hips. On highly adjustable packs, the shoulder straps converge on an anchor (perhaps an adjustable metal bar) that you can slide up or down to suit the length of your torso. The more adjustments your model allows, the longer you need to spend working out the arrangement most comfortable for you. When in doubt between sizes, go to the larger one.

When you have the right combination, the hip belt should be snug and firm; the shoulder straps should be high enough so that one shoulder can droop without the pack swinging off on that side; and the weight should be coming to bear distinctly on the lower body.

Internal-frame packs, with their flexible, close-fitting supports, allow and often require another type of adjustment: actually bending the metal stays to match your back's own shape. A knowledgeable salesperson will be willing to spend some time getting the pattern right.

Checking for quality

When you choose a pack of either basic sort, there are some details you should take time to look for. You can always get a faulty specimen of a generally excellent brand. And a quality check can help you decide whether a given model is worth its price.

If you're considering an external-frame pack, examine that frame. Some are built so strongly that you could use them for ladders. For normal purposes you don't need such high technology, and most frames, except suspiciously cheap ones, will be strong enough. To check, set the pack up with one "foot" on the floor, one raised, and press down from the upper opposite corner. This crosswise pressure catches the frame at its weakest. If you see the frame even beginning to distort under the pressure, let up quickly, and find another store.

How is the packbag attached to the frame? However it is done, there should be at least three points of attachment on each side.

Check the padded parts of the shoulder straps. The pads should be firm, almost hard, not soft and compressible.

Don't fail to examine sewing on packbags. Prestige is no guarantee of good work, though some brands are certainly more consistent than others. Stitches should be small and not too widely spaced. The Boy Scouts of Canada, in a gear-testing program, found that good strength is achieved by anything between five and twelve stitches to the inch. Rows should be straight and neat. If you see much double or triple stitching, you know standards are high. Check the end of each row of stitches. It should be bar-tacked—the line should finish in a dense band of stitches, one almost on top of another. Look at the sewing at the bottom of the pack and around the pockets. In the best packs there will be multiple stitching at these points and perhaps an extra layer of fabric in places that take extra stress, like the ends of zippers and the "root" of the storm flap.

Internal-frame packs need to be built like crazy. In such a pack, waist and shoulder straps must attach directly to the packbag, and these attachments are crucial. Sometimes straps are sewn in place; in some models they are fixed by pins that penetrate the packbag and attach to the internal frame. If the straps are sewn on, look for double and triple stitching and strong bar-tacking—several inches of strap must be sewn down. Look for leather pads, rivets, extra fabric, or other reinforcements at critical points. Get the store to tell you how the attachments are made on the packs it carries.

Daypacks

Long before you buy a full-sized pack, you will need a *daypack*—a small, uncomplicated rucksack just big enough to carry a lunch, a camera, a canteen, and the essential safety items you should never leave behind (see list, Chapter 15). You'll use such a pack, of course, for trips near home but also on long wilderness trips if you want to be able to shuck your main pack and take off on a side excursion.

The purchase of a daypack is easy. There are, naturally, competing brands and features, but, when you get right down to it, a daypack is too simple a thing to argue about. A tough fabric bag and a couple of wide shoulder straps, and you've got it. The basic daypack should weigh no more than a pound, cost no more than $30, and handle loads up to about fifteen pounds. Larger and more elaborate models are known as rucksacks.

The packbag can be of cotton or nylon (the nylon treated for water repellency). Some bags open and close with zippers, variously placed; others use straps. Some have outside pockets, some don't. A useful daypack will be not less than twelve inches wide, not less than a foot deep, and perhaps six inches thick. Since a loosely loaded bag fits more comfortably to the back than one stuffed to the limit, be generous. A "summit pack" for climbing must be much larger than a pack for simple day-hikes; many packs sold as summit packs are far too small.

The shoulder straps should have buckles for adjustment, and they should be wide enough not to cut into your back when the pack is loaded near maximum. (Some packs use padded straps.) You will sometimes find a stabilizing strap that buckles across the chest to keep the load from bouncing on your back. Whatever the variation, look for good sewing and reinforcement where the straps are sewn to the packbag.

Not all daypacks ride on the back. There's also the *fanny pack,* really a big belt with a pouch in the back. Skiers prefer them to shoulder packs on short trips because they don't bounce so much. A daypack can also serve as a backpack for a child. For more on baby-carriers and packs for kids, see Chapter 24.

Accessories

If you buy a frame with a small packbag, or one of the smaller internal-frame packs, you may find yourself cramped for space when you take a trip of unusual length or difficulty. Several things can be done to make a smallish pack carry a big load.

To a frame pack you can add a *frame extension:* a U of metal tubing that rounds off the top of the original H to give you more stowing room. You can tie objects to the tubing, or store them under the stormflap, supported by the extension.

Many packs come equipped with *tie-on patches,* squares or strips of thick leather with slits. Running thin nylon webbing through the slits, you can fasten objects securely outside. If your pack doesn't have patches where you need them, you can buy them cheaply and sew them on (with an awl); but a shoemaker does a neater job for a small price. Whenever objects have to be tied on, elastic *shock cords* are invaluable. *Extra pack pockets* can also be purchased and sewn on.

For hiking in extended rain or in long, wet snowstorms, you will just about have to have a waterproof *pack cover* ($18); for short summer storms, a multipurpose *packframe poncho* will serve ($30–$40). Pack covers are simple coated nylon shells that snap on over the pack. Once on, they're a nuisance because they block access to the outer pockets, but items inside stay dry. Wet-weather hikers should also paint *seam sealant* on the seams of their packbags—water gets in at these points no matter how water repellent the cloth. Then there's the old-timer who packs every item of gear in a plastic bag, inside her otherwise unprotected packbag, and troubles herself no further.

Bags and carriers

After the main pack itself, the most common gear containers are cloth stuffbags and plastic bags in various sizes. Take plenty of the latter, especially where it's wet. Supermarket produce bags will do, but you'll get more use out of heavy-gauge plastic bags available in gear stores.

A useful accessory is the *beltbag,* a zippered rectangular cloth pouch that rides on the belt. You can use it for ski waxes; for film and small camera accessories; for pencil and paper; for lunch; for anything you need close at hand and don't want to shift from pocket to pocket every time you add or subtract a layer of clothing. Then there's the belt-hung *bottle carrier,* which can turn any water bottle into an accessible canteen.

If you carry a camera, you face the problem of keeping it accessible and steady. Various solutions are available, including strap arrangements and special camera packs that ride on the chest. I have yet to encounter a strap arrangement that holds the camera as steady as I would like.

Packs and low impact: the question of color

When you buy your pack, you encounter the troublesome question of *color*. Wilderness gear is sold today in every shade, bright or subdued: various blues; reds and yellows and explosive iridescent oranges; leaf-greens and olive-greens, rust-browns and earth-browns and compound colors in between. Color is part of the pleasure of handling good gear, and one of the things that gives a stack of fine equipment that curiously *valuable* look.

But there's more than personal taste to consider when you choose a color. There's a question of impact as well. Simply put, do you want to stand out or blend in? Unless you're hiking in the eastern woodlands in October, a bright pack makes you highly visible. Indeed, it makes you *too* visible: the more fellow hikers you see and are seen by, the more crowded the wilderness landscape must appear. This is a problem everywhere but doubly so above timberline. A dozen hikers in an alpine basin, carrying gear in muted colors, may give you no hint of their presence—three with packs in "international orange" can make the same place seem busy. For low impact, then, you choose the soft shades.

There is a counterargument, however, and that is safety. Maybe you do a lot of traveling in popular hunting areas at just the wrong time of year and *want* to be seen. Or maybe you're thinking about a time when you could conceivably need to be rescued. Standing out as it does, bright gear can draw searchers to a lost or injured hiker.

Every backpacker must find a balance between arguments of safety and the pleasures of unobtrusiveness. If you're very concerned about the rescue angle, I would suggest this compromise: carry something brightly colored in your pack—raingear, perhaps, or a groundcloth. This you can spread on the ground, or drape on your pack, whenever you need to be seen. But a pack made of a vivid fabric is like a light you can never turn off.

7:
The Bedroll

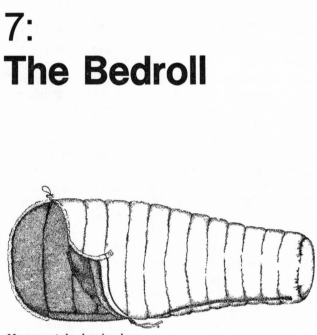

Mummy-style sleeping bag

BOOTS AND PACKS, Lord knows, are expensive
enough these days. But the chances are good that
pack and boots together will cost little more than
your third major purchase: your sleeping bag.

How do you set about choosing the right bag?
Once more, as with every major item of gear, there
are certain distinct questions to ask yourself. In
buying a sleeping bag, you need to know *how warm*
a bag you need; *what kind of insulating material*
you want in it; and *what shape and design* are best
suited to your use. Then there are certain features
you should look for in any bag.

How much bag do you need?

First things first. How cold will it get where you
plan to go? People tend to buy heavier and costlier
sleeping bags than they actually need. The bag you
choose should be about right for the temperatures
you expect to encounter frequently during the next

few years. Don't think in terms of an eventual
dream trip to Alaska. Don't even buy for the coldest
possible night in the place and season you will visit;
rather, think of a night somewhat below the average. You can make a light bag do very nicely for
the occasional chillier time, and you won't be carrying needless weight when it's warm.

On summer trips in the forty-eight contiguous
states you are unlikely to see many nights below
freezing, even in the high country, and in some regions summer nights are in the fifties and above.
Even three-season backpacking—spring, summer,
and fall—is unlikely to take you much below the
twenties Fahrenheit. If you have an idea where you
will go most often—New England mountains, say,
or the Sierra—you might check trail guidebooks or
talk to experienced hikers about the conditions they
have found.

How warm-blooded are you? People vary a good
deal. Some are obvious cold sleepers—they shiver in
sleeping bags that look like they belong on the
Greenland ice. Others find it unusually easy to keep
warm. It depends pretty much on your metabolic
rate. This is one of several good reasons for renting
sleeping bags before you buy—you learn how cold-
proof you actually are, how you compare with the
"typical" sleeper that the gear catalogs are always
talking about.

Grades of bags

Sleeping bags of a sort can be gotten very
cheap. Department stores everywhere sell rectangular bags that look like thick zippered blankets. They
have quilted seams and use cheap synthetics for fill.
These bags are inexpensive—down to a very
few dollars—but they are too cool for most wilderness camping and too heavy and bulky to tote
far.

Next up in warmth are well-made *summer sleeping bags* sold in many gear shops. These are built in
the simplest way, with sewn-through seams. The effect is something like so many pillows sewn to-

gether at the edges. Such a bag will keep you warm in nights as cool as 40 degrees Fahrenheit—maybe down to freezing if you wear all your clothes to bed. That's all you need for the Southeast in the warm half of the year or for the low-lying deserts in any season but winter. Cost: $70–$100.

Most hikers, though, will be out in a good many nights that are colder than 40 degrees. For this majority, the medium-weight *three-season bag* is the necessity. Such bags have no sewn-through seams; there is insulation all around you. No three-season bag needs more than two pounds of fill if the filler is waterfowl down, nor much over three pounds if good synthetic filler is used. A three-season down bag should weigh no more than about four pounds total, a synthetic-filled model no more than six pounds. Prices range between $80 and $180, depending chiefly on the fill material used. As the amount of fill increases, three-season bags grade into *winter* sleeping bags, marvelous constructions intended only for conditions down toward zero degrees Fahrenheit and below.

Judging the warmth of a sleeping bag

How to tell how warm a given bag will keep you? The answer is not so simple as you might expect. How warm you are on a particular night depends on half a dozen things besides your sleeping bag itself: the padding under you, the wind, humidity, protection from the open sky, how much you ate for dinner, and of course your own warm-bloodedness. Even if we forget all these variations and speak of an "average" sleeper in "ideal" conditions, it can be hard to judge the insulating power of a bag.

You have three things to go by: weight and kind of fill, manufacturer's temperature ratings, and, third and most important, *loft*.

Every sleeping bag has a fabric label attached. It tells you the total weight of the bag, the type of filler, and the weight of fill. Now if the same material is used in bags of the same design, more fill means a warmer bag. But seldom is the comparison so simple. More often you are looking at bags of different shapes filled with different substances, or with down of different grades (some insulate twice as well as others). So weight is not the key.

Manufacturers and salespeople make predictions for their bags: this one is supposed to be comfortable to freezing, that one perhaps to ten degrees above zero. The better makers are cautious, afraid to claim too much. But there is no universal standard, and certain companies, less conscientious, have made claims that are out of line. No guarantee is ever implied.

What's left is the one factor you can check for yourself: *loft*. Loft is the height to which a sleeping bag puffs up when it is nicely shaken out. Loft is insulation. Loft is warmth. Loft is what gets between you and the night. And loft is rather easily measured. Manufacturers almost always give loft figures for their bags, so you might think it simple enough to judge and compare them.

Measuring loft

But even this, the essence of the matter, is not so simple as it might be. When the makers measure loft, they do it in somewhat different ways. Some, for instance, put a slight weight on the bag—most do not. Also, a particular copy of a given model may be plumper or thinner than the average. All this means that you can't just line up official loft figures and know for sure that the seven-inch lofting bag is warmer than the six-inch version.

To cut through the confusion, you can measure loft, in a rough-and-ready fashion, yourself. Here's how to do it. If you've just pulled the bag out of a stuffsack, take hold of it at the head and shake it gently several times to get air into it. Lay it down for a few minutes; then shake it again. But if the bag has been on display for days, lie down on it first, for several minutes, before you shake it out (display bags may show more loft than you'll ever get in the field).

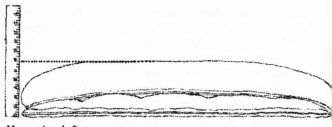

Measuring loft

After the second shaking, stretch the bag out once more. Wait another several minutes; then take an ordinary ruler and read off the height of the top of the bag above the floor. Take the reading about where the sleeper's chest would be. Bags are a little thinner at the edges, so you may have to press a little, indenting the side with the ruler, to get an accurate result.

This method, frankly, is none too precise. One could wish for a reliable industry standard. But many manufacturers actually get their own loft readings in just this unsophisticated way, and by doing it yourself you can cancel out differences in their procedures.

Now that you have a measurement, what do you make of it? How do you translate from loft to warmth? As a rule of thumb, we can say that each inch of loft is worth about ten degrees of warmth. Four inches of loft will do down to about 40 degrees Fahrenheit. Six inches will keep you warm down to about 20 degrees. Eight inches will do to about zero, and ten inches—almost the most you can buy—will carry you down to −20 degrees, or even lower.

Various tricks of bag design (see *Sleeping "systems,"* below) are designed to better this formula. As a starting point, however, it seems sound.

In the end, of course, your comfort is the only accurate measure. Each time you rent a sleeping bag—and you should try several—make a note of its loft and of the temperatures you encounter. When you find out how comfortable you are in a particular bag on a particular night, you will have more than theory to go on. And you can extrapolate: each added inch of loft will give you comfort on a night about ten degrees chillier.

What kind of insulation?

What is it that keeps you warm? Your own body heat, of course, trapped by the material around you. Anything that traps dead air will hold warmth in, and the thicker the barrier, the less heat will escape. Thus the importance of insulation thickness: loft. There is no special magic in any particular substance—even steel wool would be fine—except that some materials give you much more loft for much less weight than others.

In fact, there are now just five filling materials in wide use that are light enough and lofty enough for wilderness sleeping bags. These are *goose down*, *duck down*, and three forms of polyester: *Hollofil*, *Quallofil*, and *PolarGuard*.

Top-quality goose down is still clearly the standard. Nothing else gives so much warmth for so little weight. Nothing else compresses into such a tiny volume. Nothing else lasts so long. Nothing else costs so much. Though the very best goose down is hard to find, even poorer grades outrank other insulating materials. The nearest competitor is duck down.

What counts, of course, is the down's ability to loft. Both goose down and duck down can be good or bad. "Lofting power" can be measured precisely in cubic inches filled by a single ounce of fluffed-up down, but only top-of-the-line manufacturers enjoy giving these figures, and measurement procedures are regrettably not standard. (Just for reference, however, 550 cubic inches per ounce is considered good these days; anything much over that is premium.) The color of the down doesn't matter. Neither do the high-sounding names that makers sometimes give to the down they use: "AAA prime northern" or what have you.

When we look at the synthetic fillers, the picture is much simpler. These are laboratory products and don't vary. The warmth of a bag depends simply on design and the amount of fill. Unfortunately, even poor-to-fair down is warmer for its weight than the synthetics. It takes nearly twice as much synthetic filler to do the work of a given amount of down. The synthetic bags are not only heavier but also clumsier—they won't compress as well.

They have, however, two powerful selling points. First, they are very much cheaper. Second, synthetic bags are safer when it's wet and cold. It would be difficult to overstate how important this can be.

Down—any kind of down—soaks up water and loses nearly all its loft when it gets wet. A waterlogged down bag is not just a nuisance, it's a horror. Anyone who has ever spent a night in a wet snowstorm, two days' walk from a roadhead, with a couple of hundred dollars worth of wringing-wet goose down, can make the case for a synthetic bag. A synthetic bag loses only a small part of its loft when it gets wet. You can squeeze it out like a sponge and dry it completely, out in the wind, in half an hour.

As noted, all synthetic fills are forms of polyester. Reliance Products makes PolarGuard, a continuous filament spun like cotton candy. Dupont makes fills consisting of masses of short fibers. Hollofil fibers have a hole down the center, and Quallofil fibers an X-shaped central hollow (both designed to add surface area and keep the adjacent layer of air dead-still). There seems to be no strong case for preferring any one fill over the others. A fourth polyester fiber, *Thinsulate* by 3M, is being used experimentally in sleeping bags but seems better suited to use in clothing.

Design and construction

When you know how much loft you need, and what kind of filler you prefer, you are halfway along toward buying the right bag. What's left to consider is size, shape, design, and the finer points that show that a good job was done.

Shape. The standard is the mummy bag, a close-

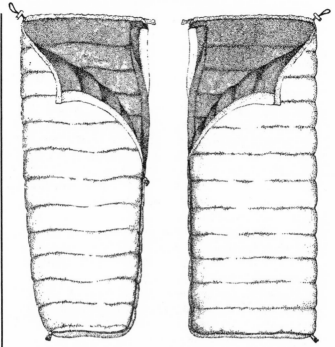

Semi-rectangular and rectangular sleeping bags (mummy style is shown at the beginning of the chapter)

cut design that is wide at the shoulders but narrows with the body to the toes. The snuggest mummies are more like sleeping garments than portable beds: when you roll, they roll with you. Mummies give the greatest warmth for the least fill. At the head there is typically a hood that can be closed around the face to leave only the tiniest of openings.

Some people find mummies unpleasantly confining. Other designs give you more room: modified mummies with and without hoods; barrel-shaped bags; semirectangular and fully rectangular models. In general, it's good to pick the narrowest bag you find comfortable. The wider the bag, the more weight it takes to give the same uniform loft.

Length. Most models come in two sizes: regular, for people up to six feet, and large. When you lie in the bag with the hood (if there is one) tightened over your face, you should be able to stretch your neck and point your toes without compressing the insulation at head or foot. When in doubt, take the longer size.

Shells. Inner and outer shells are usually made of some form of nylon. The cloth next to your skin should be pleasant to the touch: not chilly and slick to feel. If the fill is down, the shells must be woven very densely, or down particles will work their way out between the threads. (If you can blow through a fold of shell fabric, feeling your breath on the other side, the cloth is too coarse.) A few plumules always escape from a new down bag, especially at the seams—no cause for alarm unless the leakage continues. For unconventional shell materials, see *Sleeping "systems,"* below.

Internal structure. Synthetic fills come in blocks, called *battings,* that can be arranged in various ways. In one common construction, two layers of batting are installed, offset so that seams in one layer adjoin seamless parts of the other. In their attempt to approach the efficiency of down, the makers of polyester bags have produced some truly ingenious designs.

In a down bag the fill is loose. There must be internal walls, called baffles, to keep the down from shifting and opening up cold spots. These walls run horizontally around the bag, leaving the outside seams that give all down bags the familiar segmented look. In square-box baffling, now seldom used, the internal walls make right angles with the shell. More often the walls are slanted; this slant-box baffling allows fewer cold spots.

A third design adds more walls and makes small triangular compartments. This overlapping V-tube construction, heavy, expensive, and warm, is found only in expeditionary sleeping bags.

In most down bags there is a *channel block.* It runs the length of the bag, on the side opposite the zipper, and prevents down from shifting from the top to the underside of the bag. Some makers leave out the block, arguing that you can shift the down

Methods of sleeping bag construction

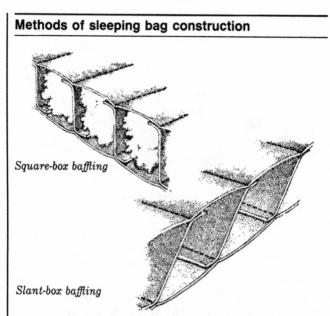

Square-box baffling

Slant-box baffling

yourself to make the bag warmer or cooler. I prefer the stability of the channel block.

The foot end. A good bag won't simply pinch out at the foot. Instead, it has an elaborately constructed bulge, a sort of a box, with room for your toes and a good thickness of insulation beyond.

Zipper. Most bags have them, typically down the sleeper's right side to about the ankle. (Some near-rectangular bags zip to the foot and along the bottom.) The zipper should work in both directions, so that you can open the foot end while leaving the upper end closed. Zippers should be nylon, not metal. There are various types, all good. Before you buy, climb into the bag and work the zipper up and down to see that it doesn't tend to snag. Bags of the same or compatible models can be zipped together to form a single, larger bed (make sure that one of them has its zipper on the *left*).

Draft tube. The zipper must have an extra flap of insulation inside it, or heat will escape. In a three-season or winter bag, check that this draft tube is not attached with a sewn-through seam; it must pro-

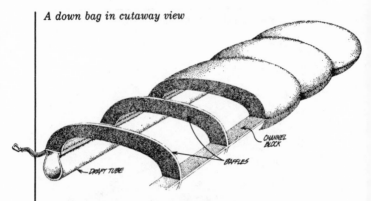

A down bag in cutaway view

CHANNEL BLOCK

BAFFLES

DRAFT TUBE

vide a thickness of insulation without a break. The draft tube should be longer than the zipper, so that no cold gap is left at the lower end.

Workmanship. There are some points worth looking at even in a costly sleeping bag. How good is the stitching? Examine a lot of it, especially where stress comes on the seams: along the zipper and around the hood where the drawstring runs in its sleeve. Double stitching, and of course strong bar-tacking, are important at these places. Check the number of stitches per inch—it should not be less than five or more than twelve. Turn the bag inside out and examine the foot end, the hardest part of the bag to sew. You can't see everything, but a bag well made where you can see it is probably sound clear through.

Sleeping "systems"

In all that goes above I have had in mind the familiar basic sleeping bag—a matter of shells and filler, with no high-technology fillips. And most backpackers will use just such uncomplicated bags.

Lately, however, the concept of the "sleeping system" has attained a certain vogue. Essentially, the idea is to supplement the insulating power of the basic bag with an assortment of shells and layers that act, in one way or another, to increase warmth. Some of these added layers may be built in; others can be added on as conditions require. The result is a layer system like the one applied to clothing.

There is an element of hype in all this (when a heretofore simple piece of gear is redefined as a "system," watch out: the price has just gone up). Nonetheless, there is value in the concept.

Here are some of the possible added layers:

Extra insulation. Some bags are built in two parts: an inner bag and a generously cut outer one. Depending on the temperatures to be faced, you can use either section or both. Two bags purchased separately may be combinable in the same way.

All-weather shells. The recently developed all-weather fabrics—water-resistant layers that "breathe," allowing sweat to evaporate—can be used to protect a vulnerable down sleeping bag. Some top-of-the-line goose down bags are built with Gore-Tex shells. For the well-funded year-round backpacker who wants to be able to do everything with one bag, this $300–$400 purchase may be worthwhile! Some bags with synthetic fills are also made with built-in Gore-Tex.

Gore-Tex bivouac bags—separate outer sheaths—can be purchased for use with any bag ($70 and up). In very cold conditions, however, these separate shells have some tendency to ice up, losing the breathability that makes them different from ordinary water-resistant cloth.

Radiant heat barriers. Ordinary sleeping bag insulation is not very good at blocking heat loss due to radiation: the infrared waves that pour from your body pass right through. A radiant barrier is a piece of reflective fabric designed to turn back these rays. Backpackers first came to know of this tool in the form of the "space blanket," a rectangle of fragile reflective cloth for use as cloak, shelter, or groundsheet. Then manufacturers began building radiant barriers into sleeping bags, and the gain here is remarkable. Field testers report that they sleep ten or fifteen degrees warmer with barrier-equipped bags than in similar bags without.

Radiant barriers have yet to be incorporated into

many down bags, for a simple reason: more warmth can be achieved by adding an equal weight of down than by adding a barrier layer. But the barriers can markedly increase the efficiency of synthetic-filled sleeping bags. They can now be purchased separately as "bivouac sacks" for use with any sleeping bag.

Vapor barriers. A vapor barrier is, simply, a waterproof layer. As noted, sleeping bags are normally built of permeable fabric, so that moisture can pass away from the skin. This has long been held to be essential for comfort. But there's another way.

The principle is this. The body works to maintain a layer of humid air next to the skin. This layer tends to dry out; we sweat partly to recharge it with moisture. As sweat evaporates, it takes a good deal of body warmth with it.

One way to conserve warmth, then, is to avoid sweating. And the way to avoid sweating is, paradoxically, to keep the moisture next to the skin from evaporating away.

If you go to sleep in some sort of waterproof sack, the layer of air next to the skin rapidly becomes humid and stays that way. You might expect to drown in perspiration. Instead, sweating slows down, and almost ceases. With a vapor barrier, enthusiasts claim, you can get much more warmth from the insulation in your sleeping bag without getting unpleasantly wet.

Some bags are built with vapor barrier liners; or separate liners are available to insert. You can even wrap yourself in a plastic bag or a groundsheet. The impermeable layer, however, must be close to your skin, say, just outside your long johns. Never put a waterproof outside your whole bedroll, or it will be soaked with body moisture.

If you are using a vapor barrier inside, there's plainly no need to have a permeable fabric in the outer shell of a sleeping bag. A fully waterproof shell can be used. Such a sleeping bag, its insulation protected between two impermeable layers, is just about weatherproof.

But is a vapor barrier, in normal conditions, either practical or necessary? For most people, the answer appears to be *no*. VB begins to make sense at deeply subzero temperatures. In general backpacking, it's an unnecessary refinement. And at temperatures above about zero Fahrenheit, many users find they feel clammy—whether or not they're supposed to.

Between you and the ground

Ground is hard. Ground is cold. Ground is often moist. To deal with these things, you need some defenses beneath you.

If you don't use a tent, you will need a groundsheet—just a rectangle of coated nylon or vinyl, available for a few dollars in any store that handles sporting goods. The more expensive ones last longer.

Besides the groundsheet, you'll want a pad. It cushions, which may be important; it insulates, which is certainly important. If your bag is down filled, the part beneath will collapse almost to nothing under your weight. Bags with synthetic fills do not compress so much, but a pad is still a good idea.

Your choice is between closed-cell foam pads, open-cell foam pads with covers, and air mattresses.

For most people, closed-cell foam pads are the choice. They are rugged and impervious to water. The best ones are made of ethyl vinyl acetate (EVA); some brand names are Evazote and Duralite. The sheets, sold in most sporting goods stores, are eighteen to twenty-two inches wide and come in varied lengths. Many summer backpackers choose a length of less than four feet. Thickness varies from one-quarter inch to three-quarters of an inch; the thinner style will do (for warmth at least) in summer, but winter campers buy the longest and thickest sheets they can find or carry two thin ones.

Open-cell foam pads, of polyurethane, generally come with fabric covers. These are both comfortable and bulky.

A third possibility is an air mattress. A mattress

with just one air valve and interconnected tubes is unreliable—one puncture and you're flat. Far better is a type made by AirLift, with a tough cloth cover and eight individual air tubes that slide into slots. If one tube fails, you still have the rest, and tubes can be cheaply replaced.

If the temperature is below about 40 degrees Fahrenheit, however, an air mattress is a liability: air circulates within it and carries away some body heat you cannot spare. To counter this problem, mattresses can be filled with something that stops air movement. Jack Stephenson makes a down-filled air mattress. Therm-a-Rest has a remarkable mattress consisting of an airtight shell around a piece of open-cell foam: when the valve is opened, the foam expands and sucks air in by itself. Many winter campers, in particular, are fond of these.

The prices of pads vary widely, according to the length, thickness, and construction. The cheapest good pad is a three-quarter-length EVA slab, three-eighths of an inch thick: these run about $10. The most expensive would be a Therm-a-Rest mattress, full length and 1.5 inches thick: about $50. Weights vary from about twelve ounces for a short EVA pad to over two pounds for a deluxe Therm-a-Rest.

Very light *hammocks* are also sold for wilderness camping, and can be useful in wooded areas when the ground is very moist. Both cost and weight are modest.

What about a *pillow?* Most people use clothing, stuffed perhaps into a cloth bag. Air mattresses may have built-in pillows. Separate inflatable pillows can also be had.

Accessories

You will need two *stuffsacks* for your sleeping bag. One, which is sold with the bag itself, will be just large enough to hold it tightly stuffed. Between trips the bedding should be stored in a big cloth bag (not airtight) or something similarly roomy.

You may want to try a *bag cover,* a big cloth

sack that pulls on over your bag to protect it from dirt (also to add warmth: as much as ten degrees). A case can be made as well for a *sleeping bag liner,* a light sheath that keeps the inside of your bag very much cleaner. This strikes most people as inordinate fussiness, but a liner can add years to the life of an expensive down bag (see below). This accessory may be hard to find. Wearing clothes to bed helps, but not as much as a liner.

Storage, cleaning, and care

A down bag should last ten or twelve years, a synthetic bag perhaps half that long. But all sleeping bags have vulnerable points.

No matter what kind of fill your bag contains, do not store it compressed. Stuffed for weeks or months, down loses part of its springiness and thus its all-important loft. Synthetic fill collapses even more dramatically. Bags with internal baffles should not be hung by the hood drawstrings; you don't want the fill bearing down on the thin internal walls for long periods. Thus the storage in a large, loose sack.

In the wilderness, too, it's good to leave a bag unstuffed as much as you can. (Depending on humidity: when the air is very moist, a loose bag with nobody in it will just get damp.) If the bag is moist and bedraggled when you put it away in the morning, you can dry it out, weather permitting, at lunch. To pack it, don't roll it; instead stuff it evenly, foot-end first, handful by handful, into its stuffsack. When you pull it out, be gentle.

Do your best to keep the bag both dry and clean. Moisture is not a threat to the synthetics, but down that is continually damp will disintegrate. It also loses insulating power as it becomes soiled: thus the advantage of using a liner inside a down bag. Air your bag thoroughly after each trip, but don't leave it lying in the sun for more than a few hours— sunlight eventually damages nylon shell material. Be extremely careful about sparks around a fire.

Cleaning a down bag is *extremely* tricky. Don't do it any more often than you have to—say once a year with frequent use. No matter how careful you are, there is a penalty: down loses a certain amount of insulating power every time it is washed.

The safest way to wash a down bag? Do it yourself in a tub with Ivory Snow soap flakes or a similarly gentle soap. Never use detergent or bleach. The water should be warm, not hot. Work the suds through the bag by pressing on it. Don't twist. Don't wring. Don't put strain on the internal baffles. When the suds have turned dark, drain the tub and start over. Do this as often as you need to until the suds are white. Then rinse again several times, making sure to get all the soap out of the bag. Then, very gently, press the excess water out. Let gravity drain most of the water from the bag; press gently to extract a little more.

Now comes the crucial move. Lift the wet bag with all the care you can. Cradle the whole soggy thing in your arms. No part should hang unsupported. If you simply grab an end and haul, the wet down will burst the baffles from one end to the other, and you'll be out your hundred-fifty bucks or so.

Don't hang the wet bag on a clothesline. Instead, tumble it in a big laundromat dryer at very low heat or no heat at all. (Caution: the "low" setting on some commercial dryers is far too hot!) Throw in a couple of dry towels and some small rubbery object—a tennis ball, a (clean) laceless tennis shoe—to help absorb water and break up clumps of down. When the bag is nearly dry, take it out and leave it in the sun for a day, turning and fluffing it now and again.

Washing a down sleeping bag, clearly, takes a lot of water, a lot of patience, and a lot of pocket-change. You can shorten the job somewhat by using a front-loading washing machine (never a machine with an agitator) set on the coolest, gentlest cycle. But most manufacturers urge you to do it by hand.

You can also get bags cleaned commercially. A

very few specialized establishments go through the hand-washing routine; most bags sent out for washing, however, get dry-cleaned. Conventional wisdom long held that certain dry-cleaning processes were acceptably gentle, but this is controversial. The simplest rule is that down bags should not be dry-cleaned, period. After all, the investment at stake is not a small one.

What about bags with synthetic fills? Here the difficulties are much less. Such a bag can be washed quite safely in a front-loading machine and dried at low heat in a large tumble dryer. But synthetic bags are never dry-cleaned, period. And you must be extremely cautious with heat. One hundred and forty degrees Fahrenheit is the "plasticizing point" of synthetic fills, the point at which the fibers lose their springiness. Some models may have still more sensitive materials (like polypropylene) somewhere in their anatomy. Read and follow the care instructions that accompany your bag.

Low impact and the bedroll

With sleeping bags, as with packs, there is just one impact question: what color? A bright-colored sleeping bag is not so obtrusive as a gaudy pack, because it will be stowed away much of the time. Even so, do you want to stand out in the wilderness like a spot of fire wherever you throw down your bag? Or do you choose rather to blend in? In the busy wildlands of the later twentieth century, the arguments seem heavy on the side of blending in. The stuffsack, at least, should not be brightly colored.

More complicated is the question of hammocks. Some advocate them as the ultimate low-impact sleeping tool: since your weight does not rest on the ground at all, you won't be damaging vegetation and compressing soil. In my view this is of interest in one situation only: if you are camping off trail, away from regularly used campsites. There it is vital that you leave *no* trace, and a hammock may make the job easier.

Most wilderness camping, however, is done on sites that have been used for years. In such spots, the price in impact has already been paid. Research shows that a campsite is altered drastically by the first few uses; after that, there is comparatively little change. Your body weight on the ground is not going to damage anything that isn't damaged already.

If you are an inveterate cross-country hiker in wooded country, you might consider a hammock on low-impact grounds. Otherwise, let comfort be your guide.

8:
Shelter

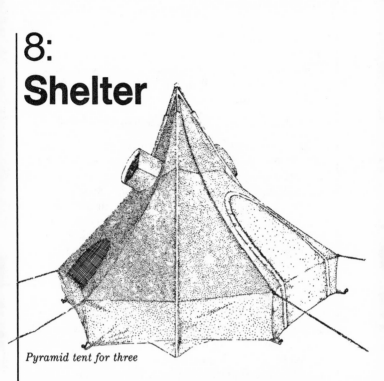

Pyramid tent for three

WHEN YOU HEAD INTO the wilderness—no matter how fine the weather at the roadhead—you must have some plan for *shelter*. And that means something carried in your pack. Don't count on improvising a lean-to, or making a bed of green boughs (unless in extreme emergency). These methods were elegant when the wilderness was vast and the population small. Jim Bridger used them, and so did John Muir, but now it is the wilderness that is tiny, the human pressure that is great. Don't count too heavily on trailside huts or lean-tos, either; some regions have them, but they afford little privacy, and when they are empty you may find them dirty or in disrepair.

What should your shelter be? In the East, in the northern Cascades, and in parts of the northern Rockies, the case is good for carrying a full-scale tent at any time of year. In the southwestern part of the United States, however, a regular tent is more shelter than you are likely to need in the summer. The weather during the southwestern hiking season is seldom wet for long. Too many expensive tents weigh down too many packs in such sunny regions as the California Sierra.

Less than a tent: poncho, tarp, and tube

The first requirement, of course, is a roof to shed rain. (It will incidentally keep dew off your sleeping bag and keep you a little warmer. In desert country you may need a sunroof for a midday stop.)

The simplest possible roof is also an item of clothing: the *poncho,* a rectangular piece of waterproof fabric with neck hole and hood. While some ponchos are made just large enough to cover the hiker's body, others are long enough in back to drape over the pack as well; these, called packboard ponchos, can be pitched as minimal one-person shelters. A poncho intended for such use should have several metal grommets along the sides and at the corners for the attachment of cords. Cheap ponchos are made of fragile plastic and are too flimsy to make workable shelters; $30 is the minimum for an adequate coated-nylon·poncho. Dimensions start at about five feet by nine feet; weight is a pound or a little over.

A *sleeping bag cover* or bivouac sack can also serve as a minimal shelter. A cover with a water-

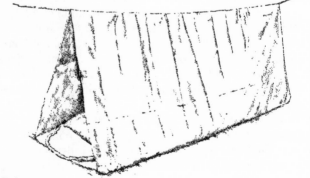

Tube tent

proof bottom and a permeable top can be flipped to make a makeshift rainroof. More practical is such a cover with a roof of Gore-Tex or other water-resistant but "breathable" fabric.

Another inexpensive shelter is the *polyethylene tube:* simply an open-ended tunnel of three-mil (.003-inch) plastic about nine feet long. Tubes come in several sizes ranging from one to three pounds and varying from three to five feet in diameter (larger ones have room for two people). Cost is under $10. To pitch a tube tent, you run a line through the tube and pull it tight between two trees or other anchors. Clothespins help in pitching. Such a shelter is only suited for the forest and for the brief rains of a southwestern summer; it won't last you through many uses.

In a tube, or in any walled shelter of waterproof fabric, you have the problem of dealing with the water that is shut in with you. The human body puts out about a pint of moisture in sweat and respiration every night, and that moisture has to go somewhere. What doesn't escape through the ends of your tube will soak your sleeping bag or condense on the waterproof walls and shower you with dew or frost in the morning.

A much more versatile shelter is the *tarp.* A tarp is simply a rectangle of water-repellent cloth. A skillful handler—it takes practice—can make it

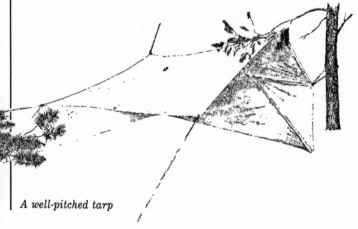

A well-pitched tarp

through a severe rain, at least below timberline, under a tarp. Good tarps are made of urethane-coated nylon, tough and grommeted. Typical sizes are ten by ten and ten by twelve feet. Weights range from two to three pounds. Prices start at $25—some, with many grommets and tabs, are sold for over $50. A regular tent fly (see below) can also be used as a tarp. Because they are open at the sides, tarp shelters avoid a serious condensation problem.

Ponchos, tarps, and tube tents can all, in theory, be pitched with nothing but cord. Actually, it is often useful to have one or two tentpoles and several stakes along; natural anchors don't necessarily come just where you'd like them. For more about pitching and living in shelters, see Chapter 18.

Tents: general

When is waterproof not waterproof?

How can you build a tent that lets body moisture out—as it has to, or you will get very damp—without letting the rain get in?

One method is to build the tent canopy of one of the recently developed waterproof/breathable fabrics, like Gore-Tex. More about this below.

Most tentmakers, however, hold to a traditional solution. These tents come in two parts: an inner shelter built largely of permeable nylon, not waterproofed, so that moisture can escape; and an additional, fully waterproof *rainfly* that is stretched just above the vulnerable structure underneath.

In most tents the two units are separate, and you can, when appropriate, leave one or the other unused. A rainfly, taken alone, can serve as a tarp, and the main tent alone may keep you dry when the only likely weather is the kind of light cold snow that won't stick to the fabric and melt.

Like boots, like sleeping bags, like backpacks, wilderness tents vary enormously in cost, complexity, and sturdiness. Generally we distinguish *three-season tents* and *winter tents*. Three-season models are intended to stop rain and keep insects out; they vary in their ability to handle high winds. Winter tents are stoutly supported, carefully tailored, and strong. A winter tent may have to resist eighty-mile-an-hour gusts or bear a weight of several hundred pounds of wet, clinging snow.

Tents are built in many sizes. The most useful for backpackers are long, narrow, boxy designs with room for two people; larger domelike tents are also popular.

A three-season backpacking tent should not weigh more than about three and one half pounds per person sheltered; makers can get that down to two and a half pounds when they put their minds to it. Prices vary more widely: you may pay as little as $50 or as much as $150 per person sheltered.

One-person tents

Tents just big enough for one—sometimes called "personal shelters"—are increasingly popular. (Some are mislabeled "bivy sacks," though true bivouac sacks are sleeping bag covers without supporting poles.) These mini-tents are low, skinny affairs, designed for easy pitching and minimal weight. Commonly they have one-piece Gore-Tex canopies or "integral" rainflies that remain attached to the inner tent. They also tend to have hefty price-tags—$150 for a well-made model is not unusual.

Two-person tents: wedge and tunnel

The typical two-person tent is long and narrow. Its floor is a rectangle or a modified rectangle. Dimensions vary, but a typical floor is about seven feet long and four and a half feet wide. The roof rises something less than four feet at the highest point. (Floor plans deviate widely from the basic rectangle. Often they will narrow at the foot, where you need less room. Some tents have prowlike "alcoves" at one end, or at both; these give you extra living room.)

There are several ways of supporting a tent's roof. The very simplest is the *I-pole:* a single, vertical post at each end of the tent. More stable and more convenient is the *A-frame.* In this design, now used less than formerly, a pole is thrust through a fabric sleeve along each side of the triangular tent end. The poles converge on a gripping device at the top, forming an "A" with no crossbar. The classic wedge-shaped summer tent has an A-frame at the door and a short I-post at the foot, where it will be less in the way.

Some modified A-frame designs add a *ridge-pole,* an additional support running from end to end to fuse the remaining members into a framework that stands up by itself. Lacking a ridgepole, the tent is held erect by the pull of *guylines,* one from the apex at each end, running to ground anchors.

A more common way of supporting the canopy is with arc-shaped, hooplike poles rather than straight ones. These poles are inserted, under tension, into fabric sleeves. The rounded shapes and elastic tension combine to pull the fabric tight, making a tent that sheds wind neatly. (Straight lines and sharp corners have become rare in tent design.)

One very popular layout is the *tunnel tent,* with rounded roof held up by several half circles of tensioned poles. There are endless variations on the basic plan: some tunnel tents slope down to the foot; some are high in the middle; in some, the arching

Classic three-season tent for two people

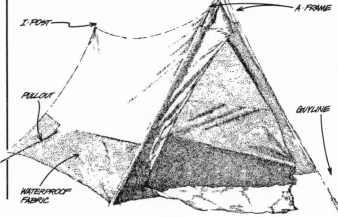

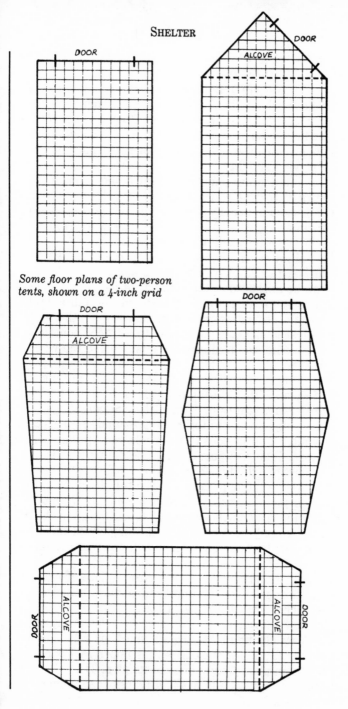

DOOR

DOOR

ALCOVE

Some floor plans of two-person tents, shown on a 4-inch grid

DOOR

ALCOVE

DOOR

DOOR

ALCOVE

ALCOVE

DOOR

poles are so arranged that the tent will stand up by itself, without the pull of guylines.

Then there is the *semidome*. In this design the poles arch diagonally over the tent, from opposite corners, forming an X. The high point of the tent is at the center, where the poles cross. This design is roomy for its weight, but is not particularly good for wind stability.

Still another support variant is the *exterior frame*. Instead of running through sleeves of tent fabric, as is usually the case, the supporting poles form a complete, freestanding framework from which the tent is hung by elastic cords.

Many tents are equipped with *pullouts*, extra lines attached to several points along the walls that can be anchored to the ground for extra stability. In older tents, these were vital to pull the fabric taut and to recover interior space that would otherwise be lost in sag; the pullouts on most good contemporary tents are used less often (say when the wind is rising).

Almost all modern backpacking tents are made of nylon, either ripstop or nylon taffeta. Tent floors are always waterproof (with the urethane-coated side up), and the waterproofing extends four inches or more up the sides of the walls and up the door or doors. This "tub floor" cannot be built without seams, but the fewer there are, the better.

Above the upper edge of the tub floor, the walls are made of ordinary permeable nylon, *not* waterproofed. This allows moisture to escape from the inside. To prevent water from invading from the outside, the tent has its second roof: the waterproof rainfly.

The rainfly is usually a separate piece of material. It drapes over the tent's supporting framework in such a way that it never touches the inner, permeable wall. It must overhang the sides enough to prevent slanting, wind-driven rain from reaching uncoated fabric. At the edges, this upper roof is held tautly in place by guylines of its own. These tensioning lines may attach to the guylines that support

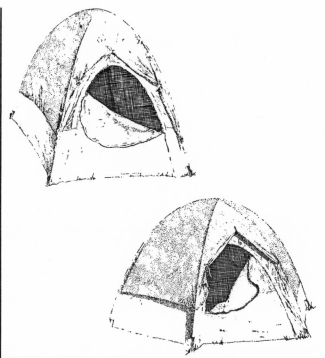

Semi-dome (above) and full-dome tents

the inner tent, to clips attached to the inner tent, or
to separate stakes in the ground.

At one end of the tent (the higher if the ridgeline
slants) is the triangular or hemispherical *door.*
Doors sometimes hinge at the bottom, sometimes at
the side. Each arrangement has advantages. If the
door is bottom-hinged, with zippers running up to
the apex on either side, the top can be opened easily
for ventilation. If the door hinges at one side and
opens along the bottom, it must zip to a raised, waterproof sill. Many tents have two doors, one at either end; this gives you a cooling breeze when both
are open.

Any tent to be used in warm weather needs *mosquito netting* over every opening and a complete
inner door of netting at each entrance. The net
should zip in the same pattern as the solid door. You

can get specialized "bug tents" made entirely of netting, except for waterproof floor and rainfly; these are ideal where rain and mosquitoes are the problems (but plainly not so good for wind and cold).

Ventilation is exceedingly important in a tent. The permeable fabric of the walls will let some moisture out, but it takes circulating air to keep you comfortably dry. Besides the door there must be at least one vent high up near the ridgeline. Two vents are better. Some tents have full-length panels of mesh.

Some tents are equipped with *vestibules*. There are several designs, but the object is to give you a rain-sheltered patch of ground just outside the main door—a sort of porch where you can cook or store gear. Some tents protect this working area with an extra-long, low-hanging rainfly; others add an extension to the roof of the inner tent. Some vestibules are built in, others add on.

Two or more *netting pockets*, hanging from the sidewalls, are essential for keeping track of small, losable objects.

Larger tents

What's the boundary between large two-person tents and small three-person models? Any tent that has a floor area much over forty square feet and a volume much over eighty cubic feet is definitely big enough for three. Almost all tents smaller than this have somewhat rectangular floors much longer than they are wide; most tents above this size have floors that are square, hexagonal, round or of some compound shape.

One common design is the *full dome*. The floor is a polygon; the canopy is supported by several curved poles that arch from side to side, intersecting in patterns that vary from model to model. One version puts the hoops outside, as an exterior frame, and hangs the tent from this skeleton—it looks something like a geodesic dome.

Another familiar design is the *six-sided pyramid*. The floor is a hexagon. Three poles slide through fabric sleeves to seat in a socketed aluminum block at the peak. Between the supporting poles, guylines pull out the walls to round out the hexagon. This design is roomy and tall enough to kneel in. (Somewhat similar but not so convenient is an older pyramid design with a tall center pole.)

Beyond the patterns of pyramid and dome, easy to visualize, still larger tents spread out into all sorts of geometric combinations. The larger the number of people to be sheltered, the more possibilities the designers find. Though some of these larger tents are good for family use, not many backpackers will be in the market for tents of such weight and size.

Tents for wind and winter

Between "three-season" tents and "winter" (or "mountaineering") tents there is no sharp line to be drawn. But there are certain features of construction and design that make a tent suitable for camps in increasingly challenging places.

Very important is *stability in wind.* Tents designed specifically for alpine gales tend to be long

Winter tent, tunnel design

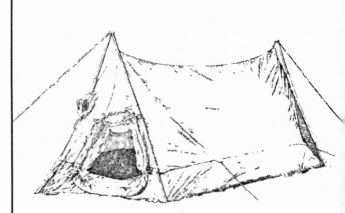

Winter tent, A-frame design

and narrow, but dome designs have also proved themselves for winter use. A winter dome must have a rather sharp summit, providing no flat spot for snow to pile up on.

Tents of the older A–frame design gain wind stability from what is called the *catenary cut*. The roofline dips steeply at the middle, in a kind of built-in sag. When the end guylines are tensioned, such a roof pulls nicely taut. (It will still make a lot of noise in a big wind, however.) Sometimes the walls are catenary cut as well, bending inward at the sides. Such hourglass designs cut down on room, but the security is worth it. The rainfly is cut to hang on a similar plunging curve.

Winter tents tend to be a good deal heavier than three-season models, for several reasons. They are often built of thicker material, and special attention must be paid to reinforcement. Also, they typically have somewhat more room than comparable three-season tents. All this gives winter tents an average weight, per person, of well over three pounds.

Some winter tents have two entrances. There may be a round opening opposite the conventional door with an extendable sleeve or *snow tunnel*. You can burrow out this exit if the zipper entrance gets blocked for some reason.

A few winter tents have *cookholes:* zippered openings in the floor, designed so that in theory you can set up an indoor kitchen on a patch of snow. Some other minor features, useful on any tent, are most common on winter models. A pair of tabs makes it easy to string a *ridge seam clothesline* for drying wet gear.

A winter tent, even more than a summer tent, *must* be well ventilated. Usually that means a vent at each end and a door that can be cracked at the top. Vents should be set in special tubes of fabric that blow with the wind and thus admit less blown snow than a simple, windowlike opening would. You do take in some powder, regardless, and vents must be closable.

With all these requirements and options, it's no wonder that winter tents are more expensive than three-season types—the average is about $275 for a two-person model.

There are two further features, found on some winter tents and available for others, that can be useful. *Snowflaps* are flanges of extra material projecting around the base of the tent on all sides. By piling snow or rocks on the flaps you can provide securer anchorage than with stakes alone. A *frostliner* looks for all the world like a bedsheet. Made of cotton or a cotton-polyester weave, it hangs on the inside of the tent, tied to special tabs along the ridgeline and on the walls. You get an Arabian Nights effect, but there's a purpose. On a cold winter trip, frost is constantly forming on the inner walls, and with each gust it shakes off: a continual light snowstorm. The frostliner traps some of this condensation or, at worst, sheds the crystals to the sides of the tent, where it is easier to deal with them.

Tents without rainflies

The double-roofed tent—breathable canopy, waterproof fly—remains the standard arrangement in wilderness tents. But other strategies have also been tried.

Jack Stephenson makes tents that are, simply, waterproof. In theory, such tents should be swamps inside, dripping with condensation. Stephenson fights condensation in two ways: by carefully engineered venting systems, to keep air moving through; and by added inner canopies (of reflective Mylar). Such an inner ceiling grows warm and so, in theory, does not cause water vapor to condense. I have not tried Stephenson's very light, very expensive tents, but many customers swear by them.

A more widespread experiment is the use of waterproof, breathable fabrics in tent canopies. Theoretically, Gore-Tex should keep rain out while allowing water vapor to escape. And in fact single-walled tents of this kind seem to work well if it is not too cold. There are frequent reports, however, that Gore-Tex canopies form thin films of ice on their outer surfaces if the temperature is below about 28 degrees Fahrenheit; when this happens, the micropores get clogged and you have, simply, a waterproof roof with the usual condensation problems.

Then there are tents that do, indeed, have flies, but come in one piece: the waterproof fly and the permeable tent wall are joined by sills with a dead-air space between them. Instead of having tent and fly, either of which you may use alone, you have a single tent with a double wall. These everything-in-one tents are warm and very easy to pitch.

Choosing a tent

The decision to buy a tent is a good decision to delay. Rental tents are easy to find (about $15 a weekend), and there are questions you need to ask yourself before you spend such a chunk of money. Do you really need a tent, or will a simple, versatile tarp give you protection enough? If you do need a tent, where will you use it most often—in rainy, mosquito-ridden woods? On ski or snowshoe trips? On summer treks above timberline? How many people should it be able to sleep? How long will you need to spend in it at a time? And how much can you afford to pay?

Sort out in your mind what your ideal tent would be like. Every tent is a compromise. The roomiest tent won't be the lightest, nor the most stable in a wind. The cheapest tent won't be the most durable, nor the easiest to pitch. And the harder the tent-maker has worked to combine different practical advantages in a single model, the higher the price is likely to be.

Size. You have a choice of shelters for one person, for two, for three or more. Within each category there is some variation. If your tent will be only a now-and-then shelter, it need only be large enough to stretch out in. But if you expect to spend days in it, during long rains or snowstorms, with much of your gear inside, you need a good deal more room.

Height. A related yet separate question. Some tents are high enough so that you can sit up in them without brushing the roof; lower ones, though, tend to be more stable in the wind. In tents that are high at each end (with a catenary sag in the middle), two people can sit up facing each other. In a tent that slopes to the foot there is only one spot with sitting room.

Ease of pitching. Some tents are easy to put up, some harder, and the difference can matter. When you consider a tent, make a list of the jobs that have to be done. (How easily could you do them with cold hands, or in the dark?)

• How many stakes must be put in to anchor the floor?

• How many poles must be slid into sleeves? Must they be inserted under tension? How hard is the final push?

• How many different guylines must be set before the tent is minimally self-supporting? (With a dome design, there may be none; most A-frame and tunnel tents require two.)

• How many pullouts—those extra lines that pull

the sag out of walls—must be anchored at the sides?

● What about the rainfly—how much extra and separate rigging does it require?

Durability. An obvious value. Durability comes from heavy materials, lots of reinforcement, and very careful workmanship—see below. It costs you something in weight and something in money.

Wind stability. If you will be camping mostly in sheltered woods, high stability may not be worth the extra money it will cost. For typical backpacking, especially in the West, you need a tent that is at least moderately stable.

Light weight. The ultimate good—or is it? Most of the other things you value in a tent mean added weight. Tent innovations are mainly aimed at getting more advantages from fewer pounds, but you can pay a great deal to shed just a handful of ounces.

Looking for quality

In buying a tent you have an extra problem. You can always get a good look at a boot, or a pack, or a sleeping bag, and see it as it is. But a tent, taken off the shelf, is a shapeless bundle of cloth and hardware. Only when you see it tightly pitched can you guess how windproof it is, how large it is, how well sewn. Catalog specifications are sometimes incomplete or wrong, and some very fine tents are sold chiefly by mail.

If you buy a tent you can't look at first, reserve the right to bring it back after setting it up indoors for a closer look. Most outfits are good about this. A tent that doesn't please, like a boot that doesn't fit, will be taken back with no hassle.

If you are concerned about wind, look carefully at the way the canopy hangs. Do deep wrinkles form? Do the walls sag despite the pullouts? Or is the cloth fairly smooth? (One caution: tents rigged in a store tend to look unnaturally perfect—tents rigged on a rug, where you can't drive stakes, always look sloppier than they really are. Make allowances.)

Look for adequate ventilation. Make sure there is at least one vent, high up.

Consider, again, how easy the tent will be to pitch.

Check to see that the bottom tip of each tent pole is seated in a grommet or a reinforced sleeve—you don't want poles sinking into damp ground or snow. Tent poles should be smooth and easy to manipulate.

Look carefully at seams. Most of them should be what the industry calls "flat fell." In a flat-fell seam, the two pieces of fabric are folded, each over the other; stitching goes through all four layers. In any seam that is not of this type, make sure that stitching is not too close to the edge of any piece of fabric (these are likely to fray). In any seam in the fly, or in a single-layer Gore-Tex tent, make sure that the joining is stable, not tending to gape when you pull on either side: a gaping seam will be difficult to waterproof. (See *Handling and care of tents*, below.)

Stitching is crucial. Less than five stitches to the inch is poor; so is more than twelve (too numerous stitches make a line of weakness that can tear). The more places with double or triple rows, the better. There should be no holes without thread in them, no loose, hanging thread ends, and no "puckered" effect where some stitches, out of line with the others, are taking extra strain. Tentmakers almost always use a *lockstitch*, so designed that the seam cannot unravel even if the thread is broken. The simpler chainstitch is to be avoided.

There should be plenty of reinforcement. Look for it wherever there is a grommet; a loop where a tent peg will seat or a cord attach; a sewn-on strap; and wherever guylines attach to the tent. At a minimum each stress point should have a heavy, doubled hem. In better tents an extra piece of material may be added, especially at the peg loops. Grommets and other metal parts should be rust-free aluminum or brass. All points of quality become doubly important in a tent intended for winter use.

Poles and stakes

Poles come with tents. There are many styles; the more common types can also be purchased off the shelf, to replace broken originals or to use with a tarp.

Many tent poles are of aluminum tubing in three sections, each a foot to eighteen inches long, linked by elastic shock cord running inside. When the pole is set up, the base of each section nests in a socket in the end of the one below. For packing, the sections pull apart, and the pole folds into a manageable bundle. Lengths, diameters, and metal gauges vary.

Other tents have thinner, lighter poles of tough, flexible fiberglass. These are typically shock-corded; segments are linked by metal fittings (permanently attached).

Some cheaper tents use telescoping poles, convenient but not so strong. To put them up, you simply extend them, as you would a standard radio antenna on a car. Stout at the bottom, these poles grow spindly at the top, where the thinnest segments are.

Pay special attention to poles when considering a tent. If metal, are they smooth and free of burrs and sharp edges? Do the segments join easily and securely? Is the shock cord firm and elastic? If the tent has the inexpensive telescoping poles, make sure that the sections slide in and out smoothly.

There are many kinds of *stakes*. The simplest are aluminum skewers with an eye at one end. Steel alloy skewers—heavier but stouter—are used in frozen or rocky ground. "Channeled stakes" are C-shaped in cross-section and will do in soft ground or consolidated snow. For loose soil there are also stout plastic stakes, I-shaped in section. For winter there's the snow stake, a light aluminum angle, V-shaped in section. There are several other variants. Weight is generally about an ounce per stake, and prices run from a few cents to a dollar apiece. If you camp in a variety of places and seasons, you will need a stock of different kinds of stakes to choose from each time you pack.

When you rig a tent, you need a way of tightening or loosening the lines without shifting the stakes. Grip-slip knots will serve, but plastic gadgets are available to do the same thing.

In pitching a tarp or tube tent that lacks a grommet at a crucial spot, you can improvise an attachment with a noose of cord and a small, smooth stone. There are commercial gimmicks that do the same thing with a plastic or rubber "rock" and a plastic or metal "noose."

Handling and care of tents

When you pitch a tent, try to locate a piece of ground without sharp rocks, sticks, or anything else that could puncture or abrade the water-resistant floor. Spread out a groundsheet under the tent. If you are lighting a fire, don't pitch the tent too close to it—nylon won't go up in flames, but sparks are likely to melt holes in it.

Cooking inside a tent, or even under its vestibule roof, is a risky business. See more about this in Chapter 19. Any tent in which you cook must have several vents, including one high up and immediately over the stove. Citrus drinks are bad for nylon, and spilled stove fuel can damage the waterproofing on your floor. Important tools in any tent that gets lived in much are a sponge for wiping up spills and condensation and a whisk broom for brushing out dirt or loose snow.

If you get a minor puncture or a leak during a trip, you can patch it with ordinary adhesive tape. Apply the patch from the outside, on a dry surface (if you can get one). Wax from a candle, or even lip balm, will stop a leak for a while. In wet country, or with a new or leak-prone tent, carry a tube of seam sealant to caulk seams.

When you break camp, get dirt and debris out of the tent, especially anything sharp or gritty. Take time to rub droplets of pitch and bird droppings off the fly and canopy (you can use white gas as solvent on the permeable fabrics only). If the tent is very wet and the weather fine, you can tie it on the outside of your pack in a loose bundle. Nylon is treated to resist mildew up to a point, but the drier you can keep it, the better.

Tents come with stuffbags of the appropriate size. Check the manufacturer's directions about stuffing: some recommend stuffing a tent into its storage bag, as if it were a sleeping bag; others want you to fold it as it was folded when you got it.

After a trip, sponge off any especially dirty spots and dry the tent thoroughly. (Dry-cleaning fluid will get rid of pitch and is safe anywhere on the tent.) If the thing is really filthy, you can take a garden hose to it. (It's best not to wash a tent in a machine: the twisting or tumbling action tends to break up the coating on the waterproof floor and fly.) To dry, hang the tent out for several days, supported at points that are built to take strain. The seams will take longest to dry.

Wipe the poles clean, too; this is especially important if you have been camping near salt water. Pay special attention to the telescoping poles and to the joints of standard sectioned poles. Finally, store everything in a dry place.

During cleaning and drying, check the tent for punctures and tears. Patching a tent is something like patching an inner tube. Kits are available, with fabric cement and patches of material, both waterproof and permeable. An air mattress repair kit will also do. For extra strength stitch around the edges of the patch—and seal the resulting seam.

Tent waterproofing is not forever. Seams or other spots in floor or fly may start leaking on their own. And in time you may have to repaint large areas with waterproof coating. REI and K-Kote are two of several companies that make products for seam and area sealing. Beware of sealants marketed in cute little cannisters with rolling-ball dispensers, like deodorants: they are useless.

In seam sealing, follow product directions. Generally, several light coats are better than one heavy one; each coat must dry thoroughly before the next is added.

Larger injuries to a tent require professional attention. A shoemaker can replace pulled-out grommets. A gear store can direct you to places and people who do more substantial repairs; some do the work themselves.

Tents and low impact

The improper placement of bed sites is one of the principal causes of damage to wilderness land. *Where* you pitch your tent is much more important than *how*. Even the weight of the tent and its occupants can compact moist ground and do long-term damage to vulnerable vegetation. For much more on impact considerations in camping, see Section E.

Is the driving of stakes a significant impact on wilderness ground? Probably not very, but the matter is worth considering. When you select stakes for a trip, choose the thinnest style the area and season make practical: in summer, the thin metal eyelet stakes work fine. It is often possible to use natural anchors instead of stakes. See also Chapter 18.

Now we come (for the third time in these chapters) to the problem of color. Do you make your campsite obvious with a tent in red, orange, or a light, bright shade of blue—or do you blend into the landscape with green or rust or brown? I recommend once more the unobtrusive colors. Nothing makes a wild landscape seem so populous as a scatter of highly visible tents—a whole seeming village where you would prefer to see no human presence at all.

Two arguments are often raised in favor of "standing out." One is convenience in choosing a camp. If you look up an open valley and see the bright blotches of tents, you know better than to plan your own camp in that area. This argument is valid but—so I believe—inadequate: the virtues of blending in are still the greater. (And what of the hiking party that passes these campsites during the day? They aren't yet ready to stop—and meanwhile their pleasure is diminished by these too obvious signs of human presence.)

More pressing is the claim of safety—the thought that a visible tent could more easily be spotted by searchers from the air. How much weight you give to this consideration must depend largely on the kind of travel you plan to do. There are places and times when a bright-colored tent seems not only prudent but also psychologically *right.* On the immense white back of a glacier, or in the middle of a violent cold storm, the orange canopy that shelters you seems somehow in scale. The greater the force and genuine danger in the environment, the less you need to be concerned about somehow asserting yourself too much.

In summer, though, or below timberline in any season, the same sense of proportion suggests tents in earthier colors. A good compromise for the safety-conscious might be a bright-colored tent with a dull-colored rainfly. In rainy woods, you can blend in; in alpine snow, you can make yourself as visible as you choose.

9:
Stove and Kitchen

Too many backpackers, in sunny regions at least, carry tents they may not need. But too few backpackers anywhere have yet formed the habit of carrying stoves. The stove, in the modern wilderness, is a necessity treated, too often, as an option or a luxury.

There is no denying the pleasures (or the uses) of the old-fashioned campfire. An evening fire is a presence: almost, strangely, a pet or a companion. It gives pleasant light, pleasant heat, pleasant noises. It is an event, an entertainment. It draws a group together around it. For many, it is a symbol of camping, a symbol of the wilderness even—a return to a far older, far simpler way of doing things.

And yet the fire, in the wilderness today, has fallen out of favor. There are simply too many of us now and too little pristine land for old habits to hold. Fires near timberline, where wood is scarce and the growing season short, are not now defensible. Nor is there any excuse for the building of new fire rings where none has been before. In the more populous wilderness landscapes, firespots mark the ground like so many black sores, and these, more quickly than anything else we leave to mark our presence, make the land look used and overused.

Thus the managers of wilderness have found it increasingly necessary to close large areas to fire. And there are times and places where no rule intervenes, but where you nonetheless feel reluctant to make a mark. Maybe you are setting up camp on a ridgeline miles from the nearest traveled trail, a place so remote and changeless that you could imagine yourself the first human being to walk there. There is no one to object to one small fire scar. There may not even be a compelling "ecological" argument against leaving one. And yet you recoil. It seems important (perhaps beyond reason) that you not leave that place diminished in any way.

The case against fire should not be overstated. There are times and places where a fire cannot, by the longest reach of conscience, be accused of doing harm: a sea beach tangled with drifted logs for fuel; a sandbar or a gravelly river bank (below the winter high-water line); an old fire ring in a moist forest littered with down wood. And even in a pristine landscape there are ways of handling a fire so that nothing visible is left behind.

But this is the point: if you have a stove, you simply don't have to worry about the propriety of the kitchen site you have chosen. You are self-sufficient. You take nothing from the land and leave nothing behind. No ashes. No rings. No blackened stones to clean or conceal. You are much more free to camp where you will.

There are other practical advantages as well. Simplicity is the main one. The next few pages will inevitably make stoves sound like complicated, rather tricky gadgets. But once you have the stove and have grown used to it, you'll find its operation quick and easy. You'll be boiling water while the wood-burner is still gathering kindling. You'll be working with a steady, controllable flame. Your pots won't even get sooty. No question about it: pleasant associations aside, stove cooking has campfire cooking beat all hollow.

And whether you choose a stove for conscience or convenience, you may in time discover something more. You may find that the stove brings with it pleasures of its own, equal, arguably, to the pleasures of a fire. A stove, too, becomes a kind of companion. It has its own rituals. It burns with a comfortable, reassuring roar. It calls to your mind, each time you light it, the other places you have used it: other camps, other journeys, other times.

But most important is that curious moment, after dark, when at last you turn the valve key and bring the stove to instant silence. There are no embers, of course, to sit by and watch fade. What happens instead is rather hard to explain. The wilderness, kept at a certain distance for a while by your noisy and lighted kitchen, appears all at once around you. The night sky comes into being over you as if its black and its brilliance had just then been invented. The colors of the night, the movements, the slight noises, become instantly present. Against all these things the wood-burning fire is a lively defense—but a defense (you may come to feel) no more to be desired than it is needed.

On some trips in some regions you can have it both ways. If you carry a stove and fuel, you can leave them in the pack when conditions are right for a fire. Maybe your first night will be spent in the rain in a low-lying forest, where wood is plentiful, a fire a real comfort. But the next night you are at timberline in a no-fire zone. Or maybe, arriving at a place where you planned to build a fire, you find there is no dead, down wood within scavenging range. Far better to carry the stove and leave it unused than to carry none and find yourself forced to choose between eating cold food and lighting a fire where no fire should be.

Stoves suitable for backpacking are small and light. They come in many different models—forty or so—but in just three essentially different popular designs. There is the old wilderness standard, the *white gas stove*. There is its variant, the *multifuel* or *kerosene stove*. Finally, there is the butane- or propane-burning *cartridge stove*, which uses prefilled, pressurized fuel cannisters.

White gas stoves

What is "white gas"? Once the term denoted a variant of automobile gasoline, available at many service stations, that was free of additives. But today this product has all but disappeared, and "white gas" is a casual name for the specially formulated camp stove fuels found in sporting goods and hardware stores. These fuels are specially refined and contain additives, different from those in auto fuel, to prevent rust and make for easy lighting. White gas burns very cleanly and leaves no residue. It can be stored for at least several years.

A gallon of white gas now costs about $4. It will

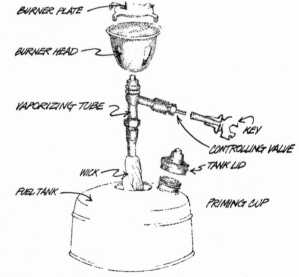

Working parts of a simple white gas stove

cook thirty meals or more for two or three campers.

The classic white gas stove is simple. There is a *fuel tank*, holding between a half a cup and a cup and a half of fuel (larger models hold more). A *wick* draws fuel out of the tank into a *vaporizing tube*, from which it passes through a controlling *valve* to the *burner.* In the burner, the stream of vapor strikes against a *burner plate* where it mixes with air and ignites. When the stove is burning, its own heat keeps the fuel flowing; the tank gets warm, and vapor pressure inside it drives fuel up along the wick. The vaporizing tube, grown very hot, transforms the liquid instantly into a gas. To get the operation started, though, you have to heat both the tank and the vaporizing tube by burning a little fuel in a special *priming cup.* The height of the flame is controlled by a *key* (or knob) that opens and closes the valve in the fuel line.

Most white gas stoves have a *pressure-release valve* set into the tank cap. This is a safety device. If, due to grossly improper operation, your stove overheats and the fuel in the tank grows excessively

Optimus 123R

hot, the increased pressure will pop this valve and spit a stream of gas into the air. Such a release is alarming, but not so dangerous as the explosion that might take place if the release valve were not present. For information on how to run a stove properly, and avoid this totally unnecessary situation, see Chapter 19.

There are two common layouts in white gas stoves. In the *upright style*, the burner sits right on top of the fuel tank, and the priming cup is nothing but an indentation in the roof of the tank. In the *separate-tank* style, the fuel tank is set a short distance away from the burner and to one side, behind a metal heat shield; the whole unit sits in a squarish metal box.

When you shop for a small white gas stove, there are just a few brands and models to consider. Most familiar is the *Optimus* line. The classic and very popular *Optimus 123R* (known widely under its former name of Svea) is an upright model. You can buy it with or without a round carrying case that serves also as windscreen. The *Optimus 8R* has a separate fuel tank and a heat shield, and rides in a side-hinged metal box. The *Optimus 99* is the same stove in an aluminum box with a tiny lid that allegedly serves as a pot. The *Optimus 199*, similar again, has a different burner style (see below). Precise International makes a parallel line of stoves: the *Phoenix Mite*, a tiny upright model weighing less than six ounces; the *Phoenix Backpacker*, a larger upright stove; and the *Phoenix Pathfinder*, similar in layout to the 8R.

Pumps and ported burners

The simple stoves discussed above use their own heat to drive fuel up to the flame: they are *self-pressurizing*. But self-pressured stoves can be hard to start and to run in severe cold. To counter this problem, some stoves are equipped with hand-operated *pumps*. With a pump, you force air into the fuel tank and drive the fuel directly to the burner. Priming is also much easier, though it is still

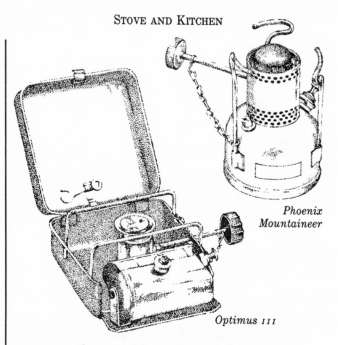

Phoenix
Mountaineer

Optimus III

necessary; the vaporizing tube must be hot before
the stove will run on its own. After starting a pump
stove, you give the pump a couple of strokes every
few minutes (say every time you stir the soup) to
keep the flame hot and bright.

Stoves with built-in pumps are generally heavier
than those without pumps, and their tanks hold
more fuel. The *Phoenix Mountaineer* (about two
pounds) is a heavy upright stove; the *Optimus III*
is a massive separate-tank model weighing close to
four pounds. The *Peak 1* by Coleman is a popular
stove with several interesting features. It can be
started without priming if conditions are perfect
(but you'd better not count on it). The *Coleman 505*
and the *Optimus 324* are similar upright models.
For these various stoves, weights without fuel run
from just under two pounds to just over three;
prices range from $40 to $100.

Then there are the nonconformists among pump-
equipped white gas stoves: the line developed by
Mountain Safety Research. These extraordinary gadgets are among the lightest of stoves—under a

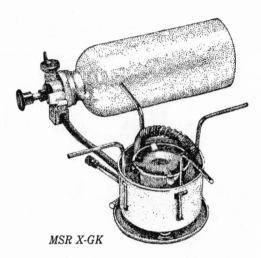

MSR X-GK

pound without fuel—but also among the most powerful. MSR uses no built-in fuel tank. Rather, the
burner draws its fuel, through a tube, from an ordinary fuel storage bottle—the type in which you typically carry your extra gasoline. You don't put fuel
into this stove—rather you plug the stove into the
fuel. There is, of course, a pump. On this principle,
MSR makes its *Model X-GK* ($80) and its *Firefly*
($60), whose big wiry burner crouches beside the
fuel bottle spider-fashion.

Two distinct styles of burners are found on
stoves equipped with pumps. MSR uses the simple,
traditional *burner plate* (also called the roarer burner). The fuel jet, striking the plate, eddies and mixes
with air. This mixing, without which there can be no
flame, does not happen unless the jet is strong.
Thus, stoves with burner plates don't throttle down
to simmering level very well. (The Firefly, due to a
very precise valve control, does somewhat better.)

The other style is the *ported burner.* Here, the
flame is divided and burns out of numerous vents;
even a small flow of fuel mixes well with oxygen.
You can simmer readily with such a stove. If you
like to do slow, home-style cooking on the trail, you

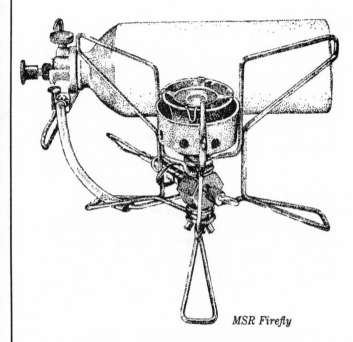

MSR Firefly

need a stove that can whisper as well as roar. Ported burners are found on the Coleman stoves, the Phoenix Mountaineer, the Optimus 111, and the Optimus 324—as well as on the little Optimus 199, the only small stove so equipped.

Stoves with pumps, high heat outputs, and large fuel tanks are sometimes labeled *mountaineering* stoves. Easy to light and operate under cold and windy conditions, they make short work of melting snow and boiling water. Of the models mentioned here, the Optimus 111, the Phoenix Mountaineer, and the two MSR stoves belong in this category.

The kerosene option

Kerosene is a far less volatile fuel than gasoline. It is slower to evaporate and slower to ignite. This makes it a bit more difficult to work with than white gas. Kerosene also has a greasy feel, evaporates rather slowly if spilled, and has a tendency to burn with smoke and soot.

It also has a selling point that no other powerful fuel can match: *it is very safe to use.* Once lit, it burns fiercely—kerosene actually yields more heat per volume of fuel than white gas does—but it must be almost persuaded to ignite. This means that spilled fuel won't flare up in a flash fire, as can happen with spilled white gas. Nor is a kerosene-burning stove at all liable to dangerous overheating. No stove can be guaranteed safe if you abuse it, but with kerosene it is much harder to provoke an accident. Partly because of the safety angle, large organized groups of hikers often favor kerosene.

You can't just pour kerosene into the tank of the typical white gas stove and fire it up. In fact, at this writing there are only four stoves that can handle kerosene: the *Mountain Safety Research X-GK,* the *Optimus 111, Optimus 199,* and the *Optimus 00.* The first three of these—discussed among white gas stoves above—are actually multi-fuel stoves and run very happily on kerosene. (The 111 and 199 burn, in addition, alcohol; the MSR can use a variety of fuels, including, according to one report, whiskey.)

It's a different story with the upright *Optimus 00* ($50), the classic among kerosene stoves. The 00 has no valve to control the height of the flame. Rather, you raise the flame by pumping and lower it by letting pressure out of a manual valve in the tank cap. White gas should not be used in an 00.

All kerosene stoves have pumps. The vaporizing tube must be *very* hot before the fluid will turn to gas; so these stoves must be primed with care. Since a pool of kerosene won't ignite readily with a match, many people use alcohol, an easy-lighting fuel, to prime their kerosene stoves. Solid fuel can also be used, or kerosene can be encouraged to burn by adding a wick of toilet paper.

Kerosene is found at a few gas stations and in hardware and sporting goods stores. Though raw kerosene has an odor unpleasant to some, most kerosene now sold is nearly odorless. Its cost is about the same as that of white gas; it weighs just slightly more, but stretches a little farther. Overseas, kerosene is sold as "paraffin" or "petroleum" and may be the only fuel available (regular gas is "benzin," while "gas" or "gaz" refers to propane or butane).

Cartridge stoves

Compared to the small but real complexities of kerosene and white gas stoves, cartridge stoves are attractively simple. That's why they now outsell all other types. Their fuel, usually butane, is sold in prefilled cartridges. The butane, which ordinarily would be a gas at room temperature, is kept liquid, under great pressure, in its solid-walled container. Open the valve, and the butane instantly streams out as vapor, ready to burn. The stove needs no priming cup, no wick; it is composed of a *stem* that plugs into the fuel cartridge, a *valve* that controls the rate of flow, and a *burner*. All cartridge stoves have ported burners and burn well at low flame. The flame is silent.

The basic parts—cartridge, stem, and burner— can be arranged in different ways. Often the cartridge sits upright and supports the burner on top

*Camping Gaz C-206
butane cartridge stove*

as in the popular Camping Gaz C-206. On other models the cartridge may form one leg of a tripod supporting the burner. It can sit under a self-supporting stove top, plug in from the side, or have a separate burner and cartridge linked by a flexible hose. The working parts are always much the same.

The cartridges differ. With certain exceptions they cannot be interchanged from stove to stove. Some must be left attached to the stove once a seal is broken; others can be removed between uses. And some cartridges contain a wick to help the fuel flow in the cold.

There's no monkey business about lighting a cartridge stove under good conditions; it's like touching a match to a burner on a kitchen range. That's what makes the design so very popular. But despite such advantages, cartridge stoves have limitations.

First, and most important, it appears that cartridge stoves are somewhat more dangerous than their competitors. Cartridges have been known to leak, to spray their highly inflammable fuel, and even to explode in use. While such accidents are surely very rare, considering the number of stoves being used, they are disconcerting because they are so random; no amount of care will prevent a faulty unit from misbehaving.

Second, cartridge stoves simply don't put out as much heat as gas and kerosene types; in fact, you're lucky to get half the heating power. This makes cartridges more suitable for summer than for winter use. Cooking times are longer.

Third, though cartridge stoves run a few dollars cheaper than gas and kerosene types, butane cartridges are much more expensive than white gas or kerosene. Since the used containers must be discarded, they are also wasteful of natural resources. And an astonishing number of people are still unconcernedly discarding their newly emptied cartridges on the spot—in the wilderness! Needless to say, *don't.*

Fourth, and crucial for some users, is the low-pressure problem. In most (not all) butane stoves,

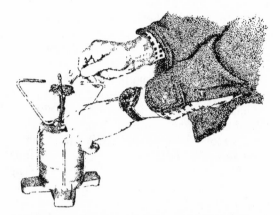

the gas streams out simply because the pressure inside is greater than the atmospheric pressure outside. But the more fuel is used, the less the inside pressure. After about the halfway point, the flame begins to weaken. It may take twice as long to boil water with a fading cartridge as with a fresh one.

And that's when the cartridge is warm. The problem becomes much worse in cold places. When the pressurized butane gets chilled, it presses outward less strongly. When it's cold enough, the stove will simply refuse to work. At sea level the failing point is about 32 degrees Fahrenheit—freezing. (Oddly enough, butane stoves do better at high altitudes. Because the atmosphere is thinner up there, there's less competing pressure from outside to block the exit of fuel from the cartridge. At 10,000 feet, a butane stove will work down to 12 degrees Fahrenheit; at the altitudes encountered on Asian expeditions, the crucial point falls below zero.)

There are several ways of getting around the chill/pressure problem. You can make a stove work, no matter how cold the air, by keeping the cartridge itself very warm. Carry the fuel next to your body; wrap it in insulation; take it into your sleeping bag—there are many possibilities. You can set up a foil reflector to bounce the stove's own heat back to the cartridge. In addition, you will need to apply heat to the stem between cartridge and burner.

Another partial answer is the *liquid-feed* butane stove. Such stoves use special cartridges that contain wicks. A wick will deliver fuel to the burner even if that fuel is liquid. Thus liquid-feed stoves function down to the freezing point of butane, which, at sea level, is 15 degrees Fahrenheit. Liquid-feed cartridges also burn somewhat more hotly than the vapor-feed type and don't suffer the same annoying fall-off in heating power. On the minus side, wicked cartridges don't last as long as vapor-feed cartridges, and they tend to flare and fade erratically on lighting, especially in the cold. Two widely available liquid-feed stoves are the *Hank Roberts Mark II Mini* and the *Optimus Mousetrap*.

Another approach to the problem is to modify the fuel. There exists a slightly different variety of butane called *iso-butane:* it is much more volatile than the normal type and remains a vapor to 15 degrees Fahrenheit. But iso-butane is not now used in stove cartridges. A similarly free-flowing fuel can be made by combining butane and propane; this mixture is utilized by Royal Robbins, Inc. in two stove-cartridge combinations. (Propane alone is used in some stoves, but it is so energetic that a heavy and thick-walled container, unsuitable for backpacking, is required to hold it.)

Cartridge stoves cost from about $15 to almost $50, with the commonest models low in that range. Weights vary widely, too, from as little as eight ounces (without cartridge) to as much as twenty-two ounces; most are under a pound. Butane cartridges typically weigh about ten ounces and contain six or seven ounces of fuel. Burning time will be in the neighborhood of ninety minutes (liquid feed) or three hours (vapor feed). Cost is about $3 per cartridge.

Other kinds of stoves

Though white gas, kerosene, and butane stoves

command the backpacking market, there are nonetheless some other possibilities.

In simple *alcohol stoves,* the fuel burns in a cup
under a housing that is both windscreen and pot
support. Minimal ones cost a few dollars. Precise International has a two-burner model for $20. The *Op-
timus Trapper* is a combination stove and cookset
with alcohol cup, windscreen, two pots, and a frying
pan; the flame can be adjusted ($50). Alcohol is easy
to work with, but it isn't cheap ($8 a gallon in hard-
ware stores), and it gives less heat than other fuels;
thus more must be carried.

Then there are *solid-fuel stoves.* These are
mostly just housings over a can of Sterno (jellied alcohol) or a fuel pellet. The rigs are cheap and simple
but lack the heating power to be of much use in wilderness cooking. Sterno is found most readily in
hardware stores, and pellet fuel (Hexamine, Esbit,
Heat Tabs) is available in sporting goods outlets.

Of special interest is the curious *Zip* solid fuel
stove; priced like a butane model, it burns charcoal
briquets, pine cones, or just about anything else,
with the help of battery-operated fan. It has a limited but enthusiastic following.

Buying a stove

What stove is best for you? The choice is broad
enough to be a bit confusing. Start by asking yourself when, where, and for whom you will be cooking. Summer? Winter? High elevations or low?
Large or small parties? Then consider these points.

Kerosene, white gas, or butane? Let's summarize. *Kerosene* is the safest and least convenient of
all the fuels; kerosene stoves are most often used
by large groups. The safety advantage is especially
great if you expect to cook frequently inside a tent
or have small children underfoot. *White gas* is safe
enough, used carefully, but gives you less margin
for error. It is slightly easier to use than kerosene,
less so than butane. *Butane,* the convenience fuel
(under ideal conditions), is perhaps best suited to

short trips in summer. It puts out less heat, costs much more, and will be harder to locate overseas.

How powerful a stove? There are three grades. *Superlight* models—butane stoves weighing under a pound with cartridge—are mainly suited for use by one or two hikers who do only the simplest cooking and go out mainly in good weather. Solid-fuel stoves and alcohol stoves are also in this group. No white gas or kerosene stoves are in this category.

Then there are what might be called *basic* stoves—the more substantial butane models and white gas and kerosene stoves weighing less than a couple of pounds with fuel. They will do admirably for summer use by small groups, and some are very usable in winter as well.

Finally, there are *mountaineering* stoves with pumps. All burn gas or kerosene. If you plan to do a lot of winter camping, a powerful pump stove will be best for the endless job of melting snow (some smaller stoves, good in summer, can only with difficulty be coaxed into boiling water in the winter). But "mountaineering" stoves can also be useful if you do a lot of cooking for groups of more than three or four, "mountaineers" or no.

Vapor-feed or liquid-feed butane? You can avoid some of the problems of butane by using liquid-feed stoves, especially in cold weather.

Boiling time. How long does it take the stove to boil a quart of water from room temperature? Under good conditions at sea level, average boiling times range from under four minutes to more than sixteen. However, the same stove will turn in widely varying performances at different times. Most stoves boil more slowly in the cold and still more slowly in wind. In bad weather, a fast boil is all-important.

Simmering ability. If you plan to cook lots of dishes that require simmering, look for a butane stove or for a white gas/kerosene stove with a ported burner.

Weight and price of fuel. How much fuel will your stove use in the course of a typical trip? A light, cheap stove that gulps fuel may not turn out to be the best bargain. Butane stoves are economical for short trips, but when you start packing extra cartridges the weight adds up quickly. And cartridges cost between five and ten times as much as white gas per hour of burning.

Time between refills. The smaller your fuel tank or cartridge and the faster fuel is consumed, the more time you will have to spend fiddling with fuel. Most stoves burn between one hour and four.

Stability. Some stoves give very good support to the pot on the burner and have low centers of gravity. But the majority are quite tippy. Look at each model and ask yourself how easy it might be to lose a pot of goulash.

Workmanship. Take a look at the fuel line from tank or cartridge to burner. Does it have rough, unfinished-looking welds? Do any screw connections tend to loosen? Generally speaking, the simpler the arrangement, the better. The best materials in stoves are stainless steel and brass.

The package. Some stoves come more or less bare, others in cunning packages. You may also find cooksets and windscreens designed to fit one particular stove or another (consider these accessories when you judge stability). There's no need to buy the package deals, but you should consider how neatly your stove will pack, how well it will fit your pots, and how it will be screened from the wind.

Care of a stove

A stove is not a difficult item to care for. Given proper use, it will almost take care of itself for long periods. For occasional maintenance you'll get, with your stove, something in the way of instructions and perhaps a tiny wrench. (MSR, which boasts that its units are "field-maintainable," provides a comprehensive parts kit.) Many gear stores will do repairs on stoves they have sold you.

When you first buy a kerosene or gasoline stove, take the time to flush out the tank with a little fuel.

Make sure that the burner plate (if there is one) is firmly attached (you'll see metal tabs that can be crimped to hold the plate more tightly to the burner head). Be sure to test the stove at home well in advance of your first trip with it (this job should be done outdoors). Burn at least a full tank or a full cartridge of butane to get an idea of how the stove behaves. How long will it burn? In the case of vapor-feed butane cartridges, when does the fall-off in heating power begin? How much does it tend to flare on ignition? (For more on starting and running a stove, see Chapter 19.)

When white gas or kerosene stoves break down, it's often because of deposits of solids in the fuel line. Do what you can to prevent them. When you fill your tank, pour the gas through a funnel with a strainer. Don't leave the tank full of fuel between trips. Over hours of burning, carbon builds up at the burner nipple where the fuel jet issues. This has to be cleaned out frequently. Many stoves have a built-in cleaning needle that probes the aperture when you turn the valve key. Get in the habit of doing this every time you cook. Every few years, you will need to take the stove apart and clean the parts (or have it serviced in a shop). Stove anatomy is not complex, but takes a little time to learn; manufacturers' instructions vary in completeness.

If you drop a stove, check it for bent connections and possible leaks. On separate-tank stoves with heat shields, make sure that the shield stands well away from the fuel tank, and keep it shiny and reflective.

Spare parts for liquid-fueled stoves are widely available. The two most important parts to carry are a spare burner plate (they do sometimes get lost) and a spare tank cap. If, for some reason, you manage to get your fuel tank so hot that the pressure-release valve blows, the valve will ordinarily reclose itself neatly. But it's reported that some caps don't. Either way, it's a good idea to replace the cap after a blowout, and indeed it should be switched every couple of years, accident or no.

Fuel and accessories

How much fuel you need depends on your stove, your cooking style, and your trip. It also depends on altitude; cooking times increase as air pressure drops. For a closer look at fuel planning, see Chapter 12.

White gas and kerosene are sold in cans much too large for trail use (though one-quart cans are now becoming available). You must transfer the fuel you need to smaller, lighter metal cans. Most used is the cylindrical *Sigg* bottle of aluminum, with its single, gasketed, screw-on cap. Sigg bottles come in liter and half-liter sizes, weigh four and five ounces, and cost $5–$7. Replacement caps and gaskets are available. MSR makes a similar bottle of intermediate size. Only Sigg and MSR bottles can be plugged into MSR stoves. Some look-alike brands exist, but avoid them if you have an MSR stove: they can't take the pressurization.

You can also get square-cornered cans of tin-coated steel. These have two openings: a broad spout with a built-in strainer, and a narrow projecting snout for easy pouring. It's a handy setup, but the two small caps are easy to lose. Cans come in quart and pint sizes and in different shapes—short and squat, tall and thin. If the tin coating is broken, they will rust.

You will need a small plastic or metal *funnel* for filling a conventional fuel tank with kerosene or gas; better get one with a built-in strainer or a replaceable filter. Several convenient *pouring spouts* and *caps* are available for use with Sigg-type bottles. With white gas stoves that lack pumps, you may also want an eyedropper to use in priming.

You very much need a screen against the wind; stoves work poorly without screening. (The Coleman stoves and the Optimus 324 have built-in screens at the burner; these seem adequate for mild breezes but need help when it really blows.) Several models come with separate, specially fitted screens, and some are made so that the sturdy screen also supports the pot. Others are commonly sold with cook-sets that include windscreens.

If your stove has no windscreen when you buy it, several kinds of separate screens are sold. Three-sided folding screens will fit most small, low stoves. Optimus's circular screen, designed for the 123R, will fit some. Mountain Safety Research makes a two-piece screen of aluminum foil—ugly but highly effective—that can be trimmed and restapled for use with stoves other than MSR's.

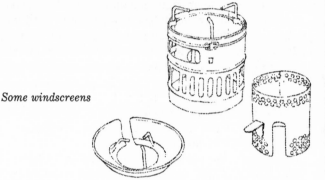

Some windscreens

Whenever you improvise a windscreen, you must take care to allow plenty of ventilation around the fuel tank. In the case of a white gas stove without a pump, the tank needs to be warm or even hot, but it should not be hot enough to burn your hand. Make sure that flame doesn't tend to blow *toward* the tank. Butane cartridges should never become more than warm.

If you are camping on snow, you will need an extra item: a small piece of *closed-cell foam* or *wood,* about six inches across. This insulates the base of the stove, which would melt a well into the snow without it—or (with some stoves) be chilled too badly to function. If a hot stove sits on a foam base, you'll need to interpose a metal layer, maybe an extra pot lid, to keep the stove from melting a hole in the insulation.

Optimus markets a special *add-on pump* that will aid in firing up its self-pressurizing stoves in cold weather. This gadget ($9) doesn't convert a small stove into a mountaineering type, but it helps adapt a summer stove to winter use. The little Optimus 199 is sold with one of these as standard equipment.

Most people who use kerosene as stove fuel bring along a separate squirt bottle of alcohol to prime with. This should be the denatured solvent form of alcohol, not rubbing alcohol, which has high water content and burns poorly. Or you can use one of several solid fuels available in gear stores in pellet or ribbon form. Whatever you use, take plenty of it, especially at first.

Carry several sets of *matches*. Put them in your kitchen gear, in your first aid or emergency kit, and in at least one other place—perhaps tucked in with some emergency food. Some stoves have built-in flint sparkers; they're nice when they work, but not cause to leave your matches home.

There are several sorts of matches to choose from. Cheapest, of course, are ordinary folder matches. They have to be dry to work, and must be struck on their own sandpapery striker pad. Then there are wooden kitchen matches, which will ignite on any dry, rough surface. Third are waterproof matches, very good to have in wet weather. Some brands can be struck on any rough surface; others require a special striker. But both match and striking surface can, in theory at least, be soaking wet. (You can also waterproof ordinary kitchen matches by dipping them in wax.) Finally, there are waterproof/windproof matches. These burn like sparklers and cannot be blown out. They are rather expensive but worth the price in stormy camping.

In dry summer climates it scarcely matters what sort of matches you take. Many people favor the strike-anywhere kitchen type, or a mixture of strike-anywheres and waterproofs. But even in summer you want your matches, and especially your backup supply, protected from damp. You can use doubled plastic bags, foil envelopes, or (for wooden matches) a plastic or metal *matchsafe*. Many people use film cans; more elaborate matchsafes cost a couple of bucks. Some have built-in strikers. Carry, regardless, several striker pads for matches that require them.

If you plan to camp in rainy country or on snow, your matches should certainly be waterproof, and you should have perhaps a handful of the more expensive windproof ones as well. Take pains to keep them dry, despite the manufacturers' claims. Regard waterproofness as insurance, not as a substitute for normal care. Experience suggests that windproof matches are *less* resistant to water than the merely waterproof type.

Auxiliary fire starters must be on your list. (In very wet weather, it takes more than matches to light a wood fire—and even a devout stove-user may someday desperately need to.) The simplest thing you can take is a segment of plumber's *candle.* Some people make little logs of wax-soaked newspaper. In gear stores you can get *fire ribbon,* a sort of incendiary toothpaste, and also *solid fuel* in tablet form.

Cookware

A single hiker can get along with a single small pot (or none, if you choose to eat cold food). In a small group you need a couple of cooking vessels. It's hard to do much with a pot of less than quart capacity, and a pair, say, one of three pints and one of five, will serve most purposes. Backpacking pots are aluminum or stainless steel and should weigh no more than twelve ounces in a two-quart size; some weigh much less. Prices range from $2 to $10 or more a pot. Cheaper ones, though less durable, may also be much lighter.

Many people buy their pots in elegant sets. The best-known cookware package is the Sigg Tourist ($31). It gives you a pair of pots that stack as a double boiler, a lid that doubles as a frying pan, a pot lifter, and a stove base and windscreen. The set comes in two versions, one designed to fit the Opti-

mus 123 and the other matched to the Coleman
Peak One. But there are other lines, some meant for
specific stoves, some usable with any. You can also
buy cheap aluminum pots in a department store and
cut off the handles, leaving only stubs.

Some pots are wide, some deep and cylindrical.
The tall, narrow pots are inefficient for cooking on
most stoves. But there is this to consider: if you are
using a separate-tank white gas stove, like the Optimus 8R, you do not want your pot completely overhanging the fuel tank. Reflecting heat back onto the
tank, a very wide pot can raise the fuel temperature
enough to provoke a safety valve blowout. As for
support, some pots have strip or wire bails, others
short handles; still others have neither, and while
these "naked" pots are bad for campfire cooking,
they work fine on a stove. Lids are important to
shorten cooking time.

You'll need, in any case, a *pot lifter*, a leather
glove, or (for pots with cut-off handles) needlenose
pliers. A bandanna will do in a pinch. When it's very
cold, a pair of light cloth gloves will take some of
the sting out of the touch of freezing metal or
spilled fuel.

What about other cooking tools? Some people
like bacon and eggs enough to carry *frying pans*
(some pots come with lids designed to double as fry-
pans). Separate pans weigh twelve to fifteen ounces
in steel or teflon-coated aluminum and cost $10 and
up. With a pan, you need an appropriate *spatula*.
Certain other gear is strictly for campfire cooking.
Lightweight backpackers' *grills* cost $3–$10 (cheap
cake racks are also good). Campfire gourmets may
take *reflector ovens*, about three pounds; these start
at $15.

As you gain in altitude, cooking takes longer.
For one thing, most stoves become less efficient in
thinner air; for another, the boiling point of water
declines. At 10,000 feet, the boiling point is about
192 degrees Fahrenheit, 20 degrees below the normal 212, and it takes more than six minutes to cook

a "three-minute" egg. Instant and just-add-water foods, of course, are affected less.

One way of speeding up mountain cooking is to use a *pressure cooker.* A four-quart cooker weighs three pounds and costs over $50. But in normal backpacking you needn't consider such a thing; cookers are mainly taken to very high altitudes or on trips so long that the saving in fuel makes up for the weight of the cooker many times over.

For the simple cooking that most backpackers do, about the only other important utensil is a ladle or *serving spoon.*

Your personal *mess kit* can be minimal. Most people carry nothing more than a plastic or metal cup and a spoon; others like plastic or aluminum plates, or bowls, or both.

For dishwashing you need a wire or teflon *pot scrubber*, and biodegradable soap (either ordinary cake soap or liquid). Detergents, of course, are never used, and washwater must be dumped well away from any lake or stream. No small party has any need for a *washbasin*, at least not for doing dishes. Dishcloth? A clean *bandanna* will do.

Containers for food and liquids

Aluminum bottles, the kind used for fuel, can also be used for other liquids; but only bottles with an anodized inner coating can be used for acids (like lemonade) or for alcohol. Your fuel cans should be plainly distinguishable from those containing drink-ables.

Other bottles are made of plastic, usually poly-ethylene. Cheap poly bottles tend to pick up flavors and hold them unpleasantly; high-density, "food-grade" polyethylene (Nalgene is a brand) resists this tendency pretty well. There are narrow-mouthed types for liquids and large-mouthed types for liquids and bulk solids. Some are round, some squarish. Prices range to $5.00, depending on size and materi-als, and weights run to four ounces. Bottles set up as canteens cost a bit more. Better patronize the gear stores here: poly bottles sold elsewhere tend to leak around the cap.

There are also large collapsible *water carriers* of several types. These can be useful around camp, and whenever a water source is not nearby. Such carriers hold from one to five gallons; they cost up to $20. Some cheaper ones tend to leak, especially if water ever freezes inside them. (If you must haul large amounts of water in your pack, ordinary gallon bleach bottles are about your best bet.) Then there's the popular wineskin or *bota bag* ($15–$20 and always entertaining).

Most solid food goes into plastic bags. You need both small, flimsy bags and larger, tougher ones, sold for a few cents apiece in most gear stores. There are also square plastic boxes with snap-on tops; flat, round, screw-top *butter dishes*; plastic *egg carriers*; and much else. *Squeeze tubes*, with a back you can open for filling, are handy for things like peanut butter so long as the weather stays warm.

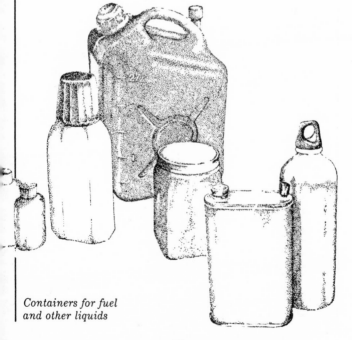

Containers for fuel and other liquids

Cheap two-part shakers are commonly taken for pepper and salt (or use film containers). If you have tin cans to open, you can use a minuscule GI-style *can opener* or simply a knife blade. Multibladed knives usually include a serviceable can opener.

In some American wilderness areas you have to protect your food from scavenging bears. This means hoisting it into a tree at night, and whenever you leave an established camp unoccupied. So your kitchen gear must include, along with plenty of cord, one or more stout containers for the hoisting. Sometimes an empty pack can be used, a tarp gathered into a sack shape, or a hammock. The modern "counterbalance" method of bear-bagging (see Chapter 19) works best with two large stuffsacks, the size you would use for a sleeping bag. Laundry bags will also serve.

10:
The Rest of the Load

CLOTHING; SLEEPING GEAR; SHELTER; cooking gear.
With these we have covered the bulk of what goes
in the pack (for food, see Chapter 12). What remains, though, is important: medical and emergency
supplies, personal items, and some tools so essential
and so useful that they demand a category of their
own.

Health and safety I: the first aid kit

Most summer backpackers need carry only a
rather basic medical kit. (Some don't even carry
that, but should.) Let's face it: today's wilderness is
small and growing smaller; most trips are quite
short; rescue is often almost literally around the corner. It's true that climbers (especially winter climbers), inveterate solo travelers, and hikers in such
true wilderness lands as are found in Alaska must
be prepared to do more than give first aid; this book
has little to tell them. But first aid, in the busy

First aid kit

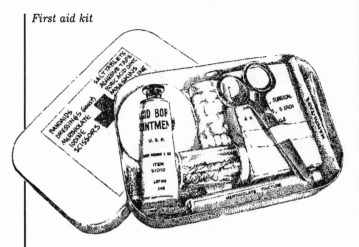

mountains of a temperate-zone American summer, is as far as you are likely ever to have to go.

Every member of the party should have a personal first aid kit and with it (perhaps in the same container) survival items for an unexpected night out. These you should keep with you at all times—on side trips and day hikes most especially. In the typical two-hiker, three-hiker, or four-hiker backpacking party, there is no group kit; larger parties in difficult country may carry more sophisticated medical supplies.

What about prepacked, commercial first aid kits? There are several on the market; prices range from $10 on up. Large suppliers also sell individual kit items and containers. But the prepacked kits have disadvantages. For one thing, their choice of items is never quite the choice you would make; second, and more important, there's nothing like putting a kit together from scratch to teach you exactly what you've got in it.

Let's run down some of the common and not-so-common components of wilderness medical kits. Items marked with an asterisk are of special importance.

The container. It's a good idea to have a rigid

box; otherwise the items in the kit can get mangled. A fairly generous kit should fit in a box of about fifty cubic inches—say two inches by four by six, though almost any shape will do.

First aid manual. Especially for people who haven't taken first aid courses, a mechanical, step-by-step routine for dealing with emergencies can be useful. There are various portable manuals, from densely printed cram cards published by the Red Cross to James A. Wilkerson's hefty *Medicine for Mountaineering,* published by the Seattle Mountaineers. One good pamphlet is Fred T. Darvill's *Mountaineering Medicine,* published by Wilderness Press and available in many stores.

Band-Aids. Several sizes. Three or more of each.

Gauze pads. Three or four pads, three or four inches square, in sterile envelopes.

Gauze bandage. One inch wide. Need not be sterile. Take not less than ten feet.

Adhesive tape. Also one inch wide and plentiful. Should be of porous, not waterproof, cloth (try REI). To save bulk, pry the ends off the roll on which the tape is wound and stamp on it to flatten the core.

Moleskin or molefoam. Stick-on pads to cushion feet where blisters show signs of developing. Moleskin is thin, molefoam thicker. Found at drugstores in three-by-four-inch pads. Take two or more sheets, depending on how easily you blister. Some people find adhesive tape works just as well.

Triangular bandage. An item with many uses; the classic arm sling. Bulky (about eleven square feet) and often missing from the small kits.

Elastic bandage. Can be useful if you *must* walk on a wrenched ankle or knee.

Soap in some form. Liquid in tube; powder in film can; or a fragment.

Antiseptic. This item, often taken, is not absolutely required. If you do carry it, remember that few preparations are considered gentle enough to use directly *on* or *in* a wound. Betadine cleanser is one of them.

Antibiotic burn ointment. Neosporin is often recommended.

Cotton swabs. Various possible uses.

*Needle. For draining blisters.

*Tweezers. Mainly for splinters. They must be very sharp and not unmanageably small.

*Scissors. Mainly for cutting dressings, moleskin, repair tape. May be on knife.

*Safety pins. Like needles, you think of these as sew/repair items, but they have uses in first aid too, as for fastening arm slings and bandages.

*Razor blade. Various uses. Can substitute for scissors. Also used to shave skin before applying tape, or the suction cup of a snake bite kit.

*Snake bite kit. An item you're most unlikely ever to need, even in prime "snake country." There is a lively debate among doctors as to whether or not backpackers should be encouraged to carry kits; for more on this, see Chapter 27. There are many good brands. All contain a constricting band, a sharp blade, antiseptic, a suction device, and directions.

*Aspirin or acetaminophen. A dozen tablets for pain and fever.

Painkiller. Many hikers carry half a dozen 30-milligram tablets of codeine/empirin, or some other prescription painkiller. Watch the expiration date and replace as needed.

Salt tablets. A very debatable item. See Chapter 28.

Antacid tablets. For indigestion.

*Personal medicines. Anything you know you need. Toothache drops . . . laxatives . . . prescription drugs . . . antihistamines. If you have a medical problem, consult your doctor before you head into wild country.

Other drugs. Many are possible, but few are needed for ordinary travel. Doctors hesitate to prescribe except for immediate need. However, on long trips it may make sense to carry a broad-spectrum antibiotic like tetracycline and a heavy-duty, narcotic painkiller. Drugs should be replaced as required.

Poison oak/ivy/sumac lotion. Can be carried for off-trail travel where these irritant plants grow thick. Unless you're really wading through the stuff, though, you can save yourself by scrubbing exposed skin with soap and water immediately after exposure.

Sting-kill ampules. Some hikers carry these where mosquitoes and stinging flies are a major problem.

Water purifier. Though hardly a first aid item, this can conveniently be stored in the kit. In some wilderness situations, hikers must disinfect the water they find on the land. Boiling will do it, but chemical treatments are often more convenient. For a discussion of the options, see Chapter 20.

Health and safety II: skin protection

These items, often listed with the first aid kit, will be used too often to be packed away.

Insect repellent. At certain times of the year, in certain places, this will seem more like a survival item than a mere convenience. The most effective preparations are those that contain the chemical n,n-diethyl-meta-toluamide (abbreviated DEET). Concentrations vary from 25 percent to nearly 100 percent; the stronger the brew, the better. In surplus stores you can find the army's "jungle juice," which is the same stuff. Buy liquid repellent, not the bulkier and more expensive aerosol or foam.

Suncream/sunblocker. Suncreams vary. Almost all preparations, however, are marked with a *sun protection factor,* a number from 1 to 15. This indicates how long you can be exposed without burning: a cream with protection factor 5, for instance, would theoretically allow you to stay in sunlight five times as long as you could without protection. At low elevations any suntan cream will do (and you may not need even that). But above 8,000 feet or so, and on light-colored rock or snow or near open water, most people need high protection. A few preparations—glacier cream, zinc oxide, clown-white makeup—will prevent *any* of the sun's ultraviolet rays from reaching your skin.

Lip balm. Most hikers will need this to prevent cracked, burned lips. Any type will do; unflavored ones won't get licked off so fast.

Other protective creams. There are creams to keep skin moist, to protect you against poison oak and the like, even to keep you warmer by reducing heat loss from the skin. None of these are very commonly used.

Health and safety III: emergency and survival

In this third group are some special items you would want to have with you if you were lost, if you had to spend an unexpected night out without normal equipment, or if you hoped to attract the attention of rescuers. There are prefabricated emergency kits ($15 or so) that contain some of the most essential items.

Whistle. A traditional item but of questionable usefulness. The theory is that you blow it, should you get lost, to summon help (three signals of any kind indicate distress, two indicate response). However, rescue workers report few cases where a whistle has actually helped much. The noise just doesn't carry far, though it *is* better than shouting. Whistles may help in keeping a large party together, and parents often give them to their kids when on long outings.

Mirror. Also recommended as a rescue signal. Does this one work any better? It seems doubtful. It is hard indeed to flash a spot of light to exactly the place where it will be seen even if you have bright sun to work with.

Signal cloth. Perhaps more to the point is a piece of bright-colored cloth—an item of clothing, a groundsheet, whatever—that you can spread out to attract the attention of aerial searchers.

Phone change. For an emergency phone call if you must hike out to a road for assistance.

Waterproof/windproof matches. A special supply in your first aid kit or emergency kit, so that you will never be caught without.

Candle stubs or other firestarters. Also essential. Fire ribbon (a paste) or fuel tablets can be used.

Emergency shelter. There are several possibilities, but the idea is simply to have something to wrap up in on a cold, wet night. Some carry reflective "space blankets"; fragile, one-use models sell for $4 or so, and somewhat stouter ones go for $10 and up. Another type of shelter is essentially a large, tough plastic bag. If you have a hooded waterproof raincoat of some sort, a shorter plastic bag, into which you thrust your legs, will serve. This is one function of the long raincoat called the *cagoule* (Chapter 8). You can pull your legs up inside it, tighten the drawstring at the hem, and make yourself almost weatherproof. A night in such a waterproof sack may not be comfortable, but you will survive it.

Snares, fishhooks, and such. Sometimes packaged with commercial survival kits, these are scarcely necessary in most travel. Food, if you're lost for a short time in wild country, is by no means the main problem: warmth and water are primary. Still, it can be entertaining to learn a few skills for living off the land: how to build a "figure 4" snare or a noose of thread or hair, how to recognize edible and poisonous wild plants, and so on. A number of books now on the market give instruction in these skills.

Manual. Prepackaged kits may contain manuals on how to stay alive. Useful, maybe, but probably not worth looking for; common sense is the key. Handbook or no, you should plan in advance just how you would conduct yourself if, separated from your party and your pack, you had to ride out a night, or several nights, with less than the usual gear.

Essential tools

Map and compass. As a rule, each member of a

party should carry both. See Chapter 16, *Finding the Way.*

Knife. You don't need a big bowie knife. Any folding pocketknife will serve. Multiple blades are nice *if* the extra tools are things you need. One popular knife, not cheap, is the Swiss Army knife, familiar with its bright red handle and imprinted cross. These come with as few as three and as many as fourteen different blades. Perhaps the most useful item of all (besides the main blade) is a small, sharp pair of *scissors.* Other blades—can opener, Phillips head screwdriver, fish-scaler—may be useful

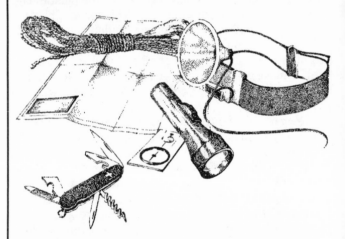

to some hikers, useless to others. You can probably do without saws, magnifiers, plastic scrapers, and metal files. Prices run from $10 to $45 depending mainly on blades. Other good pocketknives are considerably cheaper. One useful feature on any folding knife is a lock for the main blade so that it won't suddenly shut and slice a finger.

Flashlight or headlamp. It is no easy thing to find a flashlight that works, all the time and without persuasion, when you need it most. (I, for one, have trouble with *all* flashlights.) But the picture here is improving.

One strategy is to go cheap and replace lights frequently. Flat, pocketable Mallory and Durabeam flashlights cost little more than the AA cells that run them. Conventional metal C-cell flashlights are also used.

For a few dollars more you can get a flashlight that is supposed to last forever. Two lines for which high claims are made are the *Mag-Lites*, heavy and durable police-style flashlights, and the *Tekna-Lites*. The makers of the Tekna-Lite flashes have omitted the conventional on-off switch, a perennial problem spot; to turn on one of these lights, you simply twist the lens housing. Prices of better flashlights run from $10 to $25; weights without batteries vary from a couple of ounces to a full pound.

For a similar price you can get a battery-powered *headlamp*. (Fuel-burning *carbide lamps*, much used in mines and spelunking, don't work well in wind or in cold weather.) The working end of a headlamp straps to your forehead and shines wherever you are looking. The battery case may be at the back of your head, in a shirt pocket, or at your belt. Your hands are free. On the minus side, the electrical cord connecting the two parts, with its connections at either end, is a frequent source of failure.

Along with the original batteries, take a couple of extras and a spare bulb (of the original type). There are various grades of batteries to choose from. How long they last depends largely on the output of the bulb they are feeding. Generally speaking, though, AA batteries of the ordinary carbon type should run two hours or more, while C cells should burn at least five hours. Alkaline power cells last significantly longer. Finally, there are lithium cells, the most expensive and formidable power sources on the market. A single lithium cell, backed up by a space-filling dummy, can replace two ordinary batteries in most flashlights. (But some lights use *only* lithium, and the makers of certain other flashlights advise against lithium: get the story when you buy the light.) Both alkaline and lithium batteries work relatively well in cold conditions; only lithium cells can be stored for long periods without deteriorating. On the other hand, *rechargeable* batteries are nickel-cadmium. Battery prices run from a dollar for a pair of the cheapest penlight cells to $25 or more for a lithium D-size.

Be sure to reverse one battery in your light when it is not in use. You don't want it turning itself on in your pack. Alternatively, tape the switch (if any) to keep it in the off position.

Inside a tent (or snow cave or igloo) a candle can give you good light. Or you can spend $15 for a candle lantern that protects the flame from drafts. Although mainly a luxury item, this is genuinely useful under some conditions.

Cord. One of the real necessities, anywhere at all. Carry not less than fifty feet. Take more if you will use cord to pitch a tarp or tube tent or to haul your food into a tree at night (in bear country). Cord is also a repair item. It needn't be enormously strong; typical one-eighth-inch parachute cord, 550 pound test, is fine.

Axe, hatchet, shovel, trowel, saw. Not ordinarily needed, or even desirable. However, a large group may need a light shovel for digging latrines. A trowel is sometimes suggested for digging a sanitary "cat hole," but most of the time a stick will do as well. Please note this, however: the Forest Service, in some regions, requires every party to carry a small shovel or trowel if fires are to be built. Fire safety is the thought behind this little-regarded rule. If you plan a trip to one of the national forests, inquire about local regulations.

Notebook and pencil. For notes concerning route, gear problems, natural history, whatever. Also useful in emergencies to leave word for possible rescuers or for other hikers.

Essential tools: repair kit

This will vary greatly with the trip and with your gear. But these seem to be basic items:

Sewing materials. Stout thread. A couple of needles with large eyes for easy threading. A couple of buttons. A few safety pins. Larger groups may carry sewing awls for mending boots and pack straps.

Repair tape. You can buy nylon tape for making emergency patches on tents, sleeping bags, jackets. But adhesive tape from your first aid kit will work just as well.

Wire. A foot or more. Stout enough to be strong, pliable enough to bend around corners. A dozen uses in repair.

Glue. A tube of the quick-hardening, ultra strong variety. Especially valuable if you wear ultra-light boots or running shoes.

Pack fittings. Packbags are commonly held to frames by clevis pins and lock-rings. Rings can break (especially if the pack is heavy and travel rough and jolting), and clevis pins occasionally get lost. Though you can usually substitute wire, some people take a spare pin and a ring or two.

Stove tools and parts. Depending on the stove, you may need one or more of these: stove wrench, spare burner plate, spare tank cap, orifice cleaning tool.

Mattress patchkit. If you use an air mattress; will also work on a tent.

Other tools. Less often taken. Screwdriver and screws, for repairing pulled-out ski bindings; for anchoring loose boot soles. Pliers, for various uses.

Personal items

These can be few or many. Most people take a *toothbrush;* some add toothpaste and floss. Don't forget a generous supply of *toilet paper.* About the only other items almost everybody takes are a *comb,* a sliver or tube of *soap,* and several *bandannas,* one of which serves as a washrag. Some hikers like a towel. Some like a light pocket mirror. Some take handkerchiefs. Some take moistened, packaged paper washcloths. You know what you need.

Winter and technical gear

There are various items that you'll need only in snowy winter: snowshoes or skis, waxes and ski accessories, avalanche cord, perhaps snow shovel and snow saw for building igloos or snow caves. Then there's the endless range of more technical gear for mountaineers: ropes, ice axes, crampons, hard hats, protective anchors of various sorts, avalanche probes, and so on. For more about certain of these extras, see Chapters 22 and 23.

Luxuries and specialties

A list of these would be endless. While none can be called essential, there are many items that add comfort or pleasure to a trip, if you're willing to put up with the weight. Some luxuries frequently taken: camp shoes to put on when the boots come off; cameras (and all the paraphernalia that goes with them); natural history guides; tree and flower keys; geologic maps; binoculars; magnifying glasses; walking sticks; fishing gear; barometers; altimeters; thermometers; books and games; cards; chess sets; even elaborate board games.

You name it, somebody has probably loaded it into a pack, somewhere, sometime. And everyone has a short list of personal "luxuries" that seem as necessary as boots and cooking gear.

Preparing the Trip

Then find in the horizon-round
One spot, and hunger to be
there.

—Gerard Manley Hopkins

11:
Designing the Trip

THE EASIEST WAY to take your first longer trip is to sign on with an organized party (see Chapter 2). But it's when you start setting your own targets and making your own plans that the real adventure begins. The whole ritual of preparation—the packing, the planning, the study of the maps that build a landscape in your mind—is not just the dull means to the pleasant end: it is the first part of the journey itself.

Experienced packers—some of them, at least—can throw a trip together quickly. On a few hours' notice they are packed and gone, needing little time to prepack, prepackage, preplan. But at the beginning, at least, you will need to be a little more methodical.

First step: pick a place and a time

Most trips seem to start with gossip: "They say it's nice at Stonecup Basin . . . the Big Craggies . . .

Silver Falls." But if you're not tied in yet to a grapevine, you may need to do some research.

If you live in the West, or on the eastern seaboard, there is probably wild country within two hundred miles of you. If you don't know where, there are several ways of finding out quickly. You can ask at gear stores. You can consult some of the numerous area guidebooks now in print. Or you can start by writing the regional offices of the U.S. Forest Service, the National Park Service, the U.S. Fish and Wildlife Service, and the Bureau of Land Management. Some state-owned lands, especially in California, Michigan, Maine, Pennsylvania, New York, and Wisconsin, are also wild. Federal and state agencies publish maps showing roads, trails, and the boundaries of zones in which wilderness is explicitly protected. (See *Resources* appendix for these addresses.) The answers you get from agency offices in your state or region will help you focus your interest on particular parks, national forests, national wildlife refuges, and so on, and give you the local addresses you need. Then you can write those local offices for more specific help.

These sources will lead you first to the well-known, well-used landscapes. That may be just what you want at the beginning—or perhaps much longer, if you don't mind a certain amount of company. It does appear, though, that many backpackers *are* disturbed by company. You can avoid it in several ways.

You can, for instance, plan trips at odd times. Weekends in the wild are always busier than weekdays; holiday and August weekends are busiest of all. In larger or less publicized areas, and in wild places more remote from the cities, the weekends are not quite so crowded.

Outside the southwestern deserts, most wild areas get their biggest crowds in August. It is often hard to see why. Over much of the United States, autumn is a more pleasant hiking season than midsummer. In many regions, September is drier than August; and often in wooded places you get the

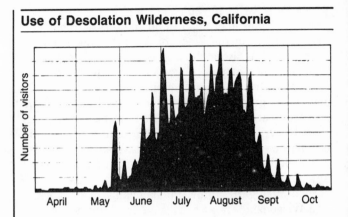

Use of Desolation Wilderness, California

Number of visitors

April   May   June   July   August   Sept   Oct

wonderful bonus of fall color. Spring, too, is lovely
and not very populous. But it should be noted that
the soils in many areas are waterlogged in the
spring, and easily damaged by human traffic. Managing agencies are moving to restrict spring hiking
in some of these fragile landscapes.

In regions where winter brings snow, that clean,
white surface, covering the fragile meadows and the
mountain roads, creates a wilderness at once more
spacious, starker, and less vulnerable to our abuse.

But even in summer, and even in the best-known
regions, people flock to a few favorite lakes, a few
peaks, a few trails. The accompanying map shows
where a Forest Service study found people going in
the Spanish Peaks Primitive Area of Montana.
Trooping along a couple of main thoroughfares, hikers left large sections almost unused. This is by no
means a bad thing. You wouldn't want all parts of
an area to be used equally. But the hiker who is
slightly more adventurous, or simply better informed, can take advantage of the unequal distribu-
tions and go where others do not.

As a rule, you can be more alone on the middle-
elevation trails that do not lead straight to picture-
postcard alpine climaxes. (Westerners, especially,
tend to be narrow-minded about scenery. They love
their peaks and lakes and glaciers—as who would

Concentration of trail traffic in the Spanish Peaks area, Montana

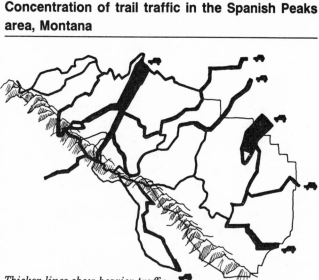

Thicker lines show heavier traffic

not?—but often overlook the beauty of their coniferous forests and woodlands.) Write the managing agency and *ask* where use is light. Both the Park Service and the Forest Service have lately begun publishing maps that show the zones of crowding in certain wilderness areas.

Then there is cross-country travel; it's more adventurous, more solitary, and more of an exploration. But this takes skill, preparation, and caution (see Chapter 22).

Informal wilderness

Now we speak of a special kind of country. In the Far West, especially, there are vast areas of what is called *de facto wilderness:* lands that are perfectly wild but which do not have official labels or official recognition. They have no legal status as national parks or wildernesses by federal law; little stands between them and exploitation. They are simply *there.* These unacknowledged wild places—the closest thing we have today to blank spots on the map—lie chiefly on lands controlled by the U.S. Forest Service and by the Bureau of Land Management. Some are used by hikers almost as much as their protected counterparts, but most are much less used, and some are all but unknown. And many are superb.

Some argue that these hidden lands should be left hidden. Are they not, in their obscurity, the truest wilderness we have? And if there were some reason to believe that de facto wilderness lands could, in the absence of public use and public interest, remain wild, that argument might be telling. But the facts are otherwise. These lands, for all their obscurity, are not truly hidden: not hidden from those who would alter and destroy them. Wherever there is a piece of wild country, there is already someone who is making plans to log it, to mine it, to build roads across it, to dam its streams—to change it in some fashion, for reasons plausible or not, from what it is. And where there is the will to exploit, there is, very often, the power. So the fragments of unprotected wilderness in America shrink year by year.

This does not mean that they cannot be defended, for they can. But protection must be formal, legal, definite. And such protection never comes—at least it comes only seldom—without a test of political strength. None of our most loved and celebrated landscapes—not the Grand Canyon, not the Smokies, not the Everglades, not Yosemite itself—was saved without a fight. If our unprotected wilderness areas are to have a chance of surviving, they must have strength on their side. They must be known by many, admired by many. They must be valued. And to be valued they must first be seen.

If you visit an unlabeled wilderness area, take a few minutes, when you get back home, to write a letter in defense of what is there. You will be doing an important service to the country you enjoyed (see Chapter 31).

How do you learn where these places—by nature underpublicized—are found? The usual source is the grapevine, but a call to the nearest office of the Sierra Club may yield some information. Government land management agencies are of course aware of these areas, too—they have inventoried and studied them repeatedly. A visit to an agency office can net you a rich catch of information, once you get past the front desk (where only the most popular hiking areas will be mentioned).

A caution: these unprotected areas are not, generally, the best destinations for your very first trips. Some of them, fascinating though they are, lack that instantly recognizable, photogenic charm that is always the first quality to be preserved. And you will need to check with the local offices of the Forest Service or the BLM about the condition of roads and trails. Maps are often out of date, and trail systems may have gone unmaintained for years. On the plus side, you can forget about wilderness permits and quotas, and chances are you can forget about crowds.

Second step: get the detailed information

There is a pleasure in going off to the woods with no very firm idea of where you'll wind up. But this is not a pleasure for the beginner. As a rule, planning makes a better trip. Besides, it's fun.

Your basic tool is always the topographic map or "topo sheet" published by the U.S. Geological Survey. These can be ordered by mail from Denver, Colorado and Arlington, Virginia (see *Resources* appendix) and cover most parts of the United States. They are webbed with thin brown lines that show elevation in feet above sea level. A further grid of horizontal and vertical lines divides the mapped territory into sections, each one mile on a side. For more about these maps and how to use them, see Chapter 16.

In addition, the agencies publish maps for each state park, national park, national forest, national wildlife refuge, or Bureau of Land Management district. These maps are small scale, show little detail, and generally lack contour lines, but they are fairly

Two kinds of maps for laying out a trip

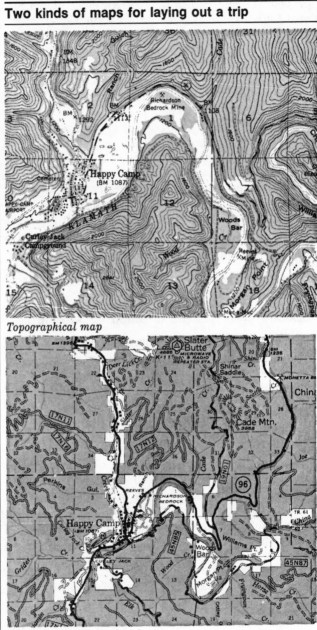

Topographical map

Forest Service recreational map

up to date about roads and trails. Of special value are the "recreation maps" published by the Forest Service for its extensive holdings. In exploring de facto wilderness especially, you will find the agency maps indispensable.

Even if you have the maps already, you will probably need to get in touch with the local office of the agency, for several reasons. First of all, there's the matter of wilderness permits (more below). Second, you may need information about weather, trail and road conditions, and—not least—about the agency's own regulations. The less well known and populous the area you will visit, the more you need to learn in advance.

Third step: map the trip

Now comes the pleasant job of laying out your trip in detail. You know how many days you have to spend—how many of those days would you like to spend resting, or on side trips out of a fixed camp? How many will you have left to use on moving forward, onward, deeper in? And how far can you walk in that time?

It all depends on the land. A crude but standard rule of thumb makes ten miles an average day on easy terrain with pack. Some people routinely do much less, others much more. Another formula runs like this: allow forty minutes for every mile of trail, plus an extra hour for every 1,000 feet you climb. This may sound slow—you may indeed find it slow in the field—but it's a good figure to start with. So you might allow eight hours of actual hiking to cover nine miles of easy trail with 2,000 feet of elevation gain—a longish day. Soon, of course, you'll know better than any book what you actually can do and want to do.

Now study the map for likely routes that take you to the places you want to see. One thing is obvious: you can enjoy a lot more country if you don't repeat yourself. Look for trails that loop back on your starting point or that bring you out to another roadhead. Sometimes a loop can be made by crossing a short gap between trails, but read the map carefully—are you going over a precipice? If you will exit at a different roadhead, you can set up a shuttle by parking a car at each end of the route; by hitchhiking between roadheads; or, in some well-provided regions, by taking the bus. Most hikers, unfortunately, go in and out on the same track.

How long is the line you have just traced? A guidebook may tell you and so may an agency's response to your request for information. If not, you can figure the distance using the map scale. A ruler won't help you much here, since rulers are straight and trails wander. The ideal tool: a pipe cleaner! Lay the pipe cleaner out along your path, bending it to fit the curves; then straighten it out and compare the length you've used with the scale. This works best on 7.5-minute topo maps, less well on maps of less detail—it's easy to underestimate the bends. I've also found this unscientific estimating trick helpful: simply add one mile to your tally every time your trail crosses one of the ruled boundaries of square-mile sections. Throw in another mile for each particularly circuitous stretch, as when the route is working up a slope with many switchbacks. This gimmick works best on trails over five miles long, because the inevitable errors tend to cancel out. When you get to the trailhead you may find mileage signs there; these are sometimes very accurate, sometimes not.

Try "walking" your entire route on the map. A skilled map-reader can get a good mental picture of the place to be visited—here there is a sharp drop, there a gentle forested valley; here an easy stretch, there a sustained ascent; here a long view over the plain, here a closed-in canyon.

Give some thought also to your camps. Be sure to find out what rules the managing agency imposes. If you plan to build wood fires, you may find yourself limited to established sites, to particular, designated locales, or to lands below a certain elevation. (Why not carry a stove and avoid the problem?) If your trip is in the desert away from a perennial stream, or along a high ridge without lakes, springs, or snowbanks, you will have to take note of water points and plan your stops with these in mind. In desert travel it is common to plant water caches in advance.

In such eastern ranges as the Catskills, wilderness sometimes lies in narrow, mountainous strips between lowland valleys. Often the long ridgetop trail will send short spurs down to roads on either side. This makes trip planning somewhat simpler, because you can make a quick exit to a road and perhaps a bus stop if the weather turns nasty, or if you get blisters, or if you simply run out of time. But in larger wildlands, you can seldom "bail out" except by going back.

If your trip will take you to high altitudes, try to allow time for adjustment to the thinner air. At a minimum, schedule a night's sleep at a high roadhead.

Wilderness permits and such

If you are going into a national park; into a designated wilderness zone in a national forest; or into certain state parks, chances are good that you will need a wilderness permit. In many cases you can obtain your permit by mail, if you write the appropriate agency office far enough in advance. (If you don't know where to write, contact regional headquarters—see *Resources* appendix.) Otherwise, you will need to stop at a field office—seldom too many miles from the roadhead—before you start your trip. If your route goes through two jurisdictions—a national park and a national forest, for instance—a permit secured at your entry point will do for both.

Why permits? Their first purpose is simply to gather information. As wilderness use increases and impact problems grow, managers have a clear need to know more about hikers, their preferences, and their habits of travel. At certain trailheads, permits are further used to limit use: only a given number of people are passed through each day. If, on some August weekend, you arrive at the local office and find the limit already filled for the day, you will be asked to take another route or to stay overnight and be the first party on the trail next morning.

When you get your permit in some national parks, you will be asked to list the general areas in which you plan to camp. A very few parks insist that you reserve a specific camping *spot* for each night, but the trend seems to be to dispense with this extra, indeed chilling, bit of regulation.

For western areas, an important information source is the series of regional guides by Wilderness Digest Publications (see *Resources* appendix). Each gives the latest word on permit requirements and other regulations in designated wilderness areas, together with plenty of sound general advice. For details on this expanding series, contact the publisher.

The wilderness permit scene is a rapidly changing one, so much so that it would be hopeless to sketch the differing procedures now common in different parts of the country. But there is an unmistakable movement toward uniform methods across the agencies and across the regions. With any luck, the matter of permits should be come somewhat simpler, not more complex, as time goes on.

One final note: even in areas that do not now require wilderness permits, you may be asked to produce a *fire permit.* These permits, available at agency offices, are commonly required not only for open fires but also for the use of stoves.

12:
Planning Food and Fuel

LIKE MANY THINGS IN backpacking, the matter of food and cooking is often made to sound more complicated than it is. Elaborate, time-consuming planning is not ordinarily required, and you can stock up for any trip of normal length at the local supermarket, with help, if you like, from a health food store. Specialized freeze-dried foods are convenient and, for very long trips, essential, but they are appallingly expensive. Most of the time you can do fine without them.

Nutrition

The main thing you require of backpacking food is that there be enough of it. That means, simply, calories to keep your body running under fairly heavy work.

Even when you are getting very little exercise, your body burns about 15 calories a day per pound of body weight. So a 170-pound man with a desk job might expend some 2,550 calories a day just living. On the trail, that goes up to 20 calories per pound; a really strenuous hike can push the rate to 25 calories or even higher. (Cold weather, too, adds to your needs.) An "average" woman, then, might need 2,500 calories a day for "average" hiking, and an "average" man about 3,500; teenagers are likely to require up to twice as much.

Few people bother to compute these things precisely. It's useful to bear in mind, though, that pure sugars and starches provide about 100 calories to the ounce in dry form. Proteins are about the same, and pure fats run 250 calories to the ounce. Most foods are mixtures of these elements and fall somewhere in between. Surprisingly enough, most breads and crackers, and candies made mainly of sugar, provide relatively little energy, no more, per ounce, than dehydrated fruits and vegetables. Fattier foods like chocolate, nuts, bacon, and dried eggs cluster near 150 calories per ounce. Margarine and oils are over 200. (If you care to know more, the U.S. Department of Agriculture publishes a book giving calories and nutritional values for just about every imaginable substance: see *Resources* appendix.)

If you analyzed a typical trail menu, you'd find something like half carbohydrates (sugars and starches), about one-third proteins, and about one-sixth fats. The carbohydrates are basic running fuel; they don't stick with you, but they keep the muscles working. Fats are energy in concentrated form and burn more slowly. In winter, and on sustained, difficult trips, backpackers carry more fatty foods. Proteins deliver about the same energy value as carbohydrates, only more gradually. Note, however, that because of something called "specific dynamic action," proteins do more to keep you warm when you are *not* exercising.

So how much food, in pounds, do you need to carry? Two pounds a day of typical lightweight foods should give you 4,000 to 5,000 calories, more than enough for most people most of the time. Children and light eaters may be happy with less than that; in winter, everyone needs a little more. If you carry almost exclusively freeze-dried foods, a pound and a half per person per day is an adequate daily ration.

While appetites go up in the wilderness, you may actually find the increase less than you expected. At dinner, for instance, two or three cups of a meaty stew will satisfy most hikers, even large and hungry hikers. Most people tend to carry too much food the first few times out, though that's much better than carrying too little. There is of course a great deal of individual variation. You'll learn from experience exactly what you need.

What about the finer points of nutrition: vitamins, minerals, balanced proteins, and such? By and large, on the trail, you can set such questions aside. You have license—strictly temporary, of course—to eat exactly what you want. Important though a well-constructed diet is over months and years, it matters little over the length of any ordinary wilderness excursion.

There are nonetheless a few matters to consider.

First, many people find that they function better in the mountains if their wilderness diet is not too different from what they eat at home. Sudden changes can upset the system and lead to diarrhea or, more commonly, to constipation. Foods with roughage are valuable in the trail diet. Some people carry laxatives as well.

Second is the question of "electrolytes." Electrolytes are the substances lost in sweat. One of these is sodium chloride—ordinary table salt—but there are others, including, notably, potassium. Since these chemicals are vital to the body, your diet must restore what has been lost. Fortunately, the foods that go into the typical wilderness diet are rich in these substances. (Many foods are salty, and meats, dried bananas and apricots, raisins, nuts, and eggs are all good sources for the other electrolytes.)

What about electrolyte drink mixes, specially formulated to replace the losses due to sweat? The consensus today is that these concoctions do little, if any, good. Salt tablets, on the other hand, may be actually harmful. The body is adept at regulating its chemical balance; if your diet is adequate, no additional quick fixes are required. (Cramps, which used to be blamed on electrolyte shortage, are now blamed simply on too little water intake.)

Third is the matter of food allergies and other toxic reactions to foods. Some people must steer clear of salt—if you are one of these, better consult your physician about your wilderness diet. Monosodium glutamate, with which many freeze-dried goods are laced, causes unpleasant reactions in some people. Depending on your personal reactions, you may need to modify your hiking diet more or less substantially.

Fourth, women who take long wilderness trips during their reproductive years may benefit from taking iron.

The wilderness meals

At breakfast some people like to fire up a stove and enjoy a full-scale meal with cooked cereal and bacon and eggs or pancakes. Others limit themselves to just-add-water foods, such as instant cereals, drinks, and concoctions like Instant Breakfast. Still others prefer cold foods like granola, crackers, cheese, and sausage. There is absolutely nothing wrong with cold cuts, at breakfast or at any other meal, but to some people they just don't seem like food.

Lunch, these days, is very seldom cooked. In fact, there may never be a formal lunch stop. Instead, the hiker nibbles all day long as appetite calls. Some travelers make no distinction between breakfast and lunch—they just keep munching. But other parties still prefer to light a stove at midday for hot drinks, soup, even for real cooking. On an exceedingly strenuous trip you may need a definite lunch stop just to make sure you take in the proper amount of fuel; nibbling isn't enough. Common lunch foods are breads with or without spreads (not dairy butter—it doesn't keep); dried fruit; sausage;

nuts; cheese; candy; and of course cold drinks made from powdered mixes.

At higher elevations—say above 8,000 feet—many hikers find it best to avoid nuts, meats, and cheeses during the day. They find these fats and proteins hard to digest without a long rest after eating and don't want to risk exaggerating any queasiness brought on by unaccustomed altitude. If you don't like to pour sugar into your mouth all day long, eat starches. They give you energy almost as quickly.

Dinner is almost always hot and is the largest meal. Commonly it begins with soup, goes on through a solid, one-pot main course, and ends with hot drinks, or dessert, or both. Often there are cold cuts on the side. You'll often see noodles and cheese, vegetable stew with beef, instant rice with meat or fish or cheese, instant puddings, and such prefabricated main courses as beef stroganoff and chicken tetrazzini. On short trips some people take fresh vegetables and salad.

But the fact is that there are no rules. So long as they are not scanty, your meals can be plain or fancy, slow or fast to prepare, meaty or vegetarian, "organic" or supermarket standard. The possibilities are endless, and most of them are good. And you're likely to find the simplest and most familiar foods tasting better, on the trail, than they ever did before.

Planning food

Who plans the meals? In a party of more than three or four members, it's customary to split into smaller cooking groups, each of which works out its own menu and carries its own stove. Only on large organization trips are you likely to find a central commissary.

Dinner, if hot, almost has to be a group project. (You can, however, find individual just-add-water dinners if you're willing to pay high prices.) The other meals are often handled individually. Each packs his or her own breakfasts and lunches, plus a

dinner for the whole group on one or several nights.
For example, if four hikers are going out for four
days, each can bring one dinner to feed four, plus
four personal breakfasts and lunches. If you do it
this way, you may want to make sure that you don't
wind up eating macaroni and cheese every night;
aside from that, little consultation is required.

Whether you're planning for one or for ten, the
first step is to work out a *menu*. Some people think
they skip this step, but in truth they don't; they
write the menu in their heads even as they push a
cart down supermarket aisles. Most of us have to be
a little more methodical, at least at the beginning.
You may find it useful to check books on backpack
cookery—there are many good ones—for recipes and
sample menus. Soon your own preferences and your
own experience will take over.

Given a menu, you can proceed to figure the
quantities of groceries you need. When you plan a
meal with several courses, it's easy to bring a little
too much of each element. Result: you have to
throw food away. Try to avoid this.

Choice of foods

You need foods that are *light in weight*—tolera-
bly light for normal trips, superlight for very long
trips. Cans, as a rule, are out (except for certain
compact and popular foods like sardines). Fresh
foods—vegetables, oranges—are practical only on
short trips or as occasional luxuries on longer ones.
You need food that will *keep*—except that perish-
ables are fine for the first day or in cold weather.
You need food that is *easy to cook*—unless you find
cooking a positive pleasure. And of course you need
food that you will enjoy eating.

You have three types of stores to work from.
Sporting goods stores stock mainly freeze-dried
meals and ingredients. Health and organic food
stores carry some useful staples that you may not
find elsewhere: fruit-flour biscuits, roasted soybeans,
various uncommon dried fruits, nuts, and seeds. But
the supermarket, in truth, can give you most or all

of what you need. There is no reason in the world to pay premium prices for such products as macaroni, granola, other cereals, dried milk, instant rice, or hard biscuits. For warm-weather trips you avoid foods that will need refrigeration; but note that firm-textured cheese, despite what it says on the label, lasts perfectly well in a warm pack.

If you use freeze-dried foods, there are several options. The easiest but most expensive method is to buy the elaborate, prepackaged multicourse meals, package within package, that are featured in gear stores. Or you can buy concentrated bulk ingredients, like dried eggs, dried peas, and meat bars, to use in your own recipes. (Some gear stores carry these, but you may have to order by mail.) A middle course is to choose freeze-dried, premixed main courses—chop suey, beans and franks, stroganoff, whatever—and round them out with cheaper foods.

Richmoor and Mountain House are familiar, widely available brands in freeze-dried food. Wee Pak is one company that tries for a "gourmet" touch; AlpineAire is one that makes a point of avoiding preservatives and MSG.

Two special forms of freeze-dried foods are of use in particular situations. One is the just-add-boiling-water meal, favored by some winter hikers and by climbers anxious to cut cooking to the minimum. The second is food not only freeze-dried but also compressed into small, flat wafers, reduced in bulk as much as in weight. These might have a place on a very long trip.

Whether you are buying food at the supermarket or in the gear store, be wary of the printed claim that such-and-such a package serves three, four, or six. With luck, a "serves four" package from the local market will serve two on the trail. While gear store meals are more generous, hearty eaters may find even these somewhat scant. The packages of freeze-dried dishes do state what the reconstituted weight will be—"two 12-oz. servings," for example—and this is the important information. Two or three eight-ounce cupfuls, whether of one dish or several, will satisfy most appetites at dinner.

At the other extreme from these highly pro-
cessed foods, there is a new interest these days in
foods you assemble yourself to eat on the trail. People are baking journey-cakes and nutritional fudges,
drying their own jerky, compounding their own pem-
micans and granolas. The Sierra Club book *Simple
Foods for the Pack* contains many such recipes.

How much should food cost per day? This can
vary hugely: $5 a day per person shows good econo-
my; $6 to $7 is not unreasonable; more than that is
getting out of line.

Packing food

There are several ways of packing food and the
ingredients of meals. One traditional method is quite
elaborate: each individual meal is premeasured, pre-
arranged, and packed in its individual, labeled plastic
bag. Everything you need for that particular job of
cooking will be there. Such packing can take a good
deal of time at home, especially if meals are cooked
from many bulk ingredients. It does save time on
the trail, makes it almost impossible to run out of
food on the last day, and eliminates any need for a
menu.

A simpler method is to pack all the ingredients
that will be used in dinners, throughout the trip, together in one large plastic bag. Needed directions,
of course, go in the same bag, and probably a menu.
Similarly, you can pack lunch and breakfast foods in
large bags of their own. Each morning before leaving camp, you pull the day's lunch out of the bag
and stow it where you can easily reach it.

Or again, you can sort foods simply by day: a
bag for Monday, a bag for Tuesday.

However you arrange things, you will have to do
some weighing and repackaging. Get rid of cardboard containers (but not the directions printed on
them) and other excess wrapping. Crackers, however, do keep better in the original packages. Purists
may want to get rid of tinfoil wrappers at this point,
but I don't go that far: just make a resolution not to

litter with these and not to toss them into fire (they won't burn).

Most foods can be stored in pint and quart freezer bags, the kind found in any supermarket. Oily items and powders should be double bagged. Cheese, which sweats, should be wrapped in butcher paper or cheesecloth, and then double bagged. Either wire twists or rubber bands are fine for closures (watch out for accidental littering again). Some bags can be tied shut with soft, loose knots in the plastic.

You can also make some use of rigid plastic boxes and bottles; a few compact foods—meats and fish—are carried in their original cans. Larger, tougher polyethylene bags, sold in gear stores, are good for keeping related items together. Heavier bags will last many uses, so wash and reuse them whenever you can. If you do a lot of weighing of bulk ingredients, you will need two scales: a postage scale for small amounts, a diet scale for larger quantities.

Emergency supply

After a few trips you will be making increasingly accurate estimates of the amount of food you actually need. But if you err, it is better to be generous and come home with unused food. While some people claim that nothing is healthier than a good hard workout during a fast, the long march to the car is not the place to make the experiment. (Many people, to the contrary, are acutely reminded when they hike that food is *fuel.*)

If it's your ambition to meter your food exactly, taking nothing not required, it's a good idea to make up a special compact package of concentrated food for an emergency; it can be largely candy, pemmican, jerky—anything that will keep a long time. Wrap it tightly in a couple of plastic bags (you might seal them shut with a hot iron), stick it in the bottom of your pack, and forget it. Ten to one you won't need it on any given trip. But if you are a serious hiker, the chances are that someday, sooner or later, you will. Once a year go ahead and eat such items as pemmican and dried meats, and replace them; they don't last forever.

Planning fuel

How much fuel do you need to cook the meals you have outlined?

That depends on your stove (some are thirstier than others) and on your cooking habits.

Let's say you plan fast-cooking meals, and light up the stove only briefly, if at all, at breakfast. Then you can reasonably expect to get by on about one-quarter cup per person per day of white gas, burned in a typical small stove. That's twenty or thirty minutes of burning time per person per day. Kerosene stretches a little further. High-output stoves like the MSR X-GK are somewhat less economical.

What about butane stoves? It takes about an ounce of butane, in a vapor-feed cartridge, to run such a stove for half an hour. With a liquid-feed cartridge, two ounces are consumed in the same period. The cartridge most often seen—the C-206 vapor-feed by Wonder—contains just under seven ounces. One such cartridge is adequate for a small group for a weekend.

If you do a lot of simmering, with perhaps substantial cooked breakfasts, your fuel needs will increase, even double. It is slow cooking that consumes the most impressive amounts of fuel. Moreover, foods that must be simmered to become fully cooked will take far longer to prepare at high altitudes. And remember to double your fuel supply on a winter trip where you will be melting snow.

Nothing can replace your own experience. Take somewhat more fuel than you think you need, and form your own impressions.

Water

On most trips water is taken for granted; there's no need to plan for it if it's plentiful along the way. But sometimes it is not so easily found. When a supply must be carried, it's important not to underestimate how much you need.

Even a person who is exercising only slightly needs two quarts of water a day, part of it in liquids, part of it from solid food. A hard-working hiker loses much larger amounts in sweat and breath. On a strenuous trip you require *a full gallon a day* or even more.

Don't wait for thirst to warn you that you aren't taking in enough water. When you're working extremely hard, as in very fast hiking or in winter travel, the mechanism of thirst seems to grow sluggish. Dehydration can set in without your knowing it, robbing your energy, and clouding your judgment. It is wise to drink more, and more often, than you actually want to. That's another good reason for carrying flavored fruit drink mixes, along with tea and chocolate and such: they keep you interested.

If you're headed for heavily used or semicivilized hiking areas, or to the desert, be sure to have a means of purifying water. For the options, see Chapter 20.

13:
Common Sense in Packing

YOU'VE GOT YOUR GEAR. It's lying in great, disorganized piles all over the living room.

You've got your trip. You're leaving tomorrow morning.

How do you get all that junk into your pack without utter confusion? How will you know where things are when you need them? How can you make sure of leaving nothing essential behind, and of taking not an ounce more than you need to take?

These are problems (if "problems" they can be called) that every backpacker must deal with. Every backpacker finds personal solutions, personal organizations, personal shortcuts and odd arrangements. What follows here is a set and rather fussy procedure to make use of, if you care to, the first few times you put a packload together.

Step one: make a list

If you are more than usually efficient, you may in time be able to pack a good pack without a list.

But it's best not to skip this step at the start. When you make your first list of objects to be taken, divide it by category. List all items connected with food and cooking in one section, all items connected with shelter and bed in another, and so on. Think carefully about the places you are going. In such a month in such a spot do you reasonably need to take a snakebite kit? Sunblocker cream? A spare pair of dark glasses? Clothing of cotton, or of wool? Imagine the situations you may be facing. As a starting point, you may find it useful to consult the accompanying skeleton list.

When you're done packing, don't throw your new list away. File it. Later, when you walk the trails, you can be making notes—mental or written, conscious or unconscious—as you go along: "Flashlight should be in outer pocket. . . ." "Did not need down jacket this trip. . . ." "Could have used another pot . . . ," and so forth. Remember which items you had but didn't need, and which you needed but didn't have. Then, when you get home, you can correct and rearrange your original list to make it a better guide next time you head into similar country at a similar time of year.

Who hasn't heard the slogan "When in doubt, leave it out"? And it's a good one. But it needs qualification. It applies properly to luxuries only. For other items—possible necessities and emergency items you may never need at all but could want desperately—the rule had better be "When in doubt, leave it in." If you aren't sure just when you'll finish the trip, take food for the longest possible period. If you aren't sure how cold it will be, put in the extra sweater.

Step two: assemble and check the gear

Here's one way. Get a big box. Locate the items on your list one by one, place them in the box, and check them off the list. If you haven't done this already, examine each item as you go for needed maintenance. (This is the point at which you find that none of your flashlights is working.) Actually,

Skeleton List

This is meant as a starting point for a precise packing list of your own. Ask yourself: Do I need . . . ? and then: Do I have . . . ?

Bed and shelter

Sleeping bag
Foam pad or mattress
Groundcloth
Weather shelter (poncho; tarp; tube tent; rainfly; full tent)

Kitchen

Stove; cookware
Method of handling pots
Spare fuel as needed
Funnel or pouring cap (liquid fuels)
Priming items (eyedropper or special fuel)
Matches
Firestarters
Personal eating tools
Provision for dishwashing

Tools

Maps
Compass
Knife
Cord
Notebook/Pencils
Repair kit
Flashlight or headlamp
Spare batteries and bulb

Personal

Toothbrush, etc.
Toilet paper
Other as needed or desired

Skin protection

Bug dope
Suncream (tanning or blocker)
Lip balm

Clothing

Boots and socks
Spare socks and underwear as desired
Clothing for cold and wind; rain and snow
Hat; glasses or goggles
Bandannas

Emergency

Signals (whistle, mirror, bright cloth)
Emergency shelter provision
Matches/firestarters
Medical kit; snakebite kit

Haulage

Stuffbags
Plastic bags and closures
Water containers
Daypack (where appropriate)

the best time to check your gear for major problems is immediately on your return from each trip, or at least while there's plenty of time to do whatever needs to be done.

Step three: combine the objects in groups

A typical pack may contain as many as 150 separate items, many of them small and losable. If you just dump them in, your confusion will be hopeless. Instead, handle them in groups. Keep all the kitchen items together, the medical kit together, the repair tools together. Or forget superficial logic and work out convenient groupings of your own. Build a pattern that enables you to find what you need when you need it. Avoid leaving tiny objects loose.

A typical frame pack, with its multiple compartments, suggests an organization. Almost everyone seems to use the lower compartment of a two-level packbag for clothing, for instance. In a pack with fewer built-in divisions, as in many internal-frame backpacks, hikers rely on cloth stuffbags to organize their gear. If you use these bags, you'll find yourself leaving much of your gear packed in them, even between trips; this shortcut can make the final packing fairly quick and easy.

Step four: pack it in

This hardly needs explanation, yet there are certain things to consider as you start the pleasant job of loading the pack, the big cloth cupboard from which, in the next few days, everything you need for life must come.

Consider the order in which you will want to get at things

Try to cut down on the number of times each day you will have to burrow deep into your pack. Thus, there needs to be an accessible slot for the food you will eat for lunch each day. A water bottle should be reachable. Camera and accessories, if you carry such, should certainly not be buried, and neither should the first aid kit. (Know exactly where to find that vital item!) Likewise sunglasses, hat, bandanna, bug dope, suncream, and whatever else you are likely to want as you go. This will never work out perfectly, and on a leisurely trip it doesn't matter, but it's nice not to have to rummage all the time. In the typical frame pack the least accessible region is the large upper compartment, under the stormflap; here you store the things you will not need till evening, like tent, dinner food, and possibly your stove (but see below).

Consider the distribution of weight

It used to be conventional wisdom that a trail hiker should carry a top-heavy pack, with weighty objects packed high and close to the back. With modern load-carrying systems, however, the importance of this method has diminished. Treadmill tests with variously loaded packs have shown *no* significant difference in ease of carrying. Consider this a matter of personal taste.

It still makes sense to avoid top-heaviness when you are packing for cross-country hiking, for climbing, or for travel over snow—especially if you are using an external-frame pack. A top-heavy load will swing disconcertingly on your back.

Weight should, in any case, be evenly divided between the *sides* of the pack. You don't, for instance, want two quarts of water and fuel in one side pocket and nothing but a sweater in the opposite one.

Consider special problems

Some objects shouldn't be packed together. Fuel and water should, when reasonable, be packed outside rather than in the main compartments of a pack; gasoline and food should never be together. Leaks can happen. Then there are a few fragile items. Some stoves, for instance, won't take much mashing. Sharp objects like tent poles shouldn't be so packed that they could poke holes in a jacket, a food bag, or in the pack itself.

Make sure you know how you will manage objects that will only occasionally be carried on your back, like skis or snowshoes for winter travel. If there is likelihood of rain, consider how you will protect pack and contents. If you have a number of items strapped on to the outside of your pack, will your packcover or poncho fit over them? If not, how will you strap them on outside the waterproof cover? It's easier to plan such things ahead of time than with water running down your neck.

In notoriously rainy areas, you will need more than one water-resistant layer to shield your pack. William Kemsley of *Backpacker* magazine offers a fail-safe system for New England weather: he puts a plastic garbage bag inside his pack; places clothing in smaller plastic bags; and carries a coated packcover to go over the whole assembly. If the pack itself is of water-resistant cloth, it's a four-layer defense! Another garbage bag protects the sleeping bag inside its (water-resistant) stuffsack.

When your pack isn't quite large enough for the load, you can make more hauling room by adding a frame extension or additional tie-on patches, as discussed in Chapter 6. Shock cords and straps with buckles are always likely to be useful and can be tightened better than simple cord. Some people use carabiners to hold things on; clothes can be dried hanging from large, sturdy diaper pins.

Travel on the Trail

. . . Followers of trails and of seasons, breakers of camp in the little dawn wind, seekers of watercourses over the wrinkled rind of the world, o seekers, o finders of reasons to be up and be gone . . .

Saint-John Perse

14:
To the Trailhead

A SIZABLE PART OF EVERY backpacking trip is spent, not on the trail at all, but on the road. And while getting to the trailhead is by no means half the fun, the drive to the edge of wilderness is certainly a pleasure in itself. On the road you are in between, anticipating, imagining, watching the land unfold around you. The work is done, the decisions made. You're both excited and relaxed. You're on your way.

I have said already: "the *drive* to the wilderness." And when trailheads lie, as they often do, on remote and rugged roads, there is really no other good way of getting there than in a car. Yet there are some wild areas that border directly on major paved highways. In quite a few cases, you can reach these by bus or—a bit less safely and plausibly—by hitchhiking.

There is regular bus service, for instance, over Santiam Pass in the Oregon Cascades and Snoqual-

mie and Stevens passes in Washington's part of that
range; along Interstate 80, which runs next to interesting roadless areas in the California Sierra and
elsewhere; and on other major western highways.
There are also services to most national parks: Yosemite and Grand Canyon, Yellowstone and Glacier,
Point Reyes National Seashore, and more. (Canadian
national parks are quite accessible by public transportation.) For good information on transit access to
wild country in the western United States and Canada, I recommend Lee Cooper's book *How to Get to
the Wilderness Without a Car* (see *Resources* appendix).

Generally, though, the carless backpacker has
better luck in the East, where public transportation
is more developed. Bus lines thread the Adirondacks
and the Catskills, run through Cumberland Gap and
across the Great Smoky Mountains, and intersect
the Appalachian Trail at many points. In the White
Mountains of New Hampshire, too, wildland trails
begin at the side of main paved roads where buses
run.

If you need to pick up a wilderness permit, perhaps at an office miles away from your trailhead,
this can complicate matters. All the same, the possibilities of public transportation are worth looking
into.

Even if you arrive by car, a local bus service can
be useful in another way; it can be your shuttle
from the endpoint of your trip back to your original
roadhead. Some national parks provide just such
shuttle buses in the heavy use season. And in such
eastern ranges as the Catskills, where the major
wild ridges lie between bus routes on the valley
roads, you can walk the whole length of such a lofty
trail, and then ride back to your car.

Planning your driving

Backpackers sometimes feel virtuous (even
smugly virtuous) compared to those other users of
the land: the people who do their "hiking" on motorcycles or in jeeps and their winter travel on snow-

mobiles. There are various reasons, some of them sound, for this professional snobbery. One common argument, in these days of energy shortage, is that the mechanized recreationist burns up a lot more gasoline than the self-powered walker of the trails.

But that is only true if the backpacker has driven a merely moderate distance to the trailhead. If you live, say, in Cleveland, and drive to British Columbia for your wilderness vacations, you may be using more gas than even the off-road vehicle enthusiast can burn.

So you might consider this balancing rule of thumb: *try to drive no more than one hundred miles (one way) for each day on the trail.* By this formula, day-trips would take you to places less than one hundred miles away; a weekend trip would lie within a range of two hundred or three hundred miles; the week-long trip within seven hundred.

You will, naturally, take as few vehicles as possible. Sometimes, though, your party will want more than one. Maybe your hike will end miles from where it began; in the absence of public transportation, you need to spot a second car at the exit point. Then there's the case of travel in remote and arid areas like the Great Basin of Nevada and Utah. Here, where driving conditions are brutal and mechanics few, it is a bit foolhardy to depend absolutely on a single vehicle. In such areas, basic mechanical knowhow and a good set of tools may serve you better than the most elaborate backpack ever made.

Leaving word

Especially if you are planning a long or a challenging trip, be certain to leave vital information at home with a friend or relative. Note where you are going, your route (so far as you know it), names and addresses of people in your party, and when you expect to return. Give also the phone number of the national park, national forest office, or local police station to be contacted if you should fail to come out of the wilderness on time.

What about that date of return? Most hikers, in telling their friends when they plan to return, ask that the alarm not be sounded unless they are *well* overdue, say twenty-four or forty-eight hours. They hate the feeling that people will begin worrying immediately if they switch to a longer route or take an extra day at an irresistible campsite. However, if you give yourself this margin, be sure to pack food and fuel for the extra time.

Permits and information

If you need a wilderness permit and haven't gotten it by mail (see Chapter 11), you will have to stop at a local land agency office before you hit the trail. Some national parks have registration booths at the parking lots where major trails begin, but in other parks and in most national forest areas, the responsible office is some miles away. You'll have to check in during business hours, which can pretty well scotch plans for an early start on the trail. Incidentally, even if you are headed for an area that doesn't require wilderness permits, you may be expected to pick up a fire permit at the local office. Not even stove-users are exempt from such requirements.

Permits aside, you may want to stop at a ranger station to ask some last-minute questions, or to double-check information you got in advance. What is the latest local weather forecast? How about the chances of flash-flooding in a desert canyon you plan to travel? How are snow conditions? Are key roads in good condition? And so forth. These questions are particularly important for unofficial de facto wilderness areas. The less you learned beforehand by phone or correspondence, the greater the need to talk to the local managers. There's a safety aspect, too: if a permit isn't required, it's a good idea to leave word of your projected route and schedule.

One more point. Many wilderness roadheads lie at the end of long, rough roads, far from the nearest service station. You may have some trouble tracing the maze of branching roads to your destination.

And rough roads eat up gasoline. Don't head into the hills without a full tank of gas.

Trailhead strategy

This trailhead business is sometimes more complicated than it seems. At many trailheads, two problems arise: first, the problem of impact and congestion; second, the problem of crime.

Some trailheads are major parking lots, designed for the traffic they get. Others are wide places in the road. People sometimes insist on parking where there is no room, and damage roadside vegetation—if they don't get stuck in ditches and mud. If there isn't room at the actual trailhead, park elsewhere along the road. Another mile on foot won't hurt.

More troubling is the problem of roadhead crime. It is no longer unusual for things left in cars to be stolen. Again, one solution is to park elsewhere than at the obvious trailhead. For best security, park at a ranger station or in a patrolled camping area (if a small fee is charged, regard it as insurance). If you drive an expensive car or plan to leave expensive items in it, this precaution is thoroughly sensible.

If you must park in a high-risk area, stash any valuable items in the trunk. Empty the glove compartment and leave it open. Wallets and such should not be left with the vehicle. (Better to leave all nonessentials at home.) Carry the keys, and don't leave spares hidden around the car. Don't leave your car unlocked, even on the night of your arrival, when you may be lying asleep right next to the vehicle.

In certain areas, it is unwise to leave a car with bumper stickers or decals that label you as a backpacker, as a conservationist, or as a college student.

The beginning

It always seems as if you could just start walking. Seldom does it work out that way. Unless you have done more planning, conferring, and prepacking than most hikers find time for, you will need to do some last-minute rearrangement. Most important, you will probably have to redivide community gear—shelter, stove and pots, food, fuel—to everyone's satisfaction. (A family group, of course, has a better opportunity to sort out such details at home.) Hikers with sensitive feet sometimes apply moleskin before the stresses of the trail begin.

If freezing temperatures are likely, be sure to leave the parking brake off (a frozen brake immobilizes the car). Nor should you set the brake if you have recently driven through water; the problem here is rust.

One more thing as you set out: pause to sign in at the trailhead register if one is provided. Even though you may have filled out a wilderness permit already, or left word with the office, the register is still the final record of who you are and where you are going.

15:
Walking with Pack

Does anyone seriously need instruction in how
to walk a trail? Probably not. Complicated though
the art of backpacking sometimes seems, the *act* of
backpacking—the moving along with a load—is almost too simple to describe. There are, nonetheless,
some points worth mentioning.

When the last stray object is stuffed into the last
pocket, when the car is locked and the maps folded,
when the boots are tightly laced, comes the Moment.
You've done it before: just grab the pack by the
shoulder straps (or, better, by the upper crossbar),
haul it up your back, and wriggle your arms, first
one, then the other, under the shoulder straps. Or
you can hoist the load first to your knee, or have a
friend hold the pack in position for you, or lean it
against a tree and sit down to shrug it on.

As you walk, you will occasionally want to adjust

the way the pack rides on your back. You might wish to tighten the hipbelt, since some rigs tend to loosen, if only slightly; or perhaps loosen the belt deliberately now and then to carry more of the load on your shoulders (just for variety). If you come to a section where you have to scramble over stones or plow through bushes, you will want to take more weight on your shoulders; the pack is less inclined to lurch from side to side that way. In a risky situation, like fording a deep, rushing stream, it's a good idea to unbuckle the waistbelt entirely—you might conceivably need to jettison the pack in a hurry.

The first time you carry a pack—and almost any time you carry an excessively heavy load—your hips and shoulders will get sore. Aside from the slight discomfort, this does no harm, and will happen less as time goes on.

The long stride and the rest step

The most comfortable trail pace for most people is not fast—at least the legs are not pumping rapidly—but it is very steady. Swing each leg as far forward as seems natural to you; three long strides take less energy than four or five short ones. (Long-legged hikers do seem to have some advantage.)

A hiker in good condition can go up a fairly steep and sustained hill without either gasping for breath or slowing down to a crawl. If the rise is severe, you may switch to the *rest step*. In the rest step you simply pause briefly every time you begin a new step, at that moment when the forward foot is planted but has not received any weight. Each leg thus gets a series of tiny rests. On a steep slope, heavily loaded packers may break stride in this manner for a second or more with each step.

Party pace and stops

Usually the members of a group hike at different rates—some go faster, some slower. Should the slower hikers puff and strain, or should the faster ones slow down? It's important to have some agreement, not necessarily explicit, among companions. It can be miserable to be the one slow member of a group that is moving at racing speed: the only one who can't take the time to look around and enjoy. So sort these things out in advance. It's important that fellow hikers be able to tell each other what they want and need. Someone who suffers in silence is likely to make a chilly companion.

Take stops, of course, whenever you like. It's not a marathon unless you happen to want to make it one. There's always a picture to be taken, a snack to be eaten, or just something worth looking at.

Physiologically, several short rests serve better than one long one. As your muscles work, they build up a waste called lactic acid. When you rest, you can get rid of about thirty percent of this waste in five to seven minutes. But fifteen more minutes of rest will eliminate only another five percent. Some people find long "flop-down" rests actually demoralizing: it can be hard to get started again, especially if tired legs have stiffened up. (But it's also true that a nap can be marvelously refreshing.)

Regulating warmth

We've already talked (in Chapter 5) about the *layer system:* the trick of staying comfortable by varying the thickness of the clothing you wear. You may start out on a chilly morning with long pants, a heavy shirt, a stocking cap, even a down jacket, but be down to boots, socks, and hiking shorts by afternoon. You learn quickly that it makes sense to start cold; however chilly the air at breakfast, you'll warm up fast on the trail. If you start hiking in the clothes that are comfortable for puttering around camp, you will be hot and sweaty in a few hundred yards.

There are two competing principles here. One is: *keep comfortable.* The second is: *don't spend all your time fiddling with clothes.* With garments that you can adjust while you wear them, like shirts and sweaters with buttons in front, you can have it both ways.

Eating and drinking

There's no "right" way of eating on the trail. Some people subsist on granola and raisins all day long. Some like to stop and eat a solid midday meal. In normal hiking your appetite will tell you what you need. Be sure to drink plenty of water, either straight or in flavored drinks. In fact, drink more than thirst suggests. Many, many hikers become at least slightly dehydrated. An insatiable "midnight thirst" is a good indication that you've taken in too little water during the day. Muscle cramps are a more unpleasant result, and dehydration can contribute to other, genuinely dangerous conditions (see Chapter 28).

Fighting blisters

The best way to handle blisters is not to get them. Make sure your boots fit properly and that they are nicely broken in before you set out with them (Chapter 4). Do enough preliminary hiking to toughen your feet somewhat. If you aren't sure you're ready, or if you know you blister easily, you will want to cover the danger points with moleskin or adhesive tape before you leave the trailhead. Pay attention to the heel, the outside of the big toe, and the sides of the foot at the base of the toes.

If you feel a spot of irritation forming as you walk—a "hot spot"—don't wait. Sit down, pull off the boot, and find out what's going on. Put on moleskin or tape; if you have some on already, make sure that it hasn't developed wrinkles (they can cause extra irritation) and add another layer. Make sure that your boots are very snugly laced, particularly in the upper part of the lacing pattern, and that your heel is not rising too far inside the rear of the boot as you stride. If the fit seems loose, try adding another pair of inner socks.

Some people find that an extremely thin pair of inner socks, about the thickness of dress socks, inside the other pairs, will help head off blisters. The thin socks slide inside the other layers—so the theo-

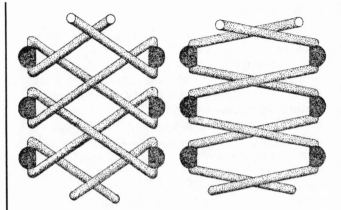

Loop pattern (left) vs. normal lacing

ry—rather than passing friction on to the skin. It's an experiment worth trying if you have consistent trouble.

Many hikers adjust the lacing of their boots depending on the slope of the hill. At the start of a climb, they loosen the toe and tighten the heel, which tends to shift and chafe in uphill travel. On the downslope they loosen the heel and tighten the toe. Again, only your experience will tell you whether you need to bother. This kind of adjustment is most easily done on boots that lace around hooks, rather than through D-rings or eyelets. The trick: run the laces around each hook in a loop. Laces set up this way won't slip around the hooks; they stay tight where you want them tight and loose where you want to ease the pressure on your foot.

On a warm day, it's good to cool your feet in a stream at lunchtime—or at any rate to pull off boots and socks for a while. Don't soak your feet for very long, though, as this can make them tender. Wet feet in wet socks blister easily. If you must ford a stream, wear your boots but not your socks; then put on dry socks after the crossing. When these are soggy, switch to a second dry pair. (Dry the wet ones on the outside of your pack if the weather's good.)

If you do get a blister, you aren't by any means crippled. Several treatments are popular. I prefer the simplest. First, wash the spot carefully with water and soap (or water and Betadine cleanser). Sterilize a needle by passing it through the blue part of a matchflame, and puncture the swollen area at one edge. When the skin is dry, cover the blister with a thin sterile pad from your first aid kit. (Some people apply antibiotic ointment.) Then put on a layer of moleskin or adhesive tape. If the blister fills with fluid again, repeat the draining after about six and about twelve hours.

Another treatment commonly recommended is the "donut patch." In this procedure, you place a ring of moleskin or tape around the blister but not on it, leaving the blister itself exposed. (An unmedicated corn pad can also be used.) Then you add a second layer of tape or moleskin, this time covering the entire area. In theory, this layer system takes pressure off the blister and prevents further irritation.

And some people swear by still a third procedure, "de-roofing": you trim the roof of the blister completely away, paint the injured area with tincture of benzoin, and cover it with adhesive.

A day's layover will help the healing process, but if this is difficult to arrange, it is by no means foolhardy to keep going. Walking a long distance such a patch can be slightly uncomfortable, but it is by no means agonizing. Though blisters very seldom lead to any further trouble, it's important to watch for signs of infection.

Trail ethics and low impact

Everybody knows it but it bears repeating: if you're hiking a trail, *stay on it.* Cutting corners, taking shortcuts, walking outside the treadway—all these break down trail edges and cause erosion and gullying. There is even some risk, on slopes, of dislodging rocks that can strike hikers below. (If this happens, yell at the top of your lungs: *Rock!*)

Not all trails are well designed, and rather few

are actually well maintained. Some are laid out so badly that it is hard indeed to avoid doing some damage; these trails push straight through boggy meadows or head directly up erosive slopes. In such places people tend to move to one side or the other to avoid the mud or the rocky footing of a gully. This is one of the main causes of *multiple trailing*, in which five or six parallel tracks scar open slopes and meadows. This is not, strictly speaking, the hikers' fault—blame it rather on bad trail layout and poor maintenance—but you can best help by gritting your teeth and keeping to the original line. Always walk single file, not side by side, on a trail. (In cross-country travel, where you wish to avoid establishing any visible track, the principle is precisely the opposite: always walk abreast, each hiker on a separate course.)

Whether on a trail or on a cross-country route, you should restrain any impulse to build ducks (small rock cairns used as route markers) or, should you have the tools, to blaze trees. Let the next travelers find their way as you did. Chances are they want it that way. (However, there is one possible exception: the mapped, designated trail that is faint from lack of maintenance. Here you may be doing a service by building an occasional duck. It's wise to find out first whether such a trail is meant to be abandoned for some good reason—this is occasionally the case.) If a trail is clearly blocked—if, for instance, a log has been carefully laid across it—respect the block.

If you meet other hikers on the trail, courtesy gives the party going uphill the right of way. When such a meeting is imminent, look for a spot where you can stand aside without scarring ground or crushing vegetation. If you meet stock on the trail, stand quietly aside—the uphill side is usually advised—and let the animals pass.

Lingering snow

In many mountain areas early in the hiking season—and in the Northwest, the Northern Rockies, and the mountains of Canada at any time—you are likely to encounter snowbanks on the trail.

Old snow is slippery stuff when cold and mushy stuff when warm. Either is difficult. Crossing a flat snowbank, you must adopt a rather tentative pussy-footing stride, lifting your feet cautiously and planting them very flatly. On hard snow, come down firmly to establish your footing. On hard-crusted snow that conceals a mushy interior, come down very gently and test the footing as you go: this should reduce the number of times you plunge in, swearing, to your knees. Be aware that snowbanks may have melted cavities underneath, especially at the edges.

Spring hikers who encounter a small melting snowbank on the trail often detour around the re-treating margin of the snow, not wanting to wade in slush. By the following weekend the snowbank has shrunk; more parties come through and detour along a different arc, and then a third, until a whole fan of tracks is worn in the moist earth. The prob-lem is so acute in some areas that managers are closing routes to public access during the thaw. If you encounter such a snowbank, don't detour (un-less you can walk on rocks or logs): put on your gai-ters and push through.

For something more about negotiating steep snowslopes in summer, see Chapter 22.

Side trips and party-splitting

There's no great harm in splitting your party—if you do it carefully, making sure that each splinter group has map, compass, and other essentials, and that everyone is clear about a place and time for coming back together.

When a party gets split by accident, problems can result. This is one danger in spreading out too far along the trail. Sometimes the people at the end of the line won't know what the leaders plan to do and will take the wrong turn at an intersection. Make sure that everyone knows what's going on. A person who simply follows, blind to the choices and landmarks of the route, runs the risk of getting lost.

You may want to vary a trip by taking side trips with nothing but a daypack. If you take such an excursion, you must be certain to have some essential items with you. Always plan for an unexpected night away from your main camp. The classic list of "ten essentials," first formulated by the Seattle Mountaineers, goes like this:

Extra clothing. This may be as little as a sweater or as much as a jacket, parka, rainpants, and cagoule. Just as you do when you're packing the main pack at home, think of clothes to keep you *warm* and clothes to keep you *dry.*

Extra food. Perhaps nothing more than a generous lunch; perhaps an emergency packet of high-energy food. It's true that a person can survive for days, even weeks, without food, and take no permanent harm, but in an emergency you need energy to work with and, still more important, to think with.

Sunglasses. Essential above timberline, in the desert, and, most of all, on snow. Snow blindness is no joke. Wherever glasses are truly essential, take a spare set as well.

Knife.

Matches. Waterproof/windproof matches are good for this purpose.

Firestarter.

First aid kit.

Flashlight or headlamp.

Topo map and perhaps others.

Compass.

To these traditional ten you may want to add some of your own. Here are some other items you may not want to risk doing without:

Provision for emergency shelter. If you don't carry a plastic sheet, footsack, reflective blanket, or the like, at least have some kind of shelter in mind.

Suncream. A probable essential wherever sunglasses are important.

Signal. Whistle? Mirror? Bright-colored item of clothing?

Toilet paper. Not a survival item but . . . take it.

Insect repellent. Important, sometimes, for sanity.

Notebook and pencil. You may want to leave a note somewhere.

Weather

The weather that hikers dread most is extended rain. Even rain, though, is troublesome only when it comes time to set up camp; walking in the rain, with the proper gear, can be a pleasure. If you have good waterproofs for yourself and your pack, you will be relatively comfortable (though it is hard to keep water out of your boots).

There is real danger for the unprepared in wet, cool, windy weather. If you don't have the gear to stay dry and warm, you run the risk of losing so much body heat that you suffer the spectacular collapse called *hypothermia.* Common sense and proper clothing, however, are all that's required to prevent such situations. For more on hypothermia, see Chapter 28.

In brief, western-style thunderstorms, you may be able to wait out a swiftly passing shower under the shelter of a tree. But make very sure it's the right tree. In thunderstorm country you have to give thought to lightning. Lightning is a definite hazard in the American wilderness, much more to be feared than, for example, the rattlesnake. Yet, like most hazards, it's easy to avoid.

Lightning doesn't strike just anywhere. It is drawn to prominent objects: the highest outcrop on a stony peak; the sharp brink of a cliff; a tall, isolated tree. When the bolt strikes, the charge spreads out through the ground, and can shock you badly many feet away from the original strike. The current tends to move along cracks in rock and down small, shallow watercourses, especially when water is running in them. (Knowledgeable readers will notice oversimplification here; the most dangerous type of lightning does not strike down from the clouds at all, but *up* from the ground. In practical terms, though, it doesn't matter.)

When you hear a thunderstorm working its way through the sky, stop for a moment and count the number of seconds that pass between a flash and the resulting thunderclap. Each five seconds that passes indicates a mile interval between you and the flash. If you are in a high or exposed place, don't wait till the last minute to start your retreat; thunderstorms typically move a mile every two or three minutes.

What are unsafe positions? A peak, of course, or a hilltop. A flat meadow or plain or rocky plateau where you yourself are a prominent object. The shelter of a tall, isolated tree. The top of a cliff but also the *base* of a cliff. A shallow cave on a slope. You are much less vulnerable at the bottom of a valley; in timber with trees of fairly uniform height; or in a deep, dry cave.

If you're trapped on a mountain top or out in the open, with no time to retreat, at least get back from the highest points and from cliff edges. Among boulders, you can crouch between rocks of similar size and low profile. Members of a party should spread apart, keeping thirty feet or more between them.

Get rid of your pack, your pocket knife, your belt, your camera, and anything else that might have metal in it. If you can, try to get some insulation between you and the ground. A rope, if you are carrying one, is good; a foam sleeping pad will help some. Crouch or kneel on the insulation. Don't lie flat. If you are inside a tent pitched in a vulnerable spot (bad planning!), do the same. If you feel a tingle, hear a buzzing from metal objects, or see, on metal, the weird flame of St. Elmo's fire, you have very little time.

If a companion has been struck by lightning, your quick action may be lifesaving: see Chapter 25.

Stream crossing

On most well-traveled trails, at least in the regular hiking season, you will find simple bridges across large streams. More primitive routes, however, don't have bridges. Lacking convenient stones, you wade.

Some people stride through such fords and keep walking, letting feet and socks and boots dry as they go. Others change socks on the far bank. Still others put on tennis shoes to cross, or take off their socks, putting their boots back on, over bare feet, to wade. Don't try to cross a stony streambed barefoot. It's bad news for a backpacker to cut a foot or stub a toe. Don't try to throw boots across a broad stretch of water.

Most fords are very innocent. But there can be genuine danger in crossing a high-volume, swift-running stream such as you may encounter at the spring thaw or in cross-country travel. Crossing a wild stream can be quite an undertaking, with rules and techniques adapted from mountain climbing. You may have to spend some time looking for a good crossing point. Often it is better to turn back, even if it means abandoning a destination or going the long way around. Ask yourself what will happen if you are swept off your feet. An astonishing number of people have been carried over the terrible verges of Yosemite's thousand-foot cataracts after they tried to cross the harmless-looking mountain streams above. Unless you know exactly what you are doing, it is not wise to tie in to a rope at a dubious crossing: the seeming protection can do more harm than good.

These dangerous situations, however, will rarely be encountered in ordinary backpacking. See Chapter 22.

16:
Finding the Way

LET'S FACE IT. Few corners of the American wilderness are now so vast, so trackless, or so primitive that they afford us much excuse for getting lost. Not truly lost, not lost without a clue, not North Woods lost. Nor are the techniques that brought the trappers in northern Canada back to their caches of more than casual use to the hiker of well-marked trails. Navigation these days is more often a simple thing, a matter of keeping track of where you are, how fast you are progressing, what landmarks you are passing. It's a matter of awareness: common sense.

Yet people do get lost, and even in serious trouble, in the most populous of wild areas. And it is a rare hiker who has not had moments of disorientation along the way. Did I miss the trail junction? When did we cross into the Horse Creek watershed? What are those cliffs up there? What happened to the trail?

Even for the hiker who never moves on anything but the plainest of paths, navigation can be fun, not so much to tell you where you are as to identify what you see.

The topographic map

The basic tool of navigation is the topographic or contour map. Add to it a compass and a little thought, and you can answer almost any question about your place in the land.

These invaluable maps—many thousands of sheets in all—are published by the U.S. Geological Survey and cover the whole area of the United States. Maps for the western United States are ordered from Denver, eastern maps from Arlington, Virginia. Similar maps for Canada can be ordered from the Department of Energy, Mines, and Resources in Ottawa. (See *Resources* appendix.) The topo maps suitable for backpacking come in two scales. "Fifteen-minute" quadrangles represent a mile of land by an inch of map and cover named areas of about thirteen by seventeen miles. "Seven-and-a-half-minute" sheets, four to each fifteen-minute sheet, cover smaller areas more minutely. ("Minute" here is a unit of space, not of time.) Both types cost $2. The fifteen-minute style is actually more useful to the hiker, more compact (fewer sheets are carried) and yet quite sufficiently detailed. Unfortunately, this series is being phased out. For some areas only seven-and-a-half-minute maps can now be obtained. At the other extreme there are a few sections of the Intermountain West that have yet to be mapped at all on a scale useful to the backpacker.

Two other types of USGS maps are of occasional interest to the backpacker. One is a relatively new series of sheets in a scale of 1:100,000, showing larger areas in less detail; these lack contour lines and give elevations in meters. The other is the 1:250,000 series, covering still vaster stretches with still less detail; but these maps do have the virtue of including contour lines and can help give you a

Topographical map, 7.5 minute scale

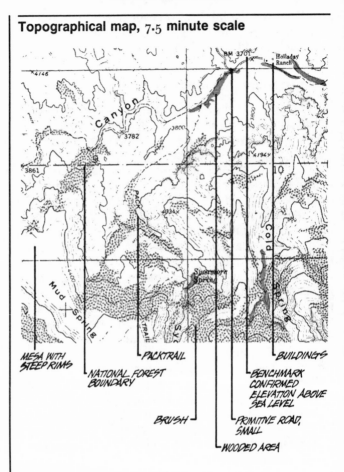

MESA WITH
STEEP RIMS

NATIONAL FOREST
BOUNDARY

PACKTRAIL

BRUSH

BUILDINGS

BENCHMARK
CONFIRMED
ELEVATION ABOVE
SEA LEVEL

PRIMITIVE ROAD,
SMALL

WOODED AREA

sense of what's topographically what in an entire region.

There are several kinds of information on a regular topo map. Most important are the thin, brown lines called "contour lines," or just "contours." These are labeled to show elevation above sea level. If you imagine the map as a three-dimensional model that could be flooded with water, the rising surface would first touch the 1,200-foot contour wherever it appears, then the 1,400-foot, and so on.

In 15 minute scale

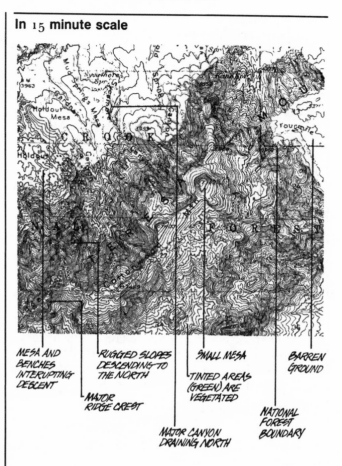

MESA AND
BENCHES
INTERRUPTING
DESCENT

RUGGED SLOPES
DESCENDING TO
THE NORTH

MAJOR
RIDGE CREST

SMALL MESA

TINTED AREAS
(GREEN) ARE
VEGETATED

BARREN
GROUND

NATIONAL
FOREST
BOUNDARY

MAJOR CANYON
DRAINING NORTH

On fifteen-minute maps, the interval between
contour lines is usually eighty feet. Every fifth line
is heavier and darker and marks a gain of four hundred feet from the last such emphatic line. On
seven-and-a-half-minute maps, the basic interval is
generally forty feet, and two hundred feet separate
the heavier lines. Don't take these intervals for
granted, however. In very flat regions smaller incre-
ments are used, and some older maps use other intervals for no special reason. (A notice at the bottom

of every sheet tells you what contour interval is being used—and the numbers printed on the heavier contour lines of course communicate the same information.)

Topo sheets ordinarily have a pale green shading to show forested areas. Green stippling indicates brush; uncolored areas are grassy or barren. Most sheets are ruled with squares a mile on a side (each with a number), called *sections.* These are the fundamental units of the national land survey. (See *More about maps,* below.)

Topo maps are highly accurate; you will find few minor and hardly any major errors, at least in the portrayal of the land itself. Manmade features, though, do change, and some of these maps were last updated in the early 1950s. Check the date in the legend. Many trails shown on these older maps have been abandoned or rerouted, and the road systems in the rugged mountains of the Far West have expanded almost beyond comprehension in the last quarter century. Looking at 1950s topo maps, you get the impression that, even so late in our history, the mountainous parts of the West were dominantly wilderness. But that has changed in most of our mountains, and changed beyond recall.

Map management

As maps get more expensive, people are looking for ways to make them last longer. Some people cut their maps into segments and mount them on backings, but this alone won't keep the pictured landscape from blurring away before your eyes in the rain. Several companies market liquid coatings you paint on map surfaces to keep moisture and mildew out; some hikers use mineral oil or acrylic varnish. And some cover the working side of the map with clear contact plastic. Another simple precaution is to store each map in a clear plastic envelope.

USGS maps come rolled, not folded. Before you start creasing away at the pristine rectangle, plan a little. How big should each segment be when you finish? If your pack has a special map pocket, how big is it? Your folded map should be a bit smaller.

It is useful to make your folds, and especially the folds that run the long way, very straight, so that these correspond to true north-south lines. The typical map gives you some help in this: both side margins and end margins are divided into thirds by little black tick marks that extend slightly onto the map itself. If you were to draw lines connecting opposite ticks, you'd have a tic-tac-toe grid. At each crossing in that imaginary grid, the mapmakers place a tiny cross on the map surface. *Most* sheets have a more obvious gridwork in the form of section lines (of which more below).

Many hikers trim the margins from their maps, leaving only the actual representation of the land. But before you do this, consider how much of the marginal data is valuable. Don't throw away the scale (though you can move it onto an irrelevant part of the map surface); do write down the name of the sheet (maybe on the back) and the declination figure from the diagram at the bottom (more on this below).

Map reading

The basic skill is the ability to build, from the map, a picture of the land—to translate swiftly, automatically, from map to land and back again. You can practice this skill most easily by buying the topographic sheet for a familiar landscape near home. Soon you'll know without thinking what a particular shape of land looks like in contour lines; that an outward eddy of lines along a slope indicates a spur ridge; that an indentation means a gully or a streamcourse; that one valley is broad and shallow, a second precipitous and deep. You will know a short, steep hill from a long, gradual one, and a plateau from a knife-edge ridgeline. It is a fascinating study. The map begins as a dead graphic, a mere representation, but it comes alive as you learn it and instructs you endlessly. The map *becomes* the country.

The perfect tool for navigation (too perfect: may

it never be invented!) would be a topo map with a built-in spot of light showing your own position—a little dot that would shift as you moved. Lacking such a gimmick, you reproduce it in your mind. Navigation, in its essence, is not a set of techniques but a habit of thought; a custom of awareness; of knowing where you are, and what the land is doing. In typical wilderness landscapes, unlike those of the city, there is seldom anything really inexplicable or arbitrary; there are broad, discernible patterns—drainages running one way and another; major and minor systems of ridges; plateaus and deep-carved canyons. If you keep alive this sense of pattern, it is rather hard to become entirely lost, whether you have a trail to follow or are striking out cross-country on a route of your own.

Some landscapes, of course, are easier than others to get lost in. Most confusing are areas that are level, rather patternless, or chaotically jumbled, and places where timber or topography cut off your long-distance views. Fog or low overcast can complicate matters, and every winter hiker knows (and somewhat fears) that brilliant-white, opaque, and snowy mist called "whiteout." But these are special cases. For more information on advanced cross-country routefinding, see Chapter 22.

More about maps

While topo maps are important, they are not necessarily the only guides you will need. Usually you also want the maps put out by the agency that controls the land you are hiking on—Park Service, Forest Service, Fish and Wildlife Service, Bureau of Land Management, or state agency. These agency maps, though mostly less detailed than topos, do reflect more recent changes in roads and trails. When you are traveling wilderness areas that have no formal protection, like so many Forest Service and BLM lands, this information is vital. Roads may be advancing, trails vanishing every year. For some designated wilderness areas, the agencies have prepared combination maps showing current roads and

trails on a topographic base—the ideal. Cost of
agency maps is typically fifty cents.

Some popular hiking areas are covered by modified topo maps, commercially printed, which incorporate more current information. Almost all maps
share with the topos a basic organization. All the
area of the United States (outside the original Colonies) is divided into squares, normally six miles on a
side, called *townships.* Each contains thirty-six *sections* of one square mile, and these are numbered
within the township in an unvarying back-and-forth
pattern:

6	5	4	3	2	1
7	8	9	10	11	12
18	17	16	15	14	13
19	20	21	22	23	24
30	29	28	27	26	25
31	32	33	34	35	36

Hikers and other people who work with the land
soon become familiar with this pattern and use it to
identify points on the map: "Looks like that must be
a real cliff in section 17!"

In the woods you will sometimes come across
yellow metal plates nailed to trees. Each is stamped
with the thirty-six section pattern shown above. A
nail through the plate tells you where you are:
highly convenient when prominent landmarks are
few.

How do maps distinguish one township from another? Townships are stacked in vertical and horizontal rows. The horizontal rows are called *extended
townships,* a term often shortened, for maximum
confusion, to just *townships* again. The vertical
rows are called *ranges.* Each extended township and
each range has a number of its own marking its position in the broader land survey. Using these num-

bers, it's possible to describe any point on the map exactly, as a location in the land survey grid. But this is not especially a hiker's game.

One final point. On most maps, true north is at the top of the sheet, east on the right hand margin, west on the left, south on the bottom. However, sometimes the field is tilted for some reason. Look for an arrow labeled *north* somewhere on the sheet and adjust your thinking if it doesn't point straight up.

The compass and how to read it

With the map, the compass is the second fundamental aid in wilderness navigation. Its function is to help you place the map in the right position, so that the map's north and the world's north are exactly the same. Then the compass helps you to read the land, from the map, with precision.

Nothing is simpler, in practice, than using a compass. Nothing is more difficult than to describe this simple act without giving an altogether spurious impression of complexity. I suggest that, after reading the next few pages, you locate a compass and review them with compass in hand. Only thus will the seeming complications disappear.

The circle of directions

Before we talk about the compass itself, we have to deal with an essential concept: the idea of the *cir-*

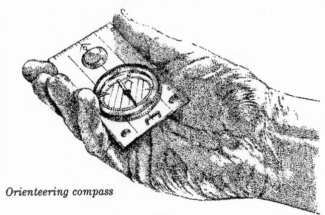

Orienteering compass

cle of directions.

Imagine yourself standing on a peak from which you can see a hundred miles in every direction. Imagine yourself turning slowly in one spot—facing north, then east, then south, then west, then north again.

How do you name the directions you have been facing? The cardinal points—north, east, south, west—are easy. For the directions in between, you can combine and say: northeast, southwest; then north-northeast, south-southwest; then north-by-north-northeast; and so on. But obviously you can only go so far with this. To simplify matters, we supplement the names with numbers. The circle of directions is divided into 360 units called *degrees*. Zero is north; 45, northeast; 90, east; 180, south; 270, west; 350, just a little west of north; and 360, north again (zero and 360, in the circle, are names for the same point).

It may seem odd at first, this use of numbers for directions, but it is indispensable for any careful navigation. It allows you to define a direction simply and quickly—using words, it might not be possible to pin it down at all.

Compass anatomy

The essential part of the compass is the magnetized *needle*. The needle does not, except by accident, point to the geographic North Pole *(true north)*. Rather, it aligns itself to point *generally* north along a wandering web of magnetic lines that converge in northern Canada, at a point *(magnetic north)* a thousand miles short of the true pole. Thus the actual direction indicated by the "North" end of a compass needle varies from place to place; it also varies over the years in a single location. The key to compass navigation is knowing where the compass needle is pointing, *this* year, in *your* wilderness—but more of this later.

There are many kinds of compasses. The type most used in backpacking is the *orienteering compass*. The needle rides on a pivot inside a round, fluid-filled plastic chamber. One end of the needle—the end that points (more or less) north—is specially marked, often with red paint. The surface of the chamber is a *dial* marked with 360 degrees running clockwise—the circle of directions. While no small compass has room for a separate mark for each of the degrees, the better models mark every five degrees, or even every two.

The needle-and-dial assembly sits on a rectangular *base plate* of clear plastic and can be rotated upon it. The bigger the base plate, the better for close navigation—five inches is good. The plate is marked with a big lengthwise *directional arrow;* this extends partway under the dial and can be seen through it. On many compasses the base plate is also marked with several *scales* to use in reading maps: inch, millimeter, and other intervals shown because, on maps of different standard scales, they represent miles or kilometers.

Good orienteering compasses without superfluous extras cost between $10 and $15. The prominent brands are Silva, Suunto, and Brunton. Very simple compasses, with small dials and no base plates, can be found much more cheaply and may in fact be sufficient for your needs. If you plan to depart from the main traveled thoroughfares of the wilderness trail system, you need a tool of greater precision. When you buy a compass, compare it with others in the store to make sure that the needle points in exactly the same direction. It is possible for a needle to be misaligned or to stick in a false position.

Compasses are confused by metal. You won't get an accurate reading from a compass held near a camera or other metallic object.

Uses of the compass

Precise compass work is rather finicky. But most of the time you will be using the tool in a simple, casual way. Just a glance at the dial, now and again, can guide you when you are uncertain or keep you from drifting off an ill-marked route. If you know, from the map, that you are supposed to be heading

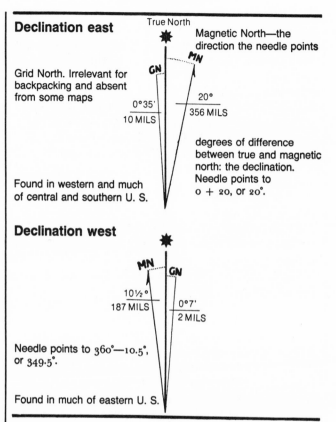

Declination east

True North

Magnetic North—the direction the needle points

Grid North. Irrelevant for backpacking and absent from some maps

GN

MN

0°35'
10 MILS

20°
356 MILS

degrees of difference between true and magnetic north: the declination. Needle points to 0 + 20, or 20°.

Found in western and much of central and southern U. S.

Declination west

MN

GN

10½°
187 MILS

0°7'
2 MILS

Needle points to 360°—10.5°, or 349.5°.

Found in much of eastern U. S.

essentially north, then something is plainly wrong if the compass shows you moving steadily east.

Now for the finicky parts:

Compass step one: knowing where your needle points

In most of the United States and Canada, compass needles point either just east or just west of true north. To make good use of your compass, you have to know *how much* east or west. The name for this difference, measured in degrees, is *declination.*

Every topographic map has, in the lower margin, a diagram that purports to give this information. The vertical line with the star represents true north; the slanted line labeled "MN" indicates magnetic north, or the direction in which the needle is actually supposed to point at the map location. The angle between them, expressed as a number of degrees, tells you how far you have to go left or right from o on your compass dial to find the number that represents the point toward which your needle will actually aim when you are in the mapped area. If the declination is "West," you'll be going around the dial toward west—counterclockwise; if the declination is "East" you'll be curving toward east—clockwise.

Got that?

There is a catch. Unless your map is very, very new, this information is out of date, perhaps so much so as to be useless for careful work! The safest thing to do, if you are really depending on your compass, is to figure out for yourself which way the damned needle is pointing—but I'll postpone discussion of this point for now.

Compass step two: orienting the dial

Suppose the declination in your map area is 19 degrees east. This means, simply, that your compass needle will point in the direction represented by nineteen degrees—about north-northeast. To orient your compass for that region, then, you rotate the dial until the number nineteen comes into position at the tip of the needle. With your compass dial thus oriented, it has become an accurate guide to all directions. True north on the compass matches true north on the land; southeast on the compass is southeast in the outside world; and so on.

In the eastern United States, compass needles lean west from true north. Say the declination is ten degrees west. Rotate the dial so that the needle rests at a point ten degrees to the west of north. This point bears the number 350: 360 (north) − 10 (declination west) = 350. (To go west from north, counterclockwise around the dial, you have to subtract degrees.)

To make orientation easy, some compasses come equipped with a movable marker for magnetic north.

By adjusting a tiny screw, you can create an obvious target for your needle to point at. Cost is a couple of dollars. Worth it? Up to you.

Compass step three: orienting the map

Once you know how to orient the compass, the next big step is to get the map lined up as well. (Remember, you are doing this in the field, standing on the territory represented by that map.) The trick, essentially, is to go back one stage and orient the compass again—this time *with* the map, as though they were one thing.

First, take the unoriented compass and rotate the dial until the directional arrow on the base plate is seen to pass through the mark on the dial that represents true north. Second, place the compass on the map, with the directional arrow in line with north on the map. (To line it up exactly, use a margin or an accurate north-south fold.) Third, hold this map-and-compass combination firmly in your hands and turn it as a unit until the compass needle points to magnetic north on the dial (the declination). You have now oriented the compass and, with it, the map. The map now parallels the land.

Compass step four: taking a bearing

Now that both map and compass are oriented, you can use them together to give you many kinds of information. Often a simple procedure will do. If you already know within a mile or so where you are on the map, it is easy to read the identities of prominent points. The big massif just east can only be General Steele's Backbone; the forested valley can only be the drainage of Horsethief Creek; what is glinting in the socket below can only be Hungry Packer Lake.

But sometimes you will need to read the land more precisely. Perhaps you don't know at all where you are; perhaps the topography is downright confusing; perhaps you must make a difficult choice of route. All these problems are reasons for taking *bearings*.

How is it done?

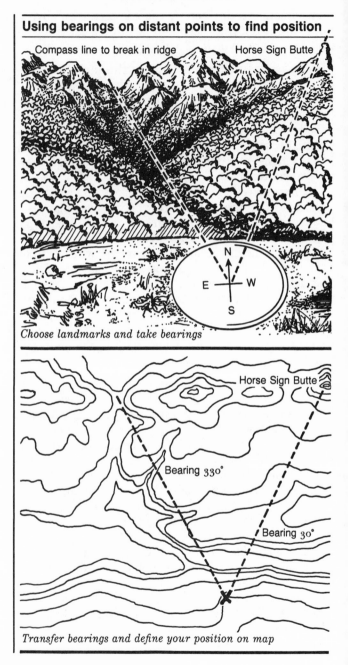

Using bearings on distant points to find position

Compass line to break in ridge

Horse Sign Butte

Choose landmarks and take bearings

Horse Sign Butte

Bearing 330°

Bearing 30°

Transfer bearings and define your position on map

The idea is to find the precise direction from you to a particular object, say, a prominent peak. Raise the compass to just below eye level. Make sure it is correctly oriented. Now, keeping the dial in that same correct position, turn the base plate underneath it so that the arrow on the plate is pointing exactly toward the object you want the bearing on. Now look down through the transparent dial. You will see that the directional arrow is visible and cuts the circle of degrees at a particular point. Read the number at that point. This is your bearing.

This information has many uses.

You know where you are and want to know what you're looking at. Take a bearing on the point you want to identify. (For convenience, say, it's a peak.) Note your own position on the map. Place the (properly oriented) compass on the (properly oriented) map with the center of its dial at your position. Say the bearing on your landmark was 120 degrees, or about southeast. Simply draw (or imagine) a line running from your position to the number 120 on the dial and on across the map. (The line printed on your compass's baseplate will do for a start.) The first height it crosses that seems of proper height and distance is the one.

You know what you're looking at and want to know where you are. Take bearings on two known peaks (or any other prominent features). The farther apart they are, the more accurate your fix will be. Placing the compass on the map as before, draw (or imagine) lines running from those landmarks at the proper angles. Where these lines intersect, you have your exact position. To double-check, you can sight on additional points.

Or perhaps you already know that you are on a certain *line* in the landscape: a major stream, a trail, a ridgeline, a road. This simplifies matters. Just one bearing, just one additional line on the map, may be enough to show you the single place where you can reasonably be standing.

You have the whole picture but want to find this place again. Say you've discovered something interesting a little way off the trail: an old cabin not shown on the map, a good shortcut, a pleasant meadow. You want to come back next year. But there's no obvious landmark along the trail to tell you where to leave it next time you come along. A bearing on a more distant landmark will do just as well. Write yourself a note: "Next time walk east along the Kangaroo Trail until Sawtooth Mountain is on a bearing of 315 degrees; then cut down the ravine to the left." You can further describe your cross-country route as a compass direction or *azimuth:* "then head downslope on a line of 125 degrees."

Determining declination

As noted above, the declination figures given on topographical maps are not always accurate, because declination varies over time. For casual compass work, the difference between a map's declination figure and the actual declination in the territory it represents may not matter much. But if you want to know for sure, your map, compass, and common sense can give you the true declination in a few minutes.

Make your way to a place that is unmistakably mapped on the topo sheet in question: a road junction, a hilltop, a USGS benchmark or whatever. Take a bearing on another unmistakable landmark. Vary the normal procedure, however, by ignoring declination: pretend for a moment that your compass needle points to true north.

Next, look at the map. Place your compass on it so that the center of the dial is at your position and "North" on the dial matches north on the map. (Forget the compass *needle* for now.) Read off the mapped bearing to your landmark.

Finally, compare the bearing you got from the landscape with the bearing you got from the map. The difference is the actual current declination. If your compass said that Landmark Peak was at 60 degrees and the map says that the peak lies at 80 degrees from your position, the real declination is 20 degrees clockwise, or east. To put it another way, when your compass needle points to 20 degrees on your dial (the point 20 degrees east of north), all the directions shown on the dial are correct in the outside world.

To check yourself, repeat this procedure several times, using different landmarks.

Substitutes for the compass

There are no very good substitutes for the combination of topographic map and compass in finding your way. It is worth mentioning, all the same, some rough-and-ready methods of determining direction. Except for the first, none of these tricks will do more than straighten you out if you are grossly turned around. For more information, I refer the reader to W. S. Kals's excellent book *Land Navigation* (see *Resources* appendix).

Polaris

Our polestar isn't always at true north, but it's close enough for emergency purposes. To locate it in a clear night sky, first find the Big Dipper. The two stars that form the end of the Dipper's "bucket," opposite the "handle," point almost straight toward Polaris, a star of medium brightness.

The sun

It's well to be aware of the arc the sun follows in the sky at a given time of year. At the equinoxes, mid-March and mid-September, the sun rises and sets very close to due east and due west. In mid-June it rises somewhat northeast and sets somewhat northwest; in mid-December, it rises somewhat southeast and sets somewhat southwest. (Exact tables, organized by date and latitude, are available to pin this down.)

Then there's the old watch trick. (It presupposes that you carry a watch and keep it running accurately.) First, set the watch to standard time (turn it one hour back if it's on daylight saving time). Second, hold the dial level and point the hour hand toward the sun (that is, toward the ground point that

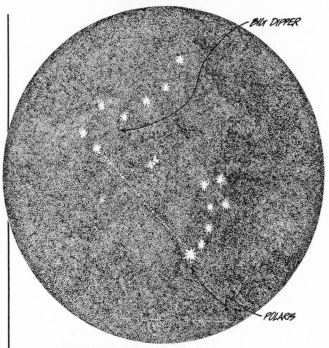

Using the Big Dipper to find Polaris

would appear to be directly below the sun). North will be a point on the watchface halfway between the hour hand and 12. Before noon, you must read backwards around the dial to find this middle point; after noon, you read clockwise. (If it's 7 A.M. standard time, north will be at about 3:30 on the dial; if it's 4 P.M., at about 8:00 on the dial. At 12 noon, north lies opposite the hour hand.) This method is none too accurate, but may be reassuring in a pinch.

Lacking a watch, you can read directions, roughly, from the shadow thrown by a straight stick. There are different versions of the technique. In the quickest procedure you plant your stick in the ground, not straight up, but slanted toward the sun, so that no shadow is thrown. Then wait until a shadow appears. This shadow will mark an approximate east-west line. The reading can be taken at any time of day and does not require a long wait.

Signs in the land

In the northern hemisphere, the north and northeast sides of objects are heated less by sunlight
each day than the south and southwest sides. Other
things being equal, then, moss *does* tend to be
thicker on the northern side of trees; timber tends
to grow lusher on north- and east-facing slopes;
snow and ice linger longest on the northern sides of
ridges. In rare cases you may also be able to guess
directions from the effects of a strong prevailing
wind: lopsided trees, sand patterns, and so on. But
all of these signs should be used with extreme caution. Local conditions complicate them, and, at best,
they are crude.

"Sense of direction"

Do human beings have a built-in "homing instinct" or sense of the proper way? Say the experts:
absolutely not. This is simply not our gift. People
who try to walk straight lines without constant cor-
rection veer in circles.

Following a trail

Ordinarily, there's no skill to following a trail.
It's there, unmistakable, and you just plod. But even
obvious trails grow faint at times and can be confused by game traces. And we have in this country
a huge network of what might be called "ghost
trails"; built in the 1930s, under the New Deal, they
have never been maintained since. (As fast as the
American hiking public is growing, our trail system
seems to be shrinking still faster.)

Faint trails, especially above timberline, may be
marked with small stacks of stones called "ducks"
or "cairns" or "birds." Occasionally these piles are
high, but most are just large enough to be clearly
artificial. Often a single stone, placed at one side of
the main stack, indicates the direction of the continuing trail.

In wooded country the guiding marks are *blazes:*
deep, clean axe cuts that have chipped out whole
sections of bark and underlying wood. Usually,

these are placed at about chest height. Often they are stacked in groups of two or three; this stacking may or may not indicate a turn. Blazes ordinarily face along the continuing line of the trail, so if you see one facing sharply off to the right, it probably marks a bend in the route. However, blazes cut by different workers at different times aren't necessarily standard.

Recently, plastic tags, metal disks, and paint spots have been much used instead of classic blazes, perhaps to avoid injuring trees. In the East, marks of different colors are much used to distinguish trails.

When the trail is clear, of course, you don't have to be too much concerned with these guides. But if it starts going hazy on you—if it disappears under patches of snow, if it threatens to dissolve in a maze of deer trails—or if the brush starts closing it over, begin watching the blazes meticulously. Don't go on for long without locating one. Stop and hunt if you must. Few of us can trust instinct, and a surprisingly official-looking trail can be made by deer and bear. Be aware, too, that natural marks can counterfeit blazes—occasionally a rock bounding down from a cliff gouges a good imitation. Yet another caution: lines of blazes are sometimes used to mark the boundaries of land survey squares, or sections, away from any trail.

When the ducks and blazes fail you, there are other signs you can look for. Have the branches of trees or shrubs been cut or clipped? Is there a terrace effect where the path was cut into a hillside? In a place where brush has obscured a route, the treadway itself may be free of new stems; plants are slow to root again on compacted ground.

If such detective work is required for long, though, you are probably no longer just bridging a difficult section of an otherwise plain path. Rather, you have to count the trail as defunct and regard the trip as a problem in cross-country routefinding. Bear in mind that the original trailbuilders may have taken the most logical line through the land-

scape; it may be worthwhile continuing on that line
even if the trail refuses to reappear.

What if you do get lost?

What *is* getting lost, anyway?

If you lose the trail in the undergrowth; if you
hesitate at a junction; if you see a landmark you
don't recognize; then you aren't lost. You're disoriented merely, and though disorientation can be the
beginning of "lost," it is not the thing itself.

You are lost when you do not know how to retrace your steps to a place where you feel sure of
your bearings. But perhaps even more than a situation, being lost is a state of mind: panic.

If you find yourself disoriented, whether you are
"lost" yet or not, sit down. Get out map and compass. Think back on where you have been in the last
hour. Think back to the last point at which you were
sure of your position. Scan the landscape for features you can reason from. Consider the lay of the
land—are you, for instance, in a valley that drains
in a certain direction? If you find yourself initially
too worried to think, start by making this a rest
stop. Eat something, take a picture, have some lemonade.

Most of the time you should be able to reconstruct where you are, or at least how to get back to
known ground. After all, a pedestrian moves only so
fast. You won't be two counties away.

And if you can't reconstruct? Sometimes, especially on flat terrain, it is appropriate to walk a
search pattern, a sort of rectilinear spiral spreading
from your starting point. This can be useful if you
are looking for something—say a trail—that is probably nearby. One caution, though: never lay down
your pack or daypack while you search. You might
not find it again, and this could turn a minor problem into a major one.

If you get lost on a side trip, away from your
party, try to make contact with the rest of your
group. Shout, blow your whistle, flash your mirror.
Three signals of any kind is a distress signal; two

signals of any kind indicates response—"We read you." Or you can light a smoky fire. (Distress or not, be careful where and how you light it. In at least one wildfire-prone area, the use of signal fires in summer and fall is explicitly forbidden.)

If none of this works, about all you can do is make yourself comfortable, keep signaling from time to time, and stay put until searchers turn up. Eventually your friends will report you missing, or an alarm will be sounded when you fail to return at an appointed time.

The first priority is *warmth and shelter.* If you are on an exposed, windy ridge in chilly country, you may have to get off it. Leave something there, though, to attract attention, like a bright cloth or a circle of stones. And don't just blunder away from the starting point. You can't afford to get still further lost. Rather, move away on a definite compass bearing. If you are hiking alone, you may have a whole packful of equipment on your back, in which case you can make yourself cozy. If you are on a side trip, you should at least have your ten essentials. If you need to cut boughs for shelter, this is justifiable in a genuine emergency.

The second priority (under some circumstances the first) is *water.* Food can wait.

As time passes, keep thinking about the land and your position in it. You may sort it out yet. But don't shift position unless you are quite sure of what you are doing. (If you do move, leave a note.) Be cautious in following such traditional advice as "Follow water downhill." It all depends on what water and what hill. Sometimes, as in the Southwest, a downhill grade leads not out of wilderness but deeper into it.

Continue signaling. Nothing attracts the interest of the authorities so quickly as smoke. Don't try to send up puffs in threes: just make sure the smoke is plentiful. (This is one situation in which there is an excuse for putting green wood or foliage on a fire.)

To repeat, however: in summer backpacking, and in our modern wilderness areas, so small and so well mapped, nothing should be easier than staying out of this kind of trouble. And in fact it is fairly rare for well-equipped backpackers, traversing the deep backcountry, to lose their way. Casual hikers, wandering away from their cars without maps, are much more at risk. If you know what you are doing, and walk with a mind aware, the land should have no unpleasant surprises for you.

Making and Managing the Camp

It is legitimate to hope that there may be left . . . the special kind of human mark, the special record of human passage, that distinguishes man from all other species. It is rare enough among men, impossible to any other form of life. It is simply the deliberate and chosen refusal to make any marks at all.

—Wallace Stegner

17:
Making Camp

Low-impact travel means many things. But among them, one is paramount: the proper making, managing, and breaking of the wilderness camp.

It is hardly surprising that the agencies responsible for our wilderness are particularly concerned with camping habits. In fact, of the guidelines they set, most have to do with campsites and camping practices. That's something of a pity. You'd prefer not to have the feeling of someone looking over your shoulder, in thought at least, when you stop for the night. But until wilderness travelers reeducate themselves to the needs of a new time, the rules can hardly be spared. When you're confronted with them, examine them; ask questions and learn from them.

Regulations are not uniform across the country. Different regions have different problems; different experts have different ideas to propose. Sometimes the managers seek to concentrate use in a few areas, leaving the rest untouched; sometimes the plan is to disperse campers widely, and this viewpoint seems to be gaining. In many areas there is a double standard. While campers who build fires must stay at designated sites, those with stoves face no such restrictions. Sometimes particular areas may be closed, not only to fires, but to any camping, all the time or at given times of year, for various good reasons (wildfire danger is one; the welfare of wildlife is another). Details of local provisions are generally printed on the back of wilderness permits.

In what follows I speak as if these regulations did not exist, as if nothing affected your choice of site but sensitive common sense. This does not mean, of course, that official advice is to be ignored; on the contrary, I hope and assume that you will follow it. Don't be put off by the way the rules change from place to place. The agency people, like conscientious hikers, are feeling their way in a complex and many-sided matter.

Choosing the low-impact camp

Where then *should* you camp? What standards can you go by—not only for low impact on the land, but for comfort and convenience as well?

We need to begin with an important distinction. There are two very different sorts of camping spots in the wilderness. First is the pristine site: the random piece of unmarked ground that, for a certain time, you make your own. If you camp in such a place, you take onto yourself a considerable responsibility. It is your job to leave that land exactly as you found it: still unscarred, still unfrayed, recognizable to no one as a place that has been used. Some sites are much more vulnerable to scarring than others, and these the low-impact camper must be at pains to avoid.

In contrast, campsites of the second type are clearly marked as areas of use. They have worn paths, fire rings, bare ground, perhaps even terraced tentpads cut from a hill. Logs and stones may have been shifted to make tables and seats. Such camps, if you find them vacant, can be both convenient and charming. And from the point of view of low impact, they have a telling advantage: they are already barren. It is relatively hard to injure them further. The price has already been paid.

It might seem that you could make very sure of doing no harm to the land by restricting yourself to sites already marked. Actually, that's only true if the developed site is in the proper place to begin with. In many open alpine landscapes you find many more firespots and tentpads than anyone needs; the same may be true along popular forest trails. Many of these excess sites, built at random by the uninformed, could not have been worse chosen if the makers had drawn up a plan for maximum impact, maximum ugliness, maximum disturbance to wildlife and land. These scars should be allowed to heal. The low-impact camper will avoid them and choose, from established campsites, the ones that are best justified upon the land.

Now the criteria:

Flatness

Surely this is the first requirement of all. A fairly level site is important, and not for comfort only; steep ground, if it is anything but solid rock, is easily disturbed and easily eroded. In steep, forested mountains, almost the only viable campsites may be artificial flats scooped from the unbroken slopes.

Surface

This is *highly* important. The best kind of ground to camp on is forest duff without vegetation; the second best is bare ground: sand, gravel, rock, rocky soil, or an area already worn bare by human traffic. Avoid damp ground and don't camp on vegetation when it can possibly be helped.

Look at almost any catalog of backpacking equipment. Chances are you'll see bright tents and sleeping bags spread out on backgrounds of green glossy meadow and windswept alpine tundra. You can't blame the photographers for composing these elegant scenes, but you can blame the equipment dealers for exploiting them. Beginning backpackers take the implied advice and camp where they should not. Meadows and tundra are the places, above all others, where camps must *not* be sited.

Plants at timberline and above live at the edge of survival. A few inches of stem and leaf may take a decade to form; a trampled heath may keep the scars for a lifetime. If you camp among the treeless peaks, find barren ground or snow. Otherwise, make your place in the woodlands below, where life has a little more margin.

Moist grasslands, especially those at higher elevations, are especially vulnerable. Trampling, the pounding in of stakes, even the weight of a sleeper (because it compacts the water-saturated soil) do them harm. Moreover, such meadows as campsites are anything but ideal. They are cooler than the surrounding uplands, mosquito-ridden, damp, lacking in privacy. Grassy ground is not even particularly soft!

The drier grasslands of high western ranges—"shorthair meadows"—are somewhat less sensitive. They can take a fair amount of pounding before damage begins to show. Unfortunately, these meadows are among the slowest plant communities to recover once damage is done.

Water supply

Few people find much charm in a camp without water somewhere. (It isn't absolutely essential, however: you can fill your containers at a handy stream in the afternoon; then make your evening stop with no need for a local supply.)

Distance from stream, lake, and trail

Land management agencies commonly make it a requirement that you camp a given distance away from streamsides, lakeshores, and trails. One hundred and two hundred feet are commonly specified setbacks.

The reasoning behind these rules is easy to grasp. Campers do tend to cluster needlessly close to water and to trails. Scarring is one result; crowding, another.

Yet I must admit to heretical thinking on this point. The camper who chooses the dispersed style may have little trouble obeying the rules; but how about the majority of backpackers who prefer to use established sites? In not a few wilderness areas, virtually all existing sites violate the letter of the law, and many of these are unobjectionable in every other respect. It is sometimes less damaging to use one of these sites than to establish a new spot on previously pristine ground. If *everyone* dispersed into the woods, the result would be more impact, not less.

Nonetheless, do your best to stay legal. If you want an established site, choose whatever available spot best fits the model. If, on the other hand, you are camping in the dispersed style (which requires fanatical attention to low-impact matters), better try to go *more* than one or two hundred feet from the trail or lake or stream. In the lake basins of western ranges, search for sites behind low trees on the hillsides, some distance back from the water. Often you will find little terraces of twiggy soil, just the right size for a small party.

Wildlife

Try to avoid disturbing the local wildlife. In arid areas, where isolated springs are vital to wild animals, you can disrupt a whole web of natural patterns by settling down near the local waterhole.

Ecotone is the ecologist's word for a place where two environments come together: the line where forest adjoins meadow, or where meadow comes down to water, or even a juncture of low brush and tall timber. These border zones are of special importance to wildlife. In them you find the species of each of the two habitats and still other species native to the ecotone itself. So campers who want to disturb the natural order as little as possible will do their best to avoid such sites as the forest edge, the streambank, the lakeshore. This may take some self-restraint, for ecotones, by their nature, are pretty places.

Privacy

Consider your own and others'. Researchers find that many backpackers prefer an uncomfortable but solitary camp to an ideal spot with neighbors. Even if you don't feel that way yourself, it's courteous to assume that others will. (Backpacking parties that meet in camp or on the trail tend to greet each other cordially, chat a moment, and then, as soon as politely possible, withdraw.) Try to stay out of earshot of the next camp. Remember, sound carries readily across lakes and meadows, less so through trees.

Safety

Be aware of possible hazards: snags or branches that might break in the wind, cliffs from which stones might fall, and, in the winter, avalanche paths. In the desert, during the thunderstorm season, be careful not to camp in dry washes; arid though they seem, a flash flood can turn them into rivers deeper than your tent is high. In bear country (and that means, above all, on wooded trails in the national parks), you should look for a proper tree to hang your food from at night. It's just as well not to drop your gear in the middle of a game trail—why draw the attention of the bears and other animal raiders? For more on the special precautions needed in grizzly territory, see Chapter 27.

Local climate

Cool air settles at night in basins; night breezes move downslope along ravines. A hillside flat or the top of a knoll may be as much as fifteen degrees warmer than lower ground. Whether you want more warmth or less, you can take advantage of these variations. Consider also the wind; you may want to escape it or use it to blow away mosquitoes. If you are hoping for an early start, a site with an eastern exposure, bringing early sun, will help.

Luxuries

If you are planning to stay in one place for several nights, you'll be somewhat choosier about the site. Now you consider the overwhelming view, the nearby swimming hole, the peaks to climb, the valleys to explore. But it is also important that you find a specially impact-free site for such an extended stay; vulnerable areas, if they must be used, should not be used long at a stretch.

Setting up the low-impact camp

When to make camp is a matter of taste—and of haste. In good weather there is nothing specially unpleasant about making camp at dusk or later, but when conditions are bad, flashlight camping may be highly uncomfortable. And an early stop gives you time for good cooking, for relaxation, perhaps for a side trip or a few minutes with a camera or a natural history guide.

If you carry a stove and water, and merely need a spot to pass the night before you press on, you can throw down your gear nearly anywhere that darkness finds you. (These brief, utilitarian camps, while perhaps not very memorable, are pleasant for their simplicity, and they impact the land very little.) If you depend on wood fires, nearby water, or both, your choice of site will be narrower. If there is some distance between suitable camps, you may have to stop somewhat earlier—or later—than you might like.

There are four essential elements to even the simplest camp. There is the *kitchen*, perhaps nothing more than a stove sitting on a boulder. There is the *water source*. There is the *sleeping area*. And there is the *toilet area* or latrine.

A small group, especially at a little-used camp, needn't specify a toilet area, so long as everyone resolves to go well away from camp, trail, and water, and uses normal care. But in a large group, it is well to select an area in advance, choosing ground that no later party is likely to pick for kitchen or bed sites. If a latrine is to be dug (done only by large groups and not always by them) it should be set up first thing, not as an afterthought.

The kitchen area must be on bare ground where trampling does no harm (this spot will get more traffic than any other part of camp). Then there's fire safety to consider (even a stove must not sit on twiggy duff!).

Normally, kitchen and bed are fairly close together, but campers in the northern Rockies, and in Alaska and Canada, learn to set up their food department at some remove from the rest of their gear. The reason is the magnificent but sometimes unpredictable grizzly bear. If a bear raids a somewhat isolated kitchen spot, it may not occur to it to rummage through the rest of the camp as well.

When you camp at a well-marked site, you try to make most use of the ground that is already bare, already stamped by human presence; a little more traffic won't alter it further. When paths and pads are there, use them. But avoid doing anything to extend the barren area. If you are at a pristine site, most especially if there is vegetation underfoot, the strategy changes. You try to avoid repeated traffic over any one piece of ground. In moving between kitchen and spring, or tent and toilet area, take a slightly different route each time, and try to walk on duff, rocks, and mineral soils. Try not to mill around too much in one place, as at the entrance of the tent or in the cooking area. If you go barefoot, or in soft camp shoes, your tread will compact the ground less. Compaction, breaking down the loose texture of the soil, stops the natural passages for air and water; the effect is almost as if the earth had been made sterile.

Engineering has no place in the design of your camp. The perfect site is found, not made. Spend your time finding the right piece of ground, not reshaping the wrong one. Don't clear brush, drive nails, build cupboards, or move any more logs and stones than is absolutely necessary. However hard you try, it is never possible to restore such objects so perfectly that the natural effect is completely regained.

What happens first when you get into camp? In the rain, or late in the day, raising the shelter has to be the first job. Otherwise, cooking often takes first place. The weather, the time of day, the number of people, the site, and personal preference decide. A large group may have to organize itself to get things done; in a smaller party, there's nothing so formal about it.

The pleasure of wilderness camping

Of necessity this chapter has contained a lot of "don'ts." Because good wilderness practices so often go against the pull of habit, it may take a little conscious effort to adopt them.

But soon enough new methods, like the old, are automatic. And you are free to enjoy each campsite you find for yourself—the smells and sounds of it, the views (short or long), the quality of its light, the taste of its water. Every campsite, when you come onto it, seems strange and even a little unwelcoming (why just here and not a mile farther on?). Every campsite, once you have eaten and slept there, becomes a known place and a comfortable one. Your camps, after all, are the spots in the wilderness of which you have special knowledge; it is your campsites that you particularly remember.

The low-impact game has added to the pleasure of wilderness camping a new, keen edge. To blunder through a landscape, never guessing that you could damage it, or that you have done so, is one thing. It is quite something else to know that you might have harmed a place and that you did not; to know that your skill and knowledge were great enough to let you use the wilderness without consuming it.

18:
Shelter and Bed

SETTING UP BEDS is exceedingly simple if the weather is fair and likely to remain so, and if the mosquitoes permit you to stay outside. Sleeping roofless, under the big, brilliant dark, is a real wilderness luxury. Without a shelter, party members can scatter, each to a separate spot of level ground; this tends to lessen impact. If you're uncertain about weather, you always have the option of setting up shelter but starting the night in a bed outside.

As for the campsite in general, so for the bed: high ground is warmer. Cold air sinks and gathers in chilly pools. Watch out for draws and hollows that might gather water in a sudden rain. If there is considerable humidity, a bed under the open sky will be coated in the morning with frost or dew; condensation will be less under the trees. A sheltered site will also be somewhat warmer.

The most comfortable sleeping surface is fine

forest duff; sand is also good, if you smooth and
shape it in advance. Grassy ground is rather hard. A
bed site should be flat, but not necessarily table
flat—lie down on it first and judge for yourself.
Then smooth and police the ground, removing sticks
and stones; the less leveling you have to do, the better. If you find a place with a natural hollow for
your hip, or if you can scoop one in sand or duff,
that's fine. The digging of hip-holes in hard ground
is no longer recommended. Spread your groundsheet—dirty side down—and mattress or pad.

Should you unpack your sleeping bag immediately, or leave it in the stuffbag? If the air is not
humid, it's good to let the bag expand as long as
possible. Down, particularly, takes quite a while to
regain its full loft. But on a cool, damp evening, the
bag may start getting clammy as soon as you expose it to the air; in this case, you're better off leaving it stuffed until you can get inside it. When you
unpack a down bag, shake it out gently to fluff the
fill.

Pitching shelter

If you are pitching shelter, you may need to take
some time locating the right spot: bare ground, as
level as possible, and, of course, well drained. With
a tarp or a flimsy tent, you may have to seek a
wind-sheltered spot; with a good tent, level ground
is more important than natural wind protection. But
if there is a chance of a considerable breeze, make
sure you have room to pitch the tent parallel to it,
rather than crosswise.

Consider anchors. With a tube tent, you ideally
need a pair of straight trees about fifteen feet apart.
For a regular tent you want ground firm enough to
hold any stakes you use but soft enough to drive
them into. Look also for rocks, trunks, and sound
snags to which you can tie guylines. A boulder or
big log may serve as one wall for a shelter made
with a tarp. A walking stick, if you use one, can
also be useful as a supporting pole.

Don't engineer the site, beyond removing rocks

and sticks, unless you are working with something loose like leaf mold, snow, or sand. Don't dig ditches in solid ground to carry off water; you don't need them, and they make all-but-permanent scars. If you are pitching a tent on stony or twiggy ground, you can save wear and tear on the waterproof tentfloor by spreading a groundsheet under it.

Tents are different from one another, but pitching methods don't vary that much. You almost always begin by staking down the principal corners of the floor. (It doesn't matter which way the entrance faces relative to wind; if the ground slopes, you probably want your head uphill.) With some designs the staking of the floor is not essential, but it is hard to finish the job cleanly if the floor is not taut and neat, and the corners must invariably be staked in wind. You may on occasion be able to replace stakes with short lengths of cord tied to stones. Winter tents often have snowflaps around the base on which stones or snow can be placed for the solidest possible mooring.

The second step, with most tents, is to insert sectioned poles into sleeves sewn to the tent canopy. Some models will stand up by themselves after this is done. With others—including the familiar rectangular A-frame and tunnel models—there follows a third step. Pulling firmly on the guylines attached to each end of the tent, you attach these firmly to stakes or other anchors. (It takes two people to do this right.) The final action is to extend additional guylines called pullouts. These are not part of the basic support, but they draw the walls out tautly, help the tent shed wind, and make it roomier inside.

When you can, it is better to use anchors other than stakes. However, no method is entirely free of impact on the land. In Rocky Mountain National Park, the managers now *urge* campers to use stakes; so many cords have been tied around timberline trees that trees are being killed by girdling! Here, not for the last time, we see how hard it is to set firm rules for the low-impact camp. What spares the land in one place may harm it in another.

Tautline hitch

Guylines tend to grow slack after they have been set. It's useful to set them up to be adjusted without moving the anchors. To do this, pass the line through the loop or grommet where it joins the tent; then double it back and tie it to itself, using one of several knots that will grip under tension but slide when you loosen the strands. The commonest is the *tautline hitch.* Adjustable loops can also be tied where the lines attach to their ground anchors, but often there is too much friction at the anchor end. Commercial gripping devices are sold to do the same job.

The tentfly, pitched over the basic tent and supported by the same poles, has guylines of its own. These are commonly tied either to the tent's anchors or to the tent's guylines a little above the anchors, using sliding knots for easy adjustment.

Below timberline you may be able to pitch a tent without poles, using overhead lines to hold it up and more or less in the intended shape. But if you are in an area where this is possible, you may not need a full tent anyway but only a tarp or tentless rainfly.

Pitching a tarp is both simpler and more tricky than setting up a tent because there are so many possible variations. You can arrange the tarp like a typical A-frame, with a long ridgeline and sloping sides; like a lean-to, with one side high and one close to the ground; or even like a pagoda, with the center raised. Your choice depends most of all on the natural anchor points you find. Most tarps come with stout grommets built in at several points along the sides. Some have tie-on cords as well. If you need an attachment where none is provided—like the middle of the sheet—you can make one by wrapping a small, round pebble in the fabric and tying it off with a noose of cord. There are also commercial devices for this purpose. If your tarp is a light one (especially if it's a plastic sheet), you'd do well not to put too much stress on any one part. For instance, run a line under the entire ridgeline rather than attaching a short line at each end and letting the sheet pull taut between them.

A tube tent would seem to offer the easiest pitching job of all: just run a line through the plastic tunnel and string it between two trees. Actually, there are not all that many perfect pairs of trees with flat, open ground between them. You may have to

Line attachment using pebble and noose

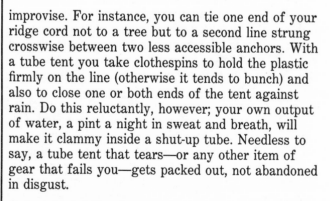

improvise. For instance, you can tie one end of your ridge cord not to a tree but to a second line strung crosswise between two less accessible anchors. With a tube tent you take clothespins to hold the plastic firmly on the line (otherwise it tends to bunch) and also to close one or both ends of the tent against rain. Do this reluctantly, however; your own output of water, a pint a night in sweat and breath, will make it clammy inside a shut-up tube. Needless to say, a tube tent that tears—or any other item of gear that fails you—gets packed out, not abandoned in disgust.

A good night's sleep

Nothing should be more automatic than a restful night in the wilderness. The harder you have worked during the day, the more luxurious the warmth and softness of the sleeping bag become;

the colder it is in the world outside, the lovelier the contrast feels.

If you've been accustomed to soft beds, however, you may find it odd and even uncomfortable at first to sleep on a thin foam pad. This is one excellent reason for beginning with an air mattress, despite the extra weight. Rolled up clothing will generally do for a pillow.

If you don't use a sleeping bag liner with a down bag, it's a good idea to wear a layer of clothing to bed. Body oils gum up the fluffy down, even if you keep fastidiously clean; the cure, washing the bag, destroys some of the all-important resiliency of down. Wear a stocking cap, or put a shirt under your head, to protect the bag from oils in your hair. (Bags filled with Polar Guard or Quallofil, however, aren't damaged either by dirt or by washing.) It's handy to leave your boots by your head, with such small objects in them as you'll want during the night or first thing in the morning. Turn them sideways if you're sleeping outdoors in the dew.

Cold and other problems

If you've planned well, you shouldn't find yourself in a sleeping bag too cool for the region you are visiting. But maybe you're testing the limits of a summer bag in winter, spring, or fall. If you do find yourself getting chilly at night, there are various things you can do about it; some have been mentioned already.

● Move under cover. Lying in the open, you radiate extra heat to the sky. Even the branches of a tree will cut that loss somewhat. And protect yourself from any chilling breeze; for instance, you can put your head downwind so that cold air won't enter the open end of your bag. A tent, protecting you in several ways, can add ten or fifteen degrees of warmth.

● Speed up your own metabolism. Take a brisk walk or get some other exercise before you crawl in. (Some people do isometrics in the bag.) If you feel warm when you lie down, your body will heat the

bag quickly and give you a good start. Don't linger
outside getting chilled. When you're cold, it's good
to eat some last thing at night, preferably protein
(the best fuel for warmth when you aren't exercising).

● But the main thing to do against cold is more
obvious: wear more clothes to bed. The single most
useful item is a head cap; the head loses more heat
than any other part of the body. Dry socks are also
important. Then come pants, shirt, sweater, mittens,
possibly a jacket—even, if required, your raingear—
until your whole wardrobe is on. Or, instead of
wearing it all, you can stuff some items into your
sleeping bag, especially at your feet, to stop air motion and add insulation.

● It may also help to add to the insulation beneath you. A wind parka, a rope, the emptied pack
itself—almost anything will help.

● If you get seriously cold, you can try sticking
your hands and feet in waterproof bags: moisture
won't escape, but neither will the considerable
warmth that is carried off with it.

If none of these ideas works, you are probably
badly underequipped for the trip you're taking. If
it's any comfort, you can lay plans for next time:
perhaps a longer, thicker foam pad, or a second pad
. . . more clothing . . . a bag cover or an inner bag
. . . even a pair of down- or polyester-filled booties
for your feet.

Whenever the wilderness world is both cold and
wet—in winter camping especially—keeping dry is
an important part of keeping warm. Sleeping gear
always gets damp at night. While synthetic bags
will keep on warming you, no matter how wet they
get, down bags will not, so you have to fight any
buildup of moisture. If the weather allows, you can
dry a bag by hanging it on a ski, a snow-free
branch, or over your pack as you walk. Where moisture is a problem, don't attempt to dry damp clothing by taking it into the sleeping bag with you.

If you should ever feel that you are dangerously
chilled, don't hesitate to say so. There is a quick

remedy: strip and get into a warm sleeping bag with a companion. (People can survive in desperate situations by pooling body heat.) Hot drinks also help; alcohol, when you're cold, only does harm. If you recognize in yourself the symptoms of what is called *hypothermia*, it's a true emergency (see Chapter 28).

But a wilderness night need not be cold to be uncomfortable. There's also the balmy night with mosquitoes; it's so warm that you can't escape them by shutting yourself up in your sleeping bag. To stop mosquitoes, you need a netted tent, or a separate piece of netting to put over your head. Repellent can prevent most of the bites, but it won't spare you the sense of being under siege. In desperation, lacking a net, you can breathe through a sweater.

19:
Fire and Food

COOKING ON A PORTABLE STOVE is, at its easiest, almost like cooking on a range at home. Yet the use of stoves, like the use of open fires, is not entirely without its problems, even its risks. Statistically slight and easily avoidable, these risks are real nonetheless. The use of a stove requires no less care and common sense than the building of a fire.

Let's start with the procedures used with white gas stoves; then turn to the somewhat different drills for kerosene and butane models. (For more about the kinds of stoves and their anatomy, see Chapter 9.)

Running a white gas stove

In operating a white gas stove there are two possible hazards to understand and avoid.

First, white gas must not be spilled near flame. White gas ignites easily and burns fiercely. Probably three-quarters of all stove accidents result from spillage of fuel.

Second, the fuel tank must not be allowed to overheat. For the stove to run properly, the fuel tank must be warm, even moderately hot, but if it grows too hot to touch, vapor pressure inside will build to dangerous levels. Should the pressure become extreme, it will force open a spring-loaded safety valve in the tank lid and send a stream of vapor into the air. This stream is more than likely to catch fire from the burner, turning your stove into something like a blowtorch. (So why do they call it a "safety valve"? Because, without it, the stove could eventually explode; a blowtorch is much easier to handle than a bomb.)

Let me repeat that normal and careful use is enough to prevent such problems. The instructions given here are cautious in the extreme and should just about remove the chance of trouble.

First, pick your site: a level wind-sheltered spot out of the line of traffic (so that nothing gets knocked over). Just set the stove on the spot. Never dig a hole for it, or bury it, or build up a hearth of stones around it—all these things will trap too much heat around the fuel tank. The stove should be some distance from any other flame, from the rest of your gear, and from burnable underbrush. The cap of the tank, with its safety release valve, should be pointed away from flammable objects. If your stove is the type that has a separate tank mounted behind a heat shield, make sure that the shield is clean and shiny, and that is has not been knocked out of alignment (there should be an air space between shield and tank). Consider wind shelter: a really good wind-screen will protect the flame in any reasonable breeze, but not all screens do the job as well as they might. If you are camping on snow, you'll need to place the stove on a scrap of foam pad or wood, with a pan lid or a piece of light metal between stove and the insulation.

Second, before each use of the stove, fill the tank. Don't overdo it; a small air space should remain. In moving the gas from storage bottle to tank, use a funnel or a pouring cap. If you spill

fuel, wipe it up and let the residue evaporate (it will
do so quickly). If your spill has soaked into the
ground beneath the stove, better shift the operation.

This is a good point in the routine to clean the
orifice where the fuel jet issues. Some stoves come
with separate cleaning needles that you insert by
hand; on others you operate a built-in needle by
turning the fuel-flow valve control to "clean" and
back again.

The third step is *priming*. When a stove is running, its own heat vaporizes the liquid fuel as it
rises from the tank—a self-sustaining process. But
in order to get the stove started, you have to apply
heat to the vaporizing tube beneath the burner. You
simply burn something—anything—in a little priming cup that is built in around the base of the vaporizing tube.

What fuel do you use? How to get it into the
priming cup? There are various answers; indeed a
whole Minor Arcanum has grown up around the
simple operation of priming.

It's traditional to make the stove cough up some
of its own fuel into the priming cup. One method:
open the fuel-flow valve; then warm the tank with
your hands and your breath until the warmed, expanding fuel rises into the priming cup. Another
method: leave the stove in the hot sun till the fuel
expands; then open the valve and let it flow. There
are other variations. On stoves with pumps there's
no need to warm the tank. You build up pressure inside it with a few strokes of the plunger.

It's not so traditional, but often convenient, to
put the priming fuel into the cup yourself. In that
case you use any burnable substance you like: white
gas, drawn from the stove tank (or a fuel bottle)
with an eyedropper; alcohol from a squeeze bottle;
bits of mashed solid fuel pellet; or toilet paper.

How much priming fire do you need? Under good
conditions a single eyedropperful of white gas, or
the equivalent, may do it. But any amount is okay
as long as you don't overflow the cup with liquid
fuel (if you do, wipe up the spill). Some bizarre

stove accidents have occurred when people drenched their stoves with several cups of fuel. They were surprised that the tanks overheated enough, in the resulting bonfires, to blow the safety valves!

Before you put a match to the priming fuel, make sure that the tank cap is screwed on firmly; that the fuel-flow valve is shut off; and that all containers of liquid fuel are capped and set well away from the stove.

Then light. If you have primed generously with white gas, the flame may rise quite high before it fades; this is normal. By the time your priming dose has been consumed, the vaporizing tube should be hot enough to do its job, and the fuel tank should be warm enough so that vapor pressure within will keep fuel flowing upward toward the flame.

The fourth step is the actual ignition. Just as the priming flame fades, open the valve to admit fuel from the tank; it should catch smoothly, powerfully, and without any flare. (Sometimes, however, especially in cold, windy weather, you will have to prime more than once.) Many stoves have metal valve keys; these must be removed from the valve while the stove is running, or they will grow too hot to touch.

Several stoves, notably the popular Coleman Peak 1, are supposed to start up without priming. And will—under perfect conditions. In the field, though, it seems better to prime them, using a solid fuel paste.

Stay with the stove as the meal cooks, just as you would stay by a campfire. With pump stoves you'll need to push the plunger a few times every now and then. Keep an eye on the temperature of the fuel tank. If you find it getting too hot to touch, better shut down the stove and see what you can do to increase ventilation. Pay special attention to this problem if you have an improvised windscreen that encloses the tank or a broad pot or frying pan overhanging it.

Wind makes problems for many stoves. A good screen can make all the difference. Be sure that the breeze is not pushing the flame around the fuel tank. Well-fitting lids will keep the wind from stealing heat and lengthening cooking time.

If your stove should spit and sputter when first lit, that's no cause for alarm. If it keeps acting oddly, however, turn it off and check it over. Has the tank gotten overhot? Are there any fuel leaks in the line between tank and burner? If the stove continues to give you trouble after you relight it, it's prudent to switch to a campfire or eat cold.

Even the smallest tank of fuel will last through one meal, maybe two, except in a winter camp where quantities of snow must be melted. If you run out of fuel in the middle of a meal, don't refill without first letting the burner grow cool enough to touch. Fuel spilled on hot metal can ignite. Do not, of course, remove the tank cap while the stove is running, to check the fuel level.

If, improbably enough, your stove should overheat and suffer a tank blowout, try to shut down the fuel flow to the burner and direct the spout away from anything burnable. Then all you can do is wait for the fireworks to stop (they will when the tank runs dry). The valve in the tank cap should close itself automatically, but reportedly valves sometimes fail to reseal perfectly; it's good to replace the cap with a spare from your repair kit.

After this catalog of possible problems, one more thing should be said. Most of the time white gas stoves, and stoves in general, work simply, swiftly, and very well indeed.

Kerosene

Most of what has been said applies to kerosene stoves (and to multifuel stoves burning kerosene). The priming routine changes somewhat, however. Most people prefer not to use kerosene as the priming fuel—it burns sluggishly and somewhat messily—and instead burn alcohol, white gas, or solid fuel. Just before the priming flame begins to fail, pump a small amount of air into the fuel tank and open the valve slightly. This sends a little fuel up through the hot vaporizing tube to the burner, where it should ignite. Then, when the priming flame dies out, pump vigorously. You should now be in business. If you get a yellow, smoky flame, you need to prime a second time.

The Optimus oo, alone among kerosene stoves, lacks any valve to control the flow of fuel; instead, you increase flow by pumping up pressure in the tank and reduce it by releasing pressure through a manual vent in the tank cap.

Kerosene is a much less volatile fuel than white gas. Nonetheless, it can ignite if spilled: an unpleasant bonfire is still a possibility. A tank blowout is not a potential hazard with kerosene.

Butane cartridge stoves

In warm summer weather, butane stoves are utterly simple to light; there's no priming or pumping, just the touch of a match.

Great care is needed, though, when you refuel. There's no liquid fuel to fuss with; instead, you remove a spent cartridge and install a full one. Follow directions scrupulously. Some cartridges must be held carefully upright. Some can be removed between uses; others, once attached, must be left until empty. Some stoves use cartridges that screw on; others plug in. With screw-on cartridges, be careful not to strip threads. Especially with the screw types, a little fuel may spray out at the moment of connection. If you hear a continuing hiss when you've completed the linkage, check the fuel line for a loose connection and the cartridge for a possible leak; even the tiniest leak will make the surface feel frosty. If you can't stop the hiss, try another cartridge. Manufacturing defects are not unknown. All in all, refueling is a good operation to handle away from tent and gear.

To light a butane stove, hold a match to the burner; then, and only then, open the valve to let the gas stream out. Cartridges which do not contain wicks—vapor-feed models—yield a smoother flow at first and light more readily than the liquid-feed types with wicks. All butane cartridges have a tendency to flare and fade erratically when first lit; the colder it is, the worse the problem. Liquid-feed cartridges, though they work at much lower temperatures than the vapor-feed type, flare badly at the lower end of their range.

In cold weather you may have to warm your cartridge before you light the stove; one method is to take it into your sleeping bag or hold it under your jacket. A cartridge should never be shaken.

Butane, like white gas, is a volatile, highly flammable fuel. Cartridges, like the tanks of gas stoves, must not be allowed to overheat. They don't have reclosable safety valves but some are equipped with wax plugs that melt out at a certain temperature. The effect, if the plug lets go, is the same as with gasoline: a spray of vapor that will probably catch fire. A cartridge should always remain cool enough to hold in your hand. Some stoves link burner and cartridge with a flexible hose; watch that neither hose nor cartridge rests too close to the flame. And never pile rocks around a cartridge, as for instance to steady a pot on the burner.

Some hikers report that partially used cartridges of the detachable sort can leak in the pack; they suggest putting tape across the orifice. Don't discard a cartridge until you have burned it dry; even then, never toss it into a fire (enough gas may be left to cause a sharp explosion). Needless to say, you pack your empties out of the wilderness with you.

Cooking in a tent

Cooking inside a tent is never free of risk. There are times, especially in winter storms, when you may not have much choice, but you shouldn't do it by preference. (If you have to do it a lot, consider a kerosene stove.)

When you light a stove in a tent, make sure the burner isn't too close to a tent wall. Tent fabrics don't exactly burn, but they do melt. If you prime with liquid fuel, watch out for any high flare of the priming flame; have a pan lid ready to interpose between the flame and your tent canopy. If fuel spills, wipe it up, let it evaporate, and air the tent before you strike your next match. All fuels are bad for the waterproofing compounds on tent floors, by the way.

Stoves put out carbon monoxide, a poison. Make sure that ventilation is good. Leave your vents open, and unzip the upper part of your door. Symptoms of monoxide poisoning are dizziness, nausea, and headache. It would be hard to get a dangerous dose in a tent at low altitudes, but in the high country the chemistry of respiration alters, and the peril becomes very real—doubly so since altitude sickness may be blamed when the symptoms appear.

Fire

Campfires these days are not popular with wilderness conservationists, nor with wilderness managers. The impact of fires on the land—so many people have come to feel—is simply unacceptable: not because any single fire does much harm, but because so many campers are lighting so many. One fire ring may be welcoming, but twenty are obtrusive, and two hundred in a single camping area constitute a plague. The trampling caused by wood foraging in popular areas is itself significant, and if the wrong sorts of fuels are selected, extra damage is done.

But in this, as in so many impact questions, there's no substitute for common sense. A fire in an old ring of stones in a middle-elevation forest littered with down wood can't possibly be called an attack on the land. A similar fire built (illegally) of green wood on a peak in the crowded Catskills, or built (illegally) against a granite boulder in an unscarred alpine meadow, is an atrocity.

What makes a fire acceptable?

An abundance of appropriate wood.

An existing fire site in a good location.

And very great care.

I would urge once more that no party set out for the wilderness without a stove so that no party will be forced, or even strongly tempted, to build a fire in the wrong place at the wrong time.

Campfire or cookfire?

If the cooking fire is in disfavor, still more, in some circles, is the pleasure fire: the comfortable blaze you sit around after the meal is done. The logic is easily seen: why use wood without the excuse of cooking? Yet, if fire has a legitimate use in the wilderness, it is not, in truth, for fixing food (stove cooking is simpler) but for fun. For fun and for something a little more than fun: for relaxation . . . for sociability . . . for the odd beauty of flames . . . as a special focus (*focus:* Latin *hearth*) of a place and time you enjoy. It may well be argued that the occasional small pleasure fire, lit as a deliberate luxury, makes more sense than a succession of cooking fires lit for a dubious utility.

Siting a fire

The fact that you find a fire ring does not necessarily mean that you should use it. In 1982, Forest Service researchers counted over two hundred fire rings in a single lake basin in the Eagle Cap Wilderness of Oregon; many of them, sited on grass at the lakeshore, should not have been built and should now, if possible, be destroyed.

Keep your fires, like your camps, on bare ground well back from water. Further, there is no case to be made for fires near timberline and above it, even if they are still permitted there. Vegetation is too fragile and wood too hard to find.

Why so many fire rings? Partly, no doubt, because many people still put value on the *creation* of a camp, the carving out of a home in the wild world. But there's another reason. Established rings are often left dirty, unpleasant, full of cans, tinfoil, and organic garbage half rotted and half charred. You'll be doing a service if you choose one of these ruined rings, clean it up, use it, and leave it clean.

Make sure that your fire is not too close to the rest of your gear. Sparks burn holes in nylon tents and sleeping bags. Make sure there are no low branches overhead and no dry brush close by. If you have a choice of rings in otherwise acceptable places, you can afford to consider such things as sun (nice for cooking in the morning, sometimes too hot for cooking in the afternoon), and the direction of the wind (typically upslope during the day, down-slope after dark).

Now, fuel. If you have settled on a well-used site, the chances are good that the woods within, say, three hundred feet will be pretty well picked over. Yet it is astonishing how much fuel you will find just outside that narrow circle. Woodhunters have been lazy.

Remember when you gather wood that, to be eligible, it must meet three tests: each piece must be *dead, down* (not attached to a tree), and relatively *small.* Larger logs on the ground have special value in the ecosystem, and rooted, rotten snags are not firewood: they are habitat and hunting territory for owls, woodpeckers, and a whole community of animals small and large. Don't use wood you can't break. Axe, hatchet, and saw are no part of the wilderness tool kit today.

Operating a fire

Get together a reasonable supply of wood, in various sizes, before you begin. Then take a final look at the weather and the site. (Has the day turned windy? Will sparks get into dry underbrush?) The risk of starting a brush or forest fire is not one you want to take.

If yours will be a cooking fire, you may want to rearrange stones and place a grate or perhaps a "dingle stick" (a sort of jib, braced at one end by stones, resting on a fireside rock or log, and protruding over the fire). From this you can hang your largest pot. (If you do much campfire cooking, you may find it convenient to rig pots with bales of thin

wire attached at *three* points around the rim, so
that they do not tip when hung.) Don't cut a green
branch for a dingle stick, or a marshmallow stick, or
for any other use.

Starting a fire is both straightforward and
slightly tricky; skills that were automatic to generations of firemakers may be less familiar in the age
of stoves. Your starting point can be paper or knife-
whittled, paper-thin shavings; *fuzz sticks*, sometimes
useful, are shaved sticks with the shavings still attached. Some firemakers always lay the whole fire,
small to large, before they touch a match to it; others start with the tiniest sticks, get them burning,
and then add larger bits and pieces gradually and
carefully. If you lay the fire in advance, don't pack
the wood in overtightly; fire needs air. Don't put on
fragments of wood larger than you can reasonably
expect to burn completely to ash.

Starting a fire in the rain is no fun, but it certainly can be done. Traditionalists look for pitchy
wood, which you can find as unrotted streaks in the
decayed trunks of fallen conifers. This stuff burns
delightfully. Firestarters of some sort—fire ribbon,
fuel pellets, wax-soaked "logs" of rolled newspaper,
candles—can also be helpful when the wood is wet.
A fragment of porous wood, left to soak in a pool of
gasoline, is another firestarter. Many people simply
drench wet kindling with white gas; more often than
not, though, the fuel flares off, leaving the stubborn
wood uncharred. If it hasn't been raining long, you
may be able to whittle the damp exterior of a fragment and find dry wood at the center. But when the
wood is truly sodden, as in rain forest country, only
the experts seem to get very far. Once the fire is
burning brightly, of course, it will dry and burn
even the most sodden logs.

Whenever conditions are drier, fire is a beast
that has to be watched with the greatest care.
Never leave one burning or even smouldering
(though a low fire may be left to consume its embers on a windless night with sleepers close by).
When you break camp, of course, the fire must be

absolutely and unmistakably cold, drowned, and drowned again with water.

Fire at an unmarked site

There is rarely either reason or excuse these days for building a fire where none has been before. This is true without exception throughout the crowded wilderness lands of the East and in well-used areas of the Far West. In remote and little-visited sections, though, even this principle may be slightly bent.

Should you ever build a fire on a pristine site, you want all traces to disappear. I don't, frankly, recommend the experiment, but the techniques that make it possible are worth discussing.

First, there are certain sites to avoid. Never build a fire in deep, woody forest duff, on peat, or on humus. Never build one next to a log or tree, next to a standing rock, or on vegetation.

Instead, find mineral soil of some sort. The ideal sites are sandy or gravelly spots where any mark that is made can be simply erased. Sea beaches and river shingles, washed periodically by tide or flood, are best of all. Given any kind of loose mineral surface, you can dig a small trench for the fire; then smooth over the site with clean material. If you're building the fire on a hard surface—like rocky soil or a stone slab—you can bring sand or gravel from another place and lay a raised base for the coals. When the fire is out, you can then sweep up both ashes and sand, leaving little trace.

What about a fire on grass? If, for some reason, you *must* make one, never light it on the living surface of the ground. Rather, cut out a square of sod and set it aside. In the hole you have created, light the fire, preferably without a lining of stones. Then, when the fire is dead out, replace the sod. The same technique will work in soft ground without sod. Dig a pit. Light the fire. Let it burn dead out. Drown it. Refill the trench with the original soil. Stamp it down. Ruffle and smooth the surface. Replace natural litter.

If a fire must be made beside a standing rock, put a smaller flat rock between the fire and the boulder to take the mark. Then the flake can be put back where you found it, blackened side down.

Obviously, these techniques—you might call them slash-and-patch methods—can only work where few parties travel. Little of this sort of thing can be done, even with extreme care, before an area begins to seem subtly scuffed and scarred. Signs of use attract more use. In some places it is already hard to find a stone not darkened by a smear of soot. Long before this point is reached, it's time to switch to stove cooking, limiting fires to definite, suitable sites.

Perhaps the greatest selfish advantage of cooking with a stove is that you need spend no time wondering just what stage has been reached in the place you choose for your camp. You know that your kitchen impinges on the landscape not at all. It's not a sacrifice you're making. Rather, you are making it easy for yourself: sparing yourself a worry, cancelling out a possible cause for concern.

Garbage

All the old rules about garbage have given way to a simple, single principle: *pack it out.* The only exception, and then only if you build a fire, is material that can be readily, totally burned: paper and also plastic bags, which combust cleanly if they are fed, a little at a time, into a very hot fire. (Allow them to smoulder, though, and you get smoke, dark, rancid, and probably poisonous.) Tinfoil won't burn: it only breaks up in fire. Watch out for packages that have a foil lining inside paper. Cans, if you have any, should be flattened; then washed or seared, and carried out.

Rarely is it proper to bury anything. (Researchers have found that an alarming percentage of today's wilderness travelers still regard it as good practice to bury garbage; it isn't.) In many mountain areas soils are shallow; animals, water, and frost-heaving expose the waste; or the ground may settle, leaving an unsightly pit. Moreover, the soil in alpine areas may never get warm enough to allow much decomposition. Whenever you find yourself with a piece of litter—even a piece as small as a gum wrapper—it goes into your pocket, a plastic junk-bag, or a fire.

What if you find yourself with a lot of organic garbage to get rid of—uneaten food, or refuse left by ignorant earlier campers? Some parties still scatter food, in small amounts, for animals to take care of. In remote areas this is probably harmless, but the land agencies have begun to advise against it. On well-traveled routes it is plainly a bad idea; you are training raccoons, bears, and other animals to scavenge and make camp nuisances of themselves. Orange peels dry to a kind of leather and last a long time; they should never be scattered. Same goes for eggshells.

It isn't generally practical to dry out extra food on the fire, and then feed it to the flames; too much fuel is required. The best answer is simply to avoid overcooking. The second best, when the excess is large, is to bury the food in an out-of-the-way location.

Dishwashing

All washing should be done well away from any spring, creek, or lake. Make sure that soap is biodegradable and nondetergent. In a small group, dishwashing can be very simple, and no dishpan is required: use your largest pot. A larger group does need a dishpan. Whenever a number of people's dishes are washed together, use plenty of soap, and scald the dishes in boiling water as a last step, to prevent any sharing of illnesses. Washwater should be dumped out of the way, among brush or stones.

Protecting your food

Depending on where you are, you will have to take more or less elaborate precautions to protect your food from animal raiders.

Many animals are inclined to piracy. Small rodents like to gnaw open food packages; porcupines will gnaw at boots and sweat-soaked packstraps, as well as salty foods; deer also like salty things. Most worrisome are the raids of bears.

Oddly enough, it is in the most used, populous, and "civilized" of our wilderness areas that wild animals become most notably a problem. In such well-used regions as the High Sierra and the Blue Ridge, and in most national parks, precautions have to be elaborate.

On snow, in winter (in regions where winter is cold), and above timberline, these problems are generally less. Even in low-elevation forests off the beaten track the question is less critical. Few large animals in truly remote areas have yet learned to scavenge human supplies.

Shelters and developed campsites attract animals. If you camp at a spot that has food lockers, metal hanging posts, overhead cables, or other built-in protective devices, better take advantage of them.

It is always a good idea to keep your camp clean so that there's no food scattered around for the taking. Where small rodents are common and bears are not, you can protect open packages by putting them under pots or in pots with the lids wired on. It's not a good idea to leave food in a pack overnight: critters may gnaw right through it.

In bear country, precautions must be much more elaborate. Where there are interested bears, hang all your food in a tree at night. Nothing short of that makes any sense. (Don't just leave your loaded pack by your bed, in your tent, or under a stack of pots as bear alarms; the modern national park bear is not so easily deterred.)

To hang your food, you need two large stout stuffsacks, not less than fifty feet of cord, and the right kind of tree. Finding the last may take a while. You need a tree with a spindly branch about twenty feet up—thick enough to support the weight of your food, but too thin to support the weight of a scrambling bear. Once you have your branch, take a good length of stout cord, tie a rock to one end, and lob it over the limb at a point at least ten feet out from the trunk. Place your food in one of the stuffsacks, and tie it to the end of the line where the stone was. Now haul the load into position, fully fifteen feet above the ground.

In the old days you finished the job by simply tying the free end of the line around a tree. But the national park bear has learned that the food comes down when it gnaws the accessible cord. For more protection, use the counterbalance method. Instead of tying off, haul on the free end to raise the load up close to the branch. Now place in a second stuffsack a weight equal to the food bag and tie it to the available line, as high up as you can reach. Wrap the remaining free line around this "counterbalance" so that nothing dangles. Finally, use a long stick to nudge the counterbalance as high as you can. Counterbalance and food bag should finally be dangling side by side, fifteen feet or more above the ground, ten feet away from the nearest trunk and five feet

Bearbagging

below the supporting branch.

To get your food back, you must push the food bag still higher, thus lowering the counterbalance to within reach. (A loop tied to the counterbalance is helpful—you can snag this with your stick to pull it down. It is also possible to wrap the extra cord in such a way that you can hook that and bring it within reach.)

Though I have spoken of "food sack" and "counterbalance," it is often most practical to divide your food and put equal weights of that on both ends of the line.

In other areas, where the problem is not so great, you will have to decide for yourself each night whether the effort of bagging is worth the security. Consider the state of your supplies. If you're two days away from the end of your trip, the loss of your food might be merely an annoyance. But if your supplies must last for another week, you don't want to take chances. In such a case it makes sense to split your larder into several caches and string them up some distance apart.

What do you do if you actually find a bear investigating your suspended cache, or, worse, heading down the trail with your food bag in his jaws? If it's a grizzly, as in the northern Rockies, you'd better simply let him have it. The brown and black bears encountered elsewhere in the contiguous United States are typically more docile; shouts, flashing lights, banging pans, and whistle blasts may make such a beast retreat or drop what it has taken. If not, you're probably dealing with a professional robber; don't argue. Never try to take food away from the creature. The more accustomed the bear has become to human beings, the less manageable it will be. And keep this in mind: a sow bear with cubs, no matter the species, is a touchy and dangerous animal.

20:
Sanitation and Clean Water

TIME WAS WHEN NOBODY DREAMED OF A WILDER-
NESS being anything other than *clean*, clean beyond
the measure of any city or town. One writer ob-
served happily that wilderness dirt was "perfectly
sanitary, being rendered so by oxygen and remoteness from human habitation." Then there was the
notion that running water purified itself every two
hundred feet.

And it is undeniable that wilderness waters are
still, in general and in most places, about the clean-
est we have. But as early as 1960 you began to hear
reports of unpleasant exceptions to the rule. Waters
along the John Muir Trail in California began to be
called *polluted*. In backpacking areas all over the
country—in Idaho, in Colorado, in the White Mountains of New Hampshire—researchers began to find
unexpectedly high counts of the bacterium *E. coli*, a
harmless organism, but one that indicates contamination by the feces of warm-blooded animals. It is

no longer unheard of for mountain hikers in this country to suffer punishing bouts of diarrhea or, much more serious, to come home with hepatitis.

Just how much of this contamination comes from human beings is not clear. But you need only spend a few days in a popular hiking area to know that many people are careless. Feces left on the surface of the ground, especially anywhere near water, can pollute an astonishingly large area. Even when the amounts of waste are very small, there is risk that diseases can be transmitted.

Precautions

What can backpackers do about this? Two things. First, each must begin to use a certain amount of caution in choosing wilderness water for drinking and personal use. Second, and absolutely vital, is this: each of us must be absolutely scrupulous in disposing of body waste.

At heavily used campsites you may find chemical or pit toilets, installed by the managing agency. These will probably become rarer, however. Many managers now hold that a site where an outhouse is needed is a site that is getting unacceptable amounts of use. And parties increasingly may be discouraged from digging their own latrines.

Still, if you are traveling in a group of unusual size, say, ten people or more, and if you plan to use one spot for several days, a latrine is probably the best solution. Site it well away from trails and water. The rules often say two hundred feet; there is no good reason not to go twice as far. And be sure not to dig the pit in a place that might appeal to another party as a bed or kitchen spot.

If you know you will need a latrine (and if regulations permit one), dig it first thing. Dig it narrow and shallow. In no case should it be more than about seventeen inches deep and a foot wide. If you need more capacity, make it longer, not deeper; go farther down, and you will get below the biologically rich "disposer" layer of the soil. It is in this layer that microorganisms convert waste to fertile humus.

Only excrement and toilet paper go into a latrine; garbage must be handled otherwise, and tampons, sanitary napkins, and disposable diapers must be packed out with you. Throw in fresh soil after every use; you don't want flies circulating between kitchen and pit.

Lacking a latrine, the hiker turns to what is rather comically labeled the "individual cat method." Dig a small hole, never deeper than about six inches. When you finish, fill it in carefully with the soil you scooped out and restore the surface to its natural appearance.

Toilet paper is slower to decompose than feces; in some cases, it is a good idea to touch a match to the paper, reducing much of it to ash. In high, cold country, where natural processes are sluggish, this is highly advisable. I also like to burn TP in some especially barren desert areas, where decomposition is slow at best. But some managing agencies are now forbidding this practice, due to the danger of fire. *Never* burn paper when your cat hole is in dry forest duff, or anywhere else where fire might conceiveably result.

With cat holes as with latrines, siting is all-important. For instance, a sandy, diggable place is probably a seasonal streambed and should be avoided. The rule is to disperse. Members of a party should go in different directions to dig their holes. If you find it practical, it's good to take care of these needs during the day, when the party is between campsites; this prevents the buildup of waste in popular areas. Around some camps, late in the season, you may find so many cat holes that it is hard to locate fresh ground. This is a sign of too much use, but also indicates a certain laziness; go far enough from camp and you won't have this trouble.

When you're traveling on snow you probably won't be able to reach the soil. You can only dig your hole in snow, and, when the thaw comes, that's no hole at all. This is a troubling problem. As winter backpacking becomes more popular, the chances of serious pollution are real. There are only two things

the hiker can do. First, you can go still farther away
from water than you would in summer. Second, you
can take special care to burn your toilet paper.
(When you come back in August to look at the place
you camped in in March, you'll see the point of this.
Toilet paper lasts much better than you'd think, and
just a few flags of tissue are enough to make a
landscape look unclean.) Further, if you can't get
the paper to burn, consider packing it away in a special plastic pouch to be disposed of later. In the cold
there won't be an odor.

It isn't necessary to be so fastidious about urina-
tion. The care you take here is mainly a matter of
courtesy. In the one way that matters, urine is surprisingly clean; that is, it contains few or none of
the organisms that can transmit diseases. Remember, the chief reason for attention to these matters
is not exaggerated prissiness; it's health.

Water, water

The pollution problem in the wilderness has
gotten a lot of publicity. It should. But you will commonly read that every drop of water you take from
the wilderness land must be boiled or treated with
iodine; and this, in my view, is nonsense.

There is no need—not yet, and probably not
ever—to forego the very special pleasure of drinking water straight from the country, flat on your
belly, sucking it from a stream, or getting its tang
across the cool rolled lip of a metal cup. Just be
somewhat cautious about where you do it.

When you look for water, *think watershed.*
Where does a stream come from? What pollution
sources might there be in its drainage area? Don't
drink downstream from a heavily used camp or trail
crossing; rather, go upstream, or find a smaller
stream draining from a pristine basin. Avoid
streams that have their sources outside wilderness,
in civilized country; this is a not-uncommon situation, especially in the Southwest. Water fresh out of
a snowbank is almost certainly safe (as well as exquisite). Watch out, though, for colored "watermelon

snow," tinted by algae that can give you indigestion.

Lakewater does not quite follow the watershed rule. Large bodies of water act as settling basins, and water from a lake outflow is likely to be safer than that from inflow streams.

What about pollution from animals? It is there—a low background level you can seldom entirely escape. A very few diseases can be transmitted from mammals to human beings. One is *giardiasis*, the famous "backpacker's diarrhea" (see also Chapter 26). This punishing ailment has gotten tremendous publicity in recent years. Whether it is actually on the increase is debatable. The only way to ensure yourself against it completely is to treat all your water; but a reasonably careful hiker will probably backpack for a lifetime without encountering it.

Some otherwise wild landscapes are grazed by livestock—even, sometimes, overgrazed and grossly spoiled. If you find a water source fouled and trampled, better treat the water. Even a few cows scattered around the landscape, especially upstream, are a modest cause for concern.

Water treatment

It is plainly a fact that every hiker in the later twentieth century needs to carry a means of disinfecting water, and the knowledge to apply it. There are various methods. The best is probably the old one: boil the water vigorously for at least ten minutes (up to twenty at high altitude).

For many purposes, though, a chemical treatment is more convenient. Treatments involving chlorine—in the form of Halazone tablets or bleach—are now out of favor. (The substance is not the most effective, and tablets lose potency quickly.) The recommended chemical today is iodine in one or another form.

Tincture of iodine. The normal dose is five drops of two percent tincture per quart of water. ("Tincture" means a solution in alcohol; the bottle you buy must say "2 percent" or "USP standard.") Let stand for half an hour.

Iodine tablets (tetraglycine hydroperiodide). Potable Aqua is one widely available brand. The normal dose is one tablet per quart. Since tablets lose potency on exposure to moisture and air, keep them in a tightly sealed container; they are less desirable than other iodine forms.

Iodine/water solution. The kit consists of four or five grams of iodine crystals in a small, tightly-capped glass bottle, capacity about one fluid ounce. (These setups are available at some gear stores; an understanding druggist can provide the items; one mail-order supplier is Insta-Pure—see *Resources* appendix.) The bottle is topped up with water. The iodine solution that results—*not the iodine crystals in the bottom*—is the treating agent. Each time you use some of the solution, replace the drawn-off water, twist on the cap, and shake the bottle: more crystals immediately dissolve and the concentration remains the same.

Dosage and treatment time depend on several factors. Most of the time an appropriate dose is 7 cubic centimeters—about two thirds of a tablespoon, or about one quarter of the one-ounce bottle. With this dosage, treatment time is half an hour. If the water looks polluted, double the dose; if it is very cold, double the treatment time; if it is both cold and ugly, double both.

A useful gadget if you do a lot of water treatment by this method is a Monoject plastic syringe marked with cubic centimeters—available at some drugstores and from doctors and veterinarians.

Filters. Now on the market are several devices that use microporous filters impregnated with a form of iodine. One comes as a straw, another as a cup. The main drawback is that it takes a long time to treat a small amount of water by this means; in addition, it may be hard to tell when the disinfectant in the filter has been used up. Units that avoid these problems are quite expensive.

After adding any chemical treatment (give tablets three minutes to dissolve), shake the water bottle with lid slightly loose, so that the threads are moistened. Very cloudy water can be strained through cloth or let to stand for several hours.

Two cautions. First, there is quite a controversy about the habitual use of iodine for water treatment. The stuff *is* toxic, in large enough doses. So don't use more than called for. Second, water that is dangerous for reasons other than its microscopic wildlife won't be made drinkable by sterilizing treatment. (Suspect a spring without insects or signs of use by animals.) This circumstance, however, is very rare.

Washing

When you wash yourself or your clothes, use biodegradable soap (never detergent), and do the washing well away from any lake or stream. Don't go swimming to get rid of a layer of suds; carry water and rinse ashore. Swimming, without use of soap, may make you feel clean enough. Too many backpackers who ought to know better are still brushing their teeth at the water's edge. And never rinse your hands in live water after using a cat hole!

If you think water is polluted, you should also treat the supply you use for dishwashing and brushing your teeth.

21:
Breaking Camp

SOME CAMPERS, VERY CAREFUL when they choose
their campsite and organize their brief life there, are
rather casual and careless when they depart. Yet it
is in breaking camp that you have a special responsibility and a special opportunity to score points in the
low-impact game.

Suppose you have camped at an established site.
It is, inevitably, a beaten-down, impacted place. That
is its great advantage. Even here you can look
around and ask yourself: How much have we added
to the problems of this place? How much can we
undo?

There is little point in getting rid of a properly
located fire ring that the next party may want to
use. But if you see a ring where no ring should
be—at the lake's edge on grass, for example—it can
be a good service to remove the stones and disguise,
as much as you can, the scar. Make sure that the
ring you used yourself is completely clean, ready,

and inviting. Otherwise you may be encouraging the next comers to start a fresh one.

Your fire must, of course, be unmistakably dead. Stop adding wood to the flames well before you are ready to leave, so that coals will burn into ashes. Never bury the fire with dirt; this may fail to kill it properly and also spoils the ring. Instead, douse fire with quantities of water. Comb through the ashes with your fingers to make sure they are cold clear through. Be certain to pull out any unburnable fragments like tinfoil. If, in spite of all care, you do have sizable chunks of wood left over, it's okay to leave them in the ring.

There is a gracious woodcraft tradition that calls for leaving a stack of wood for the next traveler. Though this may seem somewhat at variance with the current creed of "leaving no trace," it is still a nice gesture to leave wood at an obvious campsite in a forested place where fuel is plentiful.

Gather up all litter—your own and as much as you can carry of what may have been there before.

If your camp has been in a place not obviously used before, there is more to do. Your traces must be made to vanish. Some instructors in wilderness programs like Outward Bound have made a game of it. They ask their students to imagine themselves fugitives, with hostile trackers behind them examining every yard of ground for signs of their presence.

If you have used a stove, your job will be simple; with a fire, it is much more complex (see *Fire at an unmarked site* in Chapter 19). It is very important in this situation that *all* charred wood be consumed to ash. Ashes pass quickly back into the soil, but charcoal lasts so long that archaeologists count on it for dating ruins. Try not to wind up with a big, half-burned log; there is no good way of disposing of such an object.

Should fire remnants be scattered or buried? It makes sense to scatter cold ashes, if it can be done inconspicuously—the best way of getting nutrients back to the soil. Black, extinguished coals should probably be buried when your restore the ground surface at the fire site. Exception: where wildfire has left obvious traces in the scene, it probably does no harm to scatter dead embers. Sooty stones, if you have any, should be returned to the landscape, blackened side down. This does not mean scattering them about. Rocks should be reseated where you found them. Better yet, they should never be moved in the first place.

The bed site needs policing too. Restore rocks you've removed. Ruffle the smooth surface. Scatter twigs, leaves, or gravel to replace the natural litter you swept away. You won't succeed in eliminating *every* trace, but you should be able to restore the natural scene well enough to fool any casual eye. Weather, in a little time, will do the rest.

Variations

At the same time that we are earnest to explore and learn all things, we require that all things be mysterious and unexplorable, that land and sea be infinitely wild, unsurveyed and unfathomed by us because unfathomable.

—Henry David Thoreau

22:
Cross-Country Travel and Other Variants

OF ALL THE MILES THAT BACKPACKERS travel each year, ninety percent are probably hiked in summer. And of that ninety percent, ninety percent are hiked by trail. Sometimes we speak of wilderness as "crowded," but for those who are ready to take a further step into wildness—to leave behind the busy channels of the summer trails—the wild country still has room to spare.

Not that you could call these remoter lands "underused." Wilderness serves purposes beyond recreation; the lands where the hiker seldom comes may be the best preserved of all for watershed, for wildlife, for scientific study. None of the back country is wasted. Wilderness itself should have within it a deeper wilderness—wilderness, so to speak, to the second power.

Cross-country hikers are not numerous. And here's a paradox: should they ever become truly numerous, the experience they seek would vanish before them. Whenever a cross-country route begins to carry more than a handful of people a week, informal paths start to appear, and then to erode and deepen. When this point is reached, the land-managing agency has several choices: to restrict use . . . to build a formal trail . . . or (as happens too often) simply to let the land take scar upon scar. A well-built trail is not a convenience merely, but also a way of accommodating use without excessive damage to the land.

Meanwhile, the trailless outback is still there. And for a certain number of hikers, it is the only wilderness that really counts; the one experience that has the full reward.

Travel off the trail

It's hard to make rules for hiking cross-country, because "country" itself is endlessly diverse. A *trail* along a talus slope may not be so very different from a trail in a rain forest, or a trail through a thicket of rhododendron. But leave the path and you deal with the land in every shape and texture it has. Here you may struggle at half a mile an hour through an enormous, fragrant field of azalea; here you slip and slide on scree or the abominable sliding stuff called "rock mulch"; here you jump from stone to stone in the bed of a rushing stream; here you scramble up a steep rock scarp; here you clamber over and around the trunks of fallen trees.

Cross-country travel is typically slow. If two miles an hour is a lively pace with a pack on a level trail, one mile an hour is good progress through woods and brush. And yet not even this is a rule. There are open, parklike forests as well as thick and tangled ones. And on the smooth granite expanses of certain western ranges, it may be scarcely harder to move off-trail than on. In the desert, too, marked trails are rare and scarcely required.

To hike off-trail you need a genuine backpacking boot, weighing four pounds or more, the pair, in an average size, and with a good high top; lighter boots, so comfortable on easy ground, protect the ankle too little for rugged travel. Make sure you have an elastic bandage in your kit. Should you wrench a knee or sprain an ankle, the support of the firmly wound bandage can keep you mobile enough to retreat (see Chapter 26).

For travel in rough country, you will be happiest with a soft pack that rides close to the back. Frame packs, with their tendency to lurch and swing, can be harder to manage. If you have a frame already, though, it will serve. Just try to lower the center of gravity of the load. Put your heaviest objects at the bottom, reversing the traditional order, and mount the sleeping bag on top rather than underneath. On some models, you can shift the entire packbag lower on the frame. Before you wade into vegetation, make sure that zippers are shut tight, and try to get rid of any trailing loops or protrusions where bushes and branches could catch hold. Stow away any objects that are hanging on the outside of your pack, or at your belt.

For scree and loose ground, as well as for crossing snowpatches, you can borrow an item from winter camping: gaiters. These zip-on cuffs fit tightly over the gap at the top of the boot, preventing loose rocks and the like from bouncing in.

Two animal problems, common in many regions, become slightly more troublesome when you leave the trail. Ticks, which are thick in the brush, especially in the spring, are hard to avoid. Gaiters may help here, and so do dabs of insect repellent at neck, wrists, and ankles, but about the only sure defense is to strip each evening and get rid of the creatures before they get deeply attached.

Second, snakes—rattlesnakes and, in the East, copperheads and cottonmouths—are somewhat more of a hazard off the trail. Snakes can't function either in heat or in cold and are most active on warm nights and in the morning and the evening of hot days. Thus you are often warned to watch for them at those times. But in the heat of midday there is another danger; a snake, lying low, may be too torpid to move out of the way of a descending boot.

Watch where you put your feet and hands. Don't step down on the far side of a rock or log without first getting a look at the ground there.

On the plus side, the bears of remote areas, unaccustomed to human traffic, may be more timid than the average. For more about animal problems, see Chapter 27.

Routefinding and navigation

Routefinding—picking your detailed line through the landscape—is perhaps the greatest (and most fascinating) of cross-country skills. What is the easiest way through this brushfield? Which of several gullies will get us through this band of steep rock? Can we get around the head of this valley without losing too much elevation? Where is the safest spot to ford the stream? Will the going be easier up the creekbed or on the ridge to the side? Shall we pass to the left or the right of that sharp horn? Decisions are made every minute. The cross-country hiker is constantly looking both near and far; the route that looks easiest in the short run may lead you into problems later on.

It is always good, in the wilderness, to travel with a mind aware, conscious of the shapes of the land, their correspondence to the map, and your own progress among them. Even on the trail you need this skill, but don't even consider leaving the beaten path until it is automatic to you. Nobody in a cross-country group should be a passive follower. Every member must understand what's going on. It's important, among other things, to look behind you now and then, fixing landmarks in your mind, in case you must retrace your course.

In trail travel it is rather hard to get seriously lost, even if you should, at times, lose track of your exact position on the map. You know, after all, that you are on a certain *line*, or at worst (if you think you have overlooked a junction) that you're on one of several lines. Either way, you have only half a problem to solve.

Even off-trail, you may at times be following a

prominent line—a major stream, a ridgeline without confusing branches, an ocean beach. But much of the time you have no such lifeline to hold to.

In broken, mountainous country, topography—the lay of the land—is your most important guide. Your problems start when you can't see to read the land—due to fog, or clouds, or winter "white-out"—or when what you *can* see is uninstructive. Some landscapes are like that, flattish and jumbled, or flattish and forested, with no particular pattern to go by. In featureless country, as in blind weather, navigation has to go beyond the obvious. Here are a few of the tricks that professionals rely on.

Trick # 1: walking a straight line

Sometimes, with nothing else to go by, you need to walk with compass in hand, following a selected direction or *azimuth*. Even with a compass, it's hard enough to keep straight. At one point you circle left around a thicket or a massive log; at another you turn right along a stream, looking for stones to cross on; you zig and zag simply in moving among close trees.

In general you try to zig about as often as you zag. But if you have to move off course for more than a few yards, don't do it blind. Instead, plot yourself a whole new course around the obstacle. Suppose, for example, you have to turn left around a large marshy area. Simply note the bearing of your new line. As you go, count your strides. When you clear the obstacle, turn back toward the original line at the same angle you used in leaving it, and walk an equal number of paces. Then return to the old bearing. When you've done all this, you should be more or less back on track.

Trick #2: aiming for a line of destination

Nobody, no matter how careful, can walk a perfectly straight course by compass. If you try to follow a bearing to a particular point—a campsite, a car, a water cache on a sagebrush steppe—you are almost certain to miss it. You may drift left, you may drift right; you won't be precisely on target.

Plotting a course around an obstacle

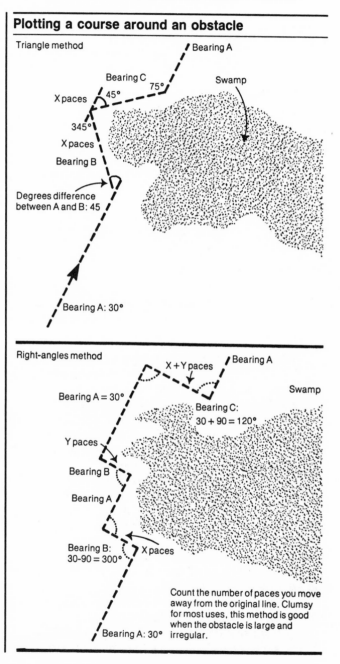

Triangle method

Bearing A

Bearing C

Swamp

75°

45°

X paces

345°

X paces

Bearing B

Degrees difference
between A and B: 45

Bearing A: 30°

Right-angles method

X + Y paces   Bearing A

Bearing A = 30°

Swamp

Bearing C:
30 + 90 = 120°

Y paces

Bearing B

Bearing A

Bearing B:
30−90 = 300°   X paces

Count the number of paces you move
away from the original line. Clumsy
for most uses, this method is good
when the obstacle is large and
irregular.

Bearing A: 30°

Using deliberate error

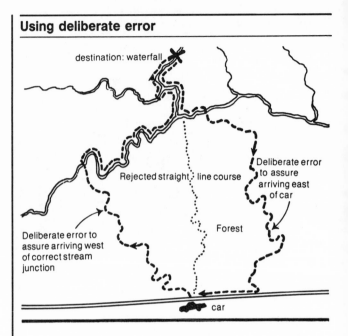

destination: waterfall

Rejected straight line course

Deliberate error to assure arriving east of car

Deliberate error to assure arriving west of correct stream junction

Forest

car

What's the answer? This: you give yourself an easier assignment. You don't try to reach one particular point; instead, you aim for a recognizable *line* on which the point is to be found. It may be a stream, a lakeshore, a ridge, a road, a trail—even (if you have long views) a compass direction to a prominent landmark (when Big Marvine Peak is at 210 degrees, you're on the intended line).

Once you're on the destination line, the problem is only halfway solved. Assuming you have no further landmarks to work from, how do you know which way to turn along the line to find whatever it is you're heading for: the car on the road, the camp on the stream, the cache on the compass line? There are two main ways of making sure you know: *deliberate error* and *bracketing.*

Trick #3: deliberate error
Though the idea takes some getting used to, this is the simplest way of protecting yourself from con-

fusion. Instead of heading straight toward your destination point, you consciously veer to one side or the other, making *an error you know about.* Let's say you're hoping to reach a car parked on a road. Angle deliberately left or right from the course that would take you to it. Don't err blindly, but use a compass azimuth, and make your error large enough so that your smaller, uncontrolled deviations won't matter. Say you've angled, consciously, to the right. You'll know, then, when you reach the road, that the car can *only* be somewhere to your left.

Here's another application. Say you are following a faint trail down a ridge toward a stream. The trace disappears in the underbrush, but you want to locate the exact point at which the old route crosses the water, in hopes of picking up a plainer trail on the other side. Now, if you try to follow the mapped line of the trail, you won't know, when you reach the water, whether you should search upstream or downstream. Unless, by unusual good luck, you're right on target, your error may have led you either way. All you can do, lacking landmarks, is wander back and forth, searching alternately in each direction.

But if, coming down the hill, you had *deliberately* angled upstream, then you'd have known to search downstream, possibly saving an hour or more of time.

Trick #4: Bracketing

Remember the problem: how do you find your destination once you've reached the destination *line?* Besides deliberate error, there's a second answer: bracketing. You establish two landmarks—two things to look for—on the destination line, one on each side of the point you are planning to reach and far enough apart so that you're sure to come out somewhere between them.

There are several kinds of brackets and several ways of "establishing" them. Sometimes you can set up your own artificial landmarks in advance. Say you've parked your car on a road through feature-

Bracketing

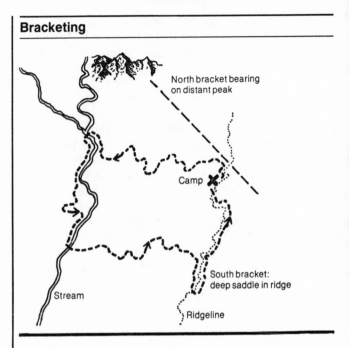

North bracket bearing on distant peak

Camp

South bracket: deep saddle in ridge

Stream

Ridgeline

less woods and have to make sure of getting back to it. Then you can simply tie rags, or leave some other markers, a mile or so away from the car in either direction. More often, though, brackets must be natural features, predicted from study of the topo map. Maybe you are trying to reach a given point on a stream; the map tells you that your destination lies between a waterfall upstream and the junction of a major tributary downstream. Or, to take a third case, brackets can be compass bearings to a landmark visible in the distance (but not visible from the destination point; otherwise there wouldn't be a problem).

It doesn't matter what your brackets are, or how you establish them. When you encounter your destination line, between the brackets, no harm is done if your guess wrong at first and head in the wrong direction. You'll soon run into one of your brackets and be turned back to the center.

Steep summer snow

In the northwestern United States and alpine Canada, snow may linger on mountain slopes for most of the summer. A snowbank is only an interruption, but what if your route simply vanishes under a steep, white snowfield? Even if you were on a trail before, you are now facing a moderate cross-country challenge.

In climbing a gently sloping snowfield, walk flat-footed, taking full advantage of the friction provided by your boot soles. As the angle increases slightly, you can point your toes outwards and waddle up duck-fashion (a maneuver that skiers will recognize as the herringbone). Steeper slopes are best ascended by traversing at an angle, making switch-backs as required. If the snow is at all firm, you will have to kick steps as you climb. Use a scraping, arching motion of the foot, and make the step no deeper than you need to feel secure. On short steep sections, head straight up the slope, kicking steps into it with your toes. If you are the first in a party, other people will be using your steps; if long-legged, restrain your stride and don't space steps too widely.

On any but very gradual slopes, you will find an *ice axe* helpful; on steeper ascents, it is essential. An ice axe consists of a stout metal or wooden shaft fitted to a head with two blades, one narrow (the pick) and one wide (the adze). For occasional use, a light, medium-weight medium-length axe is best; with the tip of the shaft on the ground, you should just be able to rest your hand on the blade. Prices start at over $40 and the weight of a typical medium-shafted axe is near two pounds.

The ice-axe is used, on an ascent, as a movable anchor. You grip its head with the hand on your uphill side and thrust the shaft deep into the snow. After a couple of steps, you pause momentarily in a stable position, remove the axe, and thrust it in again ahead of you. When you change directions at a switchback, you move the axe to the hand that is now uphill.

Descending snow slopes looks scarier than going up and is, in fact, a little trickier. On steep sections, or if nervous, you can face the slope and kick steps inward with your toes, maintaining your axe as anchor all the while. A better technique on moderate slopes is to *plunge step:* you stride downhill, facing out, legs stiff, punching into the snow with your heels. Each time your weight comes down, you compress a wad of snow and make a solid platform. It is important in this maneuver to keep erect, with your weight over your feet. Though plunge stepping takes a little getting used to, it is both easier and safer than creeping downslope in a gingerly fashion. For added security, hold your ice axe ready to plunge into the snow, shaft first, and arrest any incipient slip.

What if you *do* slip, and find yourself careening downhill? If your slope has bare rocks or a cliff at the bottom, you must be able to stop yourself quickly. The best technique requires an ice axe and is known as *self-arrest.* You throw yourself face down in the snow across your axe, with its shaft pinned beneath your chest and its pick cutting into the snow beside your head. In a good arrest, the pick creates so much friction that you stop very quickly indeed. The art, however, can't be learned from a book. Seek instruction.

Lacking an ice axe, there are other tools you can use to slow a slide. A metal Sierra Club-style cup, dug into soft snow with the bowl downhill, can generate a surprising amount of braking power. Tent pegs can be used the same way. Your hands and feet are better than nothing. Don't give up and just slide!

Unless, of course, you're *glissading:* sliding down the snow deliberately. This should only be done when you can see the course ahead and know it to be free of obstacles and sudden drops. Make sure there is a snowy run-out at the bottom of the slope, not a bruising exit onto stony ground. In a *sitting glissade* you sit down on the slope and simply coast. An ice axe, held diagonally across your torso with the tip of the shaft scraping the snow, can serve as speed control. A safer though less easily learned technique is the *standing glissade*. Here you stand erect, facing downslope, and slide on your bootsoles, using them somewhat like skis, with your axe serving again as control (or held ready for a possible self-arrest). If you feel yourself picking up too much speed, you can dig in your heels and convert the glissade to a plunge-stepping descent. Glissading, once mastered, is a fast, exhilarating way down. It is also a trifle dangerous: use with care.

To travel across very icy snow you may need an additional item: *crampons*. These are sets of spikes that fit onto the soles of your boots. Few backpackers bother with these in summer, unless they also have climbing in mind, but crampons are rather commonly seen in such regions as the North Cascades. Partial or instep crampons, with just four spikes, will do for many situations. If you use full crampons, with ten or twelve spikes, make sure that you get the two-piece type that comes with a hinge under the sole. Rigid one-piece crampons can't be worn with flexible-soled hiking boots. Cost of full crampons: $45 or more.

Lacking crampons, try to time your crossing of icy slopes for midafternoon, or whenever a particular slope has had sun on it for the longest possible time. Most summer snowfields will get soft as the day goes on.

For much more on the skills of travel on steep snow, see the Mountaineers' *Freedom of the Hills* (*Resources* appendix). Some of these techniques come naturally, or can be self-taught; but the best preparation is to travel with more experienced hikers and learn from them. Self-arrest, as noted, takes instruction and a lot of practice. If you are going into country where steep snow problems are likely, take the time to master the tricks of the trade and to review them every season.

For travel in summer-snow regions, you need moderately heavy boots, thoroughly waterproofed, with lug-type soles. Gaiters should be taken. Clothing should be of types that will stay warm if wet (wool and fiberpile, for instance). If you plan to do a lot of sitting glissades or to practice self-arrest—a wet business—take raingear with slick outer surfaces to put on in the snow (snow clings to rougher fabrics).

Stream crossing

One of the most difficult wilderness obstacles is the major, rushing stream. There is a whole craft of stream crossing and plenty of debate and disagreement about how to do it.

A slow, deep river is not a particular problem; it's usually safe enough to swim such a stream, floating your pack in front of you on an air mattress. (Note this special point in favor of the mattress—you can't float anything on a thin foam pad.)

A fast, shallow stream can be tricky if the current is fierce enough. Instinct tells you to cross slowly and cautiously, but some expert travelers prefer to hurry over, almost at a run, giving the current no chance to knock them off their feet.

But the really daunting problem is the swollen mountain stream, thigh-deep or hip-deep, fast moving and murky—just such a stream as you may encounter at the thaw. The first question to ask when you reach such a barrier is: shall we attempt it at all? For there is real danger here. It may be better to retreat or change your route. Steep, violent torrents—especially the ones that are accelerating toward dangerous rapids or falls—should be left alone.

If you decide to cross, consider both place and time. Streams fed by snowmelt will be lowest in the cool of the morning. Generally speaking, it is better to cross where the course is straight (rather than at a curve). It may also be easier to cross at a shingle, where the water is broken but shallow, than at a deeper, apparently calmer spot. Above all, consider what would happen if you were swept off your feet.

Are there dangerous spots downstream into which you might be carried? Would it be easy, downstream, to clamber to the shore? Are there shelving banks or steep, difficult slopes?

Unbuckle the waistbelt of your pack (so that, if you must, you can shed it). Stand sideways to the current, facing just slightly downstream. Set your feet wide apart and take short steps, moving one foot at a time and always keeping the same foot forward. Test each new footing before you shift your weight. A long-handled ice axe, a staff, or a pole will help you keep your balance against the tug and haul of the flow.

Several hikers, crossing together, can give each other extra support in a circle of three, with linked arms; in a line, each gripping the belt of another, facing upstream but moving sideways; or abreast, with arms linked and wrapped around a long pole, facing across the stream. In this "line-abreast" method, all move forward at once; otherwise, only one person moves at a time.

Should a river-crosser, like a climber, tie onto a rope and get a belay? You might well think so. Strangely enough, however, a rope can actually add to your danger. If you're swept off your feet, the force of the stream, dragging your weight against the rope's resistance, can press you down into the streambed until you drown. If the water's that fast, the person on the bank will have trouble pulling you to safety. There are various ways, all more or less involved, of using a rope with lessened danger. In general, though, these are specialized climbers' methods.

In a large group it makes unquestionable sense to string a rope across the water for the middle members to use as a rail or "handline"; only the first crosser and the last will then be unprotected.

These hazardous crossings are often made in winter and spring when deep, rushing streams are also bitterly cold. Wool or fiberpile clothes, which you should be wearing anyway at that time of year, will continue to insulate even when they're soaked, but you'll probably want to change socks and underwear, at least, once you're across. If someone gets dangerously chilled, he or she may have to be stripped, dried, and put into a sleeping bag, following the drill for hypothermia (see Chapter 28). Lacking a hypothermia crisis, though, the best thing to do is to eat starch and sugar and start hiking, fast and hard, to produce a lot of body heat. Wet clothes dry out fast when you hike at full speed.

On the edge of climbing

This is not a book about mountain climbing. But if you begin taking trips away from the trail, you may sooner or later want to learn at least the simplest of the climber's methods. With a rope and the skill to use it, you can deal with unexpected obstacles; more important, perhaps, you can plan trips in country where obstacles *are* to be expected. A rope-

Belaying

carrying party isn't balked if, hiking down some desert canyon, it comes to the brink of a steep, dry waterfall; or if, in some north-facing mountain gully, it has to cross lingering, slick-surfaced snow. Peaks that are out of reach to most hikers, because of a little steep rock at the top, are open to the party with a rope. Even on easy ground a rope can be a comfort, if a careless stumble could pitch someone over a dangerous edge.

The great point of the rope between climbers is this: it allows one partner, braced in a strong position, to protect a second, who is moving on hazardous ground. As the moving climber advances, the stationary partner—the *belayer*—feeds out rope. If the climber slips, the belayer can stop the climber's fall. Belaying, then, in all its elements, is the first and greatest skill to be learned.

There's another technique that can be of use in cross-country travel, and that is the *rappel*, a way of sliding, slowly and safely, down a doubled rope. This is sometimes the only way to get down a scarp without leaving the rope behind you. Running the line around a tree or knob of stone, with both ends dangling, you slide down it, and then recover the rope by pulling on one of the strands.

This isn't the place to describe these methods further, or to discuss the various knots, body stances, signals, and safety considerations that go into their use. These basics are much too important to be learned from a thumbnail sketch. Consult instead the specialized climbing texts, look for instruction (formal or informal), and practice again and again.

Low impact off the trail

Rules change when you leave the trails. On established paths, you deliberately confine your impact to places impacted already. On the trail you walk single file. In camp you build fires (if at all) at old sites. You concentrate your impact in the smallest possible area.

But in off-trail travel, exactly the opposite applies. To avoid leaving traces, you disperse. A party, walking through the woods, or on any surface where a mark could be left, should always walk abreast, each hiker in a separate line, so far as the land allows. A little impact, spread over a lot of land, will simply vanish.

Don't build cairns or ducks; don't blaze trees or break branches. Don't spoil the experience of others by reminding them, oppressively, that Kilroy has already been here. Though they may know better, walkers on the trackless ridge or in the empty forest would like to think that no one else has been in that place, at least this year. Don't kill the illusion for those who come after.

What kinds of land are most easily damaged by cross-country hiking and camping? The types are familiar: timberline vegetation of all kinds . . . wet meadows and bogs . . . erosive slopes. While subalpine meadows are known for their fragility, woody shrubs and heathers at the same high elevations are in fact more vulnerable still. Dry mountain grasslands, though slow to repair themselves, are also rather slow to scar. The rich, moist forest floors of lower-elevation wilderness may seem fragile as your boot punches down among moss and ferns, but this living fabric restores itself very well.

There's an interesting pattern in all this. Lands that are truly rich—where living things have an easy time—are somewhat resistant to abuse. And so are lands that are truly harsh: the barren peaks, the ice, the volcanic wastes of cinder and lava flow. But in between there is another class of lands, places where a seeming richness is maintained in a harsh world. Here damage is easily done but only over many years repaired, if at all.

Take the High Peaks of the Adirondacks, 4,000 and 5,000 feet high. In that region 4,000 feet is already subalpine. Yet these summits are not barren but are green with a thick fur (unlikely though it seems) of sphagnum moss—"inverted bogs," one writer has called them. Many of these peaks are trailless, and most people seem to want them that way. But so often are they ascended by cross-country hikers that their sides are striped with steep, eroding scars. These are trails in all but name, and the mossy tundras on the narrow crests are being trampled away.

What can be done in cases like this? Except where roads can be closed, reducing access, the answers seem to come down to two: either the authorities must put some sort of limit on the number of people permitted to make these climbs, or they must build formal trails and overlooks, protecting the fragile summit vegetation with railings and with signs: "Keep off the moss." Neither answer is appealing. But where there is little wilderness and many who would use it, we come to such uncomfortable choices again and again.

For the extreme case, consider Switzerland. The Swiss have set aside a single national park of about 40,000 acres—a magnificent landscape, by all accounts, but, as wild preserves are counted in America, almost untenably small. In this Swiss park hikers cannot camp, nor can they set foot off the elaborately maintained trails. It would be, to our temperament, hard to take, but it's a way.

The more wilderness we manage to preserve, the less often we will be driven to such difficult choices.

Desert

There are many kinds and degrees of desert in the United States and many kinds of desert travel. For the backpacker, there is a practical definition of *desert:* you are hiking in the desert whenever you have to think, and think hard, about *water*—when H_2O is not just a gift of the land, to be counted on, but the center of all your plans.

Much hiking done in the American deserts is not, by this measure, desert hiking at all. Most of our arid region is also basin and range country, marked by a pattern of alternating valleys and mountain masses. Some of the highlands reach 10,000, 12,000, even 14,000 feet, high enough to yield abundant water. Hiking in the Toiyabe Range of Central Nevada, for instance, or in the forested Deep Creek Mountains of Utah, you are *in* the desert only as an island is in the sea.

The desert is also interrupted, here and there, by perennial streams that flow in deep-cut canyons. Many famous "desert" treks follow these arteries: you wade the shallows and push through the green streambank thickets of an Aravaipa, an Owyhee, an Escalante River.

Take away the wet mountains and wet canyons, and what you have left is the desert itself, the real thing. It's true desert hiking when you park on the shoulder of a rugged road from nowhere to nowhere and head up a long alluvial slope toward the stark sharp shoulder of an unknown mountain range. It's true desert hiking when you clamber up the branches of a bone-dry, precipitous gorge. It's the real thing when you strike out across the featureless expanse of a *playa,* one of those dead-flat, lifeless, cream-colored sedimentary plains that fill the low points of many desert valleys.

Water

Your objective in planning desert travel must be to avoid being short of water—*ever.* Dehydration is a nasty, insidious disease. It is not something you want to take chances with.

How much water does a desert hiker need? A lot. Not quarts, but gallons—at least 1.5 gallons a day, in liquid form and in food, and sometimes much more. Figure a six-quart daily minimum and add a quart to that for every five miles to be traveled—in reasonably cool weather. In the heat of summer, figure more. In Death Valley in July, you would need nine quarts a day simply to survive, resting in the shade.

Water is heavy, over two pounds to the quart. Two days' supply at two gallons a day would already weigh some thirty-seven pounds. On the plus side, if you're hauling water anyhow, there's no need to carry high-priced freeze-dried foods.

If you have to carry *all* your water, your hiking range is necessarily limited. Many desert hikers wind up taking successions of short trips rather than one longer one—going out just for a day or two and looping back to the car between excursions. This type of travel—call it the "cluster trip"—is a desert specialty.

There are several ways of increasing your range. One is to find water on the land. Often it is there to be found. What you must *not* do, however, is to put yourself in the position of depending on a supply that may not be there. Don't count on local sources just because a map shows the blue squiggle of a spring. You may or may not find it; it may or may not be flowing. Plan your trip so that on-the-ground water will be a welcome surprise.

In addition to permanent springs, you sometimes find natural catchments or "tanks" that hold water for several days after a rain. As an emergency measure, you may be able to reach water by digging into the gravelly floor of a streambed, especially where vegetation indicates that roots are reaching the water table. In winter in high desert mountains, a ready source of water is snow.

Often desert waters must be purified. Many are polluted by domestic stock or by feral burros. A few springs are so alkaline as to be obviously undrinkable; a very few contain poisonous minerals. These are usually identified on maps, but be wary of sources that have no sign of life whatever around them. Purification, of course, is useless in such cases.

Caching water is another way of extending your range. Caching can be simple. For instance, if you will be hiking out and back on the same line, you can carry extra water and plant a generous supply a few miles up the route. For a greater extension of range, you will have to do advance work by car, planting caches near roads. Caches should be close enough together so that, if you failed to find a particular one, you would be able to reach the next. Always plan such trips with considerable margin for error.

For containers, use gallon plastic bottles (bleach bottles are good) with screw-on caps, taped shut. The tradition was once to bury the bottles or place them under cairns, but this defaces the land and now is frowned on. Try to find a concealed spot on the surface. Desert veterans take care to place caches unobserved. It is not unknown for vandals to steal or destroy supplies.

When you plant a cache, make sure that you can find the place again. Look around carefully to establish landmarks. If you have long views, take at least three compass bearings and write them down. Make a sketch of local topography. Mark the spot on your map. Try to place caches in spots that will be easy to recognize again. It is good to choose a spot on some prominent *line* on the landscape: a road or track or fenceline, the toe of a mountain slope, or the bank of a wash (but not down in the wash in summer thunderstorm season).

This is an excellent time to practice precise navigation skills. For instance, flag several locations a mile or so apart, approach the area from a new angle, and try to locate each of your flags in succession.

With due care it just won't happen. But what if the worst possible situation does somehow develop: you find yourself short of water and miles away from the next source? Research shows that a healthy person, not dehydrated to begin with, can walk about ten miles in the desert in daytime without additional water. If help or water is more distant than that, walk at night. If you have any water at all, it is better to drink it as you become thirsty and keep your body functioning well while you move toward help. To reduce water loss, remain fully clothed, even in hot weather. Do not smoke or drink alcohol. Eat only a little, and avoid salt. Talk as little as possible and breathe through your nose. If you find water that is undrinkable, you can moisten your skin with it for cooling; urine, in a pinch, can be used in the same way.

Climate and gear

We think of the deserts as hot, but that isn't quite right. The American deserts stretch a thousand miles north and south (even omitting the Mexican portion) and range 5,000 feet or more in elevation. Nowhere is it hot *all* the time. Death Valley, where the summer temperature in the shade can climb above 120 degrees Fahrenheit, is cool in the winter; in the high desert of Oregon, for instance, winter nights may be deeply subzero. By picking your hiking season, you can keep to a comfortable range.

If you steer clear of the extremes, you will need nothing extraordinary in the line of gear. For shelter, a light tent will do and often just a tarp or poncho. Nights will require warm clothes, but not massive envelopes of nylon and down. A light, three-season sleeping bag is fine. At high elevations and on snow, sunhat, suncream, and sunglasses will be essential. Do be prepared for rain (sometimes for hail or snow).

If you want to hike hot desert country in the summer—and some people do—special precautions are required. It is vital that you understand the causes of overheating or *hyperthermia* (see Chapter 28) and know how to prevent it. A period of acclimatization, of getting used to the heat, is advisable before you set out. Loose, lightly woven, light-colored clothing should be worn to reflect light and heat. Sunglasses are vital. Hikers often carry canopies to pitch for the midday stop, tentpoles to pitch them with (since vegetation may be low and sparse), and air mattresses or thick foam pads to keep their bodies off scalding ground. They may hike at morning and evening—even at night—and take a long siesta in the heat of the day.

Perhaps the most vital piece of "gear" for the desert hiker is the automobile. That vehicle is more than transportation; it is home base. Make certain it has *lots* of water in it, together with food, stove fuel, and first aid supplies. Desert driving is hard on cars. A little mechanical knowledge and a basic toolkit will serve you well. In remote areas, it is a good idea for even a small group to travel in two vehicles.

Cross-country travel

Desert travel is likely to be cross-country, without explicit trails. But navigation tends to be straightforward. Views are long; often you are following an unmistakable ridgeline or canyon; topography tends to be rather simple. Sophisticated compass work becomes important if you strike out across a featureless *playa*, of if you are aiming for a water cache. Detailed routefinding, making your way across the detail of the land, is typically easy. Vegetation is seldom so thick that you cannot work your way through it. But obstacles do occur: unexpected bands of cliffs, thickets of fiercely spined cacti, dry waterfalls in canyons. (If you plan to hike a canyon not known to be easily passable, take a rope and know how to use it.)

Flash floods are a real hazard in canyon travel. Thunderstorms, common in the Southwest through the summer and fall, reach a climax in July and August. Even if the air is dry where you are, floods may be sent down by downpours elsewhere in the watershed. Don't try to camp in streamcourses, especially in the narrows of a gorge. Never try to cross, either on foot or in a vehicle, a wash that is filling with water.

The desert has its rattlesnakes, but no more than the woods. A snakebite kit is a good thing to carry, if you know how to use it and when *not* to. Arizona travelers should inform themselves about one highly venomous scorpion, *Centuroides sculpturatus.*

Low impact in the desert

Easily scarred, slow to repair themselves, America's desert lands are taking a beating. Desert hikers are not contributing much of the damage. (It stems much more from overgrazing, from random, destruc-

tive prospecting, from off-road vehicle use and pro-
liferating roads.) The conscientious hiker, though,
will want to use care here as elsewhere.

All the familiar low-impact rules apply, and a
few more besides. One important point: don't compete with wildlife for limited water. If you draw
water from an isolated waterhole or a section of
perennial stream, don't then camp beside it, but
move a good distance away, say, half a mile or
more. This is crucial in desert mountains where bighorn sheep are struggling to maintain themselves.

In the desert, as at timberline, fires have no
place. You won't find much burnable material anyway; what you do find belongs on the land. Some
people burn their toilet paper to speed decomposition, but fires have been set that way and desert
land management agencies now commonly discourage this practice.

When crossing range fences, don't climb the
strands (which may break) but part them and slide
between. If you go through a gate, leave it as you
found it—open if it was open, shut if shut. Such
courtesies lessen friction between hikers and ranch-
ers.

Desert soil might seem to be invulnerable to any
disturbance as tiny as a hiker's footfall. But this is
not always true. Sometimes ground is covered with
a veneer of lichens and other tiny plants called
"cryptogamic crust." Once broken, this layer is slow
to heal. Where possible, avoid trampling such
ground. Avoid particularly breaking it with a tire
track—for instance, when turning around at the end
of a dead-end road.

Wading trips

At the other extreme from desert travel is the
trip on which your feet, at least, are continually in
water: the wade. Canyon travel in the West sometimes takes this form: you walk along some oasis-
making stream and ford it so frequently that you
are more in water than on land. In the swamps of
the Southeast, too, what travel is not by boat is

likely to involve some wading. Leather boots are no good for such travel: you want light footgear, like the Army's "tropical combat" boot, that lets water as readily out as in.

Wet desert canyons may pose the problem of quicksand; experienced hikers know how to *swim* the shifting sand if there's no other way to pass. Flash floods, however, are a more serious danger.

Very long trips

This is another variation on the "normal" back-pack: the trip measured not in days but in weeks. The longer the trip, the more elaborate the planning has to be. Unless you plant food caches or come out to reprovision, your food will have to be of the light-est, most compact kind. Your appetite will grow as time goes on; experienced long-distance trekkers add about half a pound per person per day to the normal ration of one and a half to two pounds. Balance in the diet—scarcely a consideration on the shorter jaunt—becomes important on a long trip.

There are various ways of placing supply caches. You can leave food on the ground in tightly sealed metal boxes (available at some gear stores) or hang it from trees in boxes or in waterproof bags (as for bear-bagging). If your route passes close enough to towns, you can mail your supplies ahead (Special Handling, Insured). You can also lay in groceries at such places. The Appalachian Trail passes quite close to many settlements, and the Pacific Crest Trail approaches a few. Along with food, you may need to replace first aid supplies and some of your minor gear as the weeks go on.

Hiking alone

"Nobody should ever hike alone."

If the land agencies had their way, if the rescue workers had their way, that's the sentence that would stand at this spot. The authorities don't wel-come anything that might encourage people to un-dertake adventures. And you can't blame them for that. They're too accustomed to retrieving—at great effort and expense—the overambitious, the overconfident, and the underprepared.

You may even hear that no party is safe with less than four people. There's a logic to this. If someone is injured, there should be one companion to stay with the patient and two (since no one should hike alone) to go together for help. When a single hiker gets in trouble, it may be quite a while before anyone knows about it, and the problems and dangers increase.

Okay, there is risk in hiking alone.

There is double risk whenever the solo hiker leaves the beaten paths—when he or she ventures into cross-country travel, or into the desert, or into the world of snow and winter storms.

And yet there are people who do all these things, matter-of-factly and without mishap, year after year. And they have their reasons. Some of the sharpest and most memorable statements of the wilderness idea—the formulations of a Muir, a Thoreau, an Aldo Leopold—have been made by the solo travelers. Whatever it is that wilderness gives you, you come back with a double dose of it when you go out alone. And then there are the practical advantages. "The man who travels alone," Thoreau observes, "can start today; but he who travels with another must wait till that other is ready, and it may be a long time before they get off."

So if you feel like taking up solo hiking, by all means do it. Do it, though, with preparation, with understanding, and even (the word is not too strong) with healthy *fear*. Things *can* happen out there. You may want to start your solo travel on frequented trails where you will meet many parties a day; later, you might find yourself drawn to remoter country, perhaps even to off-trail and off-season adventures. But take it slow. Don't overrate yourself. Don't underrate the wilderness. The wilderness is bigger.

If you do head out alone, take special care to leave a precise itinerary, both at home and with the local office of the managing agency. Take extra food and fuel (also water, if that's a consideration). For other gear, the solo traveler's rule can only be: *when in doubt, leave it in.* You'll have nobody else along this time to loan you the item you forgot, the thing you decided to do without.

23:
The Winter Wilderness

IN SNOW THE WILDERNESS grows and is wilder.

Except in the South, in the deserts, and in the foothills of the Far West, most of our wild country is snowed in during winter. The new, white surface covers scars, smooths old mistakes, shelters fragile ground. It covers the trampled campgrounds, the beaten trails of summer. And, most of all, it closes roads. In winter the California Sierra becomes once more the huge mystery that John Muir explored. Yellowstone, clean of cars and noise, is once again an amazement. In forested mountains, the labyrinth of logging roads becomes a land of flat, white corridors—still artificial but no longer ugly and (except by snowmobiles) no longer drivable. Peaks that were an hour away by summer trails become the reward of a three days' march.

Once the snowy hills were pretty much empty of travelers. Even now winter is, by comparison, the empty, spacious season. But the winter wilderness is

tracked by two species of travelers, specially
equipped, and moving with the extra vigor that
seems natural in cold places.

There are, first of all, the cross-country skiers.
Moving swiftly on narrow wooden or fiberglass skis,
they don't often push very far into the wilderness.
Most are daytrippers, lightly burdened, skiing a fast
in-and-out.

But besides the daytrippers there are those more
committed travelers, the winter backpackers.
Though their numbers are increasing, they are still
rather few. Compared to the crowds of summer,
they may always be few. Some shuffle along on
snowshoes; some slide along on skis of heavier make
than those of the daytime skiers they meet on the
first miles of trail. Some are climbers heading for remote winter summits. Some are downhill skiers,
weary of busy commercial slopes, come to shuffle up
steep peaks for the giddy, controlled ride down.
Some are simply backpackers, moving, camping, en-
joying, dealing with the white, crisp world. But
these travelers have in common a shared problem
and a fairly similar set of solutions to it.

The problem: how do you stay comfortable—and
more important, safe—in the beautiful, strange, and
unforgiving country of the cold?

Getting into winter

Winter is another world. So different are its
rules, so special its demands, that it would take a
separate book to deal with them thoroughly. Winter
gear, in particular, is full of complexities of its own.

The great reality, in snow, is *cold*. Never underestimate it. On a typical winter trip you will be cozily warm while you travel, and cozily warm once
you're lying in your sleeping bag, drinking soup.
But the times in between are rarely perfectly comfortable. Fingers get cold and disobedient. Bare
metal can be so frigid that it stings bare flesh.
Flashlights balk, cameras jam, water freezes solid in
canteens. Everything you do takes longer—and
there is more to do: more gear to deal with, more

fixing, more finding, more figuring, more rigging to be gotten through. And to add to it all there is less daylight to work with.

Then why camp in the snow? Because the world of the snow is endlessly, cleanly beautiful. Because experiences in it—the good and the bad alike—seem to happen with double intensity. Because the land is emptier, lonelier, wilder. Because you have, more than you have in any summer travel, the sense of being on a frontier.

Some backpackers value these things so much that they turn the year upside down, like downhill skiers or Australians; it is November that sets them to scanning the maps and checking out their gear, not May. Even if you don't go that far, the taste for winter camping gives you a twelve-month hiking season.

It's a real jump, the move into winter camping—almost like learning to backpack all over again. Most people will want to break into it gradually, starting with day trips, and then short overnight jaunts not far from the road. Test all your gear where the retreat is easy. If your summer stove is going to balk in the cold, you want to know about it before you're absolutely depending on the thing. Don't take on too many problems at first; there are so many. It helps to travel, the first few times, with more experienced companions. Some outings clubs offer valuable courses.

Winter gear

For winter travel you have to make some changes in your gear—some substitutions, even more additions. The most obvious new requirement is a pair of skis or snowshoes—for more on the possibilities, see the end of this chapter.

If you will be traveling on skis with three-pin bindings—the most common type—you will need special ski boots. If you plan to snowshoe, or to use skis with mountaineering style bindings (again, see below), your summer boots may or may not serve. Fairly heavy leather backpacking boots can generally be used in winter, with extra waterproofing; lighter boots, including those made of "split-grain" leather, will not. ("Split-grain" leathers are the middle layer of the animal's skin; "top-grain" leathers include the outer surface, the toughest, most water-resistant part.) The more massive the boot, and the thicker it is in the sole, the warmer you will find it.

There are several ways of increasing the warmth of a chilly boot. You can, of course, add socks—but don't overdo it (if you find the arrangement uncomfortably tight, it may be cutting off circulation to your feet, with resulting danger of frostbite). Dry socks are important in winter; take plenty of spares. You can also add inner soles.

Then there's the vapor barrier trick. Over the thin inner sock on each foot goes a plastic bag; then add whatever socks you normally wear. Over these, place a second, larger plastic bag. These plastic layers keep melted snow from working its way in to your skin. They also keep perspiration in, together with the heat you lose when sweat evaporates. The result, for most people, is feet that are no damper than they would be without the vapor barrier, and distinctly warmer. (Note: supermarket produce bags are a little flimsy for this use.)

In really extreme winter conditions, overboots ($60 and up) can help. These are tough fabric shells that cover the boot, adding insulation, and rise up the calf. Some cover the sole of the boot, others leave it free.

In the West, most non-skiing backpackers wear lug-soled hiking boots in winter as in summer. Not so in the East and the Midwest. In these regions, hikers in mud and snow often prefer the high rubber boots known loosely as "shoepacs." There are various designs. All cover most of the foot with a single piece of vulcanized rubber, so that waterproofing is total. The rest of the upper—ankle and calf—may be of leather. Heights vary. There may be detachable foam liners. The Maine Hunting Shoe by L. L. Bean is a familiar standard among shoepacs. The Army's Korean boot, known also as the Mickey Mouse, packs insulation between two layers of rubber and is exceedingly warm. Shoepacs are not for use on rough snow-free ground. They cost somewhat less than leather-and-Vibram hiking boots.

Of course you need more clothes in winter, and to some extent different clothes. Cotton is out; wool and synthetic fabrics are in. Down-filled jackets and sleeping bags are good in dry-cold climates, but dubious in wet cold, unless protected by water-resistant shells; synthetic fills are safer because they will continue to warm you if they get wet.

Most people wear long johns in winter. Various types are available: wool, angora, multilayer cotton, open net. The best material is synthetic polypropylene ("polypro"). Polypro garments wick moisture away from the skin without getting sodden themselves and dry quickly if they do get wet.

Even more than in summer, it's important to choose clothes that allow easy adjustment. You don't want to let yourself get either cold or hot—excessive sweating will chill you by evaporation later on. Front zippers or buttons, and adjustable closures at the wrists, are good. You need both wind protection (a parka or thin windproof shell) and protection against rain and wet snow (raincoat or cagoule and rain pants or chaps). In high places you may need separate wind pants as well. (If you own garments of all-weather fabric—Gore-Tex or one of its competitors—you may be able to combine rain-gear and wind protection and leave duplicate clothing at home.) The more pockets you have on your outer clothing, the handier.

It's important to have a stocking cap that pulls down over the neck, leaving a gap for the face. For colder places and above timberline, you may need a cap with a built-in facemask. For warmer days in bright sun, an ordinary hat is a good idea.

You must have dark glasses or goggles—two pairs, in fact, in case you lose the first. For the fierce, bright lands above timberline, you need glasses that protect the sides of the eyes as well as the front. Though glass lenses block more burning ultraviolet light, plastic glasses are easier to find, and they will do for altitudes to 14,000 feet. The cheapest good glasses around, made of Lexan plastic by Mountain Safety Research, cost $10 or so. Fancy glasses at fancy prices are really not required.

"Soft" backpacks with internal supports are much used in winter, especially by skiers who find standard frames awkward. Whichever kind you have, make sure you can fit all your needed gear into it, or onto it, tied to the outside. Attach pull-loops of cord to zipper tabs; these make it easier to work stubborn zippers with cold hands. (Such tiny comforts and conveniences have real meaning in the snow.)

True winter sleeping bags are heavier than summer types. As always, the key factor is not mere poundage but insulating thickness or loft. A bag with seven or eight inches of loft, in a mummy style, takes most sleepers down to about zero degrees Fahrenheit in comfort. "Three-season" bags, a little lighter, can be made to serve, especially within the protection of a tent. You do need more ground insulation than in summer. A closed-cell foam pad for winter should be half an inch thick and long enough to protect the legs and feet. (You may even want two such pads.) Still better (but expensive) is the full-length Therm-a-Rest mattress, which surrounds an open-cell foam pad with an airtight cover ($50).

For shelter you'll need a tent that can carry heavy snow weights and stand up in strong winds. Where snow is deep, you can build your own shelter—igloo, snow trench, or cave. You'll need a folding snow shovel ($25 or more) for this work; some igloo builders also carry light snow saws ($12).

Doesn't all this add up to a heavier load in your pack? You bet it does. It is difficult, in winter, to trim your packweight much below forty pounds on an overnight trip. Winter mountaineers, adding ropes and other paraphernalia, seldom carry loads of less than sixty pounds. This is one of the prices you pay.

Travel in the snow

Especially on your first trips, don't commit yourself to covering too much ground too fast. One mile an hour is a good pace on snowshoes in open country; three miles an hour is excellent progress on skis. Often you will do much less. A ten-mile day on snowshoes, when you carry a pack, is an extremely long one, as is a twenty-mile day on skis. In some situations, skis may be no faster than snowshoes.

Take into account the shortness of winter days. At the winter solstice near the Canadian border, daylight lasts less than nine hours. If you allow two hours after dawn for breaking camp and one, at dusk, for getting settled in, that leaves only five or six hours for travel.

You can simplify matters by hiking in to estab-

Wind-chill chart: effective temperature

Thermometer reading, degrees fahrenheit

	50	40	30	20	10	0	−10	−20	−30
calm	50	40	30	20	10	0	−10	−20	−30
5	48	37	27	16	6	−5	−15	−26	−36
10	40	28	16	4	−9	−21	−33	−46	−58
15	36	22	9	−5	−18	−36	−45	−58	−72
20	32	18	4	−10	−25	−39	−53	−67	−82
25	30	16	0	−15	−24	−44	−59	−74	−88
30	28	13	−2	−18	−33	−48	−63	−79	−94
35	27	11	−4	−20	−35	−49	−67	−82	−98
40	26	10	−6	−21	−37	−53	−69	−85	−100

(left margin label: Wind speed)

Read down from thermometer reading, right from wind speed, to find effective temperature in wind. Jagged line marks the degree of chill in which travel becomes dangerous; unprotected flesh can freeze.

lished shelters. It's unwise, though, to count on finding the less elaborate shelters free of snow, while those that are open will sometimes be crowded. And it is dangerous to head out so underequipped that you would be in deep trouble if you didn't make it all the way in to a distant refuge.

Whether you're on skis or snowshoes, the first problem of snow travel is keeping warm (but not hot) and, so far as possible, dry. Don't delay any changes in your armor of clothing that will keep the balance of heat production and heat loss. Allow all the ventilation you can. If there's snow in the air, you need to be wearing smooth-surfaced fabrics from which the flakes will slide; brush them off when they accumulate. Knock snow from branches *before* you pass under them.

The thermometer doesn't tell you everything about cold. What chills you is the loss of heat from the skin (as well as from the lungs), and warm but windy air will remove warmth as quickly as colder air that is still. Humid air seems colder than dry air, and if you are wet, evaporation in the wind will still further increase your loss of heat. If your body keeps on losing more heat than it can make, you will enter the dangerous and even deadly condition called *hypothermia*, described at length in Chapter 28.

Nibble starchy or sugary foods as you walk, and drink plenty of water, more than you think you want. If it's so cold that water freezes during the day, insulate the containers. For instance, you can pull a thick wool sock over the bottle. Pack canteens upside down, so that plugs of ice won't form in the necks. Water freezes more slowly when it's mixed with something; lemonade stays liquid longer than straight water.

There are certain hazards in traveling on snow. Snowshoers, in particular, need to watch out for "tree wells." Tree trunks, warmer than the surrounding snow, melt deep pits, embarrassing to fall into. There's a much more serious danger in crossing snowbridges over flowing streams. A collapsing bridge can dump a backpacker into bitterly cold, rushing water. Look for the thickest bridge you can find, and cross one at a time, testing the footing as you go. The leader should probe carefully in front with a ski pole or ice axe. Sometimes it's worth unpacking a rope and giving crossers a belay.

Avalanche!

Nothing in the winter wilderness is quite so terrifying—quite so massive, quite so inexorable—as the avalanche. In the last quarter century, about 150 people in this country have died in avalanches. There is a whole science of avalanche safety, and every winter traveler should know at least the rudiments.

Avalanches, or snowslides, are of several kinds. The most dangerous is the *slab avalanche*, the great mass of snow that breaks, all at once, from a mountainside and plunges into the valley. Slab avalanches are likeliest during, and just after, heavy winter storms. The more new snow that comes down in a storm—and the faster it comes down—the greater the risk. It's cause for concern if more than a foot is added, especially if it piles up at the rate of an inch an hour or more. High wind adds to the danger. Remember that it may be snowing and blowing much harder up the ridge you must cross tomorrow than it is at tonight's campsite in the valley.

Once snow has fallen, it immediately begins to change and consolidate, growing much more stable. If the air is warm, this will happen quite rapidly, and the risk of massive slides may vanish within hours. In very cold weather, however, the snow changes slowly, and danger can last for many days. Watch for tiny "sluffs," harmless slides of loose, powdery snow; they indicate that the snow is settling nicely.

Slab avalanches can also form without fresh snow if it's cold and windy enough. Winds over twenty-five miles an hour can build up dangerous hard drifts on the lee sides of ridges. These "hard slab" avalanches of wind-packed snow are especially important as a danger in clear but windy periods fol-

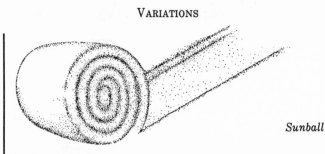

Sunball

lowing storms.

Up to a certain point, warm temperatures mean lesser risk. There is, however, such a thing as a *wet snow avalanche*. Such snowslides occur when snow becomes waterlogged and loses its grip on the surface below. This can happen whenever temperatures rise. If it's suspiciously warm, watch for "sunballs," curious wheels of snow that run down the slope, rolling up the surface layer of the snowpack in a sort of scroll. Small sunballs don't indicate much danger, but very large ones, several feet thick, suggest danger of wet avalanche. Wet-snow avalanches don't kill as many people as the slab type, but they are dangerous enough and very prevalent in the mountains of the Pacific Coast.

Avalanche defense

Before you head into the wilderness, inquire about current avalanche conditions. In some states there are Forest Service avalanche numbers to call; the National Ski Patrol will certainly have information. The land agency office nearest your destination will have reports of local conditions.

Whatever the type of avalanche, the danger is greatest on treeless slopes of middle steepness, between about thirty and forty-five degrees. Gullies and open swaths in forested landscapes are especially risky. Dense timber provides some reassurance, but a few trees on an open slope don't prove a lack of avalanches there. Avoid the lee sides of steep, high ridges. Keep out from under *cornices*, the solid waves of snow and ice that hang over the crests of windy ridges like paralyzed ocean breakers.

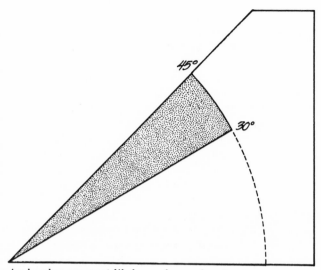

Avalanches are most likely on slopes of moderate steepness: between 30 and 45 degrees.

If an indicated avalanche path lies across your course, it's best simply to go around it. The safest method is to circle it at the top; the second best, often more practical, is to bypass the swath on gentler ground at the bottom. Ridges are safer ground than steep valleys and draws.

If you find no way around an ominous path, try to judge the risk. Is it "avalanche weather"—has it been snowing or blowing a lot? Consider also what might happen if you were caught in a slide. A short avalanche path that widens at the bottom is not quite so perilous as a long chute that funnels in. Are there rocks and trees at the bottom of the slope against which you would be crushed, or a cliff over which you would be carried? In some cases, by far the best choice is to turn back.

If you are to cross a wide avalanche path, you may be able to take advantage of natural shelters: clumps of trees and patches of bare rock. Go across one at a time. Every member of the party should watch the crosser carefully; the last to go is in no less danger than the first.

If you are crossing an avalanche path on skis, you should undo the wrist loops of your ski poles and the safety straps of your skis and set your ski bindings for easy release. If you are on snowshoes, you should undo the wrist strap of your ice axe or pole. The waiststrap of the pack, too, should be undone. Stiff encumbrances, tumbling with you in an avalanche, can drag you down. They also impede your freedom to use your arms—a very important thing. Make your shell of clothing as smooth and perfect as you can: zip zippers, button buttons, raise your parka hood, put on stocking cap and mittens.

As you cross the danger area, watch the behavior of the snow. If you hear cracking and grumbling noises, or see cracks shooting out in front of your skis, you'll do well to retreat; these are signs of an imminent break. Most victims themselves trigger the avalanches that overwhelm them.

There are several items of gear designed to improve the odds if the snow does flow. Everyone should carry an *avalanche cord,* a hundred-foot length of brightly colored cord marked with arrows ($10). You attach one end—the end toward which the arrows point—to your belt. The rest of the cord is in your pocket, wound up in a ball. In dangerous country, you trail the cord behind you. If you are buried, it will help companions locate you more quickly.

A more elaborate safety device is the *personal tracer* or peeper, a shortwave radio that broadcasts a high-pitched beep. In avalanche terrain, all members of a party thus equipped turn their units to *transmit.* If one person is buried, the other travelers turn their own units to *receive.* By homing in on the signal from under the snow, they can find the victim in short order. But there is a definite skill to this, and the multiple units are expensive.

Some ski poles are so made that they can be stripped of their baskets and screwed together into long probes: another aid in finding an avalanche victim.

Avalanche survival

If you're caught in an avalanche, things will happen terribly fast. By all accounts it's a little like being caught in a flash flood, but a flood at the same time fluid and solid. Immediately shed your ski poles or ice axe, your pack, and your skis (there's not much you can do about snowshoes). Make the motions of a swimmer; try to keep on the surface of the tumbling snow, and to work over to one "bank" of the flow. If in spite of all this you feel yourself going under, cover your face with your arms to preserve a cavity of air. When you stop moving, make an attempt to dig yourself out before the snow hardens around you. (You may have to spit to make sure which way is up; some avalanche victims have lost their orientation so totally that they started by digging *down*.) Don't bother to shout; sound carries very poorly out of snow. If you can't dig, there's really nothing to be done but discipline yourself to calmness, and wait.

If you, the person spared, see a companion carried off in an avalanche, follow these steps.

1. Mark the point where you last saw the victim. Make a quick search down the apparent main line of the avalanche. Mark the location of any pieces of gear you find. Look carefully behind trees, on ledges and benches, and wherever any obstacle might have slowed or diverted the rushing snow.

2. Next comes the careful search. Probe systematically with skis, ski poles, ice axes, or (if you have them) with avalanche probes assembled from ski poles. Reexamine the likely "traps" where the victim might have been stopped; then spread out to cover the whole surface of the avalanche.

3. When you find the victim, you may have to give artificial respiration. Get the snow out of clothing and place the victim in a sleeping bag, head downhill. Treat, as needed, for shock and hypothermia (see Chapters 25 and 28).

What about sending for help? *It is almost never*

worth the loss of time. Half of all buried avalanche victims die within thirty minutes. Unless you're right next to a ski resort, every member of your party should stay and search. Keep searching for six to eight hours. While very few victims last beyond the second hour, there have been astonishing exceptions.

Navigation on snow

In some areas, trails are as useful in winter as they are in summer. A trail may be the only tenable line through tangled woods or over a hazardous slope. Abandoned roads, healed over into simple paths, make especially good and obvious routes for snow travel in rugged country. Following a less pronounced trail can be difficult when the trace is under snow; you have to pay special attention to blazes and clipped branches, or to such signs as ducks or cairns, if they protrude above the cover.

Most of the time, though, trails simply cease to matter in the winter, except as landmarks, guides to where you are. The snow is a whole new country that you cross. One route through the trees may be as good as another. Navigation in winter is generally like cross-country navigation in summer but with special problems added.

Your views of distant landmarks will almost certainly disappear in any overcast. But much more serious are low, thick fog and the opaque misty snowstorms called "whiteouts." In a whiteout you see only a few yards. Shapes are strange, unrecognizable. You can lose all sense of place and direction. When you are thus blinded, it's terribly easy to go wrong; here as nowhere else the compass becomes your lifeline. You need to know, not only how to walk a compass course, but also how to plan a whole trek as a succession of compass lines, or azimuths as they are called—so many paces on azimuth A, so many paces on azimuth B. Keep close track of where you are on the map, so that you can plan a retreat by compass if whiteout settles in. Be sure you understand the tricks of navigation without good landmarks described in Chapter 16. Trails, even if you don't follow them, can be fine helps in navigation; you can use a line of trail blazes as a "destination line." In winter travel, as in cross-country hiking, no one can afford to be a passive follower; each person in a group must be aware.

Your detailed route over snow depends largely on the skis or snowshoes you are wearing. Skis and snowshoes, and different models of each, handle differently; some are more able, some less able, to cross icy slopes, to float in deep, soft powder, or to climb steep hills. Often the snowshoers in a party will head directly up a soft slope, while skiers will circle around, climbing in a series of switchbacks.

Camping in the snow

Let's be honest about it: no winter camp is entirely without discomfort. The snow camp can be, on balance, very pleasant or pretty miserable. It depends partly on things you can't control (like the weather), but mostly it depends on your gear, your skill, and your intelligence.

You generally have a wide choice of campsites in winter. You scarcely have to consider "low impact" when the vulnerable earth is yards beneath your feet. It is polite, though, not to set up your tent right beside the route down which other travelers will come.

One consideration is the availability of liquid water: not a necessity, if you have adequate fuel, but a luxury. You can lower water bottles to a stream rushing in a trench of snow, or maybe carve steps down to waterline. And if you dig a deep-enough well, you can get water from under the ice of any sizable lake.

If you don't find a level place, you can make one in deep snow with a little engineering. (The winter camp, of course, *can* be engineered without harm. Build a whole city, if you like—it will last, at latest, to the thaw.) Just make sure that you are out from under dead limbs and standing snags, and, of course, away from avalanche paths.

The first camp job is to pitch your tent. Without taking off skis or snowshoes, stamp out a level site. To anchor guylines in snow, you need special, broad, aluminum *snow stakes*, or you can use *deadmen*, small chunks of dead wood that are stamped into the snow and buried. Not even dead branches should be broken for deadmen, however, in popular hiking areas, or anywhere near timberline. And if you use them, make one set last the whole trip. Stakes and deadmen will quickly freeze into place, and you may well have to dig and chop to free them when you take the tent down.

You may or may not need to pitch a rainfly. If you are in Yellowstone in February, for instance, you can all but count on cold, dry snow that will slide right off the permeable surface of the inner tent. But if you are in the Cascades or the Appalachians, you can expect a wetter, more clinging snow, and you'll need all the protection you can get. A fly does also add some warmth. On long trips in foul weather, and especially if you are riding out a storm, you will be drier in a tent with a *frostliner*, a fitted sheetlike inner liner that catches and sheds the frost that forms perpetually on the inner surfaces of tents in winter.

If you have good weather and daylight, you can dig out a luxurious kitchen in the snow. Start with a natural depression, like a tree well. Straighten the vertical wall, and then dig out a waist-high "counter" for your stove and cooking gear. But when conditions are less pleasant, hikers cook and eat lying down, setting up the stove just outside the door of a tent. In truly awful weather you may be forced to cook entirely inside, but watch out for any flareup when you prime your stove, and keep ventilation generous. Most summer-type stoves are somewhat balky in cold and wind. Larger stoves with hand-operated pumps work better; Optimus's optional add-on pump makes the smaller stoves in the Optimus line more useful in bitter weather.

Winter dinners tend to be simple. Nobody wants

to deal with six-course menus in the cold. Except in the leisurely, fair-weather camp, the standard is the meaty one-pot meal, with hot drinks, possibly soup, and cold snacks on the side. (In winter as in summer, it's perfectly possible and even luxurious to forget cooking and eat a well-planned selection of cold food, but when you have to fire up the stove anyway, to melt snow for water, it's natural to cook as well.)

Melting water takes time, and it's tempting to stop after a quart or two. Don't. Make sure that each person is getting at least a full gallon of water, in food and drink, each day. As you melt snow, keep drinking; have more tea, more fruit juice, more chocolate. If you wake up with a violent thirst toward morning, it's a good sign that you've been shorting yourself.

Don't drink up the last of your old supply before you begin to melt more water. You need a few spoonfuls, at least, to moisten the bottom of the melting pot. Snow, especially dry, powdery snow, absorbs quite a bit of heat before it liquefies, and the metal of the pan may actually scorch before there's enough water to carry the heat away. (The old joke about "burning the snow" isn't just a joke.) Add small amounts of snow to your starter pool, then gradually more.

The ultimate luxury in winter is a warm, comfortable bed. Nights are long; you spend a lot of time there. If your sleeping bag isn't really intended for winter, you may wind up wearing most of your clothing to bed. Very wet clothes, though, will only chill you. It's particularly important to put on dry socks and, if you have them, insulated booties.

Certain objects need to be brought inside your sleeping bag at night: your boots (in a plastic bag, or in your sleeping bag's stuffbag—turned inside out); your flashlight or headlamp; and, if it's very cold, your camera, in several layers of plastic. If the temperature is much below freezing, water bottles will have to be brought inside or, at the least, tucked alongside your bag, away from the tent wall.

(Make sure the caps are on tight.) Alternatively, you can bury some of your bottles outside under several inches of snow—which, believe it or not, acts as insulation. (But make sure you know exactly where to dig in the morning!)

The battle against damp

Bitter-cold weather, even with wind, is not what winter campers fear. Given the right gear, they will enjoy it. But when the sky closes in, the temperature rises, and a warm, sloppy snow begins falling, they curse. Most especially if you are using down gear, you will have to keep things dry, and that can be hard work when everything around you is wet.

Avoid bringing snow into your tent with you. Keep a whisk broom and a sponge just inside the tent door. Brush yourself off as you crawl in; take your boots off at the entrance and make sure the snow is out of the laces and the spaces between lugs.

Keep air flowing through the tent. Give the humid air inside every possible chance to escape. Be quick to mop up spills. If you can cook outside the tent door, you won't have the steam to contend with.

Don't take wet clothing to bed in an attempt to dry it. The moisture doesn't vanish; it just goes into the filler of your bag. Clothes hung from a line run along the peak of the tent, inside, may dry out at least partway. While it's unpleasant to put on wet and frozen clothes in the morning, it's not as unpleasant as a wet sleeping bag. Even if it's very cold, don't cover your nose and mouth with the bag; your breath shouldn't be trapped inside. (Breathe through your stocking cap instead.)

Precautions like these are always advisable. If you are depending on a down sleeping bag without a water-resistant shell, they are absolutely vital.

Shelters made of snow

Though many never bother, every winter camper really ought to get some experience in building a shelter in the snow. These skills can be invaluable in an emergency, when there's no tent to be had, and a growing number of travelers use snow shelters all the time, saving a certain amount of weight. (Typical two-person winter tent: eight pounds; shovel and snow-saw for building a snow shelter: under two pounds.)

The simplest and quickest snow shelter is the *trench.* It's just what it sounds like, a moat, three or four feet deep, six or seven feet long, and wide enough for two or three sleepers (wider trenches are hard to cover). In the old days you would make a roof of interwoven conifer boughs. That won't do now, of course, unless a life is at stake; instead you use a tent fly, a tarp, or some such, laid on beams made of ski poles, axes, or whatever you have (down branches, should you find them, make good supports). For insulation, cover the roof with snow. Be sure to leave an opening for ventilation. Snow-trenches, in their simplicity, are perhaps the best of emergency winter shelters.

More elaborate is the *snow cave.* To build one, you need soft to medium snow—the kind that holds its shape when cut—and a good thick snowbank. Creekbanks are good places to find suitable drifts.

There are at least two ways of digging a snow cave. The traditional method is simple to describe but difficult to carry out. You burrow into the snowbank, making an entry tunnel. About four feet in, you angle the tunnel upwards; then excavate a chamber with its floor raised well above the tunnel so that warmth will be retained. The job takes three or four hours, even with a snow shovel, and the excavators get soaking wet.

It is possible to shortcut the process a bit. The trick, essentially, is to dig the snow cave with an oversize entryway, so that you have room to work without burrowing like a mole, and then to close off the extra gap. Proceed this way:

First, cut away at your snowbank to make it as close as possible to a vertical wall.

Second, dig into that wall a horizontal alcove

Snow cave construction, shortcut method

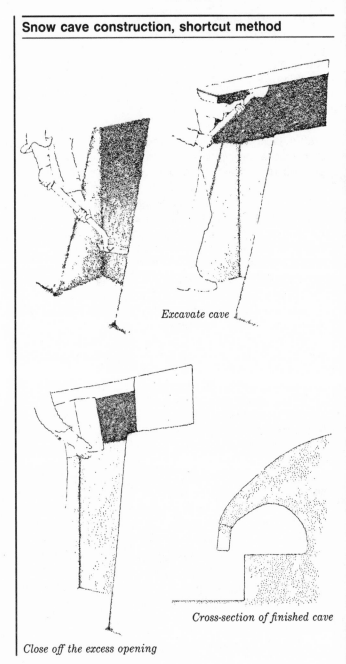

Excavate cave

Close off the excess opening

Cross-section of finished cave

about four feet wide. Make the floor of this opening level with your belt; make its ceiling about eighteen inches above. This alcove is the beginning of the cave.

Now start expanding the opening backward into the snow. Don't make the initial gap bigger; just hollow out behind it, inwards, sideways, and upwards, but not downwards. The floor should run back on a level.

When you've dug out all the snow you can get at from your first position, excavate a trench for your legs, cutting into the incomplete cave, so that you can stand up in there.

Now finish the cave. Make it as large as you like: a typical plan is more or less a rectangle, seven feet wide, five feet deep (into the snowbank), and three to four feet high. Make the ceiling a smoothly rounded dome.

What you have now is a snow cave with one side gaping open to the air, a sort of cutaway model. It remains to close off the open side. You do this by cutting several big snow blocks and placing them in the unwanted window. One of these blocks will bridge the trench you cut for your legs, turning it into a short tunnel—your permanent entry. Fill in the cracks and gaps between the blocks with loose snow.

Complex as it sounds, this method eliminates much of the misery of building a snow cave, and you don't get very wet (though it still does no harm to put on waterproofs). Practiced cave-makers can do the job this way in an hour or so.

After the shelter is essentially done—by whatever method—you "furnish" it. Cover the raised floor with a groundsheet, and cut niches and shelves for a candle, your stove, and odds and ends. Punch a ventilating shaft up through the high point of the dome and a second above the stove. Narrow to start with, these shafts will widen as heat rises through them.

An *igloo* is something like a snow cave above ground. To build one, you need snow firm enough to hold its shape in blocks cut with shovel (or shovel and saw). If loose snow is all you have, you can trample it down with skis or snowshoes, then let it set for twenty minutes or so. The bigger the blocks

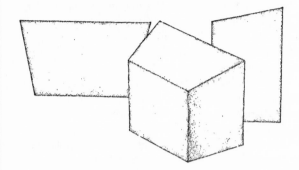

you work with, the faster the job gets done: eighteen inches by ten inches by fifteen inches is typical. Because you're building a dome, the blocks must be beveled, with top and end surfaces sloping inward.

To guide yourself, outline the base of the igloo (round or oval—an eight- to ten-foot diameter). Then choose the location of your entry. The best position is downhill and crosswise to the prevailing wind. Dig a trench from the center of your circle to the entry and several feet beyond. Remove the snow from this trench in usable blocks.

Trench dug, you begin laying blocks around the circle. (One of them will bridge the trench.) When you finish the first circuit, trim the first couple of blocks you placed to make a gradual ramp, and take the second course right on up over them, starting a spiral. Then just keep going.

Typically, one of the snow masons works outside, cutting blocks, while the second stands inside to take them, place them, and finish the shaping. Five or six courses will be required. Because of the shape of the blocks, the walls will lean increasingly inward. If the blocks are regular enough and carefully beveled, they'll support themselves clear to the final large keystone block that closes the top. When it becomes convenient, cut an arched lintel into the block

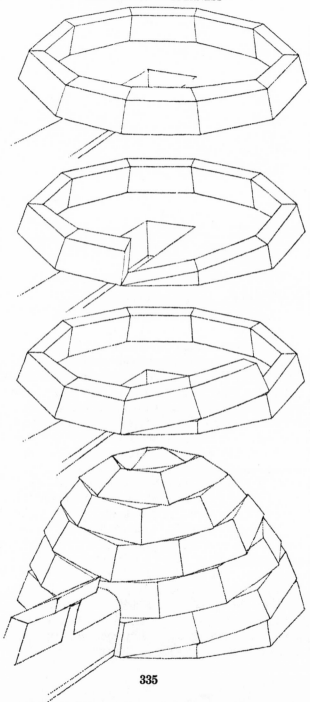

that spans the trench, making a door.

At this point you have your basic igloo. For extra protection you can add a raised roof of blocks over the trench outside the wall, making a covered entryway. Then coat the outside of the igloo with loose snow. You should be able to move inside, and out of the wind, in an hour. The structure will knit together quickly as it warms up inside. As with a snow cave, you finish the interior for convenience, punching or cutting a generous air vent at the peak.

Igloos and snow caves are quite astonishing places; they're dead silent, warm, comfortable, sheltered. No blizzard outside can touch you—can scarcely make itself heard. The snow admits daylight, a curious light, colorless, dim, yet very clear.

There are things to be aware of in any snow house. Just as in a tent, you have to make sure your ventilation is good. Don't block the air shafts or your entryway. See that the entry doesn't get sealed by drifted snow; a low, outlying shield wall of two or three blocks may trap a drift where it does no harm. Then there's the moisture problem. When stoves are running, the snowy roof will drip. Since drops collect on projections, the smoother you've made the roof, the less problem there will be. Both caves and igloos are very strong, if their roofs are properly thick.

Skis and snowshoes

For the person who wants to take up winter backpacking (as opposed to unburdened cross-country skiing) the snowshoe is the simplest tool of travel. Snowshoes aren't hard to use, they are still relatively cheap, and, unlike skis, they are practical when you carry a frame pack.

As you gain experience, you may want to switch to skis, or at least to substitute skis part of the time. It depends partly on personal taste (how much does speed matter to you?) and partly on the kind of country you visit. In lands that are largely flat and rolling, or steep but not densely timbered, nothing moves like a pair of skis. Yet in rugged, timbered, tangled mountains such as the Appalachians, skis can be clumsy; the more maneuverable snowshoes may actually serve you better. In deep, fresh powder, too, skis may lose much of their advantage. Don't be overawed by skiers who dismiss the snowshoe as a beginner's tool.

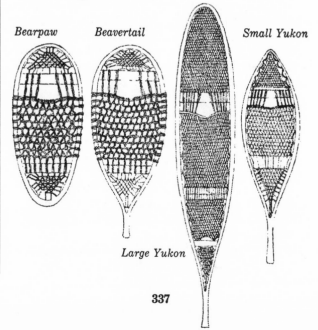

Bearpaw *Beavertail* *Small Yukon*

Large Yukon

The snowshoe

The classic snowshoe is a piece of basketwork: webbing of rawhide, neoprene, or other material stretched tightly across a wooden or metal frame. Wearing snowshoes, you walk much as you would on bare ground without them. At first you will step on yourself a few times and take some comical falls, but the skill teaches itself.

Snowshoes come in many styles and designs. The list begins with the oval *bearpaw* design: typically eight to twelve inches wide and some thirty inches long, with a rounded toe, swept slightly upward, and a rounded tail. From the bearpaw has evolved the *Western*, longer for its width, with parallel sides and sharply upturned toes: a shoe designed for the mountainous West but now found everywhere. (Sherpa is the most familiar brand.) Bearpawlike shoes that come to a point in the back are called *beavertails*. Long, narrow shoes with tails are *Maine* or *Michigan* snowshoes if the tips are flattish, and become *cross-country* or *Yukon* shoes if the toes sweep upward. Finally there's the enormous *Ojibwa* style, pointed at both ends.

Which type is best for you depends on local conditions, as well as on personal taste; consult stores in your region and rent different styles for trial. Generally speaking, long snowshoes with tails are best in open, gentle country in soft powder. Smaller, narrower shoes are suited to steeper slopes and denser snow. The more compact the snowshoe you can work with, the better off you are.

Points to consider:

Length and width. The heavier you are, and the softer the snow you traverse, the more surface area you need in a snowshoe. Seldom, however, will you want a shoe wider than one foot or longer than three. Wide shoes are awkward when you walk along a slope; long shoes are awkward when you zigzag among trees.

Style of toe. For flattish terrain and fairly firm snow, a fairly flat toe—one that curves up just slightly—will suffice. For powder snow and steeper slopes, such a toe will bury itself and trip you; you need a moderate upturn—say, three or four inches. (But short, flat tips are better for kicking steps in crusty snow.) Sharply upturned tips are good in just one circumstance: very deep, light snow on gentle terrain.

Style of tail. The tail of a classic snowshoe, dragging in the snow as you walk, helps keep the snowshoe in a straight line; tailless bearpaws tend to flop around. A firm binding that permits little twisting motion, as on the Western-style shoes by Sherpa, helps to combat this tendency.

Construction. The traditional snowshoe is built of blond ashwood and stretched rawhide; it is probably the single most exquisite object used in wilderness camping. In recent years, though, other constructions have come to dominate the market. Cording may now be of nylon or neoprene; some models have solid decks instead of webbing. Frames are often of aluminum. These alternatives have different advantages; some are more durable and require less maintenance than rawhide and ash. One material to avoid, though, is solid, molded plastic. One-piece plastic snowshoes are not now stout enough for backpacking.

Snowshoe crampons. When snow is soft, you can climb at remarkable angles in snowshoes by stamping the shoes firmly into the slope or by kicking in with the toes. On a hard or icy slope, however, you'll slip. Some shoes come with built-in gripping devices, toothed or knifelike projections mounted below the ball of the foot to grip the snow. These "snowshoe crampons" can be purchased separately ($10 or so) for shoes that lack them. In some areas, notably the Northeast, they are indispensable. They can also be made, much more cheaply, out of surplus U.S. Army crampon sets.

Maintenance. Rawhide snowshoes must be coated, now and again, with spar varnish or an equivalent (available at gear stores and nautical supply stores). If you travel mostly in deep powder, you may only need to recoat once a year, but trips on hard and abrasive snow, or on very wet snow, wear off the protective coating much more rapidly. Snowshoes of other construction may have to be painted with other coatings; metal-and-neoprene types require almost no maintenance at all.

Price. Snowshoe prices vary all the way from $30 to over $200, with the most commonly used models lying between $50 and $110.

Snowshoe boots and bindings

When you wear a snowshoe, your boot rests on webbing and is attached near the toe to a stout crossbar of some sort (the *master cord*). With each step your heel rises clear off the snowshoe, and your toe dips into an opening in the basketwork, cutting briefly into the snow below. On some models this opening lies very far forward on the snowshoe; on others it is closer to the center. A forward opening is better for climbing hills, worse for descending, and worse for wading through powder.

There are many different rigs for binding the boot to the snowshoe. A few models have very secure bindings built into the shoe. Otherwise you purchase bindings separately. (Most bindings cost $10–$20; elaborate ones by "high-tech" makers go as high as $70.) A familiar type is the "H" binding, with straps running over the foot at toe and instep and another strap wrapping lengthwise around the heel. The straps of the "H" tend to slip off and must be cinched up very tight; thus it should only be worn over a good hard boot. On the plus side, this rig leaves the sole of the boot exposed under the toe. The lugs, cutting into the snow with every step, give you some useful traction in climbing hills.

More convenient bindings are available, however. The Howe and the Beck—both variants on the "H"—cover the toe with a flap of material and grip the boot a little better; the loss of traction does not matter if snowshoe crampons are used. Bindings by Sherpa grip the whole front half of the boot and are very secure—also notably expensive.

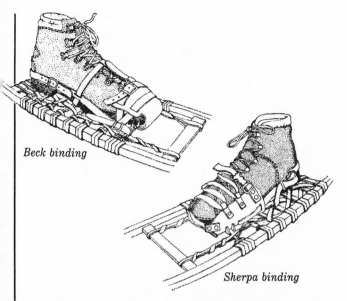

Beck binding

Sherpa binding

Most bindings give at least some trouble to beginning snowshoers. All you can do is keep on working with the harness until, as it will, it stops misbehaving. The key is getting the heelstrap tight enough, and the toe of the boot positioned properly over the toe hole: the reinforced master cord of the snowshoe webbing should be under the ball of your foot.

On snowshoes you need a third leg for balance. A ski pole will do in most terrain. If you cross steep, icy snow on snowshoes, you definitely need, instead of a pole, a long-shafted ice axe fitted out with a clip-on ski basket ($15).

Skis

Skis might seem to be simple objects. They are, after all, pretty much of one shape, without the free-form variations seen among the snowshoes. But in truth the world of skis is the more complicated one.

Most wilderness skis used to be built, handsomely, of laminated wood. A few still are, but another material, fiberglass, now dominates the market.

Cross-country skis now look like slimmer downhill skis. Unfortunately, the flashy colors of the heavier skis have been widely adopted, too.

Skis are built in a range of weights, from super-light "racing skis" used on packed, level courses up to heavy mountaineering skis and, heaviest of all, the outright downhill models. For backpacking you need a ski of medium weight, neither too light nor too narrow, in the class often referred to as "general touring" models. About the lightest skis suitable for backpacking weigh four and a half pounds the pair and are not less than fifty-two millimeters wide under the foot. If you hope to do rugged ski backpacking, or to do much downhill-style skiing in the wilderness, chances are you will need skis a good deal heavier than this minimum.

The next thing to consider, after proper weight, is *camber*. Skis are not just flat boards. Rather, they bow upwards, resisting the skier's weight. Put a pair of skis together, base to base, and you'll see daylight between. This curvature is their camber.

Skis come in a range of camber and stiffness. Some bow out very decidedly and can be flattened only with difficulty: it may take a two-handed effort to close the gap. Others are fairly limp and can be pressed together easily. Stiff, high-cambered skis glide very readily but are somewhat difficult to turn. Softer, flatter skis turn more easily but have less glide. For backpacking, choose skis toward the latter end of the scale: with moderate to low camber, not too stiff.

The next choice you face—one that hardly existed a few years ago—is whether to wax or not to wax.

In skiing cross-country you fall into a steady, gliding gait called the *diagonal stride*, which looks (and sometimes feels) practically effortless. For this technique to work, your skis must grip the snow at certain moments and glide freely forward at others. This magic can be worked in different ways.

Traditional skis have a smooth wood or plastic undersurface (or "base"). This surface you coat with one or more layers of cunningly formulated waxes. When the ski is stationary, snow crystals press into this coating and grip the ski. When you push forward, the projecting granules melt and let the ski glide. When the stride is finished, the surface refreezes and the bond is restored, giving you a firm base for the next forward push.

One wax won't serve for all temperatures and types of snow. In fact, there are a dozen or more grades of waxes for the most varied conditions. Good waxers can do marvelous things with this selection, gliding up very substantial slopes with little trouble. To many people the skill of choosing and applying the right waxes—a fascinating business—is the center of the skiing experience.

However, there are reasons for seeking alternatives to full-dress waxing. For people not caught up in the challenge of the technique itself, it seems an awful lot of trouble. There's a period of learning in which you will have trouble choosing the right goop, and even practiced waxers may have to stop and do the job anew several times a day, as conditions change. Also, there are accessories that have to be carried: scraper, cork, wax-removing solvent and rags or a butane-fired torch, and maybe some hand-cleaning lotion. Total cost of the kit can be as little as $15 if you don't shell out for a $30 torch.

Also, some regions are more hospitable to waxers than others. In the deep, dry snow of the Rockies, where conditions tend to remain the same all day, a good wax job in the morning may keep you in trim all day; but in the wet snows of the Pacific ranges or the icy, crusty packs of New England, continual adjustments will be necessary.

There are, fortunately, alternatives of three kinds: broad-spectrum waxes, climbing skins, and no-wax skis.

Broad-spectrum waxes are specially formulated for a wide range of snow conditions. Instead of a whole kit, you can get by with two or three types. They seem to work reasonably well, especially on moderate terrain.

Climbing skins are strips of fabric covered with stiff artificial hairs. To use them, you hook one end (equipped with a loop or ring) over the toe of each ski; the rest of the skin is held to the ski with a layer of strong, temporary adhesive. The bristles of the skin point backward and resist any downhill slide. With skins, you can shuffle right up a pretty severe slope.

Some ski backpackers carry both skins—to make sure they get where they're going—and broad-spectrum waxes—to use when the terrain levels out and the going is easy.

The final option is to use no-wax skis. These models have been modified so that they will slide forward but not backward, like skis with skins. Usually the gimmick is some sort of repetitive pattern on the base of the ski: plastic fish scales, minute step-like edges, or other. Other models have miniature skins—little strips of synthetic hair—built in; still others use chips of mica. These no-wax skis never perform quite as well as perfectly waxed conventional skis, but they do move.

Another ski decision concerns *edges.* Some medium-weight skis have metal strips running partway along each edge of the base; some don't. These metal corners can help in crossing icy slopes and in making turns on downhill runs; skis designed for mountaineering may have edges full length.

In choosing your skis and appurtenances, you need to distinguish between skis as transportation and skis as entertainment. If you are using skis much as you would snowshoes—to get from here to there—many of the finer points don't matter. A laden skier uses the diagonal stride, but it is a subdued, slow stride; at times you will simply trudge. If, on the other hand, you plan to pack yourself into a wilderness site and then branch out from there, skiing remote slopes with a daypack on your back, you have to weigh your ambitions and choose your gear with more care.

For much more information on ski gear and the skills of wilderness skiing, I recommend the excel-

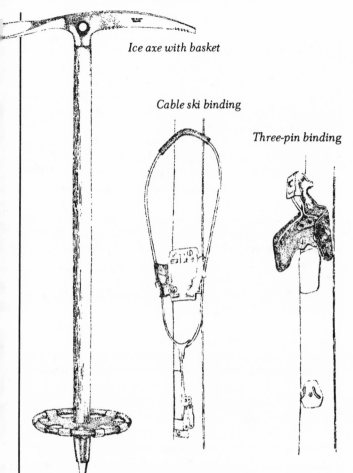

Ice axe with basket

Cable ski binding

Three-pin binding

lent book *Backcountry Skiing* by Lito Tejada-Flores (see *Resources* appendix).

Ski boots, bindings, and poles

With skis, the question of bindings and boots is quite a subject in itself. There are two major possibilities. First, and most widely used, are *three-pin* bindings with corresponding specialized boots; second are the so-called *mountaineering* bindings that can be used with any heavy hiking or climbing boot.

Three-pin bindings consist of three short pegs

mounted on the ski, a toe clamp, and a heelplate. Your boot has three small pits in the sole under the toe, corresponding to the pegs. To get into the binding, you press the toe of the boot into position, fit pegs to holes, and close down a securing clamp. You can get into such a binding quickly, and the heel of the boot rises freely, as it must for effective skiing on level or rising ground.

Some optional refinements complicate the scheme. You can, if you choose, replace the little heel plate with a V-shaped protruberance called a *heel locater.* A matching piece is mounted on the heel of your boot. When the heel is down, the locater holds it firmly in place, improving your lateral control when you ski downhill. The device is somewhat controversial—some regard it as dangerous in a fall. A *voilé plate* is a flexible plastic plate that runs back under the boot from the binding and attaches to the heel; it gives you better control if your boots are somewhat soft.

Bindings and boots are made in standard dimensions for wide interchangeability. The pattern most appropriate for backpacking is the so-called *Nordic norm.* The toe of a Nordic norm boot is a squarish projection seventy-five millimeters across and twelve millimeters thick; the holes in a Nordic norm boot match the pegs on a Nordic norm binding.

A suitable ski boot needs more than standard dimensions. It must flex readily front to back, the way the foot will bend, but resist other kinds of motion. Look for *torsional stiffness*—resistance to twisting. Hold the toe in one hand, the heel in the other, and rotate in opposite directions, as though you were wringing out a towel. A good boot will not twist very far; many on the market are entirely too limp for backpack skiing. Better boots are likely to have leather soles and a Norwegian welt (you can see lines of stitching where sole and upper join).

Some boots are light and low-cut, and thus very cool on the feet. The backpacker needs a somewhat more substantial boot with a moderately high top. Even so, most boots probably won't be warm

Cross-country ski boots

enough to beat around in when you're pitching a
tent, digging a snow cave, or cooking a meal in an
outdoor kitchen. Thus you will need to carry some
other footwear for camp: ordinary boots, soft shoepacs, or overboots. Insulated *ski overboots* are available; these have holes for the binding pegs to penetrate and thus can be worn while on skis as well as
off. (Heavy socks, worn over the boots, can also help
if you're cold while on the move.)

Bindings of the second basic type make use of
your ordinary hiking boots, if these are heavy.
These *mountaineering* bindings all contrive to give
the heels freedom to lift, like three-pin arrangements but by more elaborate means. Some use a
cable running from a toe clamp around the back of
the boot, resting in the welt (joint between sole and
upper). Other versions have a heel clamp with a
hinge arrangement that allows the heel to lift. There
is usually a means of binding the heel down firmly
for downhill runs; safety releases may be provided
at toe and heel. These rigs tend to be elaborate and
expensive. At this point, at least, there is really no
general-purpose binding made for the person, not an
ambitious skier, who simply wants to ski in hiking
boots.

You need *ski poles,* of course, usually made of
fiberglass. Short downhill ski poles won't serve.
Cross-country ski poles are longer and have tips
swept sharply back for poling in the diagonal stride.
Get a shop's advice in picking the right length.

Ski prices vary a good deal; most now run $130–$200 in the types backpackers are most likely to use. The true cost to you includes essential accessories as well. Three-pin bindings cost $10–$25, but with them you must have special boots at $60–$120. Cable bindings cost a little more, and full release mountaineering bindings may go as high as $200 (on the other hand, no special boot is required). Poles sell for $10–$60, with good ones nearer the top of the range. No matter how you choose these components, the total outlay for ski gear will probably be over $250. Special package deals, frequently offered in stores, may save you a few dollars; end-of-season sales in the spring will save you a bundle!

Repair kit

Skis and snowshoes—even the new models built of tough synthetic materials—do sometimes get broken on the trail. So you need a repair kit. For most snowshoes, especially wood and rawhide types, you should have plenty of adhesive tape, wire, and cord. For skis you also need wire, in order to hold the binding to the ski if it begins to detach. (Since most skis are now made with soft foam cores, the old remedy of replacing the pulled-out screw with a longer one no longer works.) A pair of pliers is likely to be useful. So is duct tape. You should always carry a spare tip: an emergency substitute, metal or plastic, that you can slide over the stump of your ski if you should break the point. A ski without an upturned leading edge just won't travel. If you use cable bindings, it's wise to carry a spare cable. To repair a broken pole, take electrician's tape and a spare basket.

24:
Hiking and Camping with Kids

A MAJORITY OF WILDERNESS TRAVELERS—so say the studies—are married, and most of them have children. (Interestingly enough, married couples who do *not* have children are underrepresented in the wild places.) For more and more people backpacking has become what, in earlier years, it was for few: a family sport. And more and more often, the kids, even the very young ones, are coming along.

It's perfectly practical to backpack, not only with middle-sized children, but also with babies. In fact, people who have done it—who have raised their children half in the wilderness, half at home—seem to find the process delightful.

True, you may not be able to go very far or very fast; true, you may have to carry a certain amount of extra gear and do a few extra chores on the trail and in camp. But a slower pace can be a pleasant change. And the child who has among earliest memories the woods, the streams, the far-off mountains, may well have gained an advantage that will last a lifetime. Even very young children, too, seem to value the sense of being part of the enterprise their parents are carrying out. Something important, pleasant, and adult is going on, and they are part of it, not excluded. To older children, the actual responsibilities of the trail—even scaled down to their size—are a firm link with the parents, and a kind of preview of growing up.

Parents who backpack with their children, and enjoy it greatly, warn that you mustn't expect the wrong things. A trip with kids is quite another experience than a trip with adults; it's another style of travel. It is—it has to be—more leisurely. You have to give yourself more leeway, more margin, than you would on an ordinary trip. It isn't just that children have shorter legs than their parents; they also have different attitudes. Up to a certain (and quite variable) age, kids just don't look at the wilderness the way their parents do. They enjoy it for different reasons, value different things.

Most kids are tougher, physically, than we give them credit for. They'll make out just as well in the wilderness as out of it—maybe better. They won't be as clean as they might be at home, but you quickly learn not to bother much about *that*. Otherwise, common sense is enough to keep them healthy. It's true, of course, that you're far away from the doctor. If you've put off learning first aid on your own behalf, it's a good idea to take it up when you begin traveling with children.

When you're starting backpackers small, you want to start them slow—partly for their sake, even more for yours. All those special items, all those plans for traveling with children need shaking down. It's best to start with day-hikes, very short at first, then longer. Here's where you find out about temperaments and problems. How happy is the two-year-old in the baby-carrier? How much walking does the five-year-old feel up to? Before you move on to overnight camping, you may want to test your methods on safe ground. Try cooking meals on day-trips; try a risk-free "camp" on the back lawn or at an auto campground.

As you move on to backpacking, begin with trips in familiar territory. Make plans that don't put your group under pressure, and try excursions you'll enjoy whether or not you make it all the way in to such-and-such a peak or such-and-such a waterfall. Most people who hike with young children don't fight bad weather when it catches up with them; they just go home. Don't let a youngster get the feeling that misery and wilderness belong together. The great principle is simply to take things easy.

For backpacking purposes, you can say that children come in three sizes. There are the very small ones, the *portable* ones, who aren't able to walk much yet. There are the older ones, five years and above, who (if not exactly hikers at first) are more or less *hikable.* And in between are the youngsters of two and three and four—kids who want to do things for themselves but can't very well. Backpacking parents find it most challenging to travel with children of this age. But they do it, and the young and the old seem both to enjoy it.

Portable kids

How soon do you start taking an infant into the wild country? As soon as you like. Some families backpack with babies only a month old; most wait till about six months. In some ways these youngest children are very easy to manage. You will, of course, be slowed down somewhat by feeding and diaper-changing, and most of the family's gear will have to ride in a single pack. On the other hand, the baby will go happily as fast and far as you feel able to manage.

Not all destinations are suitable, though. Because babies won't stand for wearing sunglasses, they can't very well be taken onto snowfields or to high elevations above timberline. (Sunburn, incidentally, can be quite serious in a very young child.) And the younger one is, the greater the risk of altitude sickness: infants have practically no ability to adjust to thin, high-mountain air.

What do you carry your passenger in? The choice is wide. (The old leather papoose-carrier, lined with sphagnum moss as an absorbent diaper, was elegant, but the materials are hard to find these days.) You can buy various contraptions in backpacking stores and also in department stores and through mail-order catalogs. For very young children, you can use soft slings. These hold the baby against your chest, or on your back, or at either side, depending on the model. The Japanese use a simple wide band of cotton, swathed around carrier and child, called a *kumori*. Much more elaborate rigs, including the well-known Snugli carrier, are available. Prices run from $10 to $50.

Most people start using a backpack-style carrier as soon as the child (at six months or so) can sit upright. These have seats of nylon or canvas, slung inside a metal frame. Some models have the rider facing forward, some backward. The forward-facing design—so most people find—is easier to carry. The child should be held quite close to the back. A carrier, like any other pack, should have padded hip and shoulder belts and room to strap a sleeping bag on below; the more incidental storage room there is, the better. A restraining belt, for safety, is also a good idea. Carriers run $30 and up.

Most babies, delighted by the motion, ride well in their perches. A familiar toy, tied to the frame, makes a good diversion. Not until a youngster has begun to walk does the ride seem confining and dull.

When you have a passenger on your shoulders, you obviously have to watch out for low branches and avoid leaning over (especially if there's no restraining belt). Though some babies seem amazingly warm-blooded, the rider should be dressed more warmly than you are. If it's at all chilly, you need to pay special attention to keeping the baby dry. Make sure also that eyes and skin are protected from bright sun.

The same baby clothes used at home will do on the trail. Elastic one-piece garments, lighter or heavier or doubled-up according to the season, are good. Whatever clothing you bring, carry a *lot* of changes: you can hardly bring too many. Raingear? Standard waterproof "slickers" coated with vinyl, available in department stores, work well for most children. Buy rainpants as well as long coats. (Since youngsters perspire less than adults, and don't tend to drown inside their waterproofs, you won't need to scour the stores for small-size garments in Gore-Tex.)

The various items you take to care for a baby don't add up to much, in bulk or in weight, yet it's easy to get off without some essential object. It's important, here again, to make a list.

In camp, very young children aren't likely to crawl or toddle clear away into the forest. But they are quite likely to head for the attractive flames of a fire (stove cooking is a little safer). Some people carry a tent (where they ordinarily would not) to use as a playpen. You can also make a pen out of a tarp, hung low at the middle, raised around the edges. Some parents even use a leash and a harness.

As for feeding, make it as simple as possible. Breastfeeding is of course the easiest all around. If you use bottles, make sure they're made of plastic, not of glass. Baby foods should be in cans, not jars. Quite a few freeze-dried foods are puréelike, anyway, and you can always mash solid food to make a usable paste. Kids who are just learning to feed themselves need a deep, generous cup with a big graspable handle: no Sierra Club cup, this. Also bring the usual plastic cereal bowl, bib, and washcloth. Whatever the child has been eating at home should be continued; this is no time to make big changes.

For diapering you have the choice of plain cloth diapers or "disposable" ones. Most people continue whatever routine they use at home. Do avoid, however, those disposable diapers that are made in one piece with an absorbent liner and plastic shell: this makes one of the most unredeemable pieces of garbage the human race has yet invented. Stools, of course, should be carefully buried, but not even the liners of disposable diapers should go into the cat hole—they're durable. Not many people wash diapers on the trail. If you must, keep the operation well away from natural water, use a special basin, and pour the washwater into a hole (fill it in later). Even if you do laundry, you'll need a strong, leakproof plastic bag (or several, one inside the other) for carrying soiled diapers. Take plenty—more than you expect to need—along with all the incidentals.

At night a baby can be tucked (cautiously) into a parent's sleeping bag or wrapped up and placed in a stuffsack—a comical but very sensible bed. A jacket makes a "sleeping bag" of about the right size. It's obviously better not to use down gear as bedding for young children—you'll no doubt have to launder it repeatedly, and down is damaged by washing. A plastic sheet will help.

In-between kids

It's not the infant—the object to be carried—that parents find most difficult to take to the wilderness with them. Rather, it's the two-, three-, and four-year-olds who are neither mere passengers nor quite self-operating human beings. Too heavy and restless to carry for long, the child can't walk fast or far. A four-mile day, with such a companion, is about the most you can plan on. At this stage quite a few people sign up with organized groups for aid and comfort and take mostly easy trips to accessible base-camps.

In the earlier part of this period, youngsters are of course still mastering the basic skills of being alive: learning to walk with confidence, to talk, to feed themselves, to use the toilet. Wilderness toilet methods, in particular, can sometimes upset a child who has just learned that virtue is the porcelain flush toilet. Now they're asked to squat over a hole in the ground. It may seem not only odd but also downright sinful. Some youngsters have more than a little trouble with this. It's up to the parents to stay with the child and be reassuring. Some people bring along light plastic toilet seats. (Make sure the child knows to wash hands in a basin, not in a lake or stream.)

This is the time when kids are exploring, handling things around them, getting into things. There are plenty of dangerous objects around a camp that have to be watched. But there's also a lot of gear, soft, harmless, and fascinating, for a child to play with.

Clothing gets simpler at this stage. You still need generous spares but not quite so many. For sleeping, some people give their middle-sized kids adult bags and let them flounder; there are also the short "bivouac sacks" used by climbers in combination with thick jackets. Polyester bags are best, especially for the occasional bedwetter. Though kids need some insulation under them, they're generally happy without the soft padding that many adults require.

Hikable kids

Once youngsters are able to walk at a fair clip, the problems change; some of them disappear. Older kids will wear what anybody wears on the trail, with a few differences. Boots, for instance. There just aren't any real backpacking boots in children's sizes. On easy trails in summer, high-topped tennis shoes are fine. Inexpensive work boots also do well. Few families are large enough these days for much "handing down" of wilderness gear, but sometimes several families can get together in a sort of pool. Then there are the invaluable thrift shops.

Most kids seem to enjoy carrying packs from an early age. The first "load" may be no load at all, or a favorite toy. Use a daypack or a summit pack with shortened straps. A large daypack, with sleeping bag tied on the outside, can hold a considerable amount of light gear. Kids of about nine and older have no trouble with a full load—that is, a load proportional to their weight; a small, cheap frame pack may begin to make sense at about this age.

Even after children can walk pretty well, they may think of it as a chore. It takes some encouragement to keep a young hiker going. Though your range will be longer now, you still don't want to be in the position of *having* to get to a particular, distant place. You'll need to take frequent breaks to rest, to eat, to play a game, to look at something entertaining like a stream. It can be fun to look things up in guides to flowers, trees, rocks, birds—if you aren't too high-handedly "educational" about it. Some favorite playthings should be there to fall back on.

In matters of safety your judgment will have to substitute for the youngster's—and that can take a good deal of your time. Give each kid a whistle, pinned to their shirt. (You'll have to convince them not to blow it for the fun of it.) Keep the younger children in sight and the middling ones within earshot. Older kids may want to run ahead, but have them wait at a given point (a trail junction, the foot of a slope, whatever). This is not, for that matter, a bad idea among adults.

Tell them what to do if they lose you. The rule: sit down, blow the whistle a lot, and stay put. Talk to them also about the possible hazards of the land: snakes, bears, poison oak or ivy or whatever, falling rocks, rapid currents. It can be hard to do this without making the woods sound forbidding, but it's not a step to be skipped.

Discourage kids from eating while they walk. (Some of them can't hike and chew gum at the same time, and there's a risk of getting a food fragment stuck in a windpipe.) You'll have warned them, of course, against munching the unidentified leaf or berry; still, a handbook on poisonous plants is one good item to have along.

In general, watch out for problems children may be having. Some, as you might expect, complain very readily; others, surprisingly, do not. Check now and again for developing blisters. You need to make sure that kids stay comfortably warm or cool; watch for signs of hypothermia and hyperthermia (see Chapter 28). Be alert also for altitude sickness; it isn't always harmless. Fortunately even the relatively stoic kids don't push themselves as dangerously far as adults may sometimes do.

When you get to camp, check the site for its particular problems—a steep drop, a rotten snag—and point them out. Experienced parents set limits: kids don't go beyond that creek, that rock, that stand of firs. With especially adventurous youngsters, one adult may have to spend most of the time keeping watch.

Any animals you encounter will be fascinating to the young. Teach the kids to understand them, to like them, and to respect them. But be sure to tell kids not to feed them, not to get too close. Animals that seem oddly unafraid may have something wrong with them. *Hands off the cute and furry.*

Many or most kids like to do small chores at camp. This is fine, of course, and should be encouraged. (With the younger ones, it won't speed the chores up any: contrariwise.) Wood gathering is a pleasant assignment, and so is help with tent pitching. If the weather permits, they will probably want to lay out their own bedsites. (Older kids get a lot of pleasure out of a tent of their own.) Then there's help with the cooking—safest are those jobs, like mixing a cold-water pudding, that don't get the small fry too close to fire or stove. (Be sure to tie back long hair when there's fire around.)

There's nothing special about backpacking food for these relatively grown-up children. If anything, the food you take on a trip with youngsters should be even simpler, even easier to prepare. (There is much to be said for the ease of stove cooking here.) Some foods—desserts, of course, and individually packaged hot-cereal breakfasts, and such—have entertainment value. Happily, the problem of the fussy eater is likely to solve itself on the trail.

Low impact: entertainment versus wilderness?

Though kids may enjoy a trip immensely, they aren't at first likely to enjoy it for "adult" reasons. They are more likely than adults to want to return to familiar ground. And when they're in a wild place, they look for the same sorts of entertainments they would find at home: things to *do*. Toys, cards, and games are valuable, especially for rainy days.

Since nothing can fail to be new to them, babies just coming alive to their surroundings are as fascinated by one place as by another. Older kids want places they can play in. Above all they like *water:* a stream, a pond, an ocean shore, mud, or—best of all—snow. They tend to be unimpressed by the subtle detail of the forest. The appreciation of wilderness *as wilderness* seems to come later in life.

This can lead to certain problems, for some of the things that kids find most entertaining are also hard on the wilderness they play in.

Kids (and boys especially—by nature? by social example?) are *engineers*. The first thing they want to do when they find a stream is build a dam across it; the first thing they want to do with dirt is turn it into miniature roads, walls, and earthworks. Even when no special project is underway, children, moving around as much as they do, can accomplish much more than their share of meadow trampling and path beating. This makes it all the more important, when you have youngsters in your party, to select a resilient site. And some might say there is legitimate argument for *not* taking youngsters into the wild places.

And yet there is every advantage to doing so. The taste for wilderness is best learned early, and so are the habits that protect the land. Though it may not come easily, it's never too soon to start teaching kids those wilderness manners that consist partly of courtesy, partly of safety, and partly of concern for the fabric of the country. During the day's hike, try to persuade kids not to trample down trail edges, cut across switchbacks, knock rocks down the slope, and not to collect plants at random. In camp, try to steer the games in harmless directions. Low impact can be taught as a kind of game or entertaining drama. Even adults find it sometimes useful to think of it that way, and kids have the ability to throw themselves into a fantasy without irony. *(The bad guys are after me. Did I leave any marks they can track me down by?)* At any rate it's worth a try. Think of it as an investment. You're training tomorrow's wilderness user to go gently in the fragile wild places.

The change

After all this there comes a time—a different time, for different youngsters—when the young person begins to regard the wilderness somewhat as the adult regards it. Reports vary, but clearly many children come to this change of attitude as early as eight or nine. Wilderness travel is, after all, more play than work, for anyone; the gap between child and adult is not so great here as it would be, for instance, on a visit to the office where a parent works.

Somewhere along the line, youngsters start to see the land as a place to adventure in, to admire and value for its own shape, its own interest. At this point they have already begun to be "real" backpackers, and this is the time that backpacking parents especially look forward to. At this stage some parents (fathers especially) can't resist forcing the kids to walk farther, carry more, and achieve more than they may really enjoy. This is a mistake that can just possibly spoil things. But most kids who discover for themselves the pleasure of the wilderness seem to be addicts for life.

A year or two later the situation changes again, and the kid, long-legged and energetic, will be waiting constantly for *you.*

Trouble and How to Deal With It

It must be poor life that achieves freedom from fear.

—Aldo Leopold

But it is a characteristic of wisdom not to do desperate things.

—Henry David Thoreau

25:
Trouble!

NOBODY LIKES TO THINK ABOUT TROUBLE. Still less
does anyone like to think about trouble in the wilderness. The thought throws a shadow on the pleasant landscape of memory and anticipation that is
"wilderness" in every hiker's mind. But there is a
thing that, like it or not, you can very nearly count
on: if you spend enough time in the wild places, you
will, sooner or later, have some part in dealing with
a critical emergency—someone else's or your own.

Make no mistake: the wilderness (and especially
the winter wilderness) is full of danger. Granted,
the risks, when you compare them with the hazards
of driving a car or running a power lawnmower,
don't look very large. But wilderness risks, because
less familiar, are at first more daunting.

The way to stay out of trouble is to think in
terms of trouble. This doesn't mean a hypochondria,
a fretfulness, or even a conservative unwillingness
to take *considered* risks (that's up to you). What it

does mean is awareness. Don't go out underequipped. Don't go out underinformed. On the trail keep an eye on the world around you and on yourself.

Look for certain objective outside hazards: the approaching thunderstorm, the loose rock ready to fall on companions below, the hazardous ford, the rotten snag. Some of these you will avoid, others you'll have to confront and deal with. Either way, the great virtue is simply to know what you're about. Most accidents seem to happen to people who take risks *without knowing it*, casually, carelessly, unprepared.

Watch also for physical problems in yourself, or in your companions, that could become serious if not attended to. Deal with nuisances promptly, before they become more than nuisances. A cold, drenching rain, for instance, is only an annoyance—but if you don't deal with it properly, it can lead to a life-endangering chill.

Fast trouble, slow trouble

When we think of trouble in the wilderness, we think most often of the swift, sharp blow: the avalanche, the snakebite, the falling stone, the lightning flash. And all these dangers are real.

But there is a second kind of trouble, less dramatic than the first but deadlier. This we might call "slow trouble." It doesn't happen all at once; instead, it sneaks up on you, insidious. Most often it comes with bad weather and with weariness. Altitude sickness can add to it; so can unrecognized hunger; so can unrecognized thirst. Slow trouble tends to build up out of many small problems, many small errors. And it would be inaccurate to say that the trouble finally "strikes"; rather, there comes a moment at which, with a sharp jolt of fear, you recognize the trouble for what it is.

If there is one rule for dealing with slow trouble, it is this: *catch it early.* When someone's physical condition begins to break down, or a party's morale, it is time to turn back or make an early camp. Don't try to bull it through. If your companions seem ready to tough it out, don't be reluctant to protest; they may be terribly wrong.

Few small groups ever select a leader. It goes against the informality they want. And often two or three competent friends can work together by consensus. But if there is neither a formal leader nor a lively "steering committee," a bad situation is only likely to get worse.

Obviously, there's no rule that says you can't have both "slow" trouble and "fast" trouble at once. In fact, it very often works that way. A miserable, exhausted hiker doesn't think as well as a comfortable one. Many short, sharp accidents are the result of errors made by fumbling hands and fumbling minds.

First aid

Ideally, at least one person in a party should have first aid training. In fact, *every* wilderness hiker would do well to get some, and climbers and long-distance trekkers need more medical knowledge than basic first aid courses provide. However, there is a fair amount that the unpracticed first-aider can safely do. And when there's no "expert" within three days and fifty miles, you have to work with what you have and what you know.

One of the most important items in the pack is a booklet setting out, precisely and in order, the actions to be taken when you have a seriously ill or injured person on your hands. Several guides are set up in this idiot-proof fashion. One of the best is Fred T. Darvill's *Mountaineering Medicine,* a pamphlet available at gear stores.

First aid instructions usually emphasize the treatment of dramatic injuries: wounds, broken arms and legs, and so on. They show you how to respond to sudden accident. Important though that knowledge is, it's well to remember that many wilderness illnesses are not of that sort at all. Such a slow-developing yet life-endangering problems as hypothermia, heat stroke, and pulmonary edema are discussed in Chapter 28.

If the emergency is fairly minor—and most are—you will have time to consider, to consult the manual, to talk things over with the cooperative victim. It is the major injury, or the physical collapse, that is most frightening. Such cases are rare in the extreme but so serious that it pays to think about them in advance.

Details vary, but in general there are three steps in dealing with a major wilderness injury or illness.

First, you *save life*. Some problems are so dangerous that action must be almost instantaneous.

Second, you *stabilize things*. Chances are you won't be able to treat a major injury in any fundamental way; all you can do is make the patient as safe and comfortable as possible and follow, with caution, the instructions in your manual and the dictates of common sense.

Third, you *get the victim home*. Sometimes an injured person can get out under his or her own power, slowly, and with help. If not, you'll have to send for outside aid, or, in some cases, carry the victim out yourself.

The notes that follow here are not meant to substitute for a first aid manual; still less for actual training. I've tried to select, from the long list of things the hiker needs to know, a few that seem absolutely basic. Please do consider learning more. The shortest first aid course in the world, the eight-hour Multimedia Course, is available through local Red Cross chapters for about fifteen dollars.

The first stage: saving life

As a rule, you examine the victim where you find him. (For the next few pages, let's consider the victim male.) You don't try to move him. (There are exceptions: an immediate danger from falling rock or avalanche, for instance.) You check immediately for two problems that mean instant crisis. *Has he stopped breathing? Is he losing large amounts of blood?*

Breathing. Attend to this *first*. Establish that

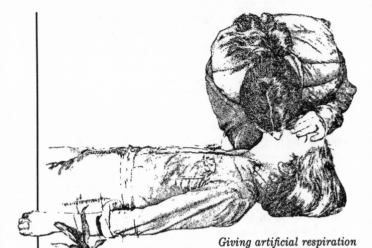

Giving artificial respiration

the victim *is* breathing. (Look for chest movement; listen for exhalation; try to feel the breath on your hand.) If you can't confirm breathing, lay him on his back. Place one hand under the back of the neck to tilt the head back sharply—this keeps the tongue from blocking the airway from the mouth to the lungs. Then begin the often-pictured technique of mouth-to-mouth artificial respiration, by far the best we have. Place your free hand on the victim's forehead and close his nostrils with finger and thumb. Seal his mouth with your own, and breathe into him. Start with four quick, forceful puffs: this may shock his lungs back into action. If not, keep going, breathing deeply into the victim's mouth about once every five seconds. Remove your mouth each time to let him exhale.

Note this, however: neck injury is likely in any accident involving force or impact. If you even suspect such a problem, don't press up under the back of the neck. Rather, place your hands along the side of the lower jaw and draw it forward, closing the nose with your two thumbs. (This jutting of the jaw may help in any case in which the airway remains blocked by the tongue.)

Bleeding. A person can bleed to death in a minute or two. And yet, in almost every case, you can stop dangerous bleeding simply by pressing on the wound with a cloth or (if nothing else is available) with your bare hand. Ten minutes of firm pressure should do it. If the wound is on an arm or a leg, it also helps to lift the limb above the level of the heart. Never remove a bloodsoaked cloth; make it the basis of the dressing you later apply.

What if the heart has stopped beating? In a wilderness situation, the chance of saving the victim is not then large. There is a technique, though, that sometimes succeeds. It combines artificial respiration with an artificial "heartbeat," supplied by rhythmic pressure on the breastbone, and is known as cardiopulmonary resuscitation (CPR). It takes practice to do CPR correctly; the Red Cross and the American Heart Association offer short, intensive courses.

Three other problems can be listed with the instant emergencies. One is *poisoning*. No matter what was swallowed, the first step is to have the victim swallow water to dilute the substance. The second step is usually to induce vomiting. (Neither of these can be done, however, if the victim is unconscious, or having convulsions.) For certain poisons—petroleum products (stove fuel!), strong acids, and strong alkalis—you do *not* induce vomiting. These substances may do further damage to the esophagus if they are vomited up; there is risk, too, of getting them into the lungs.

No less perilous is *heat stroke*, the late stage of bodily overheating or *hyperthermia*. The treatment is obvious: cool the stricken person down. For more on this problem, see Chapter 28.

The second stage: stabilizing

When the instant emergency is over, the next danger is *shock*. Shock is a collapse of the circulation of the blood. It can occur with any accident or illness, and is sometimes a sole cause of death. Thirst and sharp anxiety are common first symptoms. The skin will grow pale and cold. The heartbeat will be quick but weak; breathing will be abnormal. The victim may get dizzy or black out. In the last stage of severe shock, blood pressure drops toward zero.

Treat for shock whether or not it has yet appeared. Lay the victim flat on his back. Unless he has severe injury to the head or torso, raise his legs. Loosen constricting clothes. Keep him dry. His body will have lost much of its power to maintain its temperature; depending on the weather, you must keep him either warm or cool. If he's aware, be certain to reassure him, to listen to him, to satisfy his requests where you can. If he's awake and does not seem to have major injuries of torso or head, give him sips of a weak solution of salt or salt and soda. Don't give fluids if he's vomiting or suffering convulsions.

If you have an unconscious victim, you must watch carefully to make sure that the passage of air to his lungs remains open. Usually you can turn the head to one side. If he vomits or drools, or bleeds from facial injuries, be sure that none of the material accumulates in his mouth. Never give fluids to an unconscious person.

Along with treatment for shock, do a second, more thorough examination. Look, touch, and listen. Get all the information you can from the victim. Try to find everything: wounds, fractures, burns, dislocations, frostbite. Frequently the most serious injury is not the most dramatic.

Then decide, with deliberation, what happens next. That may be nothing more than signaling or sending companions for aid. Or you may need to apply whatever treatments you are fairly sure of, guided by common sense, a manual, the patient's own reactions, and whatever training you've had. (The idea is not to "fix the victim up," but merely to prevent further injury. Don't do a thing unless you can tell yourself *why* you are doing it.)

Do take notes on the person's condition—even a cursory "medical history" may be of value later. At some point, get "MAD." This mnemonic stands for

*M*edications (is the patient taking any?), *A*llergies (is the victim allergic to anything he knows about?) and *D*octor (is he under a doctor's care for any condition?).

Don't stop paying attention to your patient after the first crisis passes. Talk to him. Let him know what you're doing. First aid experts remark that, if you don't talk to the person in your care, you're practicing veterinary medicine!

In the excitement, don't forget the welfare of the rest of your party. Among other things, it's often important to set up a safe and comfortable camp.

Third stage: getting out

In few of our wilderness areas is there much difficulty about swift rescue, at least in summer, and at least for hikers on busy trails. If the victim can't move under his or her own power, the problem is simply to attract the attention of rescuers, or of other hikers who can send for them. If there are several healthy people in your party, send one (or better, two) for help. Beyond that, the smoke of a fire is most likely to attract the notice of authorities. Be sure the party you send out knows how to describe your whereabouts, and what signal you plan to use to draw attention.

How do you decide if an injured person can walk out? It can be hard. On the one hand, you don't want to risk further injury. On the other hand, many accident victims *can* make it out, slowly and with help. Helicopter rescues are damnably expensive. (Who pays? Policies vary. In some cases the victim and companions must pick up the tab themselves. If not, the public pays. Such a rescue should not be summoned lightly.)

One of the commonest injuries is a strained or sprained ankle. Some seemingly serious sprains will improve fairly quickly to the point where you can walk out with the help of an elastic bandage, leaning perhaps on a friend. See Chapter 26.

If you travel away from the trails, or if you visit

more remote areas in winter, it is a good idea to learn some rescue techniques yourself: how to make a litter, how to splint major body injuries, and so forth. These are set out in books on first aid, rescue, and mountaineering medicine.

26
Some Common Medical Problems

MOST OF THE TIME, MEDICAL PROBLEMS on the trail take a form much milder than the accident or collapse that demands your fast, clear-headed action. The typical complaint is a nuisance, not a danger; even serious injuries may give you time to think. Here is a list, short and by no means complete, of problems you may face sometime—the common cases, and a few uncommon ones in which a little information may be reassuring—together with the treatments that mountain medicine experts recommend for them.

Surface wear and tear

Cuts, punctures, and scrapes. You step on a nail; you skin your elbow; you gash a thumb with your pocketknife. If bleeding is copious, stop it by pressing directly on the wound. If there's almost no blood (as with a puncture), try to produce a little bleeding by kneading the surrounding flesh (object:

to wash out germs). If bleeding alone has not completely washed out the wound, finish the job with plenty of clean water. (A deep wound, one that penetrates the subcutaneous fat and goes into underlying tissues, should be washed with water that has just been purified.) You do not need to apply a dressing unless the wound would get dirty without one. A gaping cut can be kept partially closed with one or more "butterfly bandages," strips of adhesive cut in an hourglass shape, with the thin part over the cut. A minor wound is certainly not a cause to head for home; a larger one might be. (All hikers should be sure they have been immunized against tetanus.)

Burns. Whether the burn is large or small, your first priority is to *cool* the burned area by any convenient method. Immersion in cold water is ideal. This will quickly lessen the pain, inhibit further damage, and (some say) actually promote healing. Continue the cold treatment until you can remove the burn from the water without a return of pain. The burned area need not be covered with a dressing unless this is necessary to keep it clean.

Minor burns—burns that raise few if any blisters—will probably require no further attention; but do watch for infection. Burns that raise numerous blisters, or that penetrate the skin, are more serious. Be especially concerned about any blistering burn on the face, hands, feet, or genitals; any *large* blistering burn elsewhere; and any blistering burn at all on an infant. If a person has burns about the face, be aware that the breathing passages may be scorched, and watch for any breathing difficulty. People with serious burns should be evacuated.

For *sunburn* and *snow blindness*, see Chapter 28.

Eye problems. Getting a fragment of the wilderness in your eye is annoying and can be hazardous. The first thing to remember is not to rub your eye, which will only add irritation. Instead, get a wooden match or a thin twig; place it halfway up the upper lid; and peel the remainder of the lid upward around it, watching the maneuver in a pocket mirror. Foreign objects tend to stick to the inside of the lid and can be safely removed with the corner of a bandanna or a Q-tip. Sometimes the problem is no more than an inturned lash. Sometimes the irritating object has already floated away, but leaves a scratch that causes the something-in-my-eye feeling. If this persists, soothing eyedrops may be helpful; use antibiotic ointment on a persistently inflamed eye, and seek a doctor's attention as soon as you can.

If someone's eye is actually penetrated by an object, your immediate job is to calm the person and instruct him *not to move his eyes.* Do not try to remove the invading object. Cover both eyes (so that the injured eye won't move in tandem with the healthy one) and summon help.

Broken bones

Broken bones are scary and usually painful. Broken arms and legs, fortunately, are rarely very dangerous in themselves. You can recognize a fracture by discoloration and swelling around it, by deformation, sometimes, of the broken part, and by pain and tenderness. If you even suspect a fracture, assume there is one. Unless a victim's life is in danger, never move a person until all fractures, known or suspected, have been splinted.

Ways of immobilizing or *splinting* various broken bones make up a large part of advanced first aid courses. The purpose of splinting is to stabilize the broken part, to keep the broken bone ends from moving, and to make the person comfortable. In general, remember that a fracture of a bone in the arm or shoulder can usually be splinted by placing the forearm in a sling across the lower chest and binding arm and sling to the body; most fractures of leg bones can be dealt with by splinting the broken leg to the healthy one.

In some first aid courses you may be taught to leave a broken limb exactly as it is and merely to immobilize it with splinting—"splint 'em as they lie." In the wilderness, where help is more than minutes away, you may have to modify this principle. Your patient will be more comfortable, and the broken limb more stable, if you restore the limb to something like its normal shape. This means straightening to some extent. While one person cradles the limb, another can take hold of the hand or foot and pull, gently and persistently, parallel to the normal alignment of the bone. When the injured limb looks more or less like the normal one, proceed with splinting.

A particularly worrisome case is the *open* fracture, in which a wound reaches the bone, or a broken end of the bone pokes out through the skin. Should you try to clean such a wound, or scrub the bone end, before splinting? The consensus is that you should simply remove visible particles of dirt and then proceed as usual. All such fractures should be examined and cleaned thoroughly in the hospital, anyhow.

One concern you must have any time you apply a splint is that blood is reaching the part of the limb beyond the break. Locate a pulse in the healthy limb; then make sure you can find the same pulse in the broken one, both before and after you apply the splint.

Head, neck, and back. Special precautions apply whenever someone has taken a hard blow on the upper body, especially if the victim loses consciousness. First, until you know otherwise, assume the person has a broken neck; pad around the head and neck to prevent movement (the splint is a pillow or something of similar bulk, wrapped U-shape around the sides and top of the head, and secured with a binding across the forehead). Move the victim, if at all, with extreme care. Move the body as a unit, avoiding any twisting of neck and back. The danger is of damage to the spinal cord.

Second, don't neglect basic first aid: make sure that the injured person is breathing properly, and protect against shock.

Third, watch the victim's state of consciousness. Take notes. Does he become alert and then hazy

again? As time goes on, does he become more aware
and responsive, or less? If there is any pattern other
than steady improvement, it's vital to summon a rescue.

Chest. If there are one or several broken
ribs—or pain that suggests broken ribs—the best
simple treatment is to have the person lie on the injured side, preventing excessive motion.

Sprains and dislocations

A sprain is damage to the ligaments that bind
bones together in a joint: depending on its severity,
these may be stretched, torn, or actually severed. A
dislocation occurs when the bones actually move out
of their normal positions in the joint.

Ankle problems. The badly twisted ankle is
something every hiker, especially the solo hiker,
dreads. Fortunately, most ankle injuries are not immobilizing. Often the sharp pain that seemed to indicate a major problem will go away by itself. Even a
moderately damaged ankle can be walked on—with
adequate reinforcement. On the other hand, if you
mistreat a minor injury, you can just possibly make
a long-lasting problem for yourself.

You've "done something" to your ankle. Consider
it. Where does it hurt? Most of the time the painful
spot will be on the outside of the ankle, below the
bony bulge that marks the end of the smaller leg-
bone (fibula). This suggests a sprain, or, at worst, a
fracture of the fibula. These injuries will allow you
to walk out, with proper support. On the other hand,
pain at the inner side of the foot indicates a more
serious problem and you probably shouldn't plan to
do any walking.

In the case of a sprain, the immediate treatment
is to *cool* the painful area with a cold pack (snow or
a canteen of cold water, wrapped in cloth). At the
same time *compress* the area by wrapping it with
an elastic bandage. Begin at the toes and wind it
around and around the foot and clear up the ankle.
Place some padding under the bandage right at the
painful spot to increase the pressure there. The

third element of the initial treatment: *elevate* the leg to keep blood from pooling in the foot. The objective at this stage is to limit swelling.

Keep this treatment going for at least an hour—up to a full day. Then you can wrap the ankle for walking. Start by cutting a dozen strips of adhesive tape an inch wide and about two feet long. Six of these will be placed around the foot like stirrups, crossing the sole and running up the ankle on either side to a point about eight inches up the calf. The other six strips are anchors: these are placed at right angles to the stirrups, running from behind the heel forward along the foot on either side. Next, make sure that the foot is correctly positioned, at right angles to the leg. Now, beginning at the heel, apply a stirrup, then an anchor, then a stirrup, then an anchor, until the whole ankle is encased in a sort of basket weave. No tape should run entirely around the circumference of the ankle (possibly cutting circulation off). Over the tape layer goes the elastic bandage, and over the bandage, sock and boot. Lace

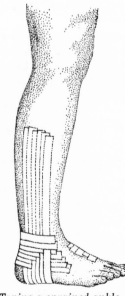
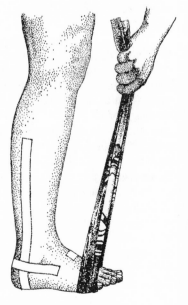

Taping a sprained ankle

the boot firmly but not ferociously. Find a stick to be used as a cane.

At this point, most people with twisted ankles find it quite possible to walk without excessive pain. A small amount of pain does not mean that it is dangerous to do so. Move along slowly. Check from time to time that the ankle is not swelling; if it is, lossen the constraining bandage slightly.

Dislocated ankle. If the ankle joint is actually torn, the foot will flop at an odd angle to the leg. This is a far more serious injury. The foot should be restored to its natural position and splinted. Wrap a jacket or other soft object around the foot in a U-shape and bind it around the ankle, not too tightly but firmly enough to keep the foot steady. In this case there is no question of trying to walk.

Dislocated shoulder. This is a rather common wilderness injury. It is relatively easy to treat a dislocated shoulder in the field, and there is good reason to do so, because it becomes much harder to treat with every hour that passes.

Of several methods of restoring a dislocated shoulder, the one most easily described and remembered is the ancient maneuver known as the "Hippocrates" or "dirty sock" technique. The injured person (having taken your best painkiller) lies flat on his back. You, the first-aider, sit beside him, facing toward him, and put the heel of your bootless foot in the patient's armpit. For about five minutes you pull on the dislocated arm with gentle, insistent pressure. You have told the patient what comes next. Now, decisively, you move the arm across the patient's body toward the center line. In most cases, the head of the upper armbone will pop back into its proper place. (If it does not, there is a backup method: have the person lie face-down on a tablelike surface with the injured arm hanging down. With tape, attach a ten to twenty-pound weight to the dangling arm. This should exhaust the arm and shoulder muscles, permitting the bone to pop back into place. Give it two hours; if it hasn't worked by then, give it up and seek help.) Not many hikers with stubbornly dislocated shoulders can be expected to walk out—the jolting is too painful.

Other dislocations. Another dislocation that can be dealt with in the wilderness is that of a *kneecap* (as opposed to a dislocated *knee,* which involves major damage to the whole joint). It is not uncommon for a kneecap to slide out of position, usually to the outside of the knee; it can be pressed back, gently but firmly, to the great relief of the owner. A dislocated *finger* is also manageable. Have the person flex the finger and press on the dislocated segment (typically the last) from below and from the backside of the hand.

By comparison with these, most other dislocations are dangerous—much more troublesome, in fact, than typical fractures. The rule is to splint them and leave them alone. But always make sure there is a pulse beyond an injured joint. (First locate the pulse in the healthy limb; then try to find it at the same spot in the injured one.) If you can't find a heartbeat out there—say in the wrist beyond an injured elbow—it may be necessary to shift the joint carefully in the hope of unkinking an artery.

Strains are injuries to muscle tissue. Minor ones are common and not serious; occasionally, though, a muscle in the calf or back will tear so badly that it cannot bear weight. There may be a considerable injury requiring medical attention. First aid is much like that for a sprain: cool, elevate, and gently compress the injured area. Some people with seriously strained muscles can walk out; some can't. A crisscross layer of tape and an elastic bandage, as with a twisted ankle, may help.

With sprains and strains, as with most other problems, the injured person himself is your best source of information. Only he can tell you how bad it feels, and whether or not he can travel on foot after your best efforts at first aid.

Bodily aches and alarms

So far we've talked of problems that arise because you are where you are, doing what you're doing: hiking in the wilderness. But other, home-grown complaints can arise out here as well as anywhere else, and sometimes do.

Headaches can usually be treated with aspirin or acetaminophen; usually insignificant, they may be connected with another problem like altitude sickness (see Chapter 28). *Earaches* tend to be due to infection; antibiotics can be taken if they persist. *Nosebleeds* are best stopped by pressing a cold compress on the bridge of the nose for as long as it takes. *Sore throats* may be a sign of another illness or may occur at high altitudes for no discernible reason; pus on the tonsils suggests that an antibiotic be taken.

Garden-variety upper respiratory infections—*colds and 'flu*—are certainly not emergencies. They're no fun, either, and if you're really under the weather, you may want to creep for home. Considering the number of people moving around in wild areas, it is truly astonishing how rare it is to encounter these common complaints.

Chest pain is alarming—everyone thinks heart attack—but can have other causes. There is little first aid for heart problems in a wilderness situation, beyond comfort and reassurance and, if required, basic life support.

Abdominal pain. A growing pain in the belly, and anybody who still has an appendix thinks *appendicitis.* If the pain does not settle in the lower right quadrant (below the navel and to the right of the midline of the body), it probably isn't an appendix that's complaining. Abdominal pain that does not increase when you press on the bothersome spot is probably superficial, not involving an organ, and not worrisome. Simple constipation can produce a suggestive pain but not the other symptoms of appendicitis: nausea, loss of appetite, and mild fever. If you do suspect the disease, start taking the antibiotic in your first aid kit and head for civilization with all deliberate speed.

Indigestion happens out here, too; antacids are good to have. Pepto Bismol, in tablet form, is about the best. *Constipation* is not uncommon; some hikers carry laxatives. *Diarrhea,* if serious, is more of a problem. You are not very likely to come down with a serious case in wild country in the United States or Canada. (Giardiasis, the infamous "backpacker's diarrhea," will not develop for at least a week after exposure—even in the unlikely case that you pick up the bug in the wilderness. If you do come down with it, you will need a doctor's care.) The essential thing to remember about any severe diarrhea is that you must replace the fluids lost.

27:
Problem Animals and Plants

THE ANIMALS OF THE WOODS and the mountains are one of the things you come for. The word "wilderness," in fact, comes from roots meaning "the place of the wild beasts." Still, animals (and some plants as well) can make problems for the hiker. Seldom are these problems more than nuisances—the bugs have probably caused many times as much misery as the snakes and the bears combined.

Mosquitoes and flies

Mosquitoes lay eggs in shallow water or damp soil and hatch when days are warm and moist. In the mountains of the Southwest, where the soil is dry by August, they vanish early. Elsewhere, and especially in wet, temperate lowlands, mosquitoes may swarm much longer. Of various repellents, the best contain the chemical n, n-diethyl-meta-toluamide (DEET). In some months and in some regions, you may want not only repellent but also a head net for walking. Netted tents and windy campsites away from water help on warm nights. Elsewhere in the world, mosquitoes are important carriers of malaria and other diseases, but this is no longer much of a problem in the United States.

Then there are the various stinging or biting flies, a whole tribe of flies. *No-see-ums* ("biting midges," "punkies"), found in low-lying areas over most of the country, are so tiny that they vanish in most lighting and can pass through all but the finest netting. The *blackfly*, famous in the north woods, is found more widely under other names. The *deer fly*, medium-sized like the blackfly, has a similarly nasty sting. There are others: horseflies, elk flies, even a type known as "green-headed monsters." The standard repellents work against some, but not all, of these species.

Ordinary, nonbiting flies can be a problem, too, especially in a camp with a latrine. Keep waste in the latrine well covered and keep food under cover as well.

Around marshes and lakes in low-lying regions, gnats can be an annoyance. The chigger, found in the eastern states, lives in grass; digging into your skin, it can cause an infuriating itch.

Ticks

These unpleasant creatures are bloodsuckers. Up to a quarter inch long and dark-colored, they are most numerous in the moist springtime of woodlands that dry out later in the year; in wet-summer regions they are a lesser problem for a longer time. Ticks climb onto you from foliage close to the ground. After riding on you for some time, they find bare skin and attach themselves painlessly. Repellents, at wrists, waist and ankles, help to discourage them. So do gaiters.

If you're bushwhacking, you can head the creatures off by examining your own and others' clothes every now and then. On a long bushwhack, hikers strip before bed and check each other for ticks. Parents should keep a close eye on children, especially very young children, for whom a tick bite can be serious.

Once a tick is well attached, getting rid of it is a bit of a project. First, touch the creature with a bandanna-corner soaked with stove fuel, mosquito dope, or sun tan lotion; this should make the tick relax its grip. Then gently remove it with tweezers. Grasp it as far toward the buried head as you can. Use a gentle rocking motion with the tweezers. Don't press or crush—you don't want to force the tick's stomach contents back into your bloodstream. Don't try to "unscrew" the tick by turning in one direction only: you run the risk of leaving the tick's mouth parts imbedded in your skin. When you have extracted the tick, wash the puncture with soap and water and watch the spot for possible infection.

Unpleasant as they are, tick bites aren't generally dangerous. They can, in some places, transmit the diseases called Rocky Mountain Spotted Fever and tick fever. These ailments, untreated, can be deadly, but antibiotics control them. There is also a condition called "tick paralysis," a mysterious weakness that afflicts some people when ticks are attached to them. When you're in tick country, any unexplained weakness calls for a careful search for ticks. If, in extracting a tick, you leave the mouth parts in your flesh, the condition may not immediately cease.

Bees, wasps, and yellowjackets

Bee stings, relatively harmless to most of us, are very dangerous to some. Bees and wasps and yellowjackets cause several times the number of deaths each year that snakes do. If you have an allergy to stings, you probably know it; if you even suspect it, be sure to get a doctor's advice on how to deal with it. Desensitization is possible for some people; the injection of adrenalin is often life saving.

If there is an allergic reaction, it will be unmistakable. In a few minutes the person will feel faint and giddy. The skin will be cool and moist. In severe cases the reaction will resemble an insanely exaggerated attack of hay fever. The tissues of the throat may swell so much that breathing is cut off. There is little the first-aider can do in such a case. If you have the allergy, carry a kit and be prepared to give yourself the life-saving injection.

If you're stung by a bee, don't pull the stinger out with tweezers or your fingernails. The venom sacks cling to the stinger, and pressure forces more of the poison into the skin. Instead, *scrape* the stinger off with the blade of a knife.

Spiders

The one really dangerous spider in the United States is the black widow. One variety or another is found in every state south of Canada. Black widows come in all shades (including white), but most are, in fact, black; all have, under the abdomen, the famous red hourglass mark. The head is small compared to the round body; front and back legs are markedly longer than those on the side. You are most likely to find these spiders in woodpiles and in old buildings like outhouses.

If you're bitten by a spider, catch it if you can. (Don't crush it.) If you're sure it's a black widow, it's prudent to head for civilization. Many people bitten by this spider have no greater problem than swelling or redness at the bite; others suffer painful

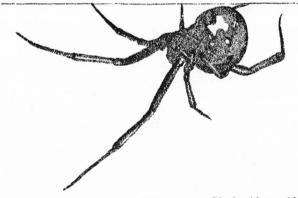

Black widow spider

and prolonged muscle cramps. In severe cases, hospital treatment is required. In about one case out of twenty there is danger of death; most victims are children.

Tarantulas, those big, elegant creatures furred like cats, have an insignificant sting (in the United States). Some other spiders—including the brown recluse and its widespread relatives—can inflict troublesome bites. If a spider bite produces a blood blister, pop it and apply antibiotic ointment. If the spot does not heal properly, seek attention when you get home. With any bite, take normal precautions against infection.

Scorpions and centipedes

Scorpions are eight-legged creatures, spider relatives, and sting with their tails. There are various species in the United States; most are found in the southwestern deserts, but they also are found as far north as Oregon and Montana. All are at least mildly venomous. One species, found only in Arizona and immediately across the border in California, can kill. The animal hunts at night. It's a good idea in any region to shake out your clothes and boots in the morning, though you seldom find anything inside them. In the daytime be careful when digging in sand or lifting rocks and logs. Though some scorpions are as long as eight inches, the dangerous ones are less than half that length; they're colored yellow

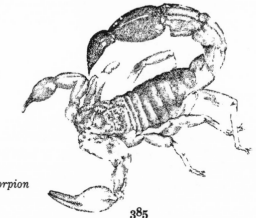

Scorpion

to yellow-green. Scorpion venom attacks the nerves; when it kills, it is through paralysis of the lungs. Though cold packs are sometimes recommended, there's actually nothing you can do in the field for a scorpion bite but wait it out.

Centipedes—many species—live under rocks and down wood. Some have a pretty good sting, though not many cases are at all serious. The harmless millipedes, sometimes confused with centipedes, have two pairs of legs growing from each body joint—the centipedes, only one.

The Gila monster

The Gila monster, found in the Southwest, is an almost harmless creature with a bad reputation. Though the bite can certainly be dangerous, the monster is not in the least inclined to attack, and almost every bite on record took place when somebody picked up a captive specimen. Incidentally, the Gila monster is an endangered species and has full protection. For its sake and yours, the rule is: leave it alone.

Gila monster

Snakes

We have four kinds of poisonous snakes in this country. Most important by far are the *rattlesnakes*, about thirty species, found somewhere in each of the forty-eight contiguous states, but there are other types: the *copperhead* in the East; the *cottonmouth* or water moccasin in the southeastern swamps; and the *coral snake*.

Rattlesnakes, copperheads, and cottonmouths are

all pit vipers. The pit vipers inject through fangs a venom that attacks via the bloodstream.

The markings of rattlesnakes vary; actual rattles may or may not be present. The snakes seldom grow longer than five feet. Rattlers become scarce above 7,000 feet in the warm Southwest and aren't found much above 3,000 feet in areas near the Canadian border. In wet, cool regions, they prefer the drier sides of ridges, especially southern exposures.

The copperhead is found widely through the East as far north as New York state. It has, indeed, a copper-colored head, and hourglass markings along its body. The cottonmouth or water moccasin lives in wetlands from Virginia south, and west to central Texas. It is a thick, dark snake, up to six feet long,

Diamondback rattlesnake

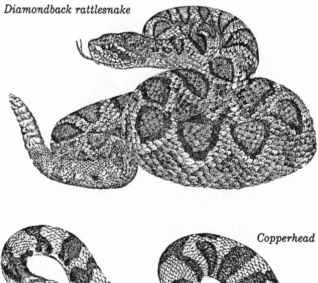

Copperhead

Cottonmouth

Coral snake

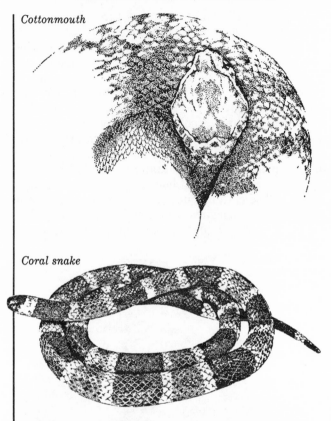

without obvious markings. Hikers aren't likely to see it, but waders and canoeists must be aware of it.

All the pit vipers have a markedly wide head swelling from a much narrower neck. The body is heavy-looking, ropy. The pupil of the eye is eliptical. Snakes not of this family, by contrast, have slender bodies merging into narrow heads with little indentation at the neck; the pupil of the eye is round.

Among those American snakes that are not pit vipers, only one is venomous: the coral snake. The coral is rather small, two to four feet long, and thin of body; it lacks the diamond head and secretes a poison that attacks primarily the nerves. Coral snakes are handsomely marked with rings of yellow, black, and red. To distinguish a coral snake from other, harmless snakes that have red bands, remember that only coral snakes have red rings adjoining yellow:

> Red on yellow, kill a fellow;
> Red on black, scratch its back.

Coral snakes in several species are found across the southern United States from the Carolinas to Arizona.

Now: how worried should you be about snakebite?

Estimates vary, but it appears that about 1,000 people are bitten by poisonous snakes each year. Not very many of these victims are hikers, by the way. About two victims in one hundred die. While healthy adults are unlikely to die from snakebite, there are many cases of permanent injury to a bitten hand or foot, when necessary treatment is not sought.

The risk, then, is not quite negligible. But it is certainly small. It is perfectly possible to blunder around the woods for years—even in good snake country—and never encounter a dangerous species at all.

Avoiding snakebite

Too much, proportionately, has been written about treating snakebite; too little has been said about the simple means of avoiding it. Different species vary in their readiness to strike, but none are out to get you. Snakes don't lie in ambush; they don't crawl into your sleeping bag. Threatened, they respond. You want to make sure that you aren't seen as a threat.

Snakes, cold-blooded animals, are active only when it is pleasantly warm. In some regions and seasons, days are too hot for them, and they do their hunting at night. If only the morning and evening hours are temperate, snakes will be moving then. Torpid snakes, however, will still strike if stepped on.

Remember these simple precautions:

First, wear long pants and high-topped boots in snake country—and especially when you leave the trail. The feet and legs are most likely to be struck. Heavy fabric gaiters help, too. If you are planning to go cross-country in snake-rich terrain, you can make tubes of thin cardboard and put them around your ankles, under the trouserlegs: clumsy but effective protection.

Second, make sure you can see where you're putting your feet and hands. Be especially careful in rock scrambling. Never thrust a hand over an unseen edge to grope for a hold.

Third, if you hear a snake rattling, stop dead still until you see where it is; then move away. Meanwhile, the snake will amost certainly be moving away from *you*.

Fourth, never pick up an unidentified snake. A large number of bites result from this.

Treating snakebite

Should you carry a snakebite kit? The experts are much divided on this question. Some feel that the risk is too slight to justify the expense. Some further argue that the use of a kit rarely helps much; and they point out that a kit, in unskilled hands, can do more harm than the bite itself. Most bites are on foot, ankle, hand, or wrist. These are dangerous places to cut, because blood vessels, tendons, and nerves lie close to the skin surface there.

But other voices, still in the majority, urge that you carry a kit and know how to use it—especially in known snake country, and in cross-country travel.

A basic snakebite kit—there are numerous brands—contains a small scalpel, a couple of suction cups, some constricting bands or ligatures, a vial of antiseptic, and a set of directions. Make sure you're familiar with these!

If someone is bitten by a snake that may be poisonous, the following steps should be followed.

First, one member of the party—let's say it's

you—must take charge. This is no time for milling around.

Second, put the bitten person in a restful position, keeping the injured limb low (below the level of the heart).

Third, try to identify the snake, or at least to determine whether it is a pit viper. Kill it, if you can safely do so, and keep the body. This may help a doctor to choose an anti-venin later on.

Fourth, place two constricting bands around the bitten limb, one above and one below the bite. Ordinary rubber bands will do. These bands, however, are not tourniquets and must not be too tight! You should be able to feel a pulse in the limb beyond the constriction. (If swelling occurs and reaches the bands, place new ones just outside the swollen area, and only then remove the first set of bands.)

Fifth, decide whether poisoning has actually taken place. If there are one or two deep, wide-spaced punctures—the fang marks—you know that a viper has struck. You do *not* know that it has left a dose of venom—in about half of all cases, none is injected! The unmistakable symptom will arrive, if at all, in a hurry: violent, increasing pain. The word "explosive" has been used. The bitten area will also swell and become discolored. The victim may sweat profusely and feel nausea, vomit perhaps (though these symptoms are sometimes caused by anxiety alone).

Sixth, once you know that venom is at work, you must act. If, by chance, you are within thirty minutes of medical help, carry the victim out or call assistance in. If the bite occured more than half an hour before, the same applies. But if the bite is fresh and assistance is far away—the typical wilderness situation—it's your job to get rid of as much poison as you can, using your snake bite kit and the incision–and–suction method.

Tell your injured friend what you are doing. Take the little scalpel from your kit and make one incision through each fang mark. The cuts should be about one quarter inch long and one quarter inch deep. Make them parallel to the body member and to the "grain" of structures in the skin. Thus on a finger, or on top of the foot, you would cut lengthwise to finger or foot. Before making each cut, bunch up the flesh around the fang mark between your thumb and forefinger, to avoid damage to the underlying tendons, vessels, and nerves.

After you have made the cuts, take the suction cups from the kit, press the air out of them, and apply them to the bleeding skin. Don't pump, but recompress them whenever they loosen. Keep up this process for thirty minutes. Never suck with your mouth, for the patient's sake, not yours (the danger of infection is great).

Now the pace can slacken a bit. If you have not done so already, send someone out for help. Place a cold pack on the bitten limb. Keep the patient comfortable, quiet, and cool. Do not give him coffee, tea, or alcohol. Depending on the amount of venom he got, he may be very sick or scarcely sick at all. Reassure him, watch him, and guard against shock.

Coral snake venom is different from that of rattlesnakes and their relatives. The cut–and–suck treatment is less effective against a coral snake bite, but is still the best thing to do if medical help can't be reached in a few minutes. Fortunately, bites by this snake are rare.

Animal bites

Even a minor bite by a wild or domestic animal can bring three possible dangers. The first is *infection;* you fight it by ordinary care in treating the wound, and later, if they are needed, with antibiotics. Second is *tetanus.* Tetanus, though a dangerous disease, is easy to prevent. A tetanus immunization shot, plus one booster every seven years, protects you. Every hiker should have this insurance.

By far the most serious of the three dangers is *rabies.* Skunks are the wild animals most likely to transmit rabies; raccoons, foxes, and bats can also carry it. Beware of any animal that acts oddly, including one that seems overfriendly.

An immunization for rabies is now available and is recommended for people, like cavers, who come into frequent contact with possible carrier animals. There is also a treatment that can prevent the disease from developing after a bite, if it is begun quickly enough.

If you are bitten by an animal that may carry rabies, try to catch it, if it is safe to do so. Kill it if you must.

The immediate treatment for the bite is simple: wash the wound thoroughly with *copious* soap and water. This will flush out many of the viruses, and if a rabies infection does occur, it will be less severe.

The next step is to get back to civilization as fast as you can. Take with you the animal's body, or at least the head. (If you can get the animal home without killing it, that's still better, but obviously difficult.) With luck, lab analysis of the animal's brain will show it not to be rabid and spare you the discomfort of the treatment. If the bite was below the neck, you have several days in which the treatment can be successfully begun. A bite on the head or neck gives you less margin.

Bears

High on the list of dangerous wilderness animals in some regions are the bears: common black or brown bruins in many states, and in the northern Rockies and Canada, the magnificent, unpredictable grizzly.

The common bears of the West and the Southeast are more nuisance than hazard, if regarded with some respect. If a black bear is trying to get at your tree-strung food, for instance, it can generally be frightened away by loud noises. Never, however, try to take food from a bear or—just as dangerous—*give* food to a bear; and give a wide berth to a female bear with cubs.

The grizzly is another matter. After years of seeming timidity, the grizzlies of the Yellowstone and Glacier regions have recently become rather aggressive; several people have been mauled, even killed. This is not a reason to cross these wilderness areas off your list—the hazard is still statistically slight—but special precautions are needed. The same precautions apply in Canada and Alaska, although it is in the comparatively crowded and civilized U.S. Rockies that the conflicts have been worst.

Park and Forest Service managers in grizzly country try to keep people and bears apart. They keep track of bears, especially aggressive ones, and close trails and campgrounds accordingly. Warning signs may be placed at roadheads, and wilderness permits will be used to steer people to safe areas. When you visit these areas, don't neglect to pick up your permit, get the official rap, and follow instructions to the letter!

In grizzly country, it is important not to make yourself an attractive nuisance. Think in terms of odor. Smelly foods—sardines, cheese and the like—should simply not be carried. When you camp, the kitchen area should be set up some distance away from your sleeping spot, and downwind from it, so that odors blow away from you and the rest of your gear. Keep in mind that breezes tend to blow downslope at night, so it's wise to sleep uphill from your kitchen. Both food and packs should be hung in trees at night, again downwind from you and several hundred feet away. Keep your camp clean and your gear as free of food smells as possible.

Apparently grizzlies are attracted by the odor of blood. This fact has given rise to a controversial piece of advice: that menstruating women should avoid grizzly country during their periods. Some women resent the suggestion and question the need, but it is a point worth considering.

A backpacker on the move has a different kind of concern: you don't want to be *too* inconspicuous. Few bears will attack unless startled; but if you suddenly appear a few yards away from one of the creatures, defensive instincts take over and the bear may charge. Hikers in grizzly country like to make some racket as they move along, banging, for instance, a spoon on a metal cup. They may avoid traveling when a noisy wind masks the sounds they make and disperses their scent.

If you meet a grizzly, much may depend on how you react, and how you read the signs present in the bear's own behavior. A grizzly that just looks at you, without making noises or laying back its ears, is checking you out. It is appropriate to stay where you are and make conversational noises. If a bear stands up on its hind legs, it is simply checking you out from a higher vantage. If a grizzly stands crosswise to you and puts its head down, it is suggesting—so experts say—that you back off. Do so. A bear that plans to attack will face you squarely, lower its head, flatten its ears, and make huffing sounds. You should move away—decisively but not too rapidly. If there is a handy tree, climb it. (Bears can climb, but they also recognize tree climbing as a mollifying retreat.)

If the situation deteriorates and you are face to face with an attacking grizzly, make yourself small. Lie down or crouch down and protect your face and neck with your arms. With luck, you may escape with only superficial injury.

First aid for a person damaged by a bear is simply first aid: maintain breathing, control bleeding, protect against shock, and seek help.

Poisonous plants

There are many, many plants in the wild that are more or less poisonous if eaten. Know exactly what you're doing before you eat any part of any wild plant, including, most especially, any mushroom. The only general first aid rule for plant poisoning is to drink water and induce vomiting.

Much more common is another kind of "poisoning": the brief, inconsequential sting of nettle or the unbearable itch of poison oak and similar toxic plants. Poison oak is hardly a danger to life and limb, but it can certainly take the pleasure out of a wilderness trip.

There are various species of *poison oak* (including the one called *poison ivy*). They are found over most of the United States at lower elevations. Some species climb like vines; others form bushes; others do both. The best field mark to look for is leaves grouped in threes. Each group of three leaflets grows out at a different point along the stem; the clusters are "alternate," not "opposite." Sometimes the leaflets are hairy, sometimes smooth; their edges may be smooth, toothed, or lobed.

Poison oak   *Poison ivy*

Poison sumac, a relative of poison oak, doesn't resemble it much in appearance. A shrub or small tree, it has smooth, pale gray bark and alternate leaves divided into seven to eleven leaflets, with smooth margins and a reddish tinge. This sumac is most common in the Great Lakes region and on the Gulf and Atlantic coastal plains. In the North it is shrubby and keeps to boggy places; in the South it is a tree up to twenty-five feet tall, growing in swamps and river bottoms.

Trumpet creeper is a woody climbing vine that grows in woods and thickets throughout the eastern United States. Like the sumac, it has divided leaves, which, however, grow in opposite pairs. The leaflets are toothed at the edges.

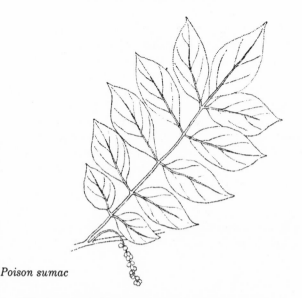

Poison sumac

All these species have the same poison, the same miserable effect. The oily sap, most plentiful in spring and summer, is the carrier. A few hours after you bruise or even brush a plant, your skin begins to itch and redden, and blisters rise. As time goes on, the irritation spreads. The problem will last for several days.

About two million people each year come down with cases of poison oak and poison ivy. Only about half the population is allergic—maybe you're in the lucky half. There is a temporary immunization that some people find effective.

Your best defense, however, is soap and water. The irritant saps are water-soluble, so you can often head off an eruption by scrubbing just after exposure. Once the reactions has begun, you can suppress the itching somewhat with poison oak lotions.

The saps of the poison oaks and ivies are transported by anything they touch, including boots, clothes, packs, and car seats. They stay potent for quite some time. To avoid infecting others or yourself at second hand, wash suspect items thoroughly with soap and water.

Nettles have a different kind of weapon. When you brush them, sharp hairs on their leaves and stems give you an "injection" of poison. There's a stinging pain, sharp but quick to pass. The plants have broad, soft leaves, rounded at the base and pointed at the tip, with coarse teeth. They are found especially along watercourses. The *spurge nettle* has the same effect but a different appearance. Its leaves are alternate, with spreading veins, and deeply lobed in three to five parts, maple-fashion. Various species are found, mainly on sandy soils, over most of the South and Southwest.

In Everglades National Park, which preserves this country's one fragment of subtropical forest, there are several irritant plants with poisons strong enough to be actually dangerous. You might inquire about them before hiking or canoeing in that region.

28:
Diseases of Heat, Cold, and Altitude

NEW BACKPACKERS ARE OFTEN too much afraid of wild animals. But they may be too little afraid of other, less obvious, yet sometimes perilous dangers: the heat, the cold, the wet, the wind, the alpine sun, the lack of oxygen at altitude. All these things affect the hiker. Some of them can make you very sick, and some can kill you. One of the "environmental" disorders—the disease called hypothermia—probably endangers more backpackers in a single year than snakes do in decades.

The body's heat machine

To keep working properly, the human body has to stay near the normal 98–99 degrees Fahrenheit. A very precise balance has to be maintained between heat gained and heat lost. If the balance shifts too far in either direction, the hiker becomes a victim, a person in trouble.

You generate heat just living. The harder you

work, the more you generate. At the same time, the body loses heat, constantly, in the breath and from the skin. Survival depends on conserving this body heat when the weather is cold and getting rid of it when it's hot. There are natural mechanisms for doing each.

What happens when the problem is *cold?* First, the muscles tense just slightly in what is called "preshivering tone"; this burns calories and generates a surprising amount of heat. (So you may be exercising in the cold without knowing it.) Then comes shivering, an even more effective heat producer. At the same time, the small arteries near the skin, where heat is radiated to the outside air, close down. Less blood approaches the skin, and less heat is lost. In dangerous cold, the body may cut off a large part of the circulation to the arms and legs, risking the limbs to keep the head and torso warm. After that the natural defenses are exhausted. To operate in cold climates, we depend on artificial ones. Clothing, our added insulation, has made us a species that can live in the Arctic as well as in the tropics, where we evolved.

If the problem is *too much* warmth, there are different mechanisms. Vessels in the skin and in the arms and legs expand, bringing blood to the surface, where its heat is lost. Perspiration begins, and sweat, evaporating, takes still more heat away. Clothes only get in the way of the cooling, except when you need to block the direct heat and burning ultraviolet rays of a hot sun.

This, oversimplified, is the machine. The diseases of heat and cold—hyperthermia, hypothermia, and frostbite—attack when this system is pressed too far.

Hyperthermia

Hyperthermia is what happens to you when your body is unable to dispose of heat as fast as it manufactures it and absorbs it from outside. As the temperature of the vital organs rises, you begin to feel sick.

The overheated person may feel faint and nauseated. The heartbeat may be fast and irregular. Sweating is profuse, yet the skin may feel oddly cool; the face is likely to be pale. The symptoms are generally those of shock. However, they don't always appear in neat packages; the most important thing to watch for is a growing indifference to surroundings. ("Whenever a person says he wants to sit down and catch up with the party later," one M.D. remarks, "it's a worrisome sign.") In this early period, the disorder is often labeled *heat exhaustion.*

As the body's core temperature rises to high-fever levels, the system goes haywire. The body may lose its ability to regulate blood flow to the skin. There may be a pounding pulse, labored breathing, and seizures. In the textbook case, the victim stops sweating: skin will be hot and dry. But experts warn that this is not always the case. Because the symptoms vary, it is most important again to focus on the person's attitude: a severely overheated hiker will lapse from indifference into major confusion. At this stage, the disease is commonly called *heat stroke.*

If the condition is far advanced, you have an instant emergency on your hands: heat stroke will kill. The treatment, early or late, is the same: rapid cooling. If there's a lake or stream nearby, lay your friend down in the water; if not, cover him with wet cloths and fan him. Keep doing these things until the victim is rational and steady. Once the person is clearly aware and able to swallow, give plenty of water.

Once the crisis has passed, you face the decision of whether to continue the trip or head for home. Except in very mild cases, the latter is probably the better choice—especially if the weather continues hot. In any event, an attack of hyperthermia is a signal to take it easy: the body has tried to handle a taxing combination of effort and heat, and failed.

How did it fail? Probably by being unable to sweat profusely enough. In hot-weather hiking, one may have to perspire *over two quarts an hour* to stay healthily cool. Hardly anybody can do this on the first hot hike of the season. But as time goes on the body adapts to heat stress, "learning" to sweat more copiously and with less loss of the salts called "electrolytes." An otherwise fit hiker needs about ı week of intermittent exercise in a hot climate to make this adjustment. If you plan to hike the desert in the warmer part of the year, bear this in mind.

Cramps, water, and salt

Many hikers experience brief, agonizing cramps, usually at night and usually in the large muscles of the leg. Traditionally, these cramps were blamed on heavy sweating and a resultant loss of salt. The answer was held to be: take salt tablets, especially on the first trips of the season. Later, the emphasis shifted from salt alone to the more complicated concept of "electrolytes," a whole variety of salts found in the blood that are lost in sweat. These we were urged to replace with specially formulated electrolyte drinks.

But as our understanding of the body's mechanisms has increased, the prescription has shifted again. Now, if a fit person has cramps, these are blamed simply on dehydration: on not taking in enough water. Dehydration plainly contributes to other wilderness ailments, too.

The importance of getting enough water into your system really can't be overstated. Thirst is not always a reliable guide. A hiker needs to take in something between a gallon and two gallons of liquid water a day! Here's a test to bear in mind: if your urine is dark, it's a sign that you should drink more water.

Keep your body fit and tanked up on water, and it should take care of the electrolytes itself.

Hypothermia: the killer

Of all the diseases of heat and cold, hypothermia has the ugliest record. In most deaths from what is called "exposure," it is hypothermia that kills. As in heat stroke, the body's defenses break down, struggling vainly not against an excess of heat but against a lack. The temperature of those organs that are vital to life—the organs of the head and torso—begins to drop. All the conserving mechanisms are tried. All fail.

How do you know when hypothermia is coming on? It can be hard to tell. Cold feet and hands are not hypothermia; neither is a generally "chilly" feeling. Take these rather as warnings: signs that you're in a hostile environment and that care is warranted.

The first more definite sign is shivering, first slight, then uncontrollable. When this begins, the body temperature is already a couple of degrees below normal. This is no ordinary shivering. It is a convulsive, alarming shuddering, growing more violent as the body continues to chill. Along with it there may be some muscular stiffness. The hiker feels miserable. Nonetheless, he is rational and capable of taking care of himself. (In fact, if uninformed about the danger, hypothermia victims may push on—"mastering themselves" when they should not, wrongly convinced that they are only a little chilly and tired.)

If the cooling process is not arrested, this borderline condition will tip over into what Cameron Bangs, an authority on the subject, calls *profound* hypothermia. Body temperature, now, has dropped to 90 degrees. The dramatic shivering has ceased or tapered off. Muscles are very stiff indeed. Most notably, the person will start acting very oddly: he will stumble, mumble, say and do peculiar things. No longer is he competent. Finally he will simply fall to the ground. If nothing is done for him, coma will follow, and then death.

If you notice the early signs of hypothermia in yourself or a companion, you take the obvious action: stop the loss of heat and make it possible for the person to warm up again. At the very beginning, it may be enough to eat some candy and take shelter from the wind. If the person has the shivers, stop. In bad weather, set up shelter. Get your friend out of wet clothes, under cover, and into a sleeping bag. It may be helpful, and it cannot hurt, for a second hiker to strip and get into the bag with the victim, sharing body warmth. Hot, sweet liquids will be comforting, if the victim can swallow them.

Profound hypothermia is not so easily dealt with. What if you come across a solo hiker semiconscious on a snowbank? In this instance, the wrong kind of first aid could kill rather than saving.

In deep hypothermia, the heart muscle is chilled. One result is that the heart is prone to go into ventricular fibrillation, a random fluttering that pumps no blood and leads quickly to death. Any shock to the system can trigger this condition!

In such a case, the sufferer must be handled *gently*, with extreme care. Do not allow him to stand up or walk. (This will shock the heart by bringing cold blood back from the limbs to the body core.) Even rewarming, if done too rapidly, can deliver a fatal shock. (A backpack party will scarcely have the means to rewarm a person too fast. But don't, for instance, place a hypothermia victim in a hot spring.)

Having avoided these errors, the actual treatment you give is the same as for the milder case. Your task is to prevent the person from getting any colder. Body-to-body contact, which will warm him very gradually, is probably a good idea. So are hot liquids, if the victim can swallow. (Never try to get food or liquid into an unconscious person, though—he may inhale it.) Mouth-to-mouth artificial respiration is good, too—not to transfer oxygen, in this case, but to transfer heat.

If someone in your party has a brush with mild hypothermia, that need not necessarily alter your plans. A hiker who has been definitely hypothermic should probably be taken home. In a case of *profound* hypothermia, move the victim as little as possible. Rather, send someone out to summon a rescue.

Generally speaking, it is in winter that you have

to be most constantly aware of the hypothermia danger. But a surprising number of cases also occur "out-of-season"—in the warmer half of the year. On New Hampshire's Mount Washington, four hypothermia cases once had to be rescued within forty-eight hours—in August! While Washington, one of the most weatherbeaten summits in the United States, is hardly typical, there is some risk in any cool region. Spring and autumn hikers in cool places are especially vulnerable, because, so often, they take gear and clothing suited only for midsummer.

Remember: it doesn't take bitterly cold air to make "hypothermia weather." The problem can arise even on a mild day if it is both *windy* and *wet.* A wet hiker, in cotton clothing, on a windswept ridge can die of hypothermia when the air temperature is in the forties or fifties.

Frostbite

Frostbite is, essentially, freezing: the freezing of a part of the body. Feet and toes are the likeliest parts, by far, to be bitten; most of the other cases are fingers and hands.

Unlike hypothermia, frostbite can only happen when the temperature is freezing. That makes it almost exclusively a winter problem (though on some peaks it can happen anytime). Winter campers, the first few times out, may worry about frostbite every time their hands or feet get unpleasantly cold. With more experience, you learn that mere chilliness isn't frostbite. Still, it's better to be oversuspicious than to be complacent.

The fact is that frostbite can sneak up on you. The *typical* pattern—a cold sensation, followed by pain, followed by no sensation at all—doesn't always hold. The best defense is to ask yourself frequently whether you have full feeling in fingers and toes, and to do something about it if you don't. It's especially important not to have your boots too tightly laced, and to loosen them further from time to time.

If you think a finger is beginning to be frostbitten, you can quickly warm it in your armpit. If you are worried about your toes, there's the belly treatment. You stop, strip off your shoes and socks, and plant your feet on somebody's warm belly—not nearly as uncomfortable for the companion as it sounds!

A part that is actually frostbitten will look waxy and discolored and, in general, *wrong*. If your toes look like that, what do you do then?

Your instinct might be to warm them up, fast. But this is often the worst thing you can do. In frostbite, the real tissue damage is done during the initial freezing and again when the flesh is thawed. While the part is actually frozen, nothing much is going on. Moreover, it doesn't hurt. (Thawed, it will hurt like hell.) People can walk many miles, without discomfort or further damage, on frozen toes and even frozen feet; but once thawing has taken place, a seriously frostbitten person must be carried.

There's another good reason for not rewarming too soon, and this is the risk of another bout of frostbite on the outward trek. Thawing and refreezing can turn a minor case into a major and crippling one.

So if you discover, in the middle of some bitter winter day, that someone in your party has a frozen toe, don't stop. Head as quickly as you can for the roadhead, or to a place from which rescue will be easy. If you must make camp, try to leave the frozen extremity cold. A frostbitten foot or hand should not be tucked into the owner's sleeping bag but left outside it. If the air inside the tent is warm, you might even have to apply a cold pack of snow wrapped in cloth to the frozen part.

What if, for some reason, you know you can't keep the part frozen? Authorities now agree that it must be rewarmed quickly, rather than gradually. Soak the injured limb in a bath of rather hot water. (Mountaineering doctors debate the recommended temperature, but the consensus puts it between 100 and 110 degrees Fahrenheit. If it's uncomfortably hot for the first-aider, it's too hot for the patient.) Keeping the water at that temperature as nearly as you can, soak the part for twenty to thirty minutes. Never pummel the damaged flesh, rub it with snow, break any blisters that appear, or try to exercise the limb. Never apply direct heat.

Remember, overtight boots can lead to frostbite when you might not expect it. Overstuffing your boots with socks, in the attempt to keep your feet warmer, may actually cut off circulation and make them colder. Tight snowshoe or crampon straps, cinched over pliable boots, can do the same. If your feet feel chronically cold, try easing up on straps and laces.

Deep frostbite is another of those subjects that *have* to be talked about, because the problem is so frightening and serious when it occurs. But frostbite simply won't overtake a well-equipped and knowledgeable backpacker.

Preventing the diseases of heat and cold

We've touched, many times in this book, on some of the basic practices that should keep you safe from the diseases of heat and cold. Reviewing them quickly:

Keep comfortable. On cold days keep warm—on hot days keep cool. Adjust your clothing whenever you need to. Don't be so strong-minded that you let yourself suffer for hours—if nothing else, you'll be wearing yourself out, and that can lead to trouble.

Drink plenty of water. Thirst isn't a reliable guide to your need for water. Drink *more* than thirst would suggest, a gallon or more a day.

Get plenty of food. This is doubly important in the cold. Nibble all day long. The body can and will run on its own fat, but this is an inefficient source of energy unless new sugar and starch are coming in.

Don't push on to exhaustion. Some readers will laugh at this advice; climbers, and others with fixed ambitions, are unlikely to follow it. But whenever heat or cold is a problem, exhaustion can help precipitate heat stroke, hypothermia, or frostbite. It can complicate other health problems as well.

Be in good condition. This means reasonable exercise at home as a matter of routine, and a good diet. Some Americans, though technically healthy, don't have the reserves of strength they would need to call on in a wilderness emergency.

Avoid most drugs. Winter campers, snug and warm at nightfall, often take a swallow or two of liquor. No harm in that. But whenever cold is becoming a major problem, it's best to stay away from that and any other "stuff." Different stimulants and depressants have different effects, but they all seem to interfere with the normal working of the body's heat machine. (Coffee and tea are okay, however.)

Deal with trouble early.

Altitude sickness

"Altitude sickness" is a name for several related physical problems. Naturally enough, it is mostly encountered in high western ranges. We're only beginning to realize how many people actually get sick at altitude, sometimes running considerable risk without ever knowing it. In one study, eighty-four percent of the people who climbed to the 14,000-foot summit of Washington's Mount Rainier were found to have at least some symptoms.

Altitude sickness is brought on by rapid rise in elevation. The farther you climb, the harder you hike, and the larger the loads you carry, the greater the chance of trouble. Though altitude problems rarely start below 9,000 or 10,000 feet, they *can* begin as low as 5,000. How fit you are doesn't seem to matter a great deal. Nonsmokers don't have an easier time of it, either.

Ordinary altitude sickness, the kind experienced by thousands, is known medically as "acute mountain sickness." Coming down with it, you will probably notice first a headache, mild or intense. If you're hiking, you'll feel exhausted and short of breath. You'll lose your appetite and may feel nauseated. In more severe cases there is vomiting. Many people get a few symptoms toward the end of a long first day that ends above 9,000 feet, feel better when they stop hiking, and wake up perfectly fit in the morning. Others are uncomfortable for several days.

All of this is a nuisance at worst—for most of us, most of the time. But acute mountain sickness can develop, on the second or third day, into one of two other conditions, both highly dangerous. For either there is only one cure: *pack up and get down the hill*—if possible, while you can still move under your own power.

Cerebral edema, a rare but deadly condition, is an accumulation of fluids in the brain. The current belief is that ordinary mountain sickness is actually a very slight cerebral edema, but the more intense form is unmistakably different. The headache turns violent. The victim will be terribly weak. He may stagger, babble, hallucinate. If he isn't taken to lower elevations, he falls into a stupor, followed by a coma and then by death.

Almost as serious, and very much more common, is *high-altitude pulmonary edema,* an accumulation of fluid in the lungs. Over one hundred people die of this disease every year, some at elevations no higher than 9,000 feet. The symptoms are somewhat like those of pneumonia. There is coughing, shortness of breath, quickened breathing, and fast heartbeat. The lungs feel tight, stiff, constricted. There will be creaking or bubbling noises in the lungs, slight at first, and then increasing. As the victim gets worse, coughing will bring up a pinkish foam. Finally, the patient goes into a stupor brought about by oxygen lack. Essentially, he drowns in body fluids.

Again, the one real answer is to go down. Sometimes a drop of a couple of thousand feet will bring a dramatic recovery. If you can't evacuate immediately, have the victim sit up, and try to keep him alert. Bed rest only makes the condition worse.

Pulmonary edema is by no means unknown in adults, but the danger is much greater for people under twenty-one. Hikers who have had it once must be on the watch for it afterwards. And here's a curious fact: people who spend a long time at high altitudes, return to sea level for several weeks, and then go up again, run the greatest risk of all.

Avoiding altitude sickness

The body has the ability to adapt, within limits, to the lack of oxygen at unaccustomed altitudes. On the typical short backpacking trip, however, this adaptation has barely begun when the party heads for home.

The more slowly you ascend, the fewer problems you will have. It's often recommended that you allow one day for each 1,000 feet you climb above the 10,000-foot line. If you must start high, try at least to get a full night's sleep at the high roadhead, and to schedule a fairly leisurely first day.

People with heart and lung problems should certainly ask a doctor's advice before setting out on trips in the high country.

Sunburn and snow blindness

About sunburn there is little to say. You know your complexion and your tolerance. In the woods, and in most American mountains when they are free of snow, sunscreen lotions will protect you, along with a broad-brimmed hat and perhaps a bandanna at your neck. Don't underdress. It's safer to cover up if you aren't well tanned. Avoid particularly a burn on your shoulders, where the pack straps ride.

The higher you climb, the more burning ultraviolet rays come through the filtering atmosphere. A moderate overcast does nothing to stop them. Be aware that burning rays bounce up from glittering granite, sand, water, or snow.

A mild sunburn is nothing to worry about. Your sunscreen lotion will also do for a salve. Severe sunburn, even though it heals, is actually a permanent injury and contributes to the apparent "aging" of human skin. In unusually bad cases there may be blistering, severe pain, even swelling, headache, nausea, fever, and chills. Such a burn can immobilize you. Moist, cool dressings will help somewhat.

Sunscreen lotions are graded according to "sun

protection factors," prominently noted on containers. A lotion with a factor of 8 would theoretically permit you to remain in the sun eight times as long, before burning, as you could with no lotion on at all; a factor of 15—the highest on the scale—would give you a fifteenfold safe period. But for a fairskinned person on snow all day, more protection still is required. *Sunblockers* are intended to shut out *all* the ultraviolet radiation. Familiar ones are zinc oxide lotion, clown-white makeup, and greasy "glacier cream." Whatever you use, don't neglect to apply lotion under your chin and around your nostrils, where rays bouncing up from below can burn you badly. Be aware that some preparations wash off with sweat, and reapply as needed.

One form of sunburn is very serious: *snow blindness*, sunburn of the eye. Snow travelers must have dark glasses or goggles (and a spare pair in the pack) and wear them much of the time even under a light overcast. The higher you climb, of course, the more important it becomes to keep protection on your eyes. Glasses for use above timberline must protect the sides of the eyes as well, with tinted glass or plastic, or with solid barriers.

Snow blindness is nothing more than sunburn of the surface of the eye. The first symptom will be a scratchy, sandy feeling. That's the time to hurry off the mountain. In another six or seven hours the eyes may swell almost shut, and the touch of light will become a physical, painful thing. At that point, to get down the mountain, you may have to be led. The first aid treatments are cold packs, total darkness, and perhaps aspirin or codeine for pain.

The Wilderness Regions

They say, Rules change in the Reaches.

—Ursula K. LeGuin

29:
Wilderness in the East

MAGNIFICENTLY VARIOUS, THE WILD COUNTRY of
North America: low and high, lush and barren, flat
and rugged, dry and wet, warm and cool. Different,
too, are the requirements it imposes on the hiker. To
the California Sierra backpacker, accustomed to
sunny summers, cool granite, and dry air, much of
America's wilderness seems foreign, difficult
even—a new and sometimes complicated world.

In most of the United States, after all, summer
is not dry and hot; it is wet and hot, or, in some sections, wet and cool. Over much of the East, Midwest, and South, the summer months are actually
the wettest of the year, and some other season—
commonly autumn, sometimes spring or winter—is
the driest time. Even in the western deserts, such
rain as falls may fall mostly in summer. And while
most hikers, in most regions, still take to the mountains in July and August, more and more are learning the advantages of the other ten months of the
calendar.

Eastern wilderness regions, including Northern Plains

Eastern beach and wetland wilderness

Say *wilderness,* and the average hiker gets a mountain in his mind. But along the Gulf of Mexico and the Atlantic coast, the great wild places are not high and rocky but flooded and flat. These are the wetlands: the swamps and marshes, freshwater, brackish, and salt.

One band of watery wilderness follows the shoreline: thousands of miles of pickleweed, needlerush, saltmeadow cordgrass, bulltongue and bulrush, spreading behind glistening barrier beaches from the mouth of the Rio Grande to the mouth of the Hudson and beyond. Barren the marshes seem when first you look at them, horizons of gray or green or dull pastel, laced with the bright arteries of tidal channels. Naturalists know better: know that these are among the most biologically productive places of the continent. You might guess as much from the throngs, the flocks, the incredible populations of birds: ducks and geese in millions, ibises, herons and egrets, terns and eagles and ospreys and hundreds of species more.

The marshes themselves have little place for the pedestrian. This is canoe territory. But between the marshes and the open sea lie long, sandy barrier islands, from Padre Island in Texas to Cape Lookout in North Carolina to Monomoy Island off Cape Cod. These can be hiked, and are.

Beach walking has its peculiarities. Typically, you'll be hiking along the ocean side of your island, next to the waves, where the sand is wet and firm. Conventional leather boots are out—you don't need them, and blisters are likely. Wear sneakers or running shoes. Water is a problem; as in the desert, you must carry or cache quite a supply. However, seawater can be used for cooking, washing, and brushing your teeth. (In some areas you can find fresh water by digging in a pocket between dunes, well back from the beachfront.) Salt on your skin and sand in all your gear will simply have to be put up with. Lack of shade makes summer an unpleasant hiking season on most barrier islands; autumn seems to be ideal.

The climate of these coastlands is in general very mild, but of course it varies greatly from the semiarid southern tip of Texas to the lush shores of Florida and the hard capes of New England where the coastal wetlands end at last. In many places autumn is the "season," the best time of year to see the flocks migrating.

Much of the continent's margin of marsh and island has been altered by dredging and diking and filling, covered with urban development, fouled by chronic pollution. But there are also large areas still pristine, and a few of them, chiefly national wildlife refuges, are protected. There are also several national seashores. Within these government-owned lands significant sections remain wild.

Inland from the shore there is another series of places both wild and wet. These are the swamps of the Gulf and Atlantic coastal plains, and of the lower Mississippi Valley, where rivers slow and spread on their travel to the sea. They are not, for the most part, open marshes, but rather water-logged forests of tupelo, bald cypress, and oak, hung with Spanish moss. Logging was never easy in the swamps, and got a late start there. Thus they contain today, if only by default, some of the grandest virgin forests in the East. Some of the best-known swamps are the Great Dismal on the Virginia/North Carolina line; the rich Congaree in South Carolina; the vast Okefenokee Swamp in southern Georgia; the Atchafalaya in Louisiana; and the Big Thicket country in Texas.

The greatest of all the eastern wetlands is neither marsh nor swamp but something unique in itself: the Everglades. Here there flows a huge, rustling river without banks—a river of sawgrass and sluggish water, finally turning salt in mangrove forests on the shores of Florida Bay. Most of this flowage is now protected in Everglades National Park and the Big Cypress National Preserve. Here is the largest wilderness of the East, and one of the most valued natural preserves in the world.

Like coastal marshes, the inland swamps are most visited by canoe or boat. But people can and do explore them on foot. Some areas have raised boardwalks; in others, old railroad routes, dikes, and "ridges" or streaks of drier ground provide dry-footed access. To really get around, though, you must count on getting your feet wet. Swamp hikers favor the Army's "tropical combat" boots (or a civilian equivalent), with mesh panels and holes in the sole through which water can drain. Gear must be water-resistant and tough. Landmarks are scarce, and skill with map and compass is essential for cross-country travel. Some swamps are habitat for bears, alligators, and cottonmouth mocassins, none of which, however, is a very serious hazard. While there is plenty of sticky mud, true "quicksand" is rare. In southern states, the months from November to mid-March are the best swamp-hiking season: cool and insect-free.

Eastern mountains: general

The Appalachians, the Ozarks, the Adirondacks— all the eastern mountain masses—are wilder today than they were half a century ago. Even the national parks in this region were repurchased from private owners after settlement and—not seldom— ugly exploitation; the forests within their boundaries are largely young growth. But the East is a well-watered, mostly temperate region. Even in the mountains, the growing season is long—as long as ten months in the south—compared to a month or so in the high western ranges. Here it does not take geological time to heal scars. Already the signs of the human past have become more charming than disturbing in otherwise wild scenes: old roads now gone to trails, old orchards still bearing fruit, the stone foundations of old houses, the rock walls around old fields.

North Carolina's Mount Mitchell, 6,684 feet high, is the tallest peak east of the Black Hills of South Dakota. Considering the moderate elevations, it is easy to underestimate the ruggedness of these ridges. Five-thousand–foot summits may still rise the larger part of a mile from valley floors below. Along with gentle trails, there are many that are steep, roughly surfaced, and demanding.

The eastern ranges are almost entirely wooded. Hardwoods—oaks and hickories, maples and beeches, birches and many more—grow almost to the summits in the southern mountains and cover valleys and foothills in the north. Above them grow coniferous forests of spruce and fir (though the hardwoods take over in this zone, too, in the first years after logging). When you travel under broadleafed trees in summer, you don't see out very often or very far. Under the trees, thick brush—especially the thickets, gorgeous in the spring, of dogwood, rhododendron, mountain laurel, briar—can make it hard to push your way cross-country. Even more than in the West, most eastern hikers stay on the trails.

If there is a time for cross-country travel, here in the East, it is fall and winter. When the leaves are off the hardwood trees and the stems of brush are bare, the landscape is transformed. You see out, see for miles, see where you are; away from the trails the going is not so hard. Besides, you'll be dressed for bushwhacking; in the warmth of summer, you may not be.

Though there are exceptions, most blocks of eastern mountain wilderness are rather small. On long trips, hikers may traverse several of them, rather than choosing a single area to explore. In such regions as the Adirondacks and the White and Green mountains of New England, whole clusters of wild areas lie close together. A great deal of hiking, too, is done on *extended trails*—pedestrian routes that traverse both wild lands and tame, and even cross (by arrangement with the owners) long gaps of private land. The Appalachian Trail is the most famous of these, and the great model, but there are a great many others: the Long Trail in Vermont, the Metacomet-Monadnock Trail in Massachusetts, the Shore to Shore trail in Michigan, and dozens more. Though this idea has been imitated in the wild mountains of the West, it seems most functional in semisettled country, where the truly wild sections are few and far between.

The small size of most eastern wilderness areas does have its advantages. Access, undeniably, is easy. It is often possible to reach wilderness road-heads by public transportation. You can't get as far away from civilization as you can in western land-scapes; thus, in the normal hiking season, you are not quite so totally on your own. However, this ease of access, this lack of great remoteness, can be deceiving. It can lead hikers to underestimate the problems that will face them on the trails—and especially those problems that are caused by weather.

Anywhere in the eastern mountains you will want a tent year-round. A tarp might serve for the rain but not for the mosquitoes of summer. And even a cool, clear night can be so humid that you need cloth above your head to catch the heavy dew. You should choose your gear with almost perpetual dampness in mind. Boots should be well treated for water-repellency, inside and out. A polyester-filled or Gore-Tex–shelled sleeping bag makes better sense than one of unprotected down. In lower parts of the more southern mountains, where summer nights are often uncomfortably warm, you may not want a sleeping bag at all in that season, but only something on the order of a wool blanket.

Throughout the East, and especially along the various long trails, you find shelters. Some, especially in the Northeast, are backcountry hostels with caretakers. Most are simple, three-sided structures. While the latter can be highly convenient, it is better, all things considered, to leave them out of your plans. These refuges are often crowded. Too often they are littered, dirty, or vandalized. Some sit in deserts of trampled, eroded ground. And nuisance animals—bears, skunks, raccoons—naturally congregate at these sites. In some areas—Shenandoah National Park, for instance—the rangers now discourage the use of shelters except on day-hikes and in emergencies. In many other places you must reserve a spot in a shelter in advance.

It's absolutely necessary to carry a stove in eastern wilderness. Fires are widely restricted, and in some places where they aren't, they should be. In the Catskills, around shelters maintained by New York State, acres have been stripped of all breakable wood, living or dead. It's an ugly scene and repeated in too many places. Don't be part of it. When the weather is wet—as it so often is—a stove may be the only practical answer anyway.

The southern Appalachians

These are the wettest of the eastern mountains. The peaks of the Smokies, with some ninety inches of annual rain, are in fact the wettest spots in the country outside the Pacific Northwest. March has the largest monthly precipitation; the summer, with torrential thundershowers, is only a little drier. Summer days are typically in the seventies or eighties Fahrenheit, though temperatures may drop to forty degrees Fahrenheit after a storm; humidity is almost always high. The typical hiking uniform in the heat is the minimum: shorts, perhaps a light shirt or net undershirt, and boots. (But you need long pants where poison ivy is dense along the trail.) On the lower slopes, nights may be only a little cooler than the days. Above 3,000 feet, however, nights drop to the sixties even in hot July.

September, October, and November are the driest and clearest months, really the best of the hiking weather. The trails are less crowded (except in popular hunting areas!) and the mosquito problem is past. In some years, the southern Appalachians get a display of fall color worthy of New England. Regular frosts begin in November.

In winter, snow is frequent but unpredictable. Since only the highest ridges stay white for very long, you will not generally have much need for skis and snowshoes. At middle elevations, rain mixes with snow and alternates with snow—it may snow at night and rain during the day. As anyone knows who has dealt with such conditions, they make for difficult camping. Freezing rain—glaze—is also fairly common. For all that, midwinter in this region is actually one of the drier times of year. Days are cool and often gray, nights subfreezing but seldom bitterly cold. Yet temperatures *can* go down below zero, winds *can* rise to gale force, and whiteout conditions are not unknown on the higher ridges.

On the slopes you find hardwood forest chiefly, or rather hardwood *forests:* there are several distinct, complex communities. (It has been said that the Great Smokies contain more species of trees than are found in all of Europe.) Spruce and fir appear above 5,000 feet. Summits may have "balds" of grass or heath, mostly rhododendron and mountain laurel.

In this southern part of the Appalachian chain, the federal government has considerable wild holdings. The most significant is Great Smoky Mountains National Park, a wilderness almost western in scale, and split by a single road. Other pieces of wild country—in Shenandoah National Park and in various National Forests—are a good deal smaller. A few are formally protected for their wilderness; most, at this writing, are not.

The Northeast

North of Virginia, the Appalachians subside for a time. Pennsylvania, with its low but still prominent ridges and plateaus, is a transition zone between southern and northern landscapes. When the land rises again in New York State, the character of the mountains has changed.

The weather is considerably cooler. While some summer days may be hot, warm nights are rare, and cold storms can come in at any time of year. Only three months—and less, in many places—are free of frost. In New Hampshire the 4,000- to 6,000-foot peaks of the White Mountains can get snow and high winds at any time of year, and the summer temperature, in bad weather, can drop as low as twenty degrees. Combined with wind and rain, such temperatures can make conditions very wintry—hypothermia weather, even frostbite weather, during summer. A surprising number of people get into trouble on summer hikes in the northeastern mountains.

Fall in the Northeast is an excellent time for the hiker. It has many crisp, clear days and is about the closest thing to a dry season. Winter is white, beautiful, and bitter. Snow camping, snowshoeing, and

ski touring are all popular here. Winter hikers
watch out for occasional storms out of the southeast, which can bring rain, usually followed by a
shift of weather, subzero temperatures, and northwest gales. Everything gets wet, and then freezes
solid. Zippers jam, tents seem welded to the ground.
Experienced winter travelers do their best to avoid
such weather.

The original forests of these mountains were almost entirely spruce and fir; only at lower elevations, as along the Hudson, did the hardwoods naturally predominate. But because almost every hillside
has been logged at some point, the transition hardwoods have taken over almost everywhere. Above
the zone of full-sized timber, there may be a thousand feet of dwarfed birch and mountain ash; then,
as low as 5,000 feet in some sections, only tundra
and stone. All of these ranges were completely buried during the last glaciation by the advancing ice;
the numerous lakes of New England and New York
are only the most obvious of the marks the icecap
made on this country.

This is the only part of the nation where the bulk
of the wild land is in the care of state agencies and
private landowners rather than of branches of the
federal government. The state of New York has
given formal wilderness protection to almost one
million acres of its vast properties in the Adirondacks and proposes another 90,000 designated acres
in its lesser empire, the Catskills. Pennsylvania has
extensive blocks of primitive state-owned land. In
Maine, too, it is the state that is responsible for the
wilderness and semiwilderness of Baxter State Park
and the Allagash Waterway, and several million
acres of private timberlands—open to limited public
use—remain remarkably wild.

The U.S. Forest Service does manage most of the
public land in the White Mountains of New Hampshire and the Green Mountains of Vermont. Even
here there is an unusual setup. Much of the work of
management—the trail maintenance, the staffing of

backcountry shelters, even some of the planning—is done by private clubs, chief among them the Appalachian Mountain Club. Westerners may be taken aback at the relative luxuries they find in some of these mountains (though they are at liberty to avoid them). Everywhere you see the traditional shelters, many of them with caretakers (and fees); there's even a system of eight elaborate backcountry hostels, or huts, where meals are served—reservations, of course, are required.

The Ozarks

West of the Appalachians, on the long, gradual slope toward the Mississippi, you find little wild land in public ownership. But beyond the great river, in the knot of low mountains called the Ozarks, there are quite a few spots where the original wilderness, once driven back, has been permitted to restore itself. There are National Forests here, and the National Park Service has narrow, linear parks along several of the major rivers.

In many ways the Ozark country resembles the mountains of the Southeast. It is only a shade more continental in climate—the summer a little hotter, the winter slightly less mild. Summer lacks the hot nights that can be so troublesome in the Southeast. Autumn is very pleasant. The wettest months are April, May, and June, and the driest (though by no means rainless) are the midwinter months of December, January, and February. There's some snow, but it doesn't last.

In the Ozarks proper, wild areas are often found on the rugged slopes between lowland valleys and plateaulike summit regions. Because the gentle highlands are settled and grazed by cattle, water in the streams below almost always has to be purified for drinking.

Lake-and-forest wilderness

Along the Canadian border, from the Adirondacks to the High Plains, there lies a great, flat tangle of blue lakes, bogs, potholes, and circuitous rivers. Many American landscapes bear the marks of glaciation; but in this flat expanse, where other obvious landmarks are so lacking, almost every feature you see was put there by the unimaginable weight and power of the ice sheets that, not long ago in geological terms, lay over it.

The ice laid down moraines and eskers and drumlins and erratic boulders; it shoved old rivers into modern courses; it scraped some landscapes bare and covered others with rich soil. Most of all, it made lakes: the five Great Lakes and uncountable smaller ones.

The result is a handsome country: mostly gentle in topography, mostly forested with hardwoods and various conifers, and in large part well settled. But scattered across the region are blocks of government land, state and federal, where wilderness remains—or is being allowed to return.

The National Park Service has some of the larger properties, wild at least in part, around the Great Lakes: three national lakeshores and one national park, splendid Isle Royale, a 100,000-acre archipelago in Lake Superior. On state lands, Michigan, Minnesota and Wisconsin have chosen areas, within their larger state parks, for protection as state-owned wilderness areas. Other fragments of roadless land remain in national forests and national wildlife refuges.

The greatest lake country wilderness lies west of the Great Lakes, in northern Minnesota. This is the famous Boundary Waters Canoe Area within Superior National Forest, about one million acres along the Canadian border. It is a wilderness of pines, red and white and jack; of waterfalls and bare rocks and waterside camps and portages; and of water itself: water in lakes, water in ponds, water in rivers. The struggle to preserve this region, not yet ended, has been going on for fifty years. Adjoining the Boundary Waters are parks in two nations: small Voyageurs National Park on the American side and the million-acre Quetico Provincial Park in Canada. Together these areas make up one of the chief wilderness reserves of the North American continent. Despite the emphasis on water travel, backpackers do find much to explore in these areas.

The climate of the lakes country is continental—hot in summer and cold in winter—but somewhat milder close to the shores of the Great Lakes. In the eastern part of the region, late summer is the rainiest time; but to the west, on the edge of the Great Plains, the rain peak comes earlier. Winters are gray and often bitterly cold. The Boundary Waters Area has six months of snow cover and some of the lowest winter temperatures recorded in the contiguous United States.

Wilderness on the plains

Little enough is left of the wild Great Plains, so little that it is almost painful to recount the fragments we have. Yet there are some, mostly in the northern part of the region, along the Canadian border.

The plains, though beautiful to the intelligent eye, lack obvious spectacle. Most of the protected areas in this vast region were set aside rather for wildlife than directly for recreation. The prairie states are spotted with wildlife refuges—some for ducks, for sandhill cranes, for pelicans, for other birds; some to preserve the bison and that other curiosity, the historic Texas Longhorn. Certain of these refuges have within them blocks of true prairie wilderness, varied sometimes by lakes, sometimes by streams, sometimes by stony hills, but always more than anything else a wilderness of grass.

In North and South Dakota, the Badlands, stark, eroded landscapes, interrupt the smooth ascent of the plains. Badlands National Monument, South Dakota, preserves a part of this country: tablelands, gulches, canyons and buttes, bright colors in the crumbling earth. The Monument also contains a very sizable chunk of rugged, roadless prairie. Theodore

Roosevelt National Historical Park, across the border in North Dakota, has smaller areas of wild ground.

As you move west across the plains, the grass grows shorter, the weather drier, and the federal holdings more extensive. Here there are many "national grasslands," lands that were badly overgrazed in private ownership, then purchased by the government for restoration. In eastern Montana there are more than a million acres of public domain land, wild in part, around the backed-up waters of Fort Peck Reservoir on the Missouri. River-carved, eroded, semiarid, these river breaks, like the Badlands, have a mountainous look. Part of this region has been named the Charles M. Russell Wildlife Range; it is one of the chief reserves of prairie wilderness.

Only a few of the wild areas of the Great Plains are large enough to reward a long hiking trip. But there's a good deal here for the weekend traveler and the day-hiker. The fascination here is of the rare. So much of the whole wild center of a continent is reduced now to so little.

Rainfall from April 1–September 30

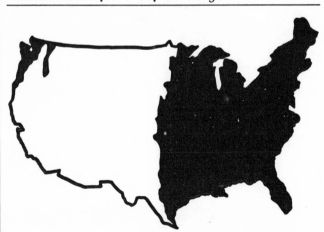

White area has 15 inches or less of summer rainfall.

In the wilderness-rich northern part of the plains, the climate is rigorous. There can be a 150-degree range in temperature over the year, from 100 degrees above zero Fahrenheit to 50 or more below. In some areas, wind is all but perpetual. Early summer is the wettest time of year.

From east to west in the plains region, annual totals of precipitation become smaller and smaller. Even the summer rains—significant, in different ways, to farmer and backpacker alike—decrease. The line where these summer rains amount to less than 15 inches will do, as well as anything, for the boundary of "The West." By that definition, the wild areas of the northern plains are already distinctly western: part of what used to be called "The Great American Desert."

For backpackers, though, the West begins a little farther along: where the plains give way to mountains once again.

30:
Western
Wilderness

MOST OF OUR WILDERNESS IS WESTERN WILDERNESS.
Wherever you are, in the eleven contiguous western
states, there is backpacking country not far away.
The problem is not to find it but to save it. Wilderness in the West, though grand, is shrinking fast.

What possible summary is there for these lands,
so varied that they might seem to belong on different continents? It is almost hard to imagine at one
time the rain forests of Washington and the red-
rock canyons of Utah—the spikes of the northern
Rockies and the chaparral mountains of Southern
California—the sagebrush steppes and the alpine
glaciers. To have all these things within a thousand
miles of each other would be astonishing enough.
But often a mere hundred miles of travel, or fifty,
or ten, is enough to take you from one world to another. There are places where you can walk, within
a couple of days, up through a luxuriant forest, over
treeless, snowy, windblown passes, and down into
desert basins on the other side.

Weather in the West

The variety of the West is very much a matter of weather; a matter of contrary climates. Many influences make these climates, but three things, in this region, are paramount. There is first the northern Pacific storm nursery, generator of winter rain and snow. Second is the warm, moist air that rides up into the Great Plains, in summer, from the Gulf of Mexico, producing thunderstorms. And third is the shape of the land itself. Western mountains don't just endure the weather; they help create it, for themselves and for the lands around them.

The winter storms bring to the West most of its snow and rain. These storms take shape in the northern Pacific and sweep southeastward onto the continent. Though their centers strike the continent at various places, the storms bear down most often on the state of Washington. South along the Pacific Coast, away from the middle of this storm track, the winter rains grow steadily shorter and steadily more intermittent.

To the east the rainfall also diminishes, but in this direction the change is not gradual. It is dramatic, abrupt. For here the storms encounter the high mountain barrier of the Cascades and, farther

Simplified map of mean annual precipitation

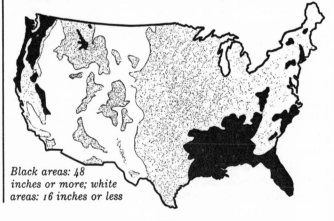

Black areas: 48 inches or more; white areas: 16 inches or less

south, the Sierra Nevada. These ranges force the clouds to rise; rising, they cool; cooling, they must let their moisture fall (chill air can't hold as much suspended water as warm air can). When the clouds at last pass beyond the crests of the Pacific ranges, they have little rain or snow left in them. And so beyond the mountains the hinterlands are dry: wide steppes, vast deserts, hard and arid hills. Only the highest mountains in the interior ranges are tall enough to force more moisture from the depleted clouds. Look at a weather map of the West, a map that shows annual rainfall, and you can tell, almost as from a topographic map, where the interior mountains are.

If there were no rains in the West besides those that come down the storm track, the interior regions would be even drier, more extensively desert, than they are. But the West, like the East, has another kind of rain: the summer thundershower. To over-simplify, thunderstorms happen when moist air, heated by sun-warmed ground, rises straight up into cooler layers of the atmosphere. The more moisture there is in the rising air, the more rain the storm will shed. The humid air that produces most of the nation's thunderstorms comes north, in the summer, from the Gulf of Mexico. Thus such storms are rather rare, and rather dry, toward the Pacific Coast but become much more important as you move inland toward the Rockies and the Great Plains.

So you could say, very roughly and crudely, that winter rainfall in the West depends on how far you are from Puget Sound in the state of Washington. And you could add that summer rainfall depends on how far away you are from the edge of the Great Plains. Having said these things, you would immediately begin to see exceptions. The tangled mountains of the West create, within the larger pattern, a thousand local climates. Most of the time, high ground is wetter than lower ground nearby, and every mountain casts, on the side away from the prevailing winds, a "shadow," not of lessened light, but of lessened rain.

Significant though it may be in arid places, the summer rainfall seldom amounts to much in absolute terms. Except for parts of the Northwest and the northern Rockies, you can safely say that the West, in summer, is a dry proposition. Even when thundershowers seem to turn the air to water, this is typically just an interruption. More than a few hours of rain are not likely; humidity stays generally low. Thus a hot day in the West is seldom as hard to take as a similarly hot, but muggy, eastern afternoon. It is for this western summer climate that much of the traditional wilderness gear is most suited. The down jacket, the down-filled sleeping bag, the tarp for shelter, the poncho against rain—they make sense for most of the West in the "normal" hiking season.

What about western temperatures? The pattern is simple. The farther north you go, the cooler it gets. The farther up the mountains you go, the cooler it gets. A rise of 1,000 feet, it has been estimated, much resembles a northward movement of three hundred miles. In New Mexico, treeline—the line where it becomes too cold for even stunted trees to grow—lies at almost 12,000 feet. In Montana it lies at about 7,000.

The forests of the West follow climate. You can divide them, with a certain neatness, into types that succeed each other as you climb a mountain slope, or as you move north into the cooler regions. There are typical (though not unvarying) forests of the lower, dryer hills; typical forests of the high and middle slopes; typical forests rising to timberline. On almost any long mountain hike you will watch the woods around you change—not once but several times—perhaps from ponderosa pine to Douglas fir, from Douglas fir to true firs, from true firs to the specialized trees of timberline. Wherever you go, however, you will find mostly the needle-bearing trees—spruces and larches, cedars and junipers and cypresses, pines and firs, redwoods and hemlocks and yews. These mix, at times, with broad-leafed trees: oaks, bays, madrones, aspens, cottonwoods,

Western wilderness regions

maples, alders, and many more. But in only a few areas in the Far West, and then mostly in California, do the broad-leafed trees make up a woodland by themselves.

The Pacific ranges

Along the Pacific Coast, just about all the remaining wilderness is found in the mountainous country. These highlands rise in two parallel north-south lines. Nearest the ocean are the tangled, many-ridged Coast Ranges. Typically rather low, these ranges nevertheless do rise, in several places, to 8,000 feet, and even to 10,000.

Parallel to the coastal ranges rise a second and greater mountain wall: the Sierra and the Cascades. The southern half of the chain is the famous Sierra Nevada. A single enormous fault block lifted as much as two miles above sea level, the Sierra slopes gently on the west but breaks abruptly to the deserts on the east in a scarp as much as 10,000 feet high. The Cascades of northern California, Oregon, and Washington are built on a different plan entirely. The basic Cascades are in fact a band of forested hills or rugged mountains of middle height. But from the green base there rise, spaced and isolated and spectacular, a dozen domes and spikes of lava, ice, and snow: the volcanoes of the Pacific Northwest. The Sierra and the Cascades are cold enough, and wet enough, to carry glaciers—small remnant ice fields among the peaks of the south, massive rivers of ice in the northern part of the Cascades. Where there are glaciers today there were, in the past, huge ice caps; these gouged out Sierra granites and Cascade lavas to make the sockets of hundreds of modern lakes.

Weather in the Pacific ranges depends on altitude and latitude. At the southern end of the Coast Ranges, in Southern California, summers are so long, so hot, and so dry that hikers tend to be out in spring and fall rather than in what would elsewhere be the "normal" hiking season. Some areas are closed to public use in the rainless months because of the extreme danger of fire. Only the highest peaks are forested; lower and middle slopes are covered with the complex and typically Californian brushfields called chaparral.

As you move north along either chain of mountains, the climate becomes steadily wetter and cooler, the forests greener, and the dry season shorter and less reliable. At high elevations, summer is pleasantly cool. In Oregon and Washington, summer rain can no longer be regarded as a surprise. In Washington there is only the ghost of a dry season (though even this rain-prone summer is not wet by eastern standards). The Olympic Mountains on the coastal side of Seattle are the wettest area in the forty-eight contiguous states: lavishly green below timberline and spotted with ice above. The North Cascades, inland across Puget Sound, are only a little drier. Hikers in this region, like hikers in the

East, go ready for rain, and count themselves lucky if they do not get it.

This pattern is varied by local factors. Both the Coast Ranges and the Sierra-Cascade chain cast rain shadows: their eastern slopes are markedly drier than their western sides. And hikers on the immediate coastline learn to count on the persistent drizzle of summer fog.

There are two kinds of winter camping in the Pacific ranges. First, there's travel below snowline—which means anything below about 8,000 feet near Los Angeles, anything below about 2,000 feet near Seattle. Here what you get is rain, or snow that melts about as fast as it falls. Higher you enter the snowy wilderness, colder, yet easier to deal with. Perhaps the least friendly zone of all is the dividing line, where the substance in the air seems neither water nor solid snow but something clinging and clammy. All snow in the Pacific ranges, though, is fairly wet; that is, it has quite a bit of liquid water within it. Such snow behaves quite differently than the dry, loose powder of the more interior ranges. Slab avalanches, though a real danger in snowy mountains anywhere, are less ubiquitous and devastating in this maritime region. An additional hazard, though, comes from wet-snow avalanches, massive amorphous slumps that occur when the temperature rises.

Winter hikers and campers have a somewhat easier time of it in the southern reaches of the Pacific ranges. In the south there are often long, clear spells between rains. But the closer you get to the Canadian border, the better your chances of running into endlessly bad weather (*bad*, I say, but it is also beautiful). It isn't unheard of in the mountains of the Pacific Northwest for snow to fall every day, most of the day, for a month.

National forests cover most of the higher ground in the Pacific ranges. National parks—Sequoia, Kings Canyon, Yosemite, Lassen, Crater Lake, Mount Rainier, Olympic, North Cascades—give more total protection to certain spectacular stretches.

If you plotted on a map the remaining roadless areas contained within these public parks and forests, you would be struck by three particularly impressive concentrations of wild land.

In the southern half of the Sierra Nevada lies the scraped-granite country, the country of John Muir, the region of Yosemite and south. Several million acres in these mountains are still roadless, undisturbed. More remarkable yet, the crest of the Sierra runs 150 miles in this region without being crossed by a single highway, a single east-west road. Only trails rise to the high passes. It was a hundred years ago that the pioneer conservationist Muir began to lobby for the preservation of these mountains. Few of the great wildernesses that existed in Muir's time have survived so well.

A thousand miles to the north, near the Canadian border, the wild areas of the Olympics and the northern Cascades surround Seattle like so many magnificent suburbs. Here too the record of preservation has been impressive.

Not as much progress has been made in the third great wilderness region of the Pacific ranges. This is the fascinating stretch of the coastal chain, partly in Oregon, partly in California, known as the Klamath Mountains. It's a rugged country, tangled, cut by rivers, forested. Botanists know it as one of the oddest corners of the United States for its rare trees and curious flowers; it has a wider, Sunday supplement fame as a home of the man-ape "Bigfoot." Little of the extensive wilderness within the Klamath Mountains has protection. Timbered wilderness is always hardest to preserve, and the virgin forests, not yet quite depleted in these mountains, draw the loggers on.

The Great Interior

We've seen how the western mountains organize the rain. The Pacific ranges make the lands to windward wetter than they would be if the continent were a featureless plain. The lands to the east they rob of water. The deep Southwest might be desert in any case, but because of the mountain barriers, an incomparably vaster area—the whole hollow center of the West—is dry. Nine states have part of this arid domain within their boundaries; one—Nevada—is almost entirely within it.

It is common to think of this enormous region as a basin, confined as it is by the Pacific ranges on the west and by the Rockies on the east. But that can give a false impression. Whatever else this country is, it is not *flat.* It is broken endlessly by mountain ranges, some rising to 12,000, even to 14,000 feet. It is broken by deep-carved canyons, where rivers run as much as a mile below the surrounding plateaus. And though all the region is more or less arid, it is full of the variety of low and high places. Mountains, cooler and wetter, are covered with forests of pinyon pine and juniper, of ponderosa pine, even of white fir and Douglas fir; summits may have timberline species like Engelmann spruce and the gnarled and undying bristlecone pine.

Here in the hidden lands, dry and not so dry, are some of the most compelling wilderness landscapes of the continent. Certain of these landscapes are as famous and admired as they deserve to be; others are almost perfectly unknown; few of them are, as yet, protected.

Lord knows the opportunity is there. Even now settlement in this country is sparse. Most of the land never passed out of the public domain. The government has so much property in the intermountain region that it is simplest to think of it as a great federal reserve, interrupted, here and there, by lands that are privately owned. Some of the higher mountains have timber and are classified as national forests; some of the grandest landscapes are national parks; some portions, habitat for the desert bighorn sheep and other endangered animal species, are national wildlife ranges. But the bulk of the land is controlled by the federal agency known as the Bureau of Land Management (see Chapter 31).

Through the center of the intermountain deserts,

the Colorado River and its tributaries have cut a ten-thousand-mile web of precipitous canyons in rock now gray, now black, now red (that famous southwestern rust or rose) or yellow. Some of these gorges are gigantic, like the Grand Canyon itself, where the Colorado cuts its unimaginable slot into the layered rock of northern Arizona. Others are closed-in, convoluted, narrow. In the greater gorges, travel is by water. The hiker may walk down to the water's edge, but there is no path along the waterline. The lesser canyons, though, are footways. And above the canyons rise mesas—isolated, flat-topped mountains, left behind in the general erosion, some of them high enough to be forested.

The canyon country has its superb wilderness; it also has its river narrows, possible dam sites that interest the engineers. Several of the most exciting stretches of the Colorado and the Green have been flooded by enormous government reservoirs (this is one of the most heavily developed river systems in the world). Even the Grand Canyon itself was almost so flooded. Some of the finest remaining stretches are protected in national parks.

The Colorado canyon system, cutting across the intermountain region from the northeast to the southwest, divides the remaining territory into ragged halves.

Northwest of the canyons, between the sunken rivers and the Pacific mountain walls that block the rain, lies the most primitive part of the Great Interior. Here hundreds of separate mountain ranges rise from the desert floor. Most of them run north and south, parallel, ranked and regular: the state of Nevada looks like one great washboard from the air. When the difference in height is enough, the valley floor and the mountain crest are contrary worlds. Standing in desert scrub, you look up as much as a vertical mile into green mountaintops that seem to have no right to be part of the same landscape. From the peaks the effect is reversed; the plain below becomes the other country.

The northern and larger part of the washboard

region is known as the Great Basin Desert; it covers most of Nevada and parts of Utah, Idaho, Oregon, and Washington. Here the valley floors themselves are rather high above sea level; the typical vegetation is sagebrush. At the southern tip of the region, mostly in southeast California, lies the lower and hotter Mojave Desert, famous for its curious Joshua trees and for the desert climax of Death Valley.

In the Mojave several large areas have been set aside for preservation: Death Valley and Joshua Tree national monuments, California's Anza-Borrego Desert State Park, and, in Nevada, the Desert National Wildlife Range. But outside this one small corner of the washboard country, very little land has yet been set aside. It is becoming imperative to catch up elsewhere in the region, as demands on the desert—demands for minerals, for oil and gas, for motorized recreation, even for firewood—begin to mount.

East and south of the dividing canyonlands there lies another vast reach of desert and desert mountain: Arizona south of the Grand Canyon, most of New Mexico, and much of western Texas. Here too the highlands rise above arid basins. Most important is the long band of mountains called the Mogollon Plateau. Ruggedly eroded, the Mogollon swings across the Southwest in an east-west arc from the Colorado to the Rio Grande. Timbered, cool, cut by canyons of its own, the Mogollon highland is attractive country. Several wilderness areas have been set aside within the national forests that cover its spine. One of these, the Gila Wilderness at the eastern tip of the plateau, was the first such area ever set aside, explicitly, with formal boundaries.

On each flank of the Mogollon Mountains—north to the canyons and south to the Mexican border— the true deserts return. To the north lies the Painted Desert; to the south, the Sonoran; to the southeast, the Chihuahuan. Each has its strange and characteristic plants, its unmistakable scenes, and its natural reserves. In the Sonoran Desert, in southern Arizona, lie Cabeza Prieta National Wildlife Range and national monuments named for the saguaro and the organ pipe cactus. In the Chihuahuan, the one large reserve is Big Bend National Park, in Texas, on an arid, spectacular bight of the Rio Grande.

Across the intermountain West the climate varies, and not only according to the height of the mountain you are standing on. The land north and west of the great canyons gets almost all its meager rainfall in the winter. But as you move east and south, the thunderstorms of summer become more and more important. In the canyon country there may be as many as sixty thunderstorms a year, and these drop a fair amount of rain—though even this falls mostly on higher ground. Southeast of the canyons, the thundershowers are even more significant. In the peak rain months of July and August, the mountains of central Arizona are among the wettest places in the West! Still farther south and east, in the Chihuahuan Desert, it is the winter storms that scarcely matter, summer that brings the whole supply of rain.

In the lowest, hottest parts of the desert—in Death Valley, for example, or along the Arizona-Mexico border—winter is the pleasant hiking season; spring and fall are reasonable; summer is impossibly hot. Farther north and at higher elevations, spring and fall can be delightful. In the canyon country, April and May, cool and clear, may be the best months of all. Water is comparatively abundant then, while the thunderstorm season, with its flash flood danger, has not yet begun. (Never camp in a streamcourse, especially in the narrows of a canyon, during the high-risk months.) Northwest of the canyons, from central Nevada north, summer in the valleys is hot but not unbearably hot; in the lofty mountain masses, it is cool. Winter can be bitterly cold, with plenty of snow on the higher ranges.

The wilderness Rockies

Beyond the deserts rises the second mountain wall: the Rockies. No simple line of peaks, the Rockies are many ranges, tangled, branching, offset one from another—a world of mountains, not a single chain.

The barrier they make is not a solid one. In New Mexico at the south, and again in southern Wyoming at the middle of the range, the Rockies subside. In each place the desert and semidesert country sweeps across the Continental Divide and merges into the dry western edge of the Great Plains. The dramatic Wyoming gap divides the Rockies into two very different mountain regions: the southern, or Colorado, Rockies, and the northern Rockies of northern Wyoming, Montana, and Idaho.

The southern Rockies don't really get started much south of the Colorado–New Mexico border. When they do rise, they go up all the way: Colorado has fifty-four peaks over 14,000 feet. The Colorado Rockies, for all their height, for all their forest cover, have a flavor of the desert still around them. They belong to the Southwest. They have the same strong thunderstorm season, in July and August, and the same rather dry winter with many clear days between storms; in the southern part of the region, more rain may fall in August than in any other month.

The northern Rockies are wetter and cooler. The winter wet season is longer and cloudier. Summers are comparatively dry, with the usual brief thunderstorms; but more substantial summer rains do sometimes occur. In the higher mountains it can snow at any time.

The northern Rockies were extensively glaciated, and a few ice fields still linger. There are swarms of lakes, especially where the bedrock is of granite. But the northern Rockies are also lower, and this somewhat mutes the contrast between them and the more southern ranges. In neither section can you count on *any* night of the year being free of frost in the high country. In Colorado, most areas can be hiked without skis or snowshoes in late June; parts of Idaho and Montana have deep snow on the ground to the end of July.

Winter in the Rockies is an exciting season. While the Pacific storms do reach these mountains, they are weak-ended here. It can be fiercely cold and windy, but not even in the northern Rockies is winter as implacably wet as in the coastal mountains. Though nighttime temperatures can go far below zero, the mountain climate is, if anything, a shade milder than that of the adjacent plains. Snow is that dry, cold, luminous stuff that skiers love—and fear, for this is the snow best suited to avalanche formation.

In Colorado and New Mexico, the virgin areas, though numerous and grandly scenic, are, by western standards, only moderate in size. It is in the northern reaches of the Rockies, from Yellowstone to the Canadian border, that we have the most remarkable treasures. The region is familiar for its sizable national parks—Grand Teton, Yellowstone, and Glacier; less known are the vast wilderness areas, protected and unprotected, that lie in the national forests around the parks. Leaving aside Alaska, these are the largest areas of wild land that remain to us in the United States. They have the splendor of the things within them—river gorges and fierce rapids, elk and grizzly, lakes, bright forests, and difficult peaks, walls of granite and layered sedimentary stone. But most of all they have the splendor that comes simply from their size. At least five of the wild areas in these mountains are larger than the state of Delaware. Here, if anywhere, you can imagine yourself, for a few days, in the continent-spanning wilderness that was.

The Politics of
Wilderness

*We are not fighting a
rearguard action, we are
facing a frontier. We are not
slowing down a force that
inevitably will destroy all the
wilderness there is. We are
generating another force, never
to be wholly spent, that,
renewed generation after
generation, will be always
effective in preserving
wilderness. . . . We are working
for a wilderness forever.*

—Howard Zahniser

31:
Battle of the Wilderness: An Orientation

IN THE UNITED STATES TODAY we are in the process of making a basic decision about our land. The results of that process—tedious, vast, dramatic, finicky, prolonged—will be with us for a very long time. *How much of our remaining wild country— its woods, its trails, its animals, its waters—will we deliberately keep the way it is? How much will we make ours forever? How much will we let go?*

This multiple decision, involving lands of every kind in almost every state, is not being made swiftly or in a single forum. The elements are being hammered out right now in crowded, noisy public hearing rooms. They are emerging on the maps and charts of federal land–use planners. But most of all, the decision is being made by a few hundred men and women in Washington: the Congress of the United States.

There is no other nation on earth right now that takes these matters quite so seriously: that has as-

444

signed the decision about the fate of wild country to its highest legislative authority. This is a remarkable, indeed a magnificent, thing.

How much wilderness?

For decades now we have been working on an answer to this question, selecting, from the wild landscapes that still exist, those areas that will be our permanent inheritance. Some wild country we have preserved explicitly, in parks and such, and we may hope that it is out of reach of exploitation. Much more formerly wild land—many times that amount—has meanwhile been developed or tamed (and in too many cases, abused) so thoroughly that we cannot imagine it returning to the wild. But there is, even now, a third great stock of lands: the wild places that have neither been saved as such nor finally made over into something else. Still wild now, but without guarantee of wildness, they are the current objects of debate.

We are getting pretty well along in this series of decisions. It will not be too many years now before we are able at last to add up the two columns and say: *This much our society chose to dominate and change. This much land it chose, by an amazing act of the public will, to leave alone.*

How will the balance look, I wonder? Will we be reasonably happy with the choices we have made? When the individual conflicts have lost their heat, will we be glad of the compromise the opposing pressures brought?

The pressures that work for the reduction of wilderness are strong, stronger perhaps now than they have been for decades. The timber industry, facing the depletion of the forests on its own western "tree farms," is lobbying incessantly for the right to cut more, cut faster, in the forests of the public lands. Miners, pointing to resource shortages, demand that no land be off limits to their bulldozers—and indeed there is not very much land that *is.* Off-road vehicle drivers, pursuing their hugely popular recreation, resent any limit on their often destructive use of public lands.

But as the supply of wild country lessens, more and more people in more and more places are moved to speak out for the preservation of what remains. Wherever the future of the land is being chosen— wherever wilderness survives but has no shield— people appear, sometimes it seems from nowhere, to defend it. Often groping at first, learning as they go along, these individuals and local groups add their weight to that of the national conservation organizations in what has become a formidable coalition.

No one who cares for the wilderness, or who travels in the wilderness, or who simply finds comfort in the fact that there is wild country out there, can afford to be ignorant of the outlines of this conflict, and the rules by which it proceeds.

The turf: the state and federal lands

Wilderness can be almost anywhere. Even in private ownership, in this country, there is quite a bit of land that remains wild. But as a practical matter, it is only on government-owned land that significant blocks of wilderness can be protected; only on government land that preservation can be made to stick in law.

State-owned lands have some share of the American wilderness. In state parks across the country, away from park roads and campgrounds, there are still odd corners of virgin land. In several states there is much more than that. The New York State Forest Preserve in the Catskills and the Adirondacks contains most of New York's wilderness; Maine, Pennsylvania, Michigan, Wisconsin, California and Alaska all have sizable pieces of wild state-owned land. But in most of the nation, it is on *federal* property, and only there, that very large areas of land have been left alone.

What and where are these federal lands?

At one time or another the federal government owned the bulk of the land in almost every state

outside the original Colonies (the greatest exception
was Texas). As a rule, when the nation annexed new
territory, the federal power was not only sovereign,
it was also the owner of all the unoccupied land. Toward that vast domain the nation, in its first hundred years, had a very consistent policy: *get rid of
it.* In theory, the Great West was to be given to
small farmers; actually, much more of it went to the
railroads, to speculators, and to state governments
that, in turn, sold it for profit. But it *went.* By 1890
only a few small enclaves of federal land remained
between the Atlantic Ocean and the first upthrust of
the Rocky Mountains.

Beyond that mountain barrier, though, the surface of the continent was sterner, not quite so readily platted out and disposed of. Well-watered agricul-
tural lands, such as there were, went into private
ownership early. So did most of the finest and most
accessible forests. But for the other land—the steep,
the rugged, the hot, the cold, the waterless, the remote—the demand was not so high. And meanwhile,
slowly and painfully, the national policy began to
change. Yellowstone National Park, first of all, was
set aside, off limits to private claims. Then followed
Yosemite, and then, faster and faster, whole systems of federal reserves. At last the public lands of
the West came to be seen, not as an expendable cur-
rency, but as a precious and permanent federal domain.

In this century there came a new development: a
movement to purchase some private land in the East
for watershed protection and for public parks. Most
of this massive repurchase program was carried out
during the Great Depression (though it has never
entirely ceased). Now the East, too, has a share in
the federal domain: a scatter of national parks, national forests, and national wildlife refuges.

Today, in most states, at least five percent of the
land is federal, if you count military reservations; in
the West the federal percentage is vastly higher. In
the forty-eight contiguous states, the federal government owns about 419 million acres altogether—

about one-fifth of all the land. Only a portion of this land, it should be understood, is wild, and most of it is quite properly open to timber cutting, mining, and other commercial uses.

Such is the empire. Within it there are four main fiefdoms, four types of land reserves, each managed under a different charter by a different government agency. These are the *national parks*, the *national wildlife refuges*, the *national forests*, and the mostly desert lands known simply as the *public domain*. They are controlled, respectively, by the Park Service, the Fish and Wildlife Service, the Forest Service, and the Bureau of Land Management.

The Wilderness Act of 1964

Before 1964, each of the four land agencies made at least a token effort to preserve examples of its wilderness. The Forest Service did most, the Bureau of Land Management, least. But as the years went on, it became clear that the job, all in all, was not getting done; the pressures to develop land were too great for the agencies, acting alone, to resist.

And so came about the Wilderness Act of 1964.

The Wilderness Act is an extraordinary law. Before it descends into the necessary mechanical detail, it is readable; it is even stirring. *"It is hereby declared to be the policy of Congress to secure for the American people . . . the benefits of an enduring resource of wilderness. . . ."* A wilderness (the Act goes on) is a place *"where the earth and its community of life are untrammeled by man, where man himself is a visitor who does not remain."*

In the Act, Congress created what is called the *National Wilderness Preservation System.* Simply put, it is a national roster of protected wild areas on the public lands. Only Congress can place areas on that roster; only Congress can remove areas from it. The boundaries of each preserve are defined with legal precision; for instance, from this peak down that ridge to this survey marker to that stream.

Within those boundaries, wilderness is made as safe as, in a changing world, it can be. Roads may not be built; timber may not be cut; jeeps and motorcycles may not enter. (Grazing is permitted in certain areas, though, and even mining, where established claims exist.) Each such protected area is known as a "Wilderness." "Wilderness" in a legal sense, "Wilderness" with metes and bounds, "Wilderness" with a capital "W."

When Congress creates a Wilderness, the designated area remains part of the national park, national forest, wildlife refuge, or other named reserve in which it lies. The same people continue to manage and control the land. Nothing changes. But changes that might otherwise take place are prevented. Strict limits are set on what the managers can do with the land—or on what they can do *to* it.

Ever since the Wilderness Act was passed, major debates about wilderness have gone to Congress for their ultimate settlement. Both sides have been lobbying hard. One faction seeks to have the largest possible amount of land placed in the formal Wilderness System; the other faction seeks to keep the largest possible amount of land out of that system.

The cast of characters changes from case to case. But among the consistent opponents of wilderness are the timber industry; the mining industry; the off-road vehicle lobby; the concessioners in certain national parks; dam builders and power companies; and chambers of commerce and local governments in rural parts of the Far West. Speaking for maximum wilderness are the various conservation groups, national and local. There are many tactics in this debate, but in the end it always comes down to a simple test of strength: which side can pile up the most mail on the legislators' desks?

By the record, it seems fair to say that the prowilderness public is the larger. It may take time, but once a proposed wilderness begins to be seriously considered by Congress, the area almost always makes it into the system. Though the bounda-

ries are usually settled by compromise, the compro-
mises tend to be more generous than miserly.

So the process, in outline, is simple. But it works
a little differently for parks than for forests, a little
differently for wildlife refuges than for public domain lands. So let's take a brief look at the record
of the Wilderness Act in each of the fiefdoms that
make up the federal lands—the different theaters, so
to speak, of the wilderness campaign.

Theater #1: the national parks

The national parks have in them some of the
grandest landscapes of the continent. They were established to preserve the land—to preserve it absolutely. And yet they were also partly intended to be
showcases, tourist attractions, "pleasuring
grounds." So no national park is entirely wild, and
most are laced with roads and spotted with buildings. There has been a great deal of controversy,
over the years, about just how tame the parks
should be allowed to become.

The Wilderness Act instructed the National Park
Service to study every large wild area in the parks
and come back with a recommendation to Congress
and to the President. This has been done. Sometimes
the planners proposed that no wilderness be classified, that lands be left open for developed use. Most
of the time they suggested wilderness, within specified boundaries. The President has passed these reports on to Congress, and Congress has most of
them before it now. Rather few wilderness areas, so
far, have been created in the parks, but many more
will come. In several cases Congress, by drawing
more generous wilderness boundaries than the Park
Service wanted, has prevented the Service from
building controversial roads.

There are about 25 million acres of national
parks in the United States south of Canada. (Many
parks are known as national monuments, national
recreation areas, national seashores, or by other
names.) Probably eighty percent of that acreage is
wild. Wilderness in the parks is not a very hotly de-

bated matter, since the land can't be logged or mined in the first place. The greater conflicts lie elsewhere.

Theater #2: the national wildlife refuges

The national wildlife refuges, though less stringently protected than the national parks, contain another large stock of pristine country. They don't get as much publicity (which is probably all to the good), and they are, on the average, less photogenic than the parks. But the refuges are supposed to be managed for the welfare of wild animals, and for many species, welfare means wild habitat.

Altogether there are about 13 million acres of refuges outside of Alaska (some are known as national wildlife *ranges*, or by other names). The Fish and Wildlife Service has some very large desert areas in the West, maintained for such species as the desert bighorn sheep and the pronghorn antelope, but also chains of smaller wetland refuges all over the country, set aside for the ducks and geese that travel north and south each year along the four continental "flyways." On the Atlantic and Gulf coasts and in the northern plains, the refuges are especially significant.

The refuges have gone through the same wilderness study process as the national parks. As with the parks, congressional action has not been especially rapid, but the situation is fairly stable. The prospect of wilderness protection has helped to discourage overdevelopment. In most areas, not too much is being lost.

Theater #3: the public domain lands

When the U.S. government stopped disposing of the public lands, it stopped by stages. First it exempted certain national parks from the giveaway. Then it established national forests. Then it began to reserve wildlife refuges. Each of these systems has grown over the years. But all of these named, designated reserves still add up to little more than half of the land the federal government owns.

What is left is mostly in a category that has no

convenient label but is known as "BLM land," "the public lands," or simply "the public domain." This territory, almost all in the West, is chiefly (though not entirely) desert: desert plain, desert peak, desert canyon. It is rugged and rough and little known—and full of wild scenery.

The agency in charge of this empire is the Bureau of Land Management. The BLM has traditionally lacked the budget of the other land agencies, the staff, and the sophistication. For years, the public domain was underappreciated, underprotected, and overgrazed to the point of devastation. Only gradually has the situation improved. The BLM and its domain were left unmentioned in the Wilderness Act of 1964.

But this omission was repaired in 1976, when Congress passed a law designed to strengthen the agency. As part of that law, it instructed the BLM, like other agencies, to make an inventory of the wild areas under its control and to study each of them, making reports to Congress.

The public domain amounts to some 174 million acres in the West, excluding Alaska. Of this, about 24 million are undergoing study for possible Wilderness status. How much of that acreage finally makes it into the National Wilderness Preservation System depends on Congress. This is a new frontier of preservation, and efforts to set aside this land, or any substantial part of it, are controversial indeed.

Theater #4: the western national forests

It was in the national forests of the West that the preservation of wilderness areas began. It was mainly on their account that the Wilderness Act was later written. It is in these forests that most of the controversy has been focused ever since. And the timbered western mountains probably contain fully half of the wild country we have left—Alaska always excepted.

In 1922, a worker in the U.S. Forest Service, a southwestern ranger named Aldo Leopold, began urging his superiors to set up wilderness preserves. While an abstract admiration for wild places had long been current, this thought of protecting them by zoning within fixed boundaries was still novel. Beginning in 1924, the Forest Service set a number of such areas aside. In the 1930s another federal forester, Robert Marshall, made it his personal cause to see vast areas of wilderness preserved. In 1937, Marshall became one of the top officials of the Forest Service. The list of protected areas was swelling. Things were moving fast.

Then, a few months after his new appointment, Marshall died. The job he had undertaken was unfinished, indeed scarcely begun.

Unfinished it remained. Only a little additional land was put into protection by the Forest Service in the next twenty-five years. Indeed, much land that had been protected under Marshall was now opened to logging. And each time this happened, pressure for an Act of Congress, a new way of saving wilderness, grew. In a sense, the Forest Service was itself responsible for the Wilderness Act of 1964.

Again leaving out Alaska, there are about 168 million acres of national forests. Unlike the parks and the refuges, the national forests have a complicated job to do. They are supposed to provide something for everyone: timber, minerals, pure water, wildlife habitat, forage for cattle and sheep, and recreation of several competing kinds. It's no easy thing to balance these demands. There is one whole group of purposes that are best satisfied when the land is left wild; another group that require roads and development. Many critics feel that the Forest Service has failed to find the balance, and that timber obsesses the agency while every other use drags on behind.

The Wilderness Act of 1964 confirmed the areas that the Forest Service had protected for their wildness under its own program, and made these units of the National Wilderness Preservation System. It also directed the service to make studies of a few specified additional areas for possible protection, with reports to Congress. What Congress did *not* require in this case, however, was a thoroughgoing inventory of all roadless lands. In the national forests, alone of the major land systems, there is no temporary protection for lands that might deserve wilderness status. Superb wild areas can be roaded and logged while the debate about their future still goes on. And are.

Because of this vulnerability, the western national forests have remained the perennial focus of the wilderness debate. Congress, responding to public demand, has acted to create a number of new Wildernesses on forest lands. In an attempt to influence these decisions, the Forest Service has twice prepared its own inventories of roadless areas and recommended some of them for Wilderness status. This unruly but productive process seems likely to continue as long as there are roadless areas left to consider.

Theater #5: national forests in the east

The story of wilderness in the eastern national forests is somewhat different. For thirty years after Bob Marshall died, the Forest Service maintained that essentially none of its land in the eastern United States could be called wild. (An exception was made for the Boundary Waters Canoe Area of Minnesota.) The eastern states, the service pointed out, had been heavily logged. Green the eastern mountains might be; lovely they might be, as the resilient forests closed over the stumps and the scars. There might be areas that seemed wild; that were, for practical purposes, wild. But in truth, the Forest Service argued, they were forever altered, tamed, impaired.

It is, or was, an interesting question. Does "wilderness" mean only land that has *never* been disturbed? Is it strictly a description? Or is it rather essentially a promise: "This land will not, *henceforth*, be disturbed"? Though there has been some disagreement within each camp, conservationists mostly prefer to regard "wilderness" as a label of intent.

After years of argument Congress decided the issue. In 1974, it began adding national forest areas east of the Rockies to the National Wilderness Preservation System.

In the East as in the West, however, there is plenty of opposition from commercial interests and from the off-road vehicle lobby—somewhat surprising when you consider the small size of most of the areas concerned. The total of national forest wilderness in the East might reach a couple of million acres, but hardly more.

Theatre #6: Alaska

In everything that has gone before, I have deliberately left out the most remarkable part of the American wilderness: the wilds of the state of Alaska. Indeed, this book has said nothing of Alaskan areas and conditions—a huge omission but a necessary one: the subject is so vast. There is certainly more wild land left in Alaska than in all the other forty-nine states of the Union combined.

There is also more *officially protected* wilderness there than in the balance of the nation: the result of the Alaska Lands Act of 1980. Until that time, most of the state was unreserved public domain controlled (very lightly) by the Bureau of Land Management. Now the state is a patchwork of national parks, national preserves, national wildlife refuges, and other specially designated areas, as well as lands assigned to the state, to Indian and Eskimo groups, and (residually) to the BLM. The pie has been carved.

There is some cause to regret the need to draw all these lines on what had been a pretty blank map. The result is an Alaska less wild, in some sense, than it was before. But the subdividing was inevitable, and it was done early enough—and intelligently enough—to ensure that Alaska will always contain our vastest wilderness reserves. The Act of 1980 added 56 million acres to the Wilderness Preservation System overnight.

Targets

Putting these pieces together, what have we got?

How much wild country is there, in fact, in the United States today?

And how much of that total should we aim to keep?

The United States is a big country. Setting Alaska aside once more, we have, in the other forty-nine states, about 1.9 billion acres of land—about three million square miles.

Adding up the inventories made by the land agencies, we find that at least 120 million acres of that land is still roadless and undeveloped. That sounds impressive, and it is. But compared to the total acreage of those forty-nine states, it's not quite so imposing—something under seven percent of all the land. By 1983 about 23 million acres—less than one-fifth of the possible total in these states—had been placed in the Wilderness Preservation System.

Growth of National Wilderness System, 1930–1982

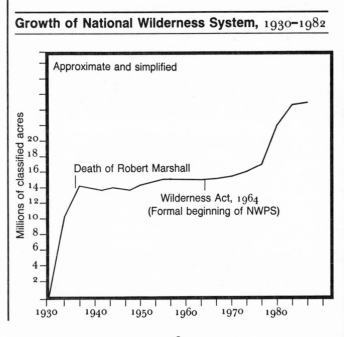

Approximate and simplified

Millions of classified acres

Death of Robert Marshall

Wilderness Act, 1964
(Formal beginning of NWPS)

20 18 16 14 12 10 8 6 4 2

1930   1940   1950   1960   1970   1980

When you add in the truly enormous wild expanses of Alaska, the figures naturally shift. Including the Alaska outback, it seems likely that about one-fifth of the total acreage in the country is still roadless and undistrubed. That is a lot. Much of that amount, clearly, will never even be considered for Wilderness status. Even the most ardent preservationist can scarcely hope for more than about 225 million acres of classified Wilderness, or just over one-tenth of the land in the fifty states.

This tithe, in my view, is a good and by no means excessive target.

But wilderness preservation does not, and cannot, proceed by quota or by some sort of master plan. It happens because people insist that it happen. It happens because individuals care about individual places. With Congress making the major decisions, the American people will probably get about the amount of wilderness they insist on getting. The answer to the question *How much?* is one we will make ourselves.

But can we afford it?

In debates about protecting wild country, you hear again and again the charge (or fear) that setting such land aside is an extravagance, a luxury beyond the means of a nation that suddenly finds itself a little less rich than it was long accustomed to think.

It is vital to remember here that the lands we are arguing about today are, by definition almost, poor in the kinds of natural resources you can extract and haul away. The public lands, after all, were the lands left over after settlers and commercial interests had selected the best and richest country for their own. And within the public lands themselves, most of the richer sections were developed long ago. With a handful of precious exceptions, the densely timbered, easily loggable areas were not left wild. Nor were the areas of obvious mineral wealth. Nobody has the comparison down in numbers, but this is very certain: if one-fifth of the United States (Alaska included) remains wild, that one-fifth contains nothing like as much as one-fifth of the commercial resources of the nation. By and large, wilderness is *cheap*. You don't give up very much, in other kinds of wealth, when you put wild lands aside.

And you gain, besides the wilderness itself, some very practical benefits. The clean water that flows from undisturbed mountains, and the fish that live or spawn in those clear streams, may have more dollar value than all the timber, all the minerals, all the grazing land those mountains contain.

Even when our wild areas have resources in them that attract exploitation, there are many cases in which the temptation ought to be resisted. And it should be resisted whether or not we care for wilderness itself. On many millions of acres the penalties of exploitation are simply greater than the gains. In the West, for instance, there are certain mountain slopes that are richly timbered, waiting, so it seems, for the saw. And yet, under the green of timber, these slopes are steep, unstable, easily eroded. When the trees are cut and the land torn up by logging roads, some of these hills will slip, slide, and lose their soil to erosion. Soil loss, on the historical scale of time, is permanent. Moreover, the sediments, clogging the streams below, can cause them to undercut steep banks and start a whole new cycle of destruction. In such a case, the land is not merely being *used*, it is being abused, impoverished, attacked.

This, then, is a question to keep in mind: how much of our currently wild country is actually *suited* to exploration? Surely the land that is poorest and most fragile ought to be left alone—left for wildlife, for watershed, for recreation value. There is often legitimate disagreement about what uses land can support; but it is helpful to remember, when you hear the complaint that commercial wealth is "locked up" in wilderness preserves, that much of that wealth may be an illusion.

What you can do

Has this ever happened to you:

Have you looked for a remembered trailhead in a mossy forest—only to find it vanished in a clearcut's tangle of slash?

Have you found, instead of a fir-shaded trail on a ridgetop, a new-carved logging road?

Have you gone back to a familiar vista of desert mountains—and stared for wordless minutes at the endless scrawl of dirt-bike tracks on the vulnerable ground?

Have you looked for the streambank flat where you once had lunch in a wilderness valley—and found not a place but the wreckage of a place, torn up by a prospector's wandering bulldozer?

Or maybe you've felt dismay at the sight of a line of survey stakes along a wild trail—marking the course of an invasion to come.

For years, backpackers, returning (as they thought) to well-loved unchanging places, have been finding this return denied them; finding that the landscapes they recall are no longer there.

It is one thing to speak, in the abstract, about the dwindling of the American wilderness. It is quite another to watch it dwindle, to see the same piece of land in both conditions; the before, and the after—the wild, and the overrun.

People react to this experience in many ways. Some are angered. Some are grieved. Some are resigned. Some make it a project to see as many beautiful places as they can "before they're all spoiled." But these people have in common—too many of them—the belief that these changes are inevitable; that they belong to some inexorable Master Plan and that nothing anyone can do will stop them. If you can't even (as the old saying goes) fight City Hall—then what hope can there be in taking on a large and determined government agency?

The feeling is quite understandable.

It also happens to be dead wrong.

If there's anything we should have learned from

the history of American conservation, it is that, if you have to, you *can* fight—or at any rate, influence—City Hall. *Any* City Hall—whether it's the one across the street, or one of the many power centers in Washington, D.C. "Inevitable" processes can in fact be changed, or turned aside. And the force that does it is usually nothing more—and nothing less—than the letter of opinion, written by the citizen to somebody who has the power to decide.

So: if you have a strong opinion about what's happening to wilderness, don't sit on it. Write. An opinion letter can either be very general—simply a statement of your feelings on the subject—or very specific. Here are a few possible courses to follow.

● When you get home from a trip, take the time to *write a letter to the agency* about the place you explored. Do this even if you have nothing in particular to write *about*. It is valuable simply to express your admiration for the land, to build up a record of interest. It can be surprisingly important, when controversy develops, to be able to prove that people *do* care about Indigo Creek, or Silver Prairie, or any of a hundred fine, endangered places. If you saw things happening you didn't like, by all means comment on them. (Calmly. Abusiveness, of course, can only do harm.) Make a point of inquiring about the agency's plans for the landscape you traversed—is it to be logged or otherwise developed? Protected, and in what way? Is planning perhaps going on right now? Ask to get on the mailing list for any announcements that appear.

(How do you know who to write? Get the address if you stop off at a local agency office, for instance to pick up a wilderness permit. If you're using an agency map, you may also find an address on that. Typically, you'll be contacting a particular national park or wildlife refuge; or a national forest; or a substate district of the Bureau of Land Management. If you're missing the address, you can contact the regional office of the appropriate agency— see *Resources* appendix.)

● *Write your representative in Congress,* and

your two senators. Tell them of your interest in wilderness in general. If you've written to an agency regarding a particular area, send your legislators a copy of that, too. You may not get a very promising response, but don't let it bother you—politicians do keep a close eye on their mail. (To reach a Senator, write Honorable _____, Washington, D.C. 20510; a Representative is Honorable _____, Washington, D.C. 20515.)

• *Locate an environmental organization* that is interested in the same issues you are. If you don't have contacts in this direction, the national offices of the Sierra Club and the Wilderness Society can help—so can some gear stores. In a number of states there are regional wilderness groups that follow the progress of wilderness controversies statewide. Then there are more local groups of wilderness advocates. You may find it worthwhile to join one of these organizations, for a few dollars. Hooked into such a grapevine, receiving current information, you know, at a minimum, who to write your letters to, and when, in order to get the largest possible effect.

At this point, of course, you can go on to get as involved as you like. Every conceivable job is waiting to be done: exploring unprotected areas, monitoring timber sales and mining claims, attending hearings, and much, much more.

But please don't be scared off: it isn't necessary to go beyond the almost effortless project of writing the occasional letter. And if only a small proportion of today's wilderness users did speak up, their common voice would be very loud indeed.

There is more than a little satisfaction in doing something, however slight, to protect the future of a place you have enjoyed. It is as though you had paid a small and proper fee for the use of the land. And if there is a tiny, unavoidable impact on the wilderness, whenever a hiker goes into it, the hiker's letter, written after the trip, can more than cancel out that debt.

32:
The
Backpackers:
Who Are They?

WHO ARE THE BACKPACKERS, ANYWAY?

We know, in a general way, what they do. But what kind of people are they?

Since about 1960, researchers have been querying the users of wilderness to find out what backgrounds they have, what their values are, and what reasons they have for leaving the motorized world behind. The results of this research are still spotty, still emerging, still somewhat contradictory. But certain patterns seem well established.

Clearly, most backpackers get started young on the trails—usually in their teens. Most of those who do get this early start continue to backpack; people who take up the sport later have a much greater tendency to drop out.

Most wilderness travelers are young or youngish. This may change somewhat as today's large generation of new converts grows older; people who have backpacked all their lives don't quit the trails at some arbitrary "retirement age."

Most wilderness users are married, and most of them have one or more children. Very many of them begin taking their children into the backlands as soon as the kids can walk, if not before. This is a fact that the makers of packs have taken optimistic note of.

The backpackers would seem to be an educated lot (or at least they have spent a lot of time in school). Two out of three, judging by most surveys, have college degrees. In the overall American population, only one out of ten have attended college. Not surprisingly, backpackers tend to work at professional or white-collar jobs.

The people who head out with gear on their backs, though choosing about the cheapest possible vacation, come mostly from the higher-income half of the population. This is true, not of wilderness travelers only, but of outdoor recreationists in general. Car camping, too, is a pursuit of the upper middle class. But the truly wealthy don't seem to be much drawn to the outdoors.

Some studies find that backpackers are disproportionately city dwellers, city bred. Others disagree. It seems to depend largely on where the questions were asked. But it does appear that city dwellers are more likely to value the wilderness *as wilderness*, to resent intrusions on it, and to think carefully about their own behavior there. City people seem to be most keenly aware of wilderness as something special, something fragile; it's not just "country" to them.

When people head into the backcountry, they go mostly in small groups—sometimes the family, sometimes three or four friends. Even today, these latter groups are typically all-male. Large organized parties are comparatively rare. Surprisingly rare, also, is the hiker who sets out alone.

Most backpackers and hikers would prefer not to have any company but the company of their own party. If they must meet other groups, they prefer to meet small ones. Thus the large organized parties are resented somewhat by the rest of the backcountry travelers, the vast majority that move in threes and fours. This is clearly a problem. And yet the larger groups appear to serve a particular and important purpose. In them you find many more children, many more people over fifty, and many more people who are venturing into the wilderness for the first time. For many, the organized trip is the introduction, the open door. And while many of the small parties are made up entirely of men, the larger groups are composed of men and women equally.

If there is wild country close at hand, hikers tend to take short trips adding up to about three weeks a year. It is surprising to find that, on most trips, people walk no more than ten or fifteen miles, altogether. Day-trips, there-and-back-again excursions on which no camp is made, account for a very large proportion of wilderness use.

Indeed, most wilderness areas are most visited by local people. Only a few well-known attractions draw people from more than a couple of hundred miles away. Nor do the hikers and packers spend a lot of money on their excursions. Not many people, these days, take horses or hire the help of professional outfitters. Though there are regions in which the use of packstock and paid helpers is traditional, this style of camping seems to be on the decline.

When they aren't in the mountains, what do backpackers like to do with their free time? According to one report, "cultural activities" (whatever those are) stand at the top of the list. At the very bottom: spectator sports, television, nonwilderness sightseeing, and other kinds of travel.

Knowing these things, it is interesting to look at the picture of the wilderness traveler that is presented, at times, by opponents of the wilderness idea. This image was reflected recently by the president of the Nevada Chamber of Commerce, as reported by the *Tahoe World:*

Hermann said that "only the rich few who have money to hike out with very expensive equipment"

*were able to enjoy the Forest Service's public
campgrounds. The Nevada Chamber President
added that camping out was something that
"none of us working people have the time, money,
or patience to do." Hermann also referred to the
Forest Service's recent purchase of the Meeks Bay
resort as useless for vacationers "unless you can
afford to be a hippie and go out and live in the
woods."*

According to such notions, the wilderness people
come only from the cities (and generally from cities
a long way away); have weeks and months of free
time to spend in wild travel; are uniformly husky
and ambitious; are filthy rich (although at the same
time hip) and, indeed, must be wealthy in order to
pursue their expensive notions of good fun.

The real picture, obviously, is more complex. The
backpackers do tend to have money (or parents with
money), and good gear is indeed a substantial cost.
Yet even the finest set of wilderness equipment
costs much less to buy, use, and maintain than a
dirt bike, a camper, or a snowmobile. The difference
is not one of means; it is a difference of taste, of attitude. As for the other points, wilderness users
most definitely do *not* come from far away; they do
not have more free time than other people; and if
they are in fact much "hipper" than the population
at large, the studies to date don't reflect it.

Why do they come?

This is not a question that troubles the backpackers much themselves. But it does interest the researchers, and they have surveyed, probed, and the-
orized for years. They have defined and traced two
dozen motives, at least, for "wilderness behavior."

There is the escape from the pressures and rou-
tines of life in the city. There is the pleasant, imper-
sonal simplicity of the jobs to be done, the chal-
lenges to be met. There is the pleasure of exertion.
There is the hunt for a trophy: the peak you
"bagged," the fish you caught, the photograph you

took, the miles you walked, the lofty passes you crossed. There is sometimes the chance to compare notes about gear (that inexhaustible conversation) or to trade stories about past adventures. In the wilderness, as everywhere, there are games people play.

But if many different attractions bring the hiker to the wild places, some of those attractions matter more; some matter less.

Except, perhaps, for climbers and river-runners, people don't seek out the wilderness with the idea of proving themselves, of testing themselves against adversity. They don't go there to meet other people, nor to add to their personal status. Even exercise and better health count only as benefits gained on the side. And while it seems certain that wilderness travel does something for balance of mind, for sanity even, it is the rare backpacker who is self-consciously "into" wilderness as people are "into" biorhythms or encounter groups.

In short, it appears that people do not treat wilderness travel, in any fundamental way, as a means to some other end; as a setting merely for some personal drama, therapy, or display.

So we come back to seeing the taste for wilderness as nothing more, and nothing less, than that—a wish to be in the wild places; to know the places themselves. The researchers have not found it easy to analyze this basic affection for wilderness into simpler, more explainable, desires. Still, they have made the attempt. Generally, they have tried to divide the attraction into plus and minus sides: are we drawn to these places because they *are wild*—or do we admire them rather for their contrast value: because they *are not tame?*

At this point (I can't help thinking) the analysis reaches the stage of diminishing returns.

33:
Problems in Wilderness Management

WHEN, AFTER DOUBT AND DEBATE, a wilderness is finally "saved"—when Congress draws around it that protecting, legal line—there's a feeling of comfort, of a thing accomplished. And the feeling is quite justified. When Congress has acted, you know that the land is safe, in its wildness, from most kinds of invasion. That is no small thing.

But when a wilderness is set aside (and sometimes even earlier than that), a whole new set of problems begins to appear. Then we encounter the other half of the wilderness challenge. How, in the face of always increasing use—welcome though that use must be—can the wilderness stay wild?

Someday, sooner or later, the last large area of unprotected American wilderness will be spoken for. Perhaps it will get protection, perhaps it will be given over to some other use, but the indecision will be done. Long before that final allocation, we will have to shift our attention to the related problem:

how to manage the wild land we have already made up our minds to preserve.

This book has said a good deal about wilderness management, as it looks from the backpacker's point of view: the annoyance (and the plain necessity) of wilderness permits; the problems caused by badly laid-out trails. And we've spoken incessantly about good practices to follow in the wild country, and how they differ from the bad.

Now it may be useful to turn the question around, to look at the problems of managing wild country as the *managers* see them. The backpackers come and go, but the professionals are always there. The Park Service, the Forest Service, and the other agencies have the wild land in their care. These people have been watching the changes that take place, year after year, in their domains. Much of what they see they do not like. They are searching—though "groping" would sometimes be a better word—for ways of handling the problems of the land. And backpackers have every right, and every need, to keep an eye on what is being done, on what is being proposed. More than anyone else, it concerns *them.*

The problem

What do the managers see that worries them so? Just what any concerned backpacker observes, but they see more of it.

They see the eroding, gouged-out trails and, across high meadows, the multiple, beaten tracks, like freeway lanes.

They see campsites turning into fields of scarred and barren ground; garbage pits and drainage ditches; grasslands pockmarked with old tentsites; trailsides and lakeshores littered with the blackened circles of old fires.

They see areas stripped not only of dead, down wood—but also of standing snags, so important to wildlife, and of all green branches small enough to break by hand.

They see the careless disposal of human waste,

and the possibility of grave water pollution in wild places.

And, hard though it is to believe these days, they see (and pick up) an astonishing amount of old-fashioned, unforgivable *litter.*

There are subtler effects that backpackers may not be aware of. Too much human traffic, at certain places or at certain times of year, can disturb or drive away such animals as bighorn sheep, can interfere with their breeding, or keep them away from scarce desert water supplies. For other animals, human presence is actually too much of an attraction; it makes nuisances, scavengers of them. Consider the bears.

Finally, quite distinct from these effects on the land and its native species, there's the matter of "overpopulation" in the wild country— "overpopulation" as judged by the backpackers themselves. Generally, wilderness travelers prefer not to have a lot of company on the trail. Increasingly, though, they find it. For many, this by itself damages the pleasure they came for and makes wilderness inadequately "wild."

It is easy to exaggerate these troubles. As yet they are obvious in rather few places. We are not yet in danger of "loving the wilderness to death"— not much of it anyway. But the problems are there, and they are growing. Now is the time to get them under control.

Put yourself in the position of a wilderness manager. What do you have to do? What are your choices? If you want to reduce the "impact," the total wear and tear on a piece of wilderness, how do you go about it? There appear to be three distinct approaches that you, as manager, can take.

- First, you can concentrate on lessening the impact each individual hiker contributes.
- Second, you can build facilities to handle heavier use than the land could take without them.
- Third, you can actually limit the number of people you allow in a particular place at a particular

time—and you can do this in various ways, subtle or direct.

In fact, of course, the wilderness manager uses all these methods constantly, relying sometimes more heavily on one, sometimes on another. The variations are endless as the land is varied. But these are the three basic lines.

Lessening individual impact

The easiest target is the obvious, outright abuse. When backpackers cut across a switchback on a trail, or build a fire against a boulder in an unscarred meadow, or use a streambank for a toilet, or set up camp ten yards from another party, they are obviously doing something drastically wrong. Almost certainly they are doing it out of ignorance. The people you meet in the wild places seldom lack a genuine affection for the land, but they may not understand what its limits are. So the problem is largely one of getting the message across.

Beyond the obvious bad practices, there are others, like the building of fires, that are fine in some places, very destructive in others. No one set of rules can be applied everywhere. A backpacker entering an unfamiliar area may need to be told what the particular problems of the region are—education again.

This is one of the functions of the "wilderness permit." When hikers pick up their permits, they get, or should get, some necessary information. Rules and recommendations are printed on the permit, and the ranger on duty is supposed to be careful in explaining the reasoning behind them. All this should be having an effect. And yet, in the backcountry, you still encounter the most blatant abuses. Clearly, a still better job of education must somehow be done.

One educational trick (a controversial one) is the "wilderness entry test." In a few places, backpackers are required to pass a multiple-choice test to show that they understand the recommended local practices. In certain other wilderness areas people are asked to take such a test if they plan to abandon the main trails for more remote travel.

Formal regulations can, of course, be enforced. In most areas of heavy use there are "wilderness rangers" who can talk to people, and, if necessary, issue citations. But wilderness areas are too big, and rangers are too few, for this traffic-cop approach to accomplish much. It's absolutely necessary that people understand the problems on their own and without coercion do what they can do to solve them. There's no other practical way.

Even when there's no question of outright abuse, some travelers contribute more impact than others. Other things being equal, the builder of a fire is taking up more room, so to speak, than someone who uses only a stove; the horseman takes up more "impact room" than the hiker. In little-used or resilient areas, these differences may scarcely matter. Elsewhere they can be crucial. One researcher has ranked the different types of parties, going from the smallest impact to the largest:

Least impact Small parties of day-hikers
Small parties of campers who build
no fires
Large parties of day-hikers
Small parties of campers who do
build fires
Large parties of campers
Small parties using horses

Most impact Large parties using horses

Some would quarrel with this ranking, but the principle is there. So a manager might well want to discourage some kinds of parties and encourage others; this is one use to which quotas (see below) can be put.

The matter of small parties versus large is sometimes more complex than it seems. There are situations in which large parties are clearly downright destructive. On the other hand, a well-run but sizable group may actually be gentler on the land than an equal number of hikers who arrive in many small parties.

Develop to preserve?

Now we come to the second of the roads you as manager can take. Along with trying to reduce the impact of people on the land, you can set out to make the landscape itself capable of handling more people. You can do this, oddly enough, by building things.

It seems paradoxical, this notion of "protecting" wild land by making it less wild, but to a limited extent it always has to be done. Even a simple trail is already a compromise with perfect wilderness; it is, in the planners' jargon, a "hardening." But a well-designed trail carries many more people than the land could support if they all scrambled cross-country. A marked and definite campsite is another kind of "hardening": barren already, it can come to little additional harm. About the next step up is the latrine. Then comes the more elaborate backcountry toilet. Taken to its extreme, this "hardening" can give you cement fireplaces; paved or graveled trails; huts and lodges; and even (as at Yosemite) back-country sewage treatment plants.

Many of these facilities have been built merely as luxuries. But they can also have a function in protecting land. The more people a manager decides to accommodate, the more facilities are needed. By concentrating use at "hardened" sites, the manager can at least in theory take some pressure off the rest of the land, the land left alone. Reasoning partly this way, the National Park Service, in particular, used to be a busy builder. In Yosemite National Park, five "High Sierra Camps" provide meals and beds in summer; the White Mountains of New Hampshire have their own system of hostels. If all the people who use these lodges were instead camping out on the land, the total impact would arguably be greater.

So why not go the whole distance? Why

shouldn't we imitate the Europeans and build whole constellations of huts and lodges? Why not "harden" the wilderness to the point where any number of people could be taken in at once?

There are several good answers. First, and most obvious: a "hardened" wilderness is always a lessened wilderness. Every time you go beyond the most basic improvements, you make the experience of wild places markedly less wild. Second, each new wilderness development is, in itself, an impact. Around a backcountry lodge, you'll probably find a ring of heavily used land, with various kinds of damage taking place in it. These facilities don't merely accommodate use—they also attract it. They may indeed lessen the impact of each person they attract, but the total effect on the wilderness can only grow as the population does.

There seems to be growing agreement that elaborate facilities are simply out of place in the deep wilderness. Backpackers themselves seem to be almost unanimous in turning down the thought of new developments in remote landscapes. As one Forest Service study concludes: "Most visitors like to take their wilderness pretty straight."

Quasi-wilderness

Most—and yet not all. When researchers interview wilderness travelers they find a certain number who really are not even looking for wilderness as it's generally understood. Rather, they want *places to hike*, pleasant places, away from roads, but not necessarily truly wild. Moreover, quite a few of them would welcome the conveniences not widely found in genuine wilderness. They'd be just as happy to have outhouses, stone fireplaces, surfaced trails, picnic tables, and whatever else the managers decided to install.

And so there arises the notion of compromised wilderness, or, as it is sometimes labeled, "Back Country." In Back Country you might have quite elaborate facilities—even perhaps service roads, closed to private cars, but open to the vehicles of the managing agency. Trails and camps would be "hardened" as required, to take very heavy use. The land would be "gardened" to repair inevitable damage, and considerable impact would simply be accepted. These Back Country areas, it is argued, could attract a lot of hikers—the ones who aren't really wilderness buffs—and thus take some of the pressure off of the deeper wilderness.

It's an attractive idea. In fact, it's an unassailable one. We will certainly need some of these less-than-wilderness zones. Indeed, we have a few, especially in the East; the long trails and hut systems of the Appalachians amount to a kind of Back Country. (It is one of the great failures of land use planning in America that we don't have more such areas. When we exploit land, we exploit it so thoroughly that the middle ground, the pleasant accessible land neither totally tame nor totally wild, disappears.)

And yet conservationists have not been in a hurry to support the Back Country concept. Not, at least, as it is usually put forward. The suggestion is most often brought up by the U.S. Forest Service; the Forest Service generally proposes to set up these compromised areas by cutting them out of larger regions that are, in fact, true wilderness, prime and pure. Thus Back Country becomes an *alternative* to formal wilderness, rather than a complement to it. Where one wins the other loses.

Limits on use

In any landscape that is used for recreation—no matter how much it has been "hardened"—there comes a point of saturation. Mountain valleys, like movie theaters, can only hold so many people. How many depends on how much damage you're willing to accept. In the wilderness, by its nature, the "carrying capacity" cannot be terribly high. As one Park Service document bluntly puts it: "If use continues to escalate, it is doubtful if *any* management activities can perpetuate the park resources . . . even with endless research and funds." There comes a point at which no amount of care, no amount of personal conscience, no amount of "gardening," can keep the land from showing signs of wear. Exactly where the limit lies can be hard to decide. It depends on different things in different places. But everyone agrees that it exists.

What do you do (as a manager) when the line is crossed? What do you do when there are simply more people in a place than a place can gracefully hold? Of all the questions that the wilderness managers have to answer, this is the most difficult and most pervasive.

There is more than one way to control the amount of use a particular piece of land receives. The most obvious (but not always the best) is the formal, flat-out *quota*. In a quota system, each wilderness, or portion of a wilderness, is judged to be capable of handling a certain number of people at one time. If more than that show up at the trailhead—most likely to happen on some sunny August weekend—some of them will be turned away, asked to take another trail, or to come back on another day. There are various ways of deciding who gets in and who doesn't: reservation systems, wilderness entry tests, lotteries, or some combination. The simplest and most usual arrangement is first come, first served.

When the land agencies began, in the early 1970s, to introduce these quotas, they did it with more than a little hesitation. They no doubt feared that the backpacking public would resent them, bitterly perhaps. Indeed there has been some resentment. Some hikers, offended by the regulation, have begun to avoid the well-known wilderness areas where these measures are being taken. Some have moved on to other wild places, unprotected and unregulated; others may simply be staying home.

And yet most hikers, a vast majority, seem to have accepted the quotas calmly, and even with some favor. Some people are frankly pleased; they find that they can now go back to old places, favorite places, that they had abandoned as the population grew.

Other ways

Despite the seemingly broad acceptance of quotas though, there's something intrinsically unattractive, inhospitable, about the wilderness numbers game. If crowding damages the wilderness experience in one fashion, regulation impairs it in another, subtler way.

That formal use limits are often necessary, often the only answer, is clear. And yet the quotas are not the only tools that can be used to guide where people go. There are several other ways of distributing use without actually turning people away.

What are they?

One of the tools is *publicity*, which can encourage people to try one place and discourage a trip to another. Suppose, for instance, you warn the backpacker that certain areas are heavily used. Since backpackers don't like a lot of company, it seems possible that many will change their plans. They will, at least, if they have the needed information well enough in advance. With this in mind, the agencies have begun publishing maps, for some areas, showing zones of heavy use. How well this will work is not yet clear.

Publicity, misused, can harm instead of help. One national forest in Oregon made the mistake of publishing a map illustrated with a photograph of an attractive lake, a steep cliff above it, an obvious campsite, and a caption naming the place. "That's the most overused spot in the whole area, now," say the local officials.

So publicity is one key. Another, still more important, is *access*. If a fragile site is getting too much use, you can lessen the problem simply by making it a little less easy to get to.

To do such a thing is to reverse the trend of decades. The wilderness, of course, has been shrinking And every time a road cuts deeper into country that was wild before, the remaining wild land becomes

that much more accessible, that much less remote.
Places that were two days away from the roadhead
may now be one day away, or one hour. When the
border of the wilderness moves inwards, so does the
zone of maximum use.

This shrinking is always significant to the wilderness manager; it increases the pressure on the inner
lands. But most of all it matters when new roadheads appear within easy hiking range of places
that are both interesting and fragile. A timberline
lake basin is exactly such a place—especially if the
lakes are stocked with fish. When such an attractive
landscape becomes easy of access, managers will either have to limit use by quotas or let the land deteriorate.

The easiest wilderness to manage is a large one,
with the most sensitive portions near the center and
buffers of less fragile country surrounding that core
on all sides. There used to be many blocks of wild
land that fit that pattern almost exactly. But in our
rush to open up access to high, spectacular places,
we have built many roads that reverse this convenient natural zoning. Too often it is the most vulnerable landscape that is now most accessible of all.

Only recently have we realized that easier access
has a price. Part of that price is more, and bossier,
regulation. Now and then, in a few special places,
wilderness managers have dared to reverse the
trend. To great public astonishment, they have actually *closed* a few established roads, restoring wilderness, or at any rate *distance*, where it had disappeared. The Park Service has been the leader in this,
but the Forest Service has begun to consider closing
down logging roads that lead to the edge of wilderness—once the logging is done.

When roads get closed, some backpackers approve heartily; others protest. It can be annoying—no question about it—to give up an easy access
you're accustomed to. The annoyance is less when
there's a decent, parallel trail, out of sight of the
road, on which you can walk. Nobody wants to hike
on a roadbed. (Couldn't you have an open road, and,

in the woods beside it, a trail for people to use who want the extra miles? You could. The problem is that nobody would use it. The hiker who has wilderness in mind doesn't get much fun out of walking to a place that other people are reaching, ten times as fast, by car.)

Better than closing roads, of course, is not to build them in the first place; it's cheaper, easier, and less controversial. From the point of view of the wilderness manager, it's important above all that the wilderness not shrink any further. For many large but dwindling wild areas, we still have a choice: we can either use the land itself to filter use, so that not too many people arrive at once in vulnerable places; or we can remove this natural buffering and increase artificial control to compensate. Each method has certain advantages. But the natural sorting out is less destructive of the freedom one hopes for in the enjoyment of the wilderness.

Disperse or concentrate?

There's a basic question that comes up again and again in wilderness management. Briefly, is it better to *concentrate* human use in certain places, leaving the rest of the landscape more or less untouched? Or should the goal be to *disperse* human presence, and human impact, as widely as possible over the land?

This question comes up in several forms. The planners must answer it, one way or another, when they set up rules on campsites and camping. In some wilderness areas dispersal is the rule. Except for certain zones that are, for some special reason, off limits, hikers can camp where they choose. But in other areas, you are encouraged, even required, to settle on certain established sites. Sometimes the managers of a wilderness will shift abruptly from one policy to another—confusing, surely, to backpackers who return to a place and find last year's *Thou Shalts* transformed into this season's *Thou Shalt Nots*!

On the face of it, concentrated camping seems

foreign to the wilderness. Heavily used sites have some particular problems too. It is near such sites that you're most likely to find pollution problems and woods exhausted of firewood.

But if dispersed camping seems more the natural order of the wilderness, it has this drawback: it takes skill and attention to choose a suitable campsite on fresh ground and use it in such a way that no scars are left behind. The camper in the established site avoids this problem.

There are intermediate policies. For instance, people who light fires are often required to use the definite sites, while people who use only stoves can camp where they like. (Some areas are closed to all camping, even to all hiking, for good reasons: for the welfare of endangered species; for scientific study; for watershed; or because of extreme seasonal fire danger.)

The same question—disperse or concentrate?—must be asked in a larger context. At present, backpackers and hikers use some wilderness areas, and some portions of wilderness areas, very much more than others. Certain trails are main highways; others are traveled little; trailless regions may get only a few visitors a year. There is a parallel variation over time. Certain summer weekends bring out fantastic crowds; certain weekdays leave the mountains almost vacant. For the informed backpacker, this is all to the good. Unless you are set on some particular destination, you can simply choose to go to the emptier places—and (if your schedule allows it) you can choose the less populous times.

Now if the demand for wilderness keeps on increasing—and there are good reasons to think that it will—more and more people will be turned away from the best-known and most populous areas. Presumably they'll learn to go to other sections. And so, as one result of regulation, use will probably spread out somewhat more evenly over the land and perhaps also over the calendar.

There's wide agreement that this will happen. But there's some question as to whether the spreading out should be promoted actively. Should the less used areas be made more easily accessible? Should access roads to such areas be improved? Should new trails be built through trailless regions of wilderness? Should little-used areas be given strong publicity?

Many wilderness management people are cautious about wholesale plans to "open up" these backlands. After all, there's no reason to want every corner of a wilderness to be visited equally. On the contrary, there's much to be said for having both the busier and the quieter corners. In some ways the least used parts of a wilderness are the most valuable parts. As wilderness use increases, we can expect to see the setting aside of *no use zones* within them—areas where the natural regime is preserved absolutely. As every corner of the world environment is modified, subtly or grossly, by the presence and technology of the human race, scientists search with increasing frustration for places to examine the original. A nonrecreational zone inside a formal wilderness answers this need about as well as anything can.

One thing is clear: if dispersal is going to be the rule, it's important to have plenty of wild land available to disperse people *into*. The problem of *managing* wilderness is in no way separate from the problem of *preserving* wilderness. The more we have, the easier it is to manage; the more the supply diminishes, the greater the manager's difficulties become.

And the first order of business is to set aside for the future as much as we can of our still grand wild inheritance. We need a generous wilderness, not a narrow, cramped, and superregulated one. We need to guard our freedom in that wilderness, and freedom, in the wilderness, means *room*.

Appendix:
Resources

1. Conservation/wilderness travel organizations

American Hiking Society
1701 18th Street, N. W.
Washington, D.C. 20009

Appalachian Mountain Club
5 Joy Street
Boston, Mass. 02108

Appalachian Trail Conference
Box 236
Harpers Ferry, West Virginia 25425

Federation of Western Outdoor Clubs
c/o Box 548
Bozeman, Mont. 59715

The Mountaineers
719 Pike Street
Seattle, Wash. 98101

Sierra Club
530 Bush Street
San Francisco, Calif. 94108

Wilderness Society
1901 Pennsylvania Avenue, N. W.
Washington, D.C. 20006

2. Federal and selected state agencies that manage wilderness land

Bureau of Land Management (BLM)
Office of Information
Department of the Interior
Washington, D.C. 20240

BLM—Arizona
2400 Valley Bank Center
Phoenix, Ariz. 85073

BLM—California
Federal Office Building
2800 Cottage Way
Sacramento, Calif. 95825

BLM—Colorado
2000 Arapahoe Street
Denver, Colo. 80205

BLM—Idaho
Box 042
Boise, Idaho 83724

BLM—Montana
Box 30157
Billings, Mont. 59107

BLM—Nevada
Federal Building
300 Booth Street
Reno, Nevada 89520

BLM—New Mexico
Box 1449
Santa Fe, N.M. 87501

BLM—Oregon and Washington
Box 2965
Portland, Ore. 97208

BLM—Utah
University Club Building
136 East South Temple
Salt Lake City, Utah 84111

BLM—Wyoming
Box 1828
Cheyenne, Wyo. 82001

National Park Service (NPS)
Department of the Interior
Washington, D.C. 20240

NPS—Alaska Region
540 West Fifth Ave.
Anchorage, Alaska 99501

NPS—Mid-Atlantic Region (Del., Md., Pa., Va., W. Va.)
143 South Third Street
Philadelphia, Pa. 19106

NPS—Midwest Region (Ill., Ind., Iowa, Kans., Mich.,
   Minn., Mo., Nebr., Ohio, Wisc.)
1709 Jackson Street
Omaha, Nebraska 68102

NPS—North Atlantic Region (N.Y., N.J., the Northeast)
15 State Street
Boston, Mass. 02109

NPS—Pacific Northwest Region (Ida., Ore., Wash.)
1920 Westin Building
2001 Sixth Avenue
Seattle, Wash. 98121

NPS—Rocky Mountain Region (Colo., Mont., N.D., S.D.,
   Utah, Wyo.)
Box 25287
Denver, Colo. 80225

NPS—Southeast Region (Ala., Fla., Ga., Ky., Miss., N.C.,
   S.C., Tenn.)
75 Spring Street, S.W.
Atlanta, Georgia 30303

NPS—Southwest Region (Ark., La., N.M., Okla., Texas)
Box 728
Santa Fe, N.M. 87501

NPS—Western Region (Calif., Ariz., Nev., Hawaii)
Box 36063
San Francisco, Calif. 94102

U.S. Fish and Wildlife Service (FWS)
Department of the Interior
Washington, D.C. 20240

FWS—Alaska Regional Office
1011 East Tudor Road
Anchorage, Alaska 99503

FWS—Albuquerque Regional Office (Ariz., N. M., Okla.,
   Texas)
500 Gold Avenue, S. W.
Albuquerque, N. M. 87103

FWS—Atlanta Regional Office (Ark., Ky., La., Tenn., and
   the remaining Southeast)
Richard B. Russell Federal Building
75 Spring Street, S. W.
Atlanta, Georgia 30303

FWS—Boston Regional Office (Pa., Va., W. Va., and the
   remaining Northeast)
One Gateway Center
Newton Corner, Mass. 02158

FWS—Denver Regional Office (Colo., Kans., Mont., N. D.,
   Nebr., S. D., Utah, Wyo.)
Box 25486
Denver Federal Center
Denver, Colo. 80225

FWS—Portland Regional Office (Calif., Hawaii, Idaho, Nevada, Ore., Wash.)
500 N. E. Multnomah Street
Portland, Ore. 97232

FWS—Twin Cities Regional Office (Iowa, Ill., Ind., Mich.,
   Minn., Mo., Ohio, Wisc.)
Whipple Federal Building
Fort Snelling
Twin Cities, Minn. 55111

U.S. Forest Service (FS)
Box 2417
Department of Agriculture
Washington, D.C. 20013

FS—Alaska Region
Box 1628
Juneau, Alaska 99802

FS—California Region
630 Sansome Street
San Francisco, Calif. 94111

FS—Eastern Region (the Northeast and the Great Lakes
states; Missouri; West Virginia)
633 West Wisconsin Ave.
Milwaukee, Wisc. 53203

FS—Intermountain Region (Nevada, Utah, southern
Idaho, western Wyoming)
Federal Building
324 25th Street
Ogden, Utah 84401

FS—Northern Region (Montana, northern Idaho,
N. Dakota)
Federal Building
Missoula, Mont. 59807

FS—Pacific Northwest Region (Oregon, Washington)
Box 3623
Portland, Ore. 97208

FS—Rocky Mountain Region (Colo., most of Wyo., S.
Dak., Nebr., Kans.)
Box 25217
Denver, Colo. 80225

FS—Southern Region (the South, incl. Okla., Ky.)
1720 Peachtree Road, N.W.
Atlanta, Ga. 30309

FS—Southwestern Region (Arizona, New Mexico)
517 Gold Ave., S.W.
Albuquerque, N.M. 87101

California Department of Parks and Recreation
1416 Ninth Street
Sacramento, Ca. 95814

Maine Department of Conservation
State House Station #22
Augusta, Maine 04333

Michigan Department of Natural Resources
Box 30028
Lansing, Mich. 48909

Minnesota Department of Natural Resources
658 Cedar Street
St. Paul, Minn. 55155

New York Department of Environmental Conservation
50 Wolf Road
Albany, N.Y. 12233

Pennsylvania Department of Environmental Resources
Box 2063
Harrisburg, Pa. 17120

Wisconsin Department of Natural Resources
Box 7921
Madison, Wisc. 53707

3. Maps and publications mentioned in text

Backcountry Skiing: The Sierra Club Guide to Skiing off the Beaten Track
Lito Tejada-Flores
Sierra Club

Backpacker Magazine
Ziff-Davis Publishing Company
One Park Avenue
New York, N. Y. 10016

Composition of Foods
Agriculture Handbook #8
U. S. Government Printing Office
Washington, D.C. 20402

Freedom of the Hills 6th ed.
Harvey Manning, Editor
The Mountaineers

Land Navigation Handbook: The Sierra Club Guide to Map and Compass
W. S. Kals
Sierra Club

How to Get to the Wilderness Without a Car
Lee W. Cooper
Box 4073
Malibu, Calif. 90265

Medical Care for Mountain Climbers
Peter Steele
William Heinemann Medical Books Ltd.
London, England

Medicine for Mountaineering, 2d ed.
James A. Wilkerson, Editor
The Mountaineers

Mountaineering Medicine: A Wilderness Medical Guide, 7th ed.
Fred T. Darvill, Jr.
Skagit Mountain Rescue Unit, Box 636, Mount Vernon, Wash. 98273

Outside Magazine
Box 2960
Boulder, Colo. 80321

Topographical maps

U.S. east of the Mississippi:
Branch of Distribution
U.S. Geological Survey
1200 South Eads Street
Arlington, Virginia 22202

U.S. west of the Mississippi:
Branch of Distribution
U.S. Geological Survey
Box 25286
Federal Center
Denver, Colo. 80225

Canada:
Department of Energy, Mines, and Resources
615 Booth Street
Ottawa, Ontario

*(USGS maps now cost $1.25 for 7.5- and 15-minute
quadrangles; maps of larger areas sell for $1.50 and
$2.00. Canadian maps range from 50¢ to $3. The USGS
provides single state indexes free.)*

Wilderness Digest series
Box 989
Lone Pine, Ca. 93545

*(Each digest describes current regulations for travel in
designated wilderness areas. Volumes now available:
Southwest, Northwest.)*

4. Gear Sources

*(My file shows more than 250 gear makers and major
suppliers. This short selection makes no claim to be
fair. I have chosen a few outfits that are large,
prominent, historic, or in some sense leaders in the
field. Many of these firms publish interesting and
informative catalogs.)*

Adventure 16
4620 Alvarado Canyon Road
San Diego, Calif. 92120

Alpenlite Wilderness Group
3891 North Ventura Avenue
Ventura, Calif. 93001

Back to Basics
1490 66th Street
Emeryville, Calif. 94608

Black Ice
2310 Laurel
Napa, Calif. 94559

Cannondale
9 Brookside Place
Georgetown, Conn. 06829

Chinook
Box 1076
Longmont, Colo. 80501

Coleman
250 North St. Francis Ave.
Wichita, Kansas 67201

Diamond Brand
Highway 25
Naples, N. C. 28760

Early Winters
110 Prefontaine Place South
Seattle, Wash. 98104

Eastern Mountain Sports
One Vose Farm Road
Peterborough, N. H. 03458

Eddie Bauer
Box 3700
Seattle, Wash. 98124

Gregory Mountain Products
4620 Alvarado Canyon Road #13
San Diego, Calif. 92120

Holubar
Box 7
Boulder, Colo. 80306

Insta-Pure (water purification kits)
Box 224
Hermosa Beach, Calif. 90254

JanSport
Building 306
Paine Field Industrial Park
Everett, Wash. 98204

Johnson Camping (Camp Trails, Silva, Eureka brands)
Box 966
Binghamton, NY 13902

Kelty Pack
Box 639
Sun Valley, Calif. 91352

L. L. Bean
3621 Main Street
Freeport, Maine 04033

Lowe Alpine Systems
802 S. Public Road
Lafayette, Colo. 80026

Marmot Mountain Works
3049 Adeline Street
Berkeley, Calif. 94703

Moss Tent Works
Box 309
Camden, Maine 04843

Mountain Safety Research
631 South 96th Street
Seattle, Wash. 98104

Optimus
Box 1950
Bridgeport, Conn. 06601

Patagonia Software
Box 150
Ventura, Calif. 93002

Precise International
Suffern, N. Y. 10901

Recreational Equipment, Inc.
Box 88125
Seattle, Wash. 98188

Royal Robbins
Box 4536
Modesto, Calif. 95352

Sherpa
2222 Diversey
Chicago, Ill. 60647

Sierra Designs
Box 12930
Oakland, Calif. 94607

SierraWest
6 East Yanonali Street
Santa Barbara, Calif. 93101

Slumberjack
Box 31405
Los Angeles, Calif. 90031

Stephenson
RFD 4 Box 145
Gilford, N. H. 03246

Trailwise
221 West First Street
Kewanee, Ill. 61443

Wilderness Experience
20675 Nordhoff Street
Chatsworth, Calif. 91311

Index

Abdominal pain, 379
Acute mountain sickness, 407–8
Adhesive tape, 42, 123, 155, 163, 205, 207, 348, 372, 376
Adirondacks, 5, 8, 26, 197, 302–3, 418, 419, 423, 446
Air mattresses, 99–100, 163, 254, 298, 307
Alaska, 247, 394, 446, 455
Alaska Lands Act, 455
Alcohol: bottles for, 150; as liquor, 256, 306, 392, 408; rubbing, 42, 43; as stove fuel, 136, 141, 142; as stove primer, 136, 147, 259, 261
Allergies, 383–84
Altimeters, 164
Altitude: adjusting to, 175; and children, 351–52; and foods, 181; and respiration, 264; and stoves, 139, 149–50; and sunburn, 157–58, 307; and sunglasses, 51, 210, 411
Altitude sickness, 264, 352, 357, 363, 379, 410
Animal problems, 271, 288–89; 381–95, 420. See also Bears
Animals: camping near, 244–45; and children, 357; and garbage, 269–70; human interference with, 469; protecting food from, 270–73; water pollution by, 278. See also Bears and other individual animals
Anoraks, 55
Antibiotic ointment, 156, 373
Antibiotics, 157, 379, 383, 385, 392
Antiseptic, 155–56
Appalachians, 5, 328, 337, 418, 421–22; 474
Appendicitis, 379
Appetite, loss of, 408
Arm sling, 155, 373
Artificial respiration, 325, 366
Athlete's foot, 42
Automobiles, 197–98, 199–201, 307–8
Avalanche cord, 324

Avalanches, 321–26, 328, 435, 442
Axe, 162, 266. See also Ice axe

Back injuries, 374–75
Backpackers, 5, 462–66
Badlands National Monument, 426
Bags. See Beltbag; Bivouac bags; Garbage; Laundry bags; Plastic bags; Sleeping bags; Stuffsacks
Balaclava, 52
Bandages, 155, 288, 372, 375, 376
Barometer, 164
Basin and range country, 303–4, 437, 438–39
Batteries, 141, 161–62
Bear-bagging, 152, 162, 271–73, 394
Bears, 273, 245, 269–70, 289, 393–95; 417, 420, 469; grizzly, 247, 273, 393–95, 442. See also Bear-bagging
Bees, 383–84
Belaying, 299, 300, 301
Beltbag, 84
Benchmarks, 230
Benzoin, 42, 43, 207
Betadine, 155–56, 207
Bindings: cross-country ski, 345–48; snowshoe, 340–41
Binoculars, 164
Bivouac bags, 97, 98, 106–7, 109
Black widow spiders, 384–85
Blazes, 208, 233–34, 302, 326, 327
Bleeding, 366–67, 371–72
Blisters: and breaking in boots, 43; and burns, 372; and children, 356; and loose boots, 39; preventing, 42, 43, 155, 201, 205; treating, 156, 205–9
Boots, 29–47; and Achilles tendon, 31; for beach walking, 416; breaking in, 12, 30, 43; buying, 29–31, 38–41; care of, 43–46, 254, 329; children's, 355; construction of, 32–38; cost of, 17, 30; cross-country ski, 41, 346–47; for cross-country travel, 287–88, 348; drying, 45; fitting, 38–40;

Gore-Tex, 30, 34–35; Korean boot, 317; lacing, 33, 206, 405, 407; leather, 30, 31, 32, 35–38, 43, 44–46; lightweight, 30, 31; and low impact, 34, 46–47; Mickey Mouse, 317; mountaineering, 30, 38; plastic, 30, 38; repairing, 44, 46, 162, 163; resoling, 44, 46; rock-climbing, 41; ski-mountaineering, 41; snowshoe, 340; for snow travel, 297–98; tropical combat, 310, 417; ultralight, 32, 33–35, 42–44; wading, 310; weight of, 17, 29–31, 33–34; for wetlands, 417; winter, 38, 41, 315–16; women's, 40

Bottles, 145, 150–51, 185, 306

Bracketing, 293–94

Breathing problems, 264, 365–66, 367–68, 408

Broken bones, 373–75

Brown recluse spider, 385

Brunton compasses, 224

Bureau of Land Management: addresses, 460, 482–83; maps published by, 167, 171–73, 220–21; and wilderness management, 170, 437, 448, 452, 455

Burns, 156, 372. *See also* Sunburn

Butane cartridges, 127, 137–40, 141–43, 146, 262–63; burning time, 140, 186; cost, 138, 140, 143; weight, 24, 140

Camera, 84, 164, 212, 224, 329

Camping Gaz C-206 stove, 137, 138

Campsites: and children, 358; criteria for, 242–46; established, 9, 241–42, 472; low-impact, 9, 241–48, 472; and mosquitoes, 382; and privacy, 245; regulations on, 240–41, 243–44, 478–79; and water, 309; and wind, 266; and wildlife, 244–45

Canoeing, 416, 417, 425–26

Canyonlands, 437–38, 440

Cape Cod, 416

Cape Lookout, 416

Carbide lamps, 161

Carbon monoxide poisoning, 264

Cardiopulmonary resuscitation (CPR), 367

Caves, 212

Centipedes, 386

Cerebral edema, 409

Channel block, 94–95

Cheese, 183, 185

Child carriers, 352

Children, 349–59; age of, and backpacking, 350–51, 354, 355; food amounts needed by, 178; and safety, 158, 356–57; and stoves, 141; and ticks, 382–83

Clevis pins, 75, 163

Climbing, 300–301

Clubs, hiking, 11–13, 315, 424, 481–82

Coast Ranges, 433, 434, 435

Codeine, 156, 411

Cold: and alcohol, 256; and batteries, 161; body's response to, 400; and butane cartridges, 263; and caloric needs, 178; clothing for, 59–62; and sleeping, 254–55

Colds, 379

Color: and low impact, 85, 103, 125–26; and rescue, 85, 126, 158, 210, 236

Compass, 210, 159–60, 222–31; and circle of directions, 222–23; and cross-country travel, 290–94; and declination, 225–27, 230–31; and deliberate error, 292–93; and following a bearing, 290–94, 326–27; and magnetic north, 223, 225–26, 227; practicing with, 12; substitutes for, 231–33; and taking a bearing, 227–30

Condensation: and frostliner, 117, 328; and Gore-Tex, 57, 118; and raingear, 55, 57; and snow shelters, 336–37; and tarps, 108; and tents, 107, 117, 118, 253, 328, 330

Conditioning, 13–14, 408

Conservation organizations: addresses, 420–21, 481–82; and "Back Country" concept, 474; and wilderness battle, 449, 461

Constipation, 179, 379, 380

Convulsions, 368
Copperhead snakes, 288, 386–87
Coral snakes, 386, 388–89, 392
Cord, 152, 162, 251, 271–72
Cotton, 27, 59, 61, 317, 405
Cottonmouth snakes, 288, 386–87, 417
CPR, 367
Crampons, 297, 339, 340
Cramps, 180, 205, 402
Crater Lake National Park, 435
Cross-country travel, 286–312; boots for, 30, 34, 287–88; compass use, 230; in eastern mountains, 419; and low impact, 208, 301–3, 472; noting down route, 230; packs for, 70, 288; in swamps, 417
Cuts, 371–72

Day-hiking, 11, 12, 154
Daypacks, 68, 82–83, 355
Declination, 225–27, 230–31
Dehydration, 187, 205, 402
Deserts: acclimatizing to, 402; and quicksand, 310; and sunglasses, 210; and sun shelters, 106; travel in, 303–9; unmarked trails in, 287, 308; and water, 27, 174–75, 187, 304–7; and wilderness lands, 437–40, 452
Diarrhea, 179, 275, 278, 380
Dingle stick, 266–67
Direction finding, 214–37
Dishwashing, 150, 270, 280
Dislocations, 375, 377–78
Distress signals, 235–36
Dizziness, 264, 368
Down: dry-cleaning, 103; jackets, 53, 54, 62, 317, 432; sleeping bags, 91–92, 98, 317, 432; vests, 54; washing, 102; wet, 92, 101, 317, 330
Dry-cleaning gear, 103
"Ducks" (route markers), 208, 233, 302, 326

Earache, 379
Edema: cerebral, 409; high-altitude pulmonary, 409–10

Electrolytes, 179–80, 402
Emergencies: distress signals in, 210, 235–36; essential items for, 158–59, 210–11; and evacuation, 365, 369–70, 372, 391, 406; extra clothing for, 49, 52, 210; first aid kit for, 153–57, 191–92, 210; getting lost, 209–10, 214, 220, 235–37; leaving word on trip plans, 198–99, 201, 311; shelters for, 159, 210, 236, 331; steps in dealing with, 365–69. See also First aid
Environmental organizations. See Conservation organizations
Evacuation, 365, 369–70, 372, 391, 406
Exhaustion, 407, 408
Eye problems, 372–73

Fanny packs, 83
Federal agencies: addresses, 460, 482–86; maps published by, 167, 171–73
Federal lands, 446–58
Fever, 156
Fiberpile, 53, 61, 65, 298, 299–300
Field guides, 164, 356
Fire ribbon, 148, 159, 267
Fire rings, 128, 264, 265, 281–82
Fires, 264–69; burying, 282; and children, 353, 357; in desert, 309; drowning, 268, 282; and low impact, 9–10, 26, 127–29, 264–66, 268–69, 471; permits for, 176, 199; regulations on, 128, 162, 174, 236, 241, 479; and safety, 247, 266, 267–68, 282; and shovels, 162; signal, 236, 369; and sleeping bags, 101, 266; and tents, 123, 266
Firestarters, 148, 159, 210, 267
First aid, 364–411
Fish and Wildlife Service. See U.S. Fish and Wildlife Service
Flash floods, 245, 440
Flu, 379
Foam pads, 99, 100, 146, 258, 307, 318
Food, 177–87; amount needed, 24, 178–79, 183–84;

bear-bagging, 152, 162, 271–73, 394; caches, 273, 310; canned, 182; for children, 353, 357; compressed, 183; containers for, 150–51; cost of, 18, 184; drink mixes, 123, 150, 179–80, 181, 187, 320; emergency supplies, 185–86, 210, 311; and energy, 407; freeze-dried, 177, 179, 180, 183; fresh, 181, 182; and high altitude, 181; mail-ordering, 183; menus, 182; monosodium glutamate in, 180, 183; and nutrition, 177–80; packing, 151, 184–85; protecting, 270–73; shopping for, 182–83; and warmth, 255, 320, 403, 404; weight of, 18, 24, 178–79, 182, 185

Forests: eastern, 418, 421–22, 423, 425; western, 432–33. See also *National Forests*

Forest Service. *See* U.S. Forest Service

Frostbite, 316, 405–7

Frostliner, 117, 328

Fuel, 130–47 *passim;* amount needed, 24, 145, 186; extra, 312; packing, 192; spilling, 123, 257–64 *passim;* swallowing, 367. *See also* Alcohol; Butane cartridges; Kerosene; White gas

Fuel pellets, 141, 159, 259, 267

Gaiters, 42, 61, 209, 288, 298, 382, 390

Garbage, 9, 193, 265–66, 269–70

Gear suppliers, 20–21, 167, 487–90

Giardiasis, 278, 380

Gila monster, 386

Glissading, 296–97, 298

Gloves, 52, 61, 149

Goggles, 59, 317–18, 411

Gore-Tex: bivouac bags, 97; boots, 30, 34–35; mitten shells, 61; raingear, 56–58; sleeping bag covers, 107; sleeping bag shells, 97, 420; tents, 109, 118, 121; and winter travel, 317

Grizzlies, 247, 273, 393–95, 442

Grommets, 121–22, 123, 125, 253

Groundsheets, 99, 123, 158, 251, 333

Guylines, 110, 112, 116, 119, 121, 123, 250, 251

Halazone, 278

Hammocks, 100, 103–4

Hatchet, 162, 266

Headache, 264, 379, 408, 409

Headgear: balaclava, 52; hats, 51, 307, 317; head nets, 51, 381; hoods, 54, 55–56; rainhats, 56; stocking caps, 52, 255, 317

Head injuries, 374–75

Headlamp, 161, 210, 329

Heart: attack, 367; conditioning, 13–14; problems, 14, 410

Heat: balance, 62–64; exhaustion, 401; stroke, 367, 401–2

Heel locators, 346

Hepatitis, 275

Hexamine, 141

High-altitude pulmonary edema, 409–10

Hiking clubs, 11–13, 315, 424, 481–82

Hollofil, 91, 92

Hostels, 424, 472

Huts, 105, 424, 473, 474

Hyperthermia, 307, 357, 367, 400–402

Hypothermia, 402–5; and avalanche victim, 325; and children, 357; and rain, 211, 363, 405; and stream crossing, 300; and winter camping, 320

Ice axe, 295–96, 297, 298, 299, 321, 324, 325, 341, 345

Igloos, 318, 333–37

Immunizations, 372, 392, 393, 397

Impact problem, 5–6, 468–72, 478–80. *See also* Low impact

Infection, 207, 372, 379, 383, 392

Insect repellent, 157, 211, 256, 288, 381, 382

Insects, 381–83, 384

Iodine, 277, 278–80

Iso-butane, 140

Jackets: down, 53–54, 62, 317, 432; repairing, 163; synthetic-filled, 53–54
Jerky, 185–86

Kals, W. S., 231
Kemsley, William, 193
Kerosene, 135–37, 142, 143–44, 147, 261–62, 263; amount needed, 186; safety of, 141; weight of, 24
K-Kote, 124
Kneecap, dislocated, 378
Knickers, 61
Knives, 152, 160, 210, 212
Korean boot, 317

Lactic acid, 204
Lakes: camping near, 243–44; drinking water from, 278; and sound, 245
Lamps, 160–62
Latrines, 162, 246–47, 275, 382, 472
Laundry bags, 152
Laxatives, 179, 380
Lean-to, 105
Leather, 23, 28, 35–37, 45
Leopold, Aldo, 452–53
Lightning, 211–12
Lights, 160–62
Lip balm, 123, 158
Litter, 469
Lock-rings, 75, 163
Loft, 88–91
Loop trips, 173–74
Losing your way, 209–10, 214, 220, 235–37
Lowe packs, 77, 489
Low impact: and breaking camp, 281–83; and campsites, 241–48, 472; and children, 358–59; and color, 85, 103, 125–26; and cross-country travel, 301–3, 472; and desert travel, 308–9; ethics of, 7–10, 26–27; and fires, 128, 264–66, 268–69; and groups, 471–72; and hammocks, 103–4; and lug soles, 46–47; and regulations, 478–79; and sleeping, 249; and snow, 29; and tents, 125–26;

and trail ethics, 207–8; and wilderness management, 469–72
Lug soles, 34, 46–47
Lung problems, 409–10

Mag-Lites, 161
Magnifiers, 160, 164
Malaria, 382
Map reading, 216–20
Maps, 215–22; agency, 167, 171–73, 220–21; as essential, 159–60, 210; geologic, 164; mail-ordering, 171, 215, 487; preserving, 218; showing wilderness use, 476; topographic, 12, 171, 172, 210, 215–20, 221; using a compass with, 222–31
Marshall, Robert, 453
Matches, 147–48, 159, 210
Mazamas, 12
Meadows, 9, 212, 243, 245, 302
Medical problems, 371–80, 399–411. See also First aid
Medical supplies, 153–57
Mess kits, 148–50
Mildew, 44, 45, 124
Mining, 445, 449, 451
Mirror, 158, 163, 210, 235, 373
Mittens, 52, 61
Moleskin and molefoam, 42, 155, 201, 205, 207
Mosquitoes, 381–82; 9, 49, 51, 157, 243, 245, 256, 420, 421
Mosquito netting, 51, 113–14, 381
Mountaineers, 12, 155, 210, 297, 481
Muir, John, 10, 105, 311, 313, 436
Mylar, 118

National forests, 448–50, 452–55; addresses, 460, 484–85; eastern, 422, 424, 425–26, 447, 454–55; and fire regulations, 162, 176; maps for, 167, 171–73, 220–21; use of wilderness in, 4; western, 435, 437–38, 439, 442, 452–54; and wilderness permits, 175–76, 199

National grasslands, 427
National historical parks, 426–27
National lakeshores, 425
National monuments, 426, 439, 440, 450
National parks, 447–51; addresses, 460, 483; in Alaska, 455; and bears, 245, 271; bus service in and to, 197; in Canada, 197; eastern, 418, 422, 424, 425; maps for, 167, 171–73, 220–21; shelters in, 420; in Switzerland, 303; western, 5, 251, 435–42 *passim;* and wilderness permits, 175–76, 199
National Park Service: addresses, 460, 483; maps published by, 167, 171–73, 220–21; and wilderness management, 448, 450, 468, 472, 477
National preserves, 455
National recreation areas, 450
National seashores, 197, 417, 450
National Wilderness Preservation System, 448–57
National wildlife refuges, 448–50, 451; addresses, 460, 483–84; in Alaska, 455; eastern, 416, 425, 426, 427, 447; maps for, 167, 171–73, 220–21; western, 437, 439–40
Nausea, 264, 408
Neck injuries, 374–75
New York State Forest Preserve, 446
North, magnetic and true, 222–227 *passim*
Nosebleeds, 379
Nylon, 112, 124

Optimus stoves, 131–36 *passim*, 140, 141, 145–49 *passim*, 262, 328; address, 489
Outward Bound, 282
Ovens, 149
Overboots, 316, 347

Pacific Crest Trail, 310
Pack covers, 84, 193
Packframe ponchos, 55, 84
Packlist, 17–18, 64–66, 188–90

Packs, 67–85; accessories for, 83–84; backbands, 73, 76; buying, 68–69; color of, and low impact, 85; child carriers, 352; children's, 355–56; cost of, 18; for cross-country travel, 288; daypacks, 68, 82–83, 355; fanny packs, 83; fitting, 75–77, 80–81; external-frame, 69–77, 81, 288, 377; flexible-linkage-frame, 72; frame extensions for, 83, 193; hipbelts, 14, 73, 76, 78–79; how to wear, 202–3; internal-frame, 69–71, 77–82, 318; increasing capacity of, 193; organizing, 188–93; packbags, 73–75, 81–82; plastic-frame, 71; pockets, 41, 75, 82, 84; putting on, 202; renting, 68; rucksacks, 82; size of, 74; ski-carrying, 79; soft, 70, 78, 288, 318; sternum straps, 446; stitching, 28, 81–82; summit, 83; tie-on patches, 83–84, 193; weight of load in, 18, 24–25, 192, 318–19; winter, 218; wrap-around-frame, 72, 77
Pain medication, 156, 157, 411
Pants, 49–50, 59, 61
Parkas, 55, 56–57, 59. *See also* Jackets
Patching, 123, 124
Peaks, 211, 212
Pemmican, 185–86
Personal gear, 18, 163–64
Phoenix stoves, 132, 133, 135
Plants: edible, 159; poisonous, 159, 395–97
Plastic: bags, 84, 151, 159, 185, 316; bottles, 185; boxes, 151, 185; egg carriers, 151; pack frames, 71
Pockets: pack, 41, 75, 82, 84; pants, 50; tent, 114
Poisoning, 367
Poison ivy, 157, 396–97, 421
Poison oak, 157, 395–97
Poisonous animals and plants, 308, 381–98 *passim*
Poison sumac, 157, 396–97
Polaris ("polestar"), 231, 232

Pollution, water, 274–80, 305, 479

Polyester fills, 53–54, 91–92, 103

Polypropylene, 59, 317

Ponchos, 55, 58, 84, 106, 432

Porcupines, 271

Propane, 137, 140

Public domain, 448, 451–52, 455

Pulmonary edema, 409–10

Puncture wounds, 371

Quallofil, 53, 91, 92, 254

Quicksand, 310, 418

Quota system, 7, 471, 475–76

Rabies, 392–93

Radiant heat barriers, 97–98

Rain: and down, 92; in the East, 421–28 passim; freezing, 421; and hypothermia, 211, 363, 405; national distribution of, 430; summer, 27, 414, 421–35 passim, 440, 441; starting a fire in, 267; walking in, 211–12; in the West, 430–35 passim, 440

Raingear, 54–58; children's, 353; and snow travel, 298, 317, 333

Rattlesnakes, 42, 288–89, 308, 386–87

Red Cross, 155, 365

Regulations, 6–8, 10, 175–76, 470, 474–75; and access, 477–78; and campsites, 240–41, 243–44, 478–79; and fires, 128, 174, 236, 241, 479; and impact, 478–79; and quota system, 7, 471, 475–76; and wilderness permits, 7, 10, 175–76, 199, 394, 470

Repairs, 28, 44, 46, 123, 124–25, 162–63, 348

Rescue, 369–70; of avalanche victim, 325–26; and colors, 85, 126, 158, 210, 236; signaling for, 158, 369

Ripstop nylon, 112

Rocky Mountain Spotted Fever, 383

Rope, 212, 255, 299, 300–301, 308, 321

Routefinding, 214–37, 289–94, 326–27

Route markers, 208, 233–35, 302

Rucksacks, 82

Safety: campsites, 245; children, 356–57; fires, 247, 266, 267–68, 282; health, 155–58; leaving word on trip plans, 198–99, 201, 311; stove, 131–33, 136, 138, 141, 149, 245, 257–58, 260, 261, 263–64; survival, 158–59, 210; tents, 123, 141, 212, 263–64, 266, 328

St. Elmo's fire, 212

Salt, 156, 180, 306, 402

Sanitation, 162, 274–78, 353–55

Scorpions, 308, 385–86

Scree, 33, 288

Seams: bar-tacking, 81–82, 96; boot, 43–44; jacket, 54, 62; flat-fell, 121; and number of stitches to the inch, 81, 121; pack, 28, 81–82; pants, 61; sleeping bag, 87–88, 96; tent, 112, 121, 123, 124–25

Seam sealing, 44, 58, 121, 123, 124–25

Seizures, 401

Sewing kit, 162–63

Sheep, bighorn, 46, 309, 451

Shells: all-weather, 57; mitten, 61; sleeping bag, 87, 317; wind, 58–59

Shelters, 105–26; branch, 26, 236; emergency, 159, 210, 236; established, 320–21, 420, 424; snow, 318, 330–37

Shirts, 51, 52, 54, 58, 61

Shivering, 400, 403

Shock, 325, 367–68

Shock cords, 84, 122, 193

Shoepacs, 41, 316–17, 347

Shoes, light, 16, 18, 31, 33–34, 42, 164, 213, 416

Shoulder, dislocated, 377–78

Shovels, 162, 318, 331

Sierra Club, 12, 171, 461, 486

Signals, distress, 158, 210, 235–36

Skiing, cross-country, 337, 341–48; beltbag, 84; crossing

avalanche path, 324, 325;
daytripping, 314; packs for, 79;
rate of travel, 319; route
choice, 327
Ski mountaineering, 41, 344, 345,
347, 348
Skin protection, 157–58, 210,
307, 351, 352, 410–11
Sleeping bags, 86–104
Sleeping pads, 99–100, 212
Snakebite, 389–92
Snakebite kit, 156, 308, 390
Snakes, 42, 288–89, 308, 386–92,
417
Snow: camping in, 276–77,
313–19, 327–37; gear for,
61–62, 116–17, 315–19;
melting, 142, 186, 261, 329;
stoves in, 146, 328–29; travel
on, 208–9, 295–98, 319–27,
337–48; "watermelon," 277–78.
See also Winter wilderness
Snow blindness, 51, 210, 411
Snow caves, 318, 331–33, 336
Snowshoeing, 70, 319, 324, 325,
337–41, 348
Soap, 150, 155, 163, 270, 280
Socks, 42, 61, 205–6, 213, 316,
407
Solo hiking, 153, 310–12, 463
Space blankets, 97, 159
Spiders, 384–85
Splinting, 373–74, 377
Sprains, 375–77
Spring hiking, 167–68, 209, 382,
424, 434, 440
Springs, 270, 305
Stakes, 108, 122–23, 125, 251,
296, 328
Sterno fuel, 141
Sternum straps, 80
Stoves, 127–44; accessories for,
145–48; alcohol, 136, 141, 142;
and altitude, 139;
battery-operated, 141; burner
styles, 134–35; butane
cartridge, 24, 127, 137–40,
141–43, 186, 262–63; buying,
141–43; care of, 143–44, 259;
cooking on, 257–64; costs, 133,
134, 140–43 *passim;* and fire
permits, 176, 199; vs. fires,
269; kerosene, 135–37, 141,
142–47 *passim,* 261–62, 263;

liquid-feed butane, 140, 142;
and low impact, 26;
mountaineering, 135, 142;
multi-fuel, 136; overheating,
131–32, 136, 149, 258, 260,
261, 263; packing, 192;
priming, 131, 132–33, 136,
147, 259–60, 261–62, 264, 328;
pump, 132–35, 142, 146–47,
259, 260, 328; repairing, 28,
143, 163; safety, 131–32, 136,
138, 141, 149, 245, 257–58,
260–64 *passim;*
self-pressurizing, 130–32;
solid-fuel, 141, 142; spare parts,
144, 163, 261; stability, 143;
testing, 144; weight, 18,
133–34, 140, 142; white gas,
130–35, 141, 142–46 *passim,*
257–61; windscreens for, 132,
141, 143, 145–46, 148, 260,
270; winter, 142, 328
Strains, 378
Streams: camping near, 243–44;
crossing, 203, 206, 212–13,
298–300, 320–21
Stuffsacks, 84, 100, 103, 152,
191, 271–72
Summit packs, 83
Sunburn, 157–58, 351, 410–11
Suncream, 157–58, 210, 307,
410–11
Sunglasses, 51, 59, 210, 307,
317–18, 411
Survival items, 158–59, 210–11,
224
Sweaters, 52–53, 61
Sweating, 317, 401–2
Synthetic fills: dry-cleaning, 103;
in jackets, 53–54, 317; in
sleeping bags, 27, 91–92, 254,
255–56, 317, 420

Tarp, 107–8; as desert shelter,
307; pitching, 123, 162, 250,
253; poncho as, 55; and snow
trench, 331
Temperature, body, 399–400
Tents, 108–26
Tentsites, 250–54
Tetanus, 372, 392
Thermometers, 164
Thirst, 363, 367

Thunderstorms, 211–12, 308, 431, 440, 441
Ticks, 285, 382–83
Timberline: and animal problems, 271; camping at, 9, 243; fires near, 265; vegetation at, 9, 243, 251, 302
Toilet paper, 163, 210, 245, 276, 277, 309
Trail ethics, 207–8
Trail guides, 167, 174
Trail markers, 208, 233–35, 302
Trees: blazing, 208, 233–24, 326, 327; camping under, 245; and cord damage, 251; cutting for shelters, 26, 236; and direction finding, 214; and lightning, 211–12
Tundra, 243, 303

Ultra-Seal, 45
Unconsciousness, 368
Underwear, 51, 59–61, 317
U.S. Department of Agriculture, 178, 486
U.S. Fish and Wildlife Service: addresses, 483–84; maps published by, 167, 220, 448; wildlife refuges, 451
U.S. Forest Service: addresses, 484–85; and avalanche information, 322; and "Back Country" concept, 474; and fire regulations, 162; and fire-ring research, 265; maps, 150, 167, 173, 215, 220; and wilderness management, 170, 423, 452, 468–80. See also National Forests
U.S. Geological Survey, 171, 215, 230, 487. See also Maps, topographic

Vapor barriers, 98–99, 316
Ventilation: in tents, 114, 117, 118, 123, 124, 328, 330; in snow shelters, 331, 333, 336
Vomiting, 368, 408

Wading, 209–10
Walking sticks, 164, 299, 377

Warmth: and food, 255, 320, 403, 404; regulating, 62–64, 204; in sleeping bags, 254–56; in winter, 320
Wasps, 383–84
Water: amount needed, 186–87, 205, 329, 402, 407; and beach walking, 416; caching, 175, 305–6; camping near, 243–44, 309; carriers for, 151; carrying, 26; and cramps, 180; and desert travel, 27, 175, 187, 304–7, 479; placement of, in pack, 192; pollution of, 274–80, 305, 479; purifying, 157, 187, 278; siting fires near, 265; and snow camping, 142, 186, 261, 320, 327, 329–30; weight of, 24, 304
Water moccasin snake, 386–88
Waterproofing: problems with, 28, 54, 58, 107, 123, 124, 264; products for, 124. See also Seam sealing
Wet clothing, 256, 300, 330, 405
Wetlands, 415–18, 451
Whistle, 158, 210, 235, 273, 356
White gas, 130–31, 141–46 passim, 257–61; amount needed, 186; as firestarter, 267; weight of, 24
Whiteouts, 290, 326
Wilderness: access to, 477–78; in Alaska, 455; cost of, 457–58; debate on saving, 444–61; de facto, 169–71, 173; development of, 472–73; in the east, 414–28; educating about, 470–71; federal lands in, 446–57; figures on, 456–57; "hardening" of, 472–73; limits on use of, 474–76; management of, 467–80; meaning of, 6; natural resources of, 457–58; no-use zones in, 480; opponents of, 449; problems of, 467–80; in public domain, 451–52; quasi-, 473–74; restoration of, 477; state lands in, 446; in the west, 429–42. See also Regulations; Wilderness permits
Wilderness Act, 448–50, 452, 453

Wilderness land management agencies, 448, 482–86
Wilderness permits, 7, 10, 175–76, 199, 394, 470
Wilderness Preservation System, 448–57
Wildlife. *See* Animals; National wildlife refuges
Wind: and avalanche danger, 321; and campsites, 245, 266; clothing for, 317; and fires, 266; and hypothermia, 405; and matches, 147–48; and sleeping site, 254; and snow shelters, 334; and stoves, 148, 260–61, 270; and tent design, 109, 112, 115–16, 120, 318

Wind chill, 319
Windscreens, 132, 141, 143, 145–46, 148, 260, 270
Winter hiking, 419, 421–24 *passim*, 435, 440
Winter wilderness, 313–48
Wood for fires, 9, 266, 267
Wool, 27, 52, 59, 61, 65, 66, 298, 299–300, 317

Yellowjackets, 383–84

Zinc oxide, 158, 411
Zippers, 28, 75, 82, 95, 318
Zip stove, 141